Born in Chiswick in 1946, the son of a wartime RAF pilot, Brian was educated at Hounslow College, attaining five GCE O-Levels.

A few years later, as a Xerox salesman, his exceptional selling skills helped him acquire the sponsorship necessary to embark on what was to become a professional race-driving career. These same skills eventually took him to Formula 1, as the marketing director of the Lola Ferrari and the Benetton Grand Prix teams. In a fascinating career, Brian also became the founder of the prestigious Motorsport Industry Association, manager of the Kyalami F1 Circuit in South Africa, a Sky TV motorsport presenter, a guest lecturer for the World Academy of Sport and the author of two highly acclaimed sponsorship books.

Awarded an Honorary Doctorate in 2018 by Birmingham City University, in recognition of his outstanding contribution to the motorsport industry, Brian has recently been appointed the Motorsport Industry Consultant to the University of Wolverhampton. He now lives in Shrewsbury with his South African born wife, Liz.

This book is dedicated to Lizzie, my wonderful wife, who had never even watched a motor race when we first met in Cape Town, back in the 1980s. Over the years, we've shared some wonderful adventures together, thanks mainly to my motorsport related activities.

Without Liz's on-going encouragement, support, enthusiasm, patience and belief in the project, I would not have been able to write this book.

Brian Sims

YOU DON'T HAVE TO BE A CHAMPION... TO BE A WINNER!

A JOURNEY FROM XEROX TO FORMULA 1

AUSTIN MACAULEY PUBLISHERS™

LONDON · CAMBRIDGE · NEW YORK · SHARJAH

A CIP catalogue record for this title is available from the British Library.

ISBN 9781528934053 (Paperback)
ISBN 9781528967716 (ePub e-book)

www.austinmacauley.com

First Published (2019)
Austin Macauley Publishers Ltd
25 Canada Square
Canary Wharf
London
E14 5LQ

I would like to thank Claire, at Austin Macauley, for listening to me when I made initial contact in August 2017 with a view to writing this autobiography. She then encouraged me to write the book. Also thanks to the Editorial Department at Austin Macauley, as well as the team who worked with me to bring it to fruition.

Prologue

From a very early age, there was never any doubt that I would one day become a fighter pilot.

I took charge of my first squadron in 1953, at the age of seven. There were six other pilots, all school chums, and the squadron's strategic threat involved running around the playground of Dare House School in Farnham Common, in close formation, arms outstretched, screaming like banshees in an attempt to sound like jet planes. In the process, the squadron scared not only many of the young girls at our school but possibly brought about the early retirement of a couple of teachers.

I knew even then that I would have to wait another ten years before I could try to emulate my father's wartime career and apply to join the Royal Air Force; but in the meantime, this was good practice.

As I led my young squadron around the school playground, little did I know then that in reality, I would never fly a real aircraft, neither in the Royal Air Force nor in any other capacity. At that age, I just assumed that if you wanted something badly enough, it would happen. My dad had been an RAF pilot, and that was good enough for me.

Our Dare House School squadron was eventually disbanded in 1954, in accordance with the sign at the school's main gate, stating that it offered education for boys and girls up to the age of eight. Having reached that magic figure, I was moved on to the local primary school. A couple of years later, my parents moved to Isleworth and arranged for me to take the entrance exam to a small private school, Hounslow College. To their relief, I passed the exam and started in a class which might be misinterpreted in the current era, but was then called 'Transition'. To everyone's delight, the school was well-served by an Italian ice cream parlour, just across the road, which belonged to the mother of one of the boys. It also boasted a constant stream of noisy aircraft flying overhead, into what was then called London Airport. The disruption that this brought to classes always went down well with us if not with the teachers.

My RAF dream continued when my parents took me to the cinema to watch films, such as the *Dam Busters* and *Reach for the Sky*. I also recall us visiting a close wartime friend of my dad, Gordon Storey, who was the squadron leader of a Fighter Command unit, based at Waterbeach in Cambridgeshire. Unlike my father, Gordon had opted to stay on in the RAF after the Second World War and was now flying *Hawker Hunters*. To my great delight, I was allowed to sit in the cockpit of what was then considered to be the most advanced jet fighter in the world. My abiding memory, however, even at such a young age, was the way in which that visit affected my dad. I could see that he would have loved to have been back in uniform and flying again.

Hounslow College made no apologies for focussing almost exclusively on securing university places at either Oxford or Cambridge, for those wanting to be academics, lawyers, doctors or bankers. Dr Hindle, the headmaster, never did come to terms with the fact that a potential fighter pilot had somehow scraped through the very specific entrance exam process.

Fortunately, if you liked sport and happened to be of a reasonable standard, Hounslow College was a good place to be, and my endeavours in football, cricket and athletics meant that I soon found myself in the school teams for all three disciplines. In 1960, my sporting status, such as it was, qualified me to join pupils from some of the other grades in attending a special lunch at a local restaurant in Osterley. We were there to meet a former pupil, who'd become a school legend by winning Olympic gold.

Don Thompson, nicknamed Little Mouse because of his petite stature, went to the Rome Olympics in 1960 and upset all the odds by securing a stunning victory in the 50 kilometre walk, enduring the extreme summer heat and humidity that shattered many of the more acclimatised competitors.

I sat fascinated as Don explained how he trained in the kitchen of his tiny flat in Hounslow, with a kettle boiling all the time and a gas heater on full bore, trying to simulate the humid conditions that he expected to face in Rome. We sat, spellbound, as he related how he often endured severe light-headedness during the kitchen training sessions, brought on, he believed, by the intense heat. Only later did he discover that it was actually a mild form of carbon monoxide poisoning, caused by a faulty heater.

My abiding memory that day was of Don Thompson bidding us farewell, putting on his bicycle clips and a scruffy beige raincoat before heading up the road on his rickety bike. How times have changed. If he had waited another 40 years or so, he would have been whisked off to Buckingham Palace in the back of a Bentley to receive his MBE from the Queen.

Don Thompson's extraordinary determination stayed in my mind for a long time. It was probably my first realisation that if you want to achieve something special, talent alone is rarely enough without there being an extraordinary level of determination to go with it. I wanted to be an RAF pilot, but fate would decide otherwise.

I'd enjoyed a good childhood, living in Isleworth; gone to school in Hounslow, supported Brentford Football Club and partied in Richmond. I was 13 and a half when the 1960s arrived, just the perfect age to make the most of what would be an iconic decade.

There was the music for a start. The late '50s had given us a taste of what was to come, with Elvis, The Everly Brothers, Duane Eddy, Buddy Holly, Connie Francis and many others, all producing sounds that were a million miles away from anything we'd previously heard.

Thanks to a crystal radio set that my dad built for me, I'd been able to tune in to Radio Luxembourg on 208 AM, listening through a set of head phones under the sheets at night when I was meant to be sleeping. It enabled me to keep up-to-date with the latest top 20 hits from a string of new artists, such as Bobby Vee, Cliff Richard, The Shadows, Billy Fury, Helen Shapiro and Adam Faith. During school lunch-hours, together with my schoolmate Barry Pratt, I'd go to one of Hounslow's three record shops and listen in a sound-proofed booth to a stack of vinyl 45s, before parting with what was meant to be my lunch money, to buy the latest hit from yet another rock favourite.

A new innovation in the 1960s offered teenagers a hugely popular way of socialising. Sixties' coffee bars were very different to the Costas and Starbucks that fill our towns and cities today. In those days, coffee bars served mainly espresso, frothy coffee; and most of them offered the added attraction of a jukebox, providing a cheap way of spending fun evenings, listening to amazing music. Coffee bars were also the place to go to find out where the good parties were going to be held that weekend and proved to be a great place for taking girls to on a first date. Some bars even let us dance to the music.

By the early 1960s, Richmond in Surrey had more than its fair share of coffee bars; with Pronto's and the open air L'Auberge being two of the most frequented. L'Auberge was situated right next to the Odeon Cinema, facing Richmond Bridge, and was quite popular with the members of a group that played locally, the Rolling Stones. The mods preferred Pronto's, where, throughout the weekend, hundreds of scooters would be parked outside on the road. Mods could be distinguished by their slick clothing style and back-combed hair styles, copied from many of the music groups of the day, such as The Who and The Small Faces. Mods rode scooters, mainly Lambrettas or Vespas, which were invariably adorned with a plethora of chrome-plated spotlights and crash bars, whilst a tall, flexible aerial on the back of the scooter was mandatory. Attached to these aerials, you would normally see fur fox tails or pennants. Across the back of the parka, garments worn by mods on their scooters, was a stencilled set of letters, spelling out their hometown.

Richmond also had a superb ice-rink; and together with Barry Pratt, would spend most Saturday afternoons there, in our flashy ice hockey boots, checking out all of the female skaters, who tended to circulate the ice in pairs, whilst the music system belted out the latest chart hits. Now and then, we'd be lucky enough to persuade a couple of girls to join us for a coffee in the cafeteria, where we would spend a few bob playing the latest hits on the jukebox, in a hope that they would be impressed.

As far as I can remember, alcohol played only a very small part during my teens, unlike the binge-drinking culture that we see all too often today. For a start, most of us simply couldn't afford it, and secondly, it just didn't seem important. We usually took some beers with us to parties, but that was about it. I knew even then that drugs were a part of the scene for some of the people who frequented the live music gigs at venues, such as Eel Pie Island and the Craw Daddy; but as far as I was aware at the time, it rarely went beyond a few magic smokes. In hindsight, I may well have been wrong.

Another coffee bar that I went to on a couple of occasions was in London, Soho to be precise. The 2i's had become well known as a breeding ground for future music stars, including a certain Harry Webb who, as Cliff Richard, set the music world alight. With him on his incredible journey was his backing group, The Shadows.

Hank Marvin and Bruce Welch had left school in Newcastle at 16, to travel down to London to try and launch a music career as guitarists. They met up with Harry Webb, who had just secured a recording contract with EMI, which meant he'd be going on tour and would need a professional backing group. He talked to Hank and Bruce, whom he knew well by then, and invited them to join up with him. They in turn recruited bass-guitarist, Jet Harris and drummer, Tony Meehan. After a short stint as the Drifters, they became The Shadows. It was a fortuitous move for them, and they went on to become the most successful instrumental group in history. During my career, I was able to go to several of the Shadows' live shows and have always been a huge fan since first hearing their famous, number-one hit, Apache, back in 1960.

Many years later, in 2017, I had the pleasure of meeting Bruce Welch for lunch in Richmond. To hear his stories of life in the music industry, over seven decades, was both fascinating and a real privilege.

Another memory that comes to mind involved the infamous Bank Holiday Monday battles that took place at a few well-known coastal resorts, including Margate, Southend and Brighton. On the one side, you had the mods, all of whom headed down to the resorts from the Greater London area in a cavalcade of scooters. It wasn't mandatory in those days to wear helmets, and the mods didn't, not wanting to spoil their mid-parting and back-combed hair styles. Waiting for them would be the rockers, easily recognisable by their black leather jackets, jeans and motorcycle boots. These guys had arrived in town on their Triumph Bonnevilles, Nortons, BSAs and Ariels. For them, helmets were mandatory.

The resulting skirmishes, as the mods and rockers faced up to each other on the South Coast beachfronts, hit the headlines in virtually every newspaper and TV news bulletin of the day. Not surprisingly, the public soon steered clear of these resorts over a Bank Holiday, knowing that getting caught up in the running battles could be particularly harmful to one's health. Subsequent investigations have put forward convincing arguments that some of the media at the time actually played a role in stirring up the mods vs rockers battles, generating good copy in the process! This even involved paying some of combatants to re-enact the battles of the day.

Talking about motorbikes and scooters, as soon as I was legally old enough to ride one, I had bought myself a moped. It was a welcome step up from a Raleigh bike that my folks had given me for passing the entrance exam to Hounslow College School, way back in 1958.

Contrary to my expectations, however, the 50cc moped did very little for my street cred! The sight of me pedalling like mad to get the motor started, followed by a cloud of blue smoke when it did eventually fire-up, generated more laughter from the girls at the youth club in Osterley than adulation. After a few months, the lack of reliability had frustrated my parents as much as it had me, and I opted to use some of my school-holiday job earnings to replace it with a small James 198 cc motorcycle, restoring some, if not all, of my street creed.

Football had become a big part of my life by that stage. I was playing in goal for the school team; and at weekends, together with another school friend, Keith Adcock, we'd head off to Griffin Park in Brentford on our motor bikes, to watch the majority of Brentford Football Club's home matches. Playing in the third division at that time, the club would attract around 4000 to 5000 spectators. Although I've been a life-long supporter of Wolverhampton Wanderers, Brentford's results are the next that I always look for.

All too soon it was exam time, or to be more specific, GCE O-Level time. To the surprise of a lot of people, my two best subjects leading up to these exams, in 1962, were mathematics and advanced mathematics. My worst was history, to the extent that I failed the mock-GCE exams in that subject and wasn't allowed to take it when the real exams came along. I have no doubts as to why this happened. In the year leading up to the GCEs, our history teacher was Jack Watts, who doubled up as the assistant sports master. Whilst he was a good guy in many ways, his forte was not for teaching history, in my opinion. Our lessons comprised him reading out aloud to us from H G Wells' *Short History of the World*, which bored me rigid. In particular, the seemingly endless section of the book that dealt with the geological formation of the planet was the worst.

What rather irks me is that since leaving school all those years ago, I've developed a great passion for history and have spent many holidays and weekends exploring and researching certain periods of our past that I find fascinating. Looking back, I often wonder whether I might have pursued an academic career in the subject, had I been more inspired at school. Such is the power of teaching, both in a positive and negative way.

I saw these formative years of my life and schooling as simply being a way of gearing up for my primary ambition; to follow in my father's footsteps and join the Royal Air Force. I've explained that I was aware of my dad's regret of leaving the RAF at the end of the war, but what I didn't mention is that I was partly responsible for this.

I was born in Chiswick Maternity Hospital on 12 June 1946. Dad had flown home from Singapore, where he was based at end of hostilities, to be there for my birth. What he hadn't anticipated was that, within a few weeks, I would develop a very serious case of gastro-enteritis, still a worrying disease in babies, even today. At that time, it was often fatal.

I was transferred to West Middlesex Hospital and stayed there for several months until I fully recovered. It was touch and go for a while, to the extent that I was christened in hospital once it looked as though I wouldn't pull through. To be able to stay at home with my mother Eileen during these difficult times, Ken opted to leave the RAF. He eventually went on to build a career in the chemical industry, but would always wonder what would have become of his life if he had stayed on. He was so excited when I first told him that I too wanted to join the RAF.

I was first allowed to apply when I was 16 and a half years of age. The application form was duly posted, and I prepared myself for the day that I would head off to the Air Crew Selection Centre at RAF Biggin Hill, for a week of assessment.

I'll never forget the morning when an official brown envelope was popped through our letter box, a few weeks after I had sent in my RAF application form. It lay on the carpet, staring up at me, and I handed it to my dad to open. His face said it all. I'd been rejected.

I don't know who was the most disappointed, me or my father. His first reaction was to suggest a career in civil aviation, but after researching the possibilities, he reluctantly came to the conclusion that it would cost a lot of money; and he and my mother just weren't in a position to afford it, much as they would have liked to. He made a few enquiries and found out the reason why I had been turned down.

He explained to me that having been born in June 1946, a year after VE Day, I was a baby boomer. Apparently, this is what they called the millions of babies born just after the war years. With the emotional return to peace in Britain, following seven years of utter turmoil, it wasn't surprising that there was a huge increase in the subsequent birth rate, with so many families being reunited, often after years apart.

When my application to join the RAF was submitted late in 1962, it was just one of a vast number received from this baby boomer group. As a result, the RAF could

13

be extremely choosy about whom they invited to attend an initial interview, and they chose not to invite me! Apparently, my minimum qualification of five GCE O-Levels was bettered by a high number of applicants. It seemed, however, that I would be allowed to re-apply prior to my 21st birthday.

I felt as though my dream had been shattered. Not only did the letter of rejection bring about a feeling of massive disappointment, it also created a huge void in my life.

My folks eventually suggested that a change of school might be a good thing, and, after thinking it over, I took their advice. I moved to the sixth form of the nearby Isleworth Grammar School to study for my A-Levels prior to making another attempt at joining the RAF, believing that next time I would be better equipped academically. I never thought for one moment that it might lead to me becoming a rock star!

During my short spell at Isleworth Grammar, I'd got together with three guys in my class and formed a pop group, The Victims. You can imagine the comments that followed our choice of name! The Victims comprised two singers and two guitarists. I couldn't play the guitar, but neither could I sing. We tossed for it, and I became a singer. It's probably an indication of our singing talent that we won the Isleworth Grammar School Music Competition with an instrumental number, our rendering of the Tornados' instrumental number-one hit Telstar.

This involved a keyboard lead, and none of us could play a keyboard of any sort. We managed to solve this little hiccup, firstly by appointing me as the fall guy, then solving my lack of keyboard ability by taping strips of paper, on which numbers were printed, onto the keys of the school's electric organ. It was hoped that I could do the musical equivalent of painting by numbers. It worked well in rehearsals, and on the big day, we confidently walked onto the stage of the assembly hall, where the school organ sat prominently in the corner, all taped up with large numbers.

It wasn't my fault that, with such a large audience, the temperature in the hall had risen. It certainly wasn't my fault that there was no air-conditioning. How was I to know that a couple of teachers would decide to wind down some of the highest windows along one entire side of the hall? I tried my best; but about two-thirds of the way through the chart-topping instrumental, it became obvious that we hadn't used a strong-enough Sellotape. How we got through the final 60 seconds of Telstar, I'll never know. We were as surprised as everyone when it was subsequently announced that we had won the instrumental category of the School Music Awards. Maybe it had something to do with the fact that we were the sole entrants in that category.

Nevertheless, this achievement led to a professional booking. It was our first "gig" and turned out to be our last but one "gig".

Our bass guitarist, Phil Morris, also acted as our "agent", and you can probably imagine the excitement that erupted when he told us that he'd secured our first booking, with a fee included. OK, so £5 doesn't sound much today, but it was a lot of money in 1963. Our debut performance was to be at Heathrow Airport, playing at BOAC's staff dance in the new terminal building facility. Wow! Once the initial excitement abated, we got around to the thorny question of how we would get to airport with all our gear. Luckily, there was a solution.

I'd passed my driving test that year, and my mother was kind enough to loan me the Mini that she was so proud of. I'll never understand how the four of us, with sound system and two guitars, managed to fit in the Mini, but we did.

I wish I could describe how wonderfully well our debut went down, but there was a slight hitch; a misunderstanding might be one way of describing it. We'd been asked to get there at 2:30, which we thought was a bit early, as the event wasn't due to commence until 7:00 p.m. However, it seems that our "agent" had got it wrong, and it wasn't actually the BOAC staff dance that we'd been booked for but rather the BOAC children party, which was the precursor for the evening event!

Instead of playing our version of Billy J Kramer's "Do You Want to Know a Secret?" and stunning the audience with a unique rendering of Brian Poole and the Tremeloes' chart topper "Do You Love Me?", we ended up playing Ring a Ring of Roses and other well know children's favourites.

Looking back, it was probably a good thing that The Victim's then decided to split up, due to our all-too-obvious differences of musical appreciation! However, with the demise of the Victims, my one and only chance of becoming a musical superstar disappeared into thin air.

Although I made some good friends at my new school, I really didn't enjoy studying applied maths or English literature; and towards the end of my second term, I made it clear to my folks that it wasn't for me. I wanted to leave school and get a job. The big question was what sort of job would excite me?

In my school holidays, I'd been employed in a number of temporary jobs. One involved washing-up in the kitchens of Forte's new Heathrow Airport restaurant. The management didn't explain that it would also involve scraping the chewing gum off the underside of tables. A far more enjoyable job was being a van boy for one of London's leading laundries. This involved delivering and installing the roller towels in the clubs, theatres and cafes of Soho and the West End. Quite an education for a 15-year-old! Every morning, the driver would stop at a greasy spoon café, and we'd enjoy a bacon sandwich together before hitting the road. They sure were fun times.

Later, wanting a bit more money from a holiday job, I was lucky enough to get some help from my mother, Eileen. The job was with a company owned by the Taylor Woodrow Group. Greenham Tool Company had its head office in Isleworth, where Eileen was employed as PA to the sales director. Greenham's had branches across the UK and sold building and civil engineering equipment, including protective clothing, road signs, shovels, forks and a host of small tools. I started as a holiday fill-in, mainly as a filing clerk, which, although not too difficult, was decidedly tedious. Nevertheless, it subsequently paid for an overseas holiday in Austria, a brand new Dansette record player, Lonnie Donegan's hit single of The Battle of New Orleans and lot more. That was really all that mattered at that age.

During my time there, a chance conversation took place between my mother and her boss about my failure to get into the RAF. It led to him mentioning a new management trainee scheme within the group, and he wondered whether it might be of interest to me. That evening, Eileen told me about this possible new role and suggested it might be a smart career move. She added that there was one major drawback to consider; the job that her boss had in mind for me was based at the company's Southampton branch. This would mean that I would have to leave home.

Looking back, I think it might have been a blessing for both my folks and for me! Like all teenagers and particularly being an only child, I wasn't always an easy person to live with. Through her work, Eileen knew the manager of the Greenham branch in Southampton, Jack Heller, and arranged for us to travel down and meet him there one weekend. It would give me the chance to look at the city, at accommodation and, of course, at the branch itself.

I liked what I saw of the maritime city and got on well with Jack when I met him. It seemed that my life was in for a big change.

What I didn't realise at the time was that, in the course of my work for the Greenham Tool Company, to give it its full name, I would be learning a range of skills that would ultimately help me succeed in a totally different career, in one of the most exciting, glamorous and fiercely competitive sports in the world.

Chapter 1

Digs, Cars and Margaret Thatcher

Life after school started for me on 6 January 1964, on a bitterly cold Monday morning in Southampton. I'd already moved into Mrs Reid's boarding house in the Shirley district of the city, or digs, as such places were called in those days. It was located just up the road from The Dell, home of the Saints, Southampton Football Club. My folks had driven me down a few days before, wanting to be sure that I settled in OK, bringing my clothes and my bike with them.

After a delicious English breakfast in the front dining room, I cycled the mile or so to Avenue Road, where the Southampton branch of Greenham's was situated. In my determination not to be late on my first morning, I got there nearly 20 minutes before it was due to open, finding that the steel gates were locked with a huge padlock, and there were no lights on in the building. Trying to ignore the cold, I sat on my bike, leaning against the wooden fence. For the first time since arriving in this famous maritime city, I began to worry that maybe my choice of career hadn't been so clever. It was probably a serious case of homesickness, but I beginning to feel that I'd made a dreadful mistake.

My fingers and toes were frozen, and I was tired, not having slept more than three hours the previous night. My roommate in the digs was a ship worker from the Clyde, who was working on a contract in the Southampton dockyard. In those days, it was full of ships, many of them luxury liners, such as the *Windsor Castle*, *Queen Mary*, *United States* and the SS *France*, providing a thriving source of employment across a wide range of trades. It hadn't gone un-noticed that he kept a huge pile of coupons on his bedside table, but it was only when I first saw him light up a Woodbine that I realised the coupons were the rewards of his smoking habit. In the night, I discovered that he suffered from a vile smoker's cough, the cause of my lack of sleep.

As I wrapped my scarf even tighter to keep out the chill wind, my mind drifted back to happier days, and I wondered how my school friends were spending their last few days of the school holidays. They were now in the sixth form, on course for their GCE A-Levels. I also wondered how my parents would be feeling, now that I'd left home. I smiled to myself when I came to the conclusion that they probably feeling liberated. Then a few drops of what looked ominously like snow started drifting around in the strong wind. It didn't make me feel any better. What was I doing here, I thought, sat on a bike in the freezing cold, waiting to start my business career in an industry that had no real appeal for me? Actually that's not quite true, I would be earning £7.50 a week, out of which £4.50 would go on what was referred to then as full board and lodgings.

Then the sound of an exceptionally loud air horn grabbed my attention. Looking around, I saw a young guy of about 20, sliding the back wheel of his bike precariously close to where I was huddled on my own bike, leaning against the fence. Sticking out a hand towards me, he introduced himself as John Barrow, before asking me if I was the new kid from London. Yes, I confirmed, realising that he was the important person who had the keys to open up. It seemed that phase two of my life was about to commence. I suddenly felt very nervous.

Within an hour of Greenham Tool Company opening for business on that bitterly cold morning in January 1964, I was handed my first assignation as a management trainee. It was a task which I didn't really feel offset the huge disappointment of not becoming an RAF fighter pilot. Nevertheless, I had to admit that without the front wheel being fitted to a steel industrial standard barrow, it wouldn't be much use to anyone. The problem was that there were about a 100 wheelbarrows that needed "wheeling", and as I've described, it was a cold winter morning, with ice on the ground. The barrows were stacked up against the wall in the open yard in front of the corrugated tin warehouse and office building. I made a start.

By 12 o'clock on that Monday morning, I was ready to hand in my notice, head back to Mrs Reid's guest house, pack my bags and catch a train back home. Fortunately, common sense eventually got the better of me, and I decided I would stick it out for the rest of the day. After all, I hadn't yet met the boss, Jack Heller. I wanted to tell him that I hadn't come all this way to fix wheels on wheelbarrows, in the company of John Barrow. Was there possibly a clue in that name?

I've mentioned that Jack Heller knew my mother quite well, as he often met her whilst attending sales meetings at the Isleworth head office. When he learnt that her son would be joining the company and working for him in Southampton, he assured her that he would make sure that I was OK.

He was true to his word. Later that morning, he arrived back from a meeting, just before my designated lunch hour. He got out of his green Ford Zephyr and walked straight across to where I was fitting my 39th miserable barrow wheel. To my surprise, after welcoming me to Southampton, he asked me if I'd like to go out to lunch with him. He didn't have to ask twice, and after washing off the grease and grime, I jumped into his company car and was immediately surprised to find a bench style front seat and a column gear change, which certainly wasn't the norm in any of the cars my father had driven.

Jack's choice of lunch venue was a coffee bar on London Road called The Kasbah, very close to where we were working. It was located in a basement beneath a car showroom in the city centre. Coffee bars of the type in which I had spent so much of socialising in Richmond and Twickenham were still all the rage. It seemed that they were just as popular in Southampton.

I was just about getting the feeling back into my frozen fingers as I walked down the stairs into the Kasbah. Halfway down, I was greeted by the sound of the Dave Clark Five belting out their huge hit, *Glad All Over*, from a juke box under the stairs. The place was quite full, and the overpowering feeling was one of warmth. Maybe it wouldn't be too bad in Southampton after all. I should add that I refrained from telling Jack where to stick his job.

After two days of fitting barrow wheels, I moved on to learn the more interesting skills needed to carry out a stock-check. This entailed working in the big warehouse, which was heated by a paraffin heater that looked like a jet engine in reverse, and I was starting to enjoy my work.

I spent a lot of time in my early days at Greenham's working alongside John Barrow. We got on well, and he took delight in telling me about the best places to go to meet girls, as well as those places to be avoided. He also organised my first ever blind date, which not only turned out to be a total disaster but nearly ended with me being assaulted by the girl's drunken father.

Although I was feeling much happier than on that first day, I was aware that the main purpose of the work in which I was engaged was to initially become a sales representative for the company and then hopefully go on to become a branch manager. There were times, however, when I wondered whether I'd ever get to sell anything. I'd learned from John how to go about the business of stock-taking, and how to put wheels on wheelbarrows, which I felt I could do in my sleep. I could write out a sales invoice when John or one of the other staff members sold an item at the trade counter, and I'd gained a lot of knowledge about how road signs were made, about safety clothing, including hard hats, and I'd even learned how to use a brick chasing machine, a powerful electrical piece of equipment that enabled builders to cut channels into which cables could be concealed. All of this would be helpful, but I hadn't yet learned about this important skill which Jack Heller referred to as "the real world of face-to-face selling".

That opportunity eventually came when Jack called me into his office one day and told me that he was going to promote me from being a trainee to being a "telephone salesman", working under the guidance of Arthur Rook, who had been with company for many years and was seemingly a font of all knowledge about the mystic art of selling over the telephone. This bit of good news was followed, later in the same week, by some more.

A phone call informed me that my application had been accepted for an evening job, which I hoped would allow me to earn enough to move into a decent apartment in the city. Being a chef in a Wimpy Bar might not be the most special of jobs, but it paid quite well and included a free evening meal. What I hadn't realised about the job was that by the time I'd spent a couple of hours cooking burgers and frankfurters, the thought of sitting down for a free meal which comprised those very same ingredients, didn't have the same appeal that I'd expected. It also didn't help my social life. On a couple of occasions, after the Wimpy Bar closed at 10:00 p.m., I went on to one of the city's popular dance venues. It didn't do a lot for my self-confidence when I was repeatedly asked by girls, with whom I danced, why I reeked of onions.

I was really enjoying my new daytime role as a telephone salesman and was given a lot of help by both Arthur and Jack. Computers were unheard of in such jobs at that time. To maintain and update what we now call a customer database, we used a very simple device called a RotaDex, which comprised a high number of lined cards being attached to a central spindle, so that it could be spin around to access contact details on each card. The cards contained all of the contacts details, including address, phone number, names, titles and any discounts that had been agreed. All data had to be entered by hand.

Within a few months, I had really taken to the art of using the phone as a sales tool, making contact with companies and hopefully taking orders for stock items which would then be delivered by one of our two delivery drivers. I'd also liaise with the sales rep who had responsibility for the geographical region, in my case Peter Brown, who was out on the road in his company car most of the time. Mobile phones were unheard of, and so Peter would use public phone boxes when he wanted to phone in the orders that he'd taken during the day.

I often had lunch at the Kasbah with Jack Heller. I remember, on one occasion, that when we arrived, it was extremely busy, and we asked a couple of girls if they would mind us sharing their table. It turned out that they both worked in the parade of offices next to the coffee bar. One rather took my fancy, not just for her Cilla Black hairstyle, but because I liked her catchy Hampshire accent. I decided to play it cool and hoped that we'd meet her another day when we came down for lunch.

Within a month, I asked Margaret out, and to my amazement, she'd accepted. However, when she told me that she'd been going out with one of the Manfred Mann group, who were now regular chart-toppers, with hits such as 5-4-3-2-1, Pretty Flamingo and Semi-Detached Suburban Mr James, I feared that my tales about telephone selling wouldn't offer the same charm. The group often played at the Concord Jazz Club in Southampton, one of several great live music venues in the city.

Margaret's previous relationship rather worried me in another way, as I didn't even have a car at that stage and wondered how long before she got fed up with going out, either in a hire car, which I forked out for a couple of times, or by bus or train. On one occasion, however, I splashed out some of my hard-earned cash to buy a bright red Berkeley sports car, which was powered by a 350cc Ambassador motorcycle engine. It was pre-owned and going very cheap. Sucker as I was, I believed everything that the salesman told me about the car.

Margaret was in the passenger seat, the sun was out, and there we were about to set off for the New Forest. We got about 400 metres down Thornbury Avenue when the front bonnet flew off, nearly decapitating my passenger in the process. I stopped the car, ran back and collected the flying missile and tried fixing it back in place. I could immediately see that the brackets were rusted through and had broken. That was that!

The very next day, I got a full refund, and it was back to buses and bikes for a while.

I needn't have worried about trying to impress Margaret; she had a wonderful sense of humour, and we went out together for a couple of years. I recall another incident involving a car, but this one had a less amusing outcome. My mother had sold her 850 cc Mini, in which I had passed my test at the first attempt prior to heading to Southampton. It was the Mini in which I had ferried The Victims to our only two gigs. She'd replaced it with a brand new white Vauxhall Viva, which had red seating. Snazzy little car! We'd been up to stay for a weekend with my folks, who were then living in Maidenhead, so that we could attend the Greenham Group annual dinner dance, which was being held in a function room within the new Queen's Building at Heathrow Airport.

We'd been loaned my mother's brand new Vauxhall for the evening. On the way home, well after midnight, we were driving through the Berkshire countryside, not far from home, when we took a wrong turning. In an attempt to turn around, in the days before reversing lights, I reversed into the gravel drive of a large detached house. Two factors then combined to create a disaster. For a start, it had been raining for most of the day, and to add to that, it transpired that the owner of the house had laid a new drainpipe under his drive. The weight of the car as I turned in was too much for the filled-in gravel, and the car lurched down on one side, the passenger side. Its wheels sunk in deeply and then became wedged, meaning that when I got out, I immediately sank in ankle-deep mud. I discovered that the passenger door couldn't be opened, as the bottom of the door was firmly wedged in the ditch. To make matters worse, Margaret was wearing a stylish evening dress and high-heel shoes and had to clamber over the driver seat to get out of the car.

It was pitch dark, and it was unlikely there'd be a lot of passing traffic at that time of night. I wished that mobile phones had been invented, but they hadn't. Fortunately, within a few minutes, the sight of distant headlights approaching gave us hope. We were lucky. Not only did the car stop, but the two guys in the car had a tow rope. We would soon get out of this predicament and head home.

That's what should have happened, but sadly it didn't. Instead of pulling the Viva out of the mud slowly, in the right direction, and making sure that the deep ditch on the other side was avoided, the tow car jolted forward, and then started sliding sideways. In the process, we were dragged out of the one hole and slid across the drive into the even deeper ditch on the other side. Now we were in an impossible situation. It was at the point that our good Samaritans decided they'd had enough, but not before we were able to persuade them to drop us at a phone box. They then sped off up the road.

By the time that the taxi, that we were able to eventually book, arrived, it was pouring with rain, and we must have looked like two bedraggled rats as we clambered into the back of the cab.

We crept in to the house, showered and turned in, me in a sleeping bag on the lounge floor, and Margaret in a single bed in the spare room. Those were the days!

Breakfast was a terse affair as we explained that we had left the brand new Vauxhall Viva, car stuck in a ditch. My father eventually sourced a local garage that owned a tractor. He then spent the next couple of hours helping to get the car out of the awful mess in which they had found it, in broad daylight. It was then ignominiously towed to the garage, whereupon high pressure hoses attacked the thick, sticky mud.

The fact that I survived this incident is testimony to the fact that I had very loving parents. Luckily, no lasting damage had been done; and looking as good as new, the car was driven home. The entire saga eventually faded into one of those anecdotes that families tend to look back on with a mixture of relief and humour. It hadn't seemed at all funny at the time.

You may have noticed that I haven't mentioned my girl-friend's full name. It was Margaret Thatcher. People often ask me if it was THE Margaret Thatcher, and I always answer in the affirmative. For two years of my life, she was very much THE Margaret Thatcher. She eventually moved on and married my boss, Jack Heller. Today, she still lives in Southampton, where she became a magistrate for 27 years, being honoured in 2018 with an MBE for her services to the bench and also her extensive charity work. She has become a very good friend of my wife Liz and mine, and we often get together and have a good laugh at what were our formative years back in the 1960s, which included watching TV together when England won the 1966 World Cup!

As you can probably imagine, mention of the fact that I had dated Margaret Thatcher in my youth always brings an interesting reaction at social gatherings!

Chapter 2
Mary Quant, Tyres and Photocopiers

Jack Heller, the Southampton Branch Manager, was a very good salesman, and I learned a great deal from him over the next couple of years. He taught me the value of building relationships with key individuals and of being totally straight with people, even if you lost a potential sale as a result. He also sent me on a couple of telephone selling training courses, which boosted my confidence, no end.

Then a major change came about in my career. One of the two sales representatives working out of the Southampton office handed in their notice. Mike Joyce was a larger-than-life character who had always been very supportive of me, as I was learning the business of selling. We got on really well, and I was genuinely sorry to hear of his impending departure.

When Jack Heller asked me out to lunch one day, just after Mike had left Greenham's, I assumed that he was going to tell me about his replacement. The word amongst the staff was that it would be one of the sales reps from another branch, who would be transferred to Southampton. They were wrong. To my astonishment, Jack asked me if I felt that I was ready to move from telephone selling and take over Mike's role, as the sales representative for Hampshire and Dorset.

I was still only 19 years of age and would be the group's youngest salesman. It would mean that I would also take over Mike's car, a relatively new Ford Cortina Estate car, in British racing green. That might not seem worthy of mention today, but in the mid-1960s, having a car at the age of 19 was quite unusual, and I was beginning to realise that my choice of career hadn't been such a bad one after all.

I spent four really enjoyable years at Greenham's, with Jack Heller proving to be an excellent manager from whom I learned a huge amount, both in terms of selling techniques and also about life skills. He helped me build up my self-confidence and instilled in me the pride that being a successful, professional salesman can bring. In the process of living on my own from an early age, first in digs, before moving into a number of small apartments as my earning s grew, I learnt how to become totally self-sufficient. It was a valuable lesson.

I was very sad, many years later, to hear that Jack had been diagnosed with terminal cancer. I have a special memory of being invited to lunch with Margaret and Jack at their house in Chilworth, Southampton, together with my mum and dad. Eileen, of course, had worked with Jack all those years ago and had survived a long bout of cancer treatment and surgery herself. Jack passed away not long after that. I have a lot to thank him for, and I know he would have been so proud of Margaret receiving her MBE from the Queen.

Over the next few years, I continued to progress in the field of professional selling. I spent some time working as a sales representative for the Gala Cosmetic

Group, initially selling the Outdoor Girl brand to retail chains, such as the Boots and House of Fraser, as well to individual chemists and shops. I then moved on to represent the high-profile Mary Quant brand. I remember attending the Gala Group sales conference at the Grand Hotel in Eastbourne. Together with several colleagues, I was standing just outside reception when a silver Rolls Royce pulled up alongside us and out climbed a diminutive, very-striking Mary Quant, accompanied by her husband. He had a name you don't forget, Alexander Plunkett-Green. In the 1960s and 70s, Mary Quant was a fashion icon.

That evening, the cabaret featured a TV personality who I must admit to not liking very much, Bob Monkhouse, who hosted several TV quiz shows. Having said that, when I saw him live on stage, in a totally different environment, Bob Monkhouse proved to be one of the funniest comedians that I have seen; and his jokes just flowed like a machine gun, all funny, all tailored to suit the audience whom he had obviously researched in advance, without the need to resort to foul language.

Fun as my job with Mary Quant was, I didn't find it very stimulating or challenging and had made up my mind to start looking for a job that would do help me move forward with my sales career. During my ongoing search, an advert in the *Daily Telegraph* caught my eye. Goodyear Tyre Company was recruiting trainee area managers. I liked what I read and felt that if I could succeed as a professional salesman within such a prestigious global organisation, it would be an advantageous career move.

However, according to the job adverts, there was a strong likelihood that successful applicants would be posted to regions where there were vacancies, rather than being able to choose where they worked. This was an important consideration, as I could no longer just think about what I wanted; there was someone else in my life whom I haven't yet spoken about. It's now time to do so.

I had moved up the ladder somewhat in terms of my living accommodation whilst based in Southampton. Whilst living in digs worked well for me for a while, providing a good platform for moving from home to standing on my own two feet, it soon lost its charm, and I wanted to be on my own somewhere. I tried a couple of small flats before spotting an advertisement in the local paper for someone to share a luxury apartment with two "professionals". It was in a block called Carlton Court, situated right next to the Hampshire County Cricket Ground, in a very pleasant area of Southampton.

The two professionals were both school teachers. I would have my own room in a very modern, spacious apartment, with off-street parking. It seemed ideal, and the two guys seemed OK. It would prove to be very convenient, being able to walk into the city centre very easily. It was also close to the ice rink, the Top Rank Dance Hall and the Dell, home of Southampton Football Club. I decided to give it a go. Little did I realise when I moved in, that as a result of this decision, I would very shortly meet my future wife.

Melanie Kveta Skucek and I first met when we bumped into each other, literally, as she came down the indoor staircase of Carlton Court from the apartment she shared with her mother, father and two younger brother. It was on the floor directly above mine.

A couple of weeks later, I ran out of sugar. Guess where I went to ask if I could have a small amount, which I would, of course, replace? Yes, you're right! Then a few days later, as I was heading towards my car, I saw that Melanie and her young brother, Royston, were walking through the car park. We had a quick chat about the weather, or something else as equally unimportant, before Melanie looked at her watch and told me that they would have to go, as she was walking Royston to his school. Being a gentleman, I offered to run them there in my car, but Melanie turned the offer down. Royston didn't go a bundle on this and tugged at her arm, asking why not, until a short whisper in his ear from his sister shut him up.

We went out on a date after about four weeks and 18 months later, got engaged. Melanie was Czechoslovak, as was her father and three of her four brothers, two of whom lived away from home. Her mother was English. They were a fun family, and we shared some amazing times together. In particular, Melanie's father, Joseph, was such a laugh. We got on extremely well together. Royston became the young brother that I never had, and we shared a love of Subbuteo, the football game, which we would spend hours playing together. Three years after we first met, Melanie and I were married at the nearby Ampfield Church, not far from Romsey in Hampshire.

Now you can understand why it had to be a joint decision as to whether I applied for a position that would probably mean a move from Southampton to literally anywhere in the UK. Fortunately, we both agreed that it was too good an opportunity career wise to miss out on. I completed and then posted off the relevant application forms.

It was a surprisingly tough selection process, comprising about 20 applicants. It took place at Goodyear's head office, in the form of a board meeting style event. Throughout what seemed a long and tiring day, we all had to complete a series of tests, including each one of us standing up and talking for five minutes about a topic, chosen at random. We then had a lunchtime cocktail reception with some of Goodyear's directors, to check out our individual social graces and conversational ability. More written tests followed the reception.

It meant a lot to me to hear that I had been successful, after such a tough selection procedure. I think they took on eight of the original 20 applicants, all of whom would be attending an eight-week residential training course at Goodyear's massive Bushbury plant in Wolverhampton. This meant being away from home for quite a while, other than weekends. We were all booked into the Fox and Hounds, a pub on the Ring Road in Wolverhampton. At some stage, we would individually be sent away to learn how to check and fit bus tyres. In my case, this meant a week at Portsmouth bus depot.

It was a long and often quite stressful training course, but I thoroughly enjoyed it. On the final day, we were all feeling quite elated, whilst at the same time, wondering where we would be posted to begin our careers as Area Managers for the Goodyear Tyre Company. In those days, e-mail was unheard of, and so we had to wait on a letter that would give us this important news.

I can still remember waiting for the postman each morning. We were convinced that we would be heading off to Middlesbrough, Liverpool, Stoke or some other far away destination. When I read that it was, in fact, Maidstone in Kent, juts two hour's drive from Melanie's folks in Southampton and mine in Maidenhead, we breathed a sigh of relief. Of course, it still meant relocating, but nothing of the magnitude we were expecting.

I took an instant dislike to the person for whom I would be working, which wasn't a good sign. He wasn't the regional manager, but had been with the company a long time and would be overseeing my progress. I found him to be totally lacking in humour and incredibly supercilious. Nevertheless, I had no choice but to get on with my work and hope that he would eventually get tired of training me and leave me to my own devices. In my second year with Goodyear, I was both surprised and delighted to discover that I had become the top UK Area Manager, based on my sales figures. In my opinion, it was despite the efforts of my mentor rather than because of them that I was successful. I think he would have liked to see me fall flat on my face.

The only problem with the tyre industry, certainly at that time, was that it didn't pay well. Melanie and I had bought a house in the Medway town of Rainham in Kent, but wanted to find something a bit more up-market. It was a struggle financially.

Then one evening, I went out after work for a drink with Melanie, and we bumped into Simon, a guy that I knew from my Mary Quant days. He was with his girlfriend Susan, and they were interested to hear that I had also moved on from the Gala Cosmetics Group. They asked what I was doing career-wise, which I briefly explained to them. Whilst I nipped outside for a couple of minutes, Melanie told them more of my success at Goodyear, including the top UK salesman achievement. When I returned, Susan asked me a bit more about my work and suggested that I must be earning a lot of money. I didn't comment on that at the time, but she continued by inviting me to meet the regional manager of the company, for whom she and Simon both worked. She explained that they were always looking for skilled professional sales people, then really grabbed my attention by adding that their sales force earned well above average income. The company was Rank Xerox.

Quite frankly, the prospect of selling photocopiers didn't really turn me on. However, she was adamant that I should come into their Maidstone regional office and see for myself what the opportunities might be. *What do I have to lose by having a chat?* I thought.

The sheer scale and style of the Xerox offices and showroom impressed me, as did my conversation with John Liddle, the regional manager. The potential to earn two or three times the salary I was currently on, in itself, was an incentive; but when I learned about the various incentive programmes that Xerox operated, I became quite excited. I heard that if you hit target for the year, you could attend Xerox international conferences in exotic venues, such as the Bahamas or Mexico. If you exceeded target, the venue became even more exotic.

What really appealed to me was the fact that everything in Xerox was geared to achieving sales of high quality, top of the range, state-of-the art printing and copying equipment. If I joined, I would attend a residential three-week course at the company's Newport Pagnell sales training school, to prepare me fully for the role. John Liddle went on to tell me that such was the focus on sales, even the showroom's receptionist, who turned out to be Susan, Simon's partner, attended the courses. Xerox rightly believed that the receptionist was very often the starting point of a sales enquiry. The company's engineers and customer service representatives also attended scaled down sales courses.

I didn't need any more persuading. This is what I was looking for. It was also pointed out to me that the attitude of the Rank Xerox chairman, Haimish Orr-Ewing, was very unusual. He believed that if a salesperson was performing at a level which resulted in them earning more than he did, as chairman, it was a situation to be applauded, not prevented or frowned upon, which is sadly the case in a high number of companies. Xerox encouraged its staff to be proud to call themselves professional sales people. It rewarded success.

Chapter 3
Pan's People, 3-Day Weeks and Victoria's

The three week Rank Xerox training course that I attended in Newport Pagnell was an extraordinary revelation. It introduced me to the Xerox PSS Course, for a start. Professional Selling Skills was a multi-module sales training programme that broke the entire sales process into its constituent parts and encouraged the sales person to develop a two-dimensional interactive sales strategy rather than the accepted "tell is best" method used by a high percentage of sales people. Remember, this was in an era way before the advent of social media.

Such was the reputation of the Xerox PSS programme that Xerox Learning Systems was established in its own right to sell those courses to other companies throughout the world.

In addition to sales training, Xerox taught a phenomenal way of demonstrating its product range to individuals or groups of people. I wonder why, some four decades on, it is still a rare occurrence when a salesperson in a retail store displays any ability to demonstrate a technical product in a dynamic, professional way. If Xerox could do it all those years ago, what is the problem stopping companies today using the latest digital training to improve the poor standard of product demonstrations?

It wasn't all hard work at Xerox. Another area in which the company excelled was in motivating its sales force in a range of different ways. Each year, all of the sales personnel (around 1500 at its peak) were invited to a glamorous event at which the company presented the forthcoming year's sales incentive programme. Xerox did nothing by halves; I recall one particular event that not only was one of its most successful but which has proved extremely beneficial to me many years later.

This particular event was held in London, in 1973, and was themed "the Race of Champions". It comprised two parts. In the afternoon, we were invited to the Theatre Royal in Drury Lane. The incentive programme was presented by means of a dynamic audio-visual presentation, linking the sales targets, which we would be expected to achieve in 1974, to the Formula 1 World Championship. Sales personnel who achieved 100% of target or above, at specific times during the year, would qualify for a number of exciting awards, including a day at a racing school, tickets to the British F1 Grand Prix and other motorsport related activities. Then the top prize was dramatically announced for the salesperson with the highest percentage over target at the end of the year. Onto the stage, driving a brand new MGB GT V8 sports car, appeared Stirling Moss. He climbed out of the car and held out the keys towards the audience, asking who was going to win this beauty. It really brought the house down, and you could say that the 1500 members of the Xerox sales force were in a buoyant mood as they herded back on the street, ready to head off to the second part of the day, which comprised a gala dinner later that evening at the Grosvenor Hotel in Park Lane.

With everyone seated at their tables prior to the meal being served, they listened to an address from Haimish Orr-Ewing, the Rank Xerox chairman. He told us what a fantastic sales force we were, how we'd exceeded our national sales targets in the year to date and generally inspired us all with his speech; he then accepted a few questions from the floor. I'll never forget one particular salesman stood up and took advantage of the invitation. He thanked Orr-Ewing for the praise that he'd lavished on the sales force and then asked a question which generated a few gasps from the assembled sales force. Why, he asked, if they were such great salespeople, were they given two-door 1100cc Ford Escorts as company cars? Without any hesitation whatsoever, the chairman told the person in question that the reason was very simple; it was because he hadn't yet persuaded Ford Motor Company to build one-door Ford Escorts!

I seem to recall that everyone got to their feet to applaud the much-appreciated humour of the chairman. I was liking this company, liking it a lot!

The cabaret that evening comprised two well-known acts. The first was the unforgettable Pan's People, BBC *Top of the Pops* resident dance group, whilst the main act was Ronnie Corbett, of the Two Ronnie's fame. Sadly, for some reason this world-class funny man just didn't perform as we all knew he could; and a Xerox sales force can be very intimidating, believe me. As he delivered what seemed like a below-par performance, a few bread rolls started to fly through the air towards the diminutive comedian. Corbett, not unnaturally, took umbrage and turned on the audience before storming off the stage. It wasn't good to experience this mutual lack of respect, but fortunately, the compère then quickly changed the mood of the audience by informing us that Pan's People would be returning to the stage. That would have been quite adequate, but he then made a regrettable error by asking if a few of the salespeople would like to join Pan's People on stage and dance with them. It wasn't a good idea, as salesmen got to the stage by any means they could. It was a disaster, and Pan's People had to leave the stage at a rapid pace.

Nevertheless, the day had been memorable for me, and I learned a lot about the way in which sales people can be motivated by a well-designed sales incentive programme. That knowledge came in very useful throughout my career.

I will always be grateful to Rank Xerox for providing me with a set of skills that subsequently enabled me to move into a totally different environment and reach the highest level in one of the world's most fiercely competitive and overtly commercial sports. During my first couple of years at Xerox, I was able to earn at a very high level and revelled in the job. Had I not met Simon and Susan that evening in the pub, I would have missed something very special.

Then something happened that was way outside my control. It was to have major effect on the Xerox sales force.

The Prime Minister at that time was Edward Heath, who is always associated with a phenomenon that shocked the UK, when in December 1973; he introduced what became known as the **3-Day Week.** This provided legislation preventing companies operating for more than three days each week. It was based on a need to conserve electricity, which was severely restricted due to industrial action by coal miners. From 1 January 1974 until 7 March, commercial users of electricity were limited to three specified consecutive days' consumption each week and prevented from working longer on those days. Hospitals and other essential services were exempt. In addition, TV companies were required to cease broadcasting at 10:30 p.m.

As a direct result of the 3-day week legislation, Rank Xerox took the drastic decision to reduce the size of its sales force in what were obviously very difficult times. We all waited nervously to hear whether the proverbial thumb would be pointing up or down in our own individual situations. Fortunately for me, the thumb was up, and I was promoted to the role of major account executive. This meant working with major corporations and also government departments. It was a huge relief, and I felt very sorry for many of my colleagues who lost their jobs. It wasn't going to be easy to find another source of employment in the current circumstances.

Interestingly, around this time, one of my colleagues was called into John Liddle's office, to be told that he would no longer be selling photocopiers. Alan Hinton was a very good salesman, but that almost goes without saying at Xerox. He wondered what, if anything, he'd done wrong. The answer was nothing; in fact it was just the opposite. John told Alan that he been selected to take on the selling of a brand new product that Xerox were launching. It was exciting and innovative product, called a facsimile machine, offering the telephonic transmission of scanned printed material, both text and images. Alan's face when he came out of the meeting was a picture. He was clearly not a happy bunny. He told us what he'd been offered and added the comment that he couldn't understand why anyone would sign up for fax machine if no one else had yet got one? It was going to be a tough job. Little did he know how much he was going to earn over the next decade, as the fax era took off in a huge way.

Unfortunately, despite the good news that I was staying on with Xerox, there was a negative aspect resulting from the sales force reduction. Xerox took the decision to reduce recruitment, which meant that the training school at Newport Pagnell would be cut back in terms of staffing. This would have an impact on my plans. It was mandatory within Rank Xerox that no one would be promoted to a management position without having spent a minimum of six months as a training officer at the sales training school. I'd been looking forward to that role and had spoken to my regional manager, John Liddle, about the possibility. However, the imposed staff reductions meant that there would be a greatly decreased need for training instructors, and this would put paid to my moving in that direction.

I wasn't too down-hearted; after all, I had been promoted, and I would earn more money as a result. Nevertheless, I needed to look for a way to fire myself up again. The solution presented itself within a very short time.

Whilst I had been working at Xerox, Melanie and I had spent a weekend with her eldest brother Chris and his wife Jacky, who lived in Birmingham. He was employed by British Leyland and had been part of the team headed up by Alec Issigonis, designer of the original Mini. I was keen to spend some time talking to Chris, as Melanie had mentioned that he was involved in some form of motor racing. She thought that he owned a Lotus 7 and competed mainly at Silverstone, in what she referred to as club racing.

On this particular weekend, Melanie had suggested that we should go and watch Chris compete. It wasn't my first visit to a race track; as many years before, when I was about 15, I'd been taken to the Boxing Day race meeting at Brands Hatch in Kent. I remember it being a bitterly cold day and, together with some friends, stood huddled on the bank at Clearways Corner, fascinated by the close racing that was going on. The thought of being able to have a go at this myself one day never even entered my head. For a start, it would have been way beyond my budget level.

Apart from that event, I'd also been to watch a couple of F1 Grand Prix, both of which really blew my mind. The first was at Brands Hatch in 1968, where I managed to wriggle into a space right by the fence on the outside of Druids Hairpin. It was a stunning vantage point, from which I could see cars come through Paddock Hill Bend and up the hill towards me. I'd never witnessed anything like it. The noise and sheer speed of these awesome-looking machines thrilled me to the core. I remember that the American racer, Dan Gurney, was wearing the first ever full-face helmet to be seen in F1. Up to then, drivers had worn open-face helmets with goggles and Nomex face masks. That day, the British Grand Prix was won by the Swiss driver Jo Siffert, in Rob Walker's Lotu49B. It was the first of two Grand Prix victories that he would celebrate. Three years later, driving a Yardley-sponsored BRM in a non-world championship F1 race, also at Brands Hatch, Jo Siffert was tragically killed.

Ironically, whilst writing these words about the 1968 British Grand Prix and, in particular, Dan Gurney's full-face helmet, I heard the sad news that that the popular American driver had passed way at the age of 89. In his era, not every F1 driver would survive and go on to enjoy such a long retirement. F1 was a very dangerous sport, with fire being one of the greatest risks. It was good to know that such a great personality and doyen of the sport should live to enjoy the respect and recognition of his peers and public.

Maybe it was a sign of things to come, but my abiding memory of that British Grand Prix in 1968 was the fact that for the first time ever, the race cars carried commercial advertising. In particular, I was impressed with the Gold Leaf Team's Lotus cars of Graham Hill and Jackie Oliver, even with the extraordinary aerodynamic wings that were perched above the car, fore and aft. Colin Chapman, the boss of the Lotus Team, ever the businessman, was the first to exploit a significant rule change in motorsport. Up to that time, cars had been painted in the colours of their home country. The French cars were blue, Italian cars red; British were green and so on. When the decision to allow advertising on race cars was taken, with effect from 1968, Chapman proposed to tobacco giant John Players that he should run his two F1 cars in the world championship, carrying the livery of their Gold Leaf brand. It was the start of a sponsorship revolution that would not be restricted to Formula 1 but quickly spread across a host of other sports as well.

Another race meeting that I attended was the 1969 British Grand Prix. In those days, it was alternated between Silverstone and Brands Hatch, so for 1969, the venue was the Northamptonshire track, where I was privileged to watch the historic race between Jackie Stewart, in his Matra-Ford, and Jochen Rindt in the Gold Leaf Team Lotus. I was watching from the outside of Copse Corner and became aware of the fact that I was only able to see the two protagonists every one minute twenty seconds, and even then, only for a few seconds. For the rest of the time, I had to rely on the antiquated PA system to keep me updated. I thought back to Brands Hatch the previous year, where I had been able to see so much more of the action, from wherever I stood. This was due to the amphitheatre style of the circuit. I wondered then, and I still wonder today, why more F1 track designers don't recognise this. People want to see as much of the action as possible, especially when they are paying so much for the pleasure of being there. These flat, airfield style circuits really don't do much to grow the popularity of the sport.

I know that most people watch on TV, but for those who spend hundreds of pounds to gain access to a circuit, only to be forced to watch most of the action on big screens, I think it's a bit off. Then again, I suppose the more cynical amongst us will say that with the increasingly boring nature of many races, these people are not actually missing much action.

I enjoyed my day at Silverstone with Melanie and her family, watching Chris race. It was very different to watching a Grand Prix, but on the short club circuit, the action came thick and fast. There was also a totally different atmosphere, but the level of enthusiasm was hard to match. As I watched Chris battling with a host of similar cars, it struck me that this level of participation might actually be achievable for me, both from a skill and a financial level.

Over the next few weeks, I started researching the most feasible way of putting my toe in the water, in terms of going racing. It occurred to me that it might be helpful to visit the Racing Car Show, which was then held annually in London. One of the exhibitors was Motor Racing Stables, the racing driver school at Brands Hatch, which had set up a Formula 3 simulator on its stand. It was incredibly basic compared to today's high-technology versions, but I was encouraged to try my hand in it. I noticed a big sign, informing me that the person achieving the fastest lap of the day would get a free lesson at Brands Hatch. My first lap in this somewhat dated simulator wasn't very encouraging, as the wooden steering wheel came off in my hands. Nevertheless, after three laps, I climbed out of the car, determined that somehow I would find a way of driving one of these single-seater cars on a track. Later in the day, I went back to check the times and discovered that I had set the fastest time, probably because I got the steering wheel back on quicker than other contestants had managed! On the stand were two Formula 1 drivers, Trevor Taylor and Peter Arundel, both employed as instructors at Motor Racing Stables. They issued me with a voucher, entitling me to a free lesson at the school. I remember thinking that if two such well-known F1 drivers thought that I was quick, who was I to argue with them? Of course, looking back now, I'm fully aware that it was just a simple marketing exercise, and I'm sure that most of those who had paid their ten bob were told they had the fastest time of the day and were given a voucher to get them to visit the school and part with more money.

Eventually, the big day arrived, and I headed off to Brands Hatch. I have to say that it proved to be somewhat of a disaster. Not that I didn't find the two hot laps in a TVR 1600 Vixen, driven by F1 racer Peter Arundell, exhilarating, but the condition of the very early model Formula Fords in which I would complete my five laps, left a lot to be desired. Everything was shaking, seemingly to pieces, as I found my way around the short club circuit, including one mirror that spun precariously on its bracket. Other much faster cars were also lapping the track, but seeing them approaching in my mirrors was a near impossibility. I had built up some speed and tried too hard to keep out of their way, in the process, embarrassingly spinning in the middle of the bend. The car stalled, and I waited for the instructor to reach me, like a naughty schoolboy who has spilled ink over his exam papers.

That was it. I was told my day was over, as spinning was "not allowed". You'd think I'd done it deliberately, the way I was spoken to. It wasn't a pleasant experience, and quite frankly, I found the attitude of the staff at the school that day very poor. It didn't destroy my racing ambitions, but it surely would have done for a lot of people, and I don't think that is what a commercial operation like MRS should be doing. It wasn't the fact that I'd been crapped out, it was the "totally bored with the whole business" attitude shown towards all of us novices from a bunch of guys who should have known better. I would go onto set my own racing school many years later, in South Africa, and I always made sure that my instructors never adopted a "rather bored with it all" attitude shown by the Brands Hatch guys that day.

My intrepid "spin" hadn't put me off wanting to race one of these single-seater cars, just the opposite in fact, so I carried out some more research on how else I might go about the task. Many of the people, to whom I spoke in the process, suggested that I should get in touch with the Jim Russell Racing Driver School, based at the Snetterton Race Circuit, not far from Norwich. From what I could find out, remember Google wasn't there to help me, the schools' reputation seemed good; and so Melanie and I headed up the A11 and booked into the cosy Bunwell Manor Hotel, as recommended by the school's brochure, which had been sent to us in advance. The hotel was owned by one of the instructors, and nearly all of the guests were either involved in racing of some sort or pupils at the school.

I was determined not to make the same mistake as I had at Brands, but I needn't have worried. The welcome that all 20 of us received on that trial day was of the highest standard. Our instructor on that first lesson was John Kirkpatrick. Looking back, I think the primary difference between this school and that at Brands Hatch was that John was not a budding young racing driver or even an experienced racing driver, trying to earn a few bob. He was a professional instructor, and therein was the difference.

I've now known John Kirkpatrick as a friend for over 40 years. You'll discover later in the book, that I worked closely with him many years after my first lesson at his school, in a ground-breaking development within the motorsport industry. John also went on to set up ARDS, the Association of Racing Driver Schools, in the process bringing in a much-needed standard to licensing for racing schools and the instructors working for them.

Over a few months, Melanie and I spent many enjoyable but often freezing-cold weekends at the Snetterton Circuit, where I learnt the skills to drive a skittish Formula Ford racing car around the track at high but consistent speeds. I eventually qualified and got my certificate. I was all ready to go racing, except for one major issue. Not only couldn't I afford to buy a Formula Ford race car, I didn't have the infrastructure or the technical knowledge to prepare it for racing.

Whichever way I looked at it, it seemed that my desire to go motor racing would have to go on hold for a while. I came to the conclusion that it made sense to rather concentrate on my career with Xerox and make some serious money. The potential was there to do just that, so I forced myself to forget about race driving and focus on selling Xerox's comprehensive range of photocopying and printing equipment.

For the next few months, I worked my butt off and achieved some good results for the company. I was learning more and more about professional selling and felt very fortunate that I'd joined a company that put so much focus on on-going training. Even today, when I talk to business people about the reputation that Xerox had for producing highly successful sale personnel, there is an agreement that it was very special. Interestingly, Clive Woodward, who became famous for his management exploits with England in Rugby Union, was also a Rank Xerox salesman in his time.

Then one day, as I was driving along the A20 from Maidstone to Ashford, on the way to meet a potential customer, I noticed a large hoarding that was being erected at the side of the road by some workman. The sign advised motorists that in a few weeks' time, a new night-club would be opening on the site. It was to be called Victoria's.

Why, I don't know, but the name Victoria's stuck in my mind for the rest of the day. The next morning, I drove back to the site of the new club and jotted down the details that were on the sign. An hour later, I was on the phone to a young lady who told me that she was Victoria's PR executive. I learned from her that the club was owned by a Yugoslavian, whose name I think was Mr Jorkov. She told me that Victoria's would comprise a restaurant, a casino and a substantial dance floor. Importantly, she confirmed that the new club was targeting the business sector within a 20 mile radius. She added that it would be opening in about six weeks away. I thanked her and turned my thoughts back to my next business meeting.

That evening I told Melanie about my phone call to Victoria's, to which she registered some surprise, reasoning that neither of us were exactly night-clubbers. I explained that I wasn't thinking of us becoming members, but rather that Victoria's should become a motorsport sponsor. I went on to outline my thought process, which was based on showing the owner of the new club how we might help him sell membership subscriptions for Victoria's in an innovative, measurable way.

Despite the fact that I would be making my very first approach to a business in terms of trying to acquire sports sponsorship, I had no comprehension at the time that it would prove pivotal in my eventually embarking on a new career path.

Over the next week or so, I spent my evenings developing a strategy that I hoped would generate interest from Victoria's owner. It was based on a combination of the information I'd gleaned from the PR person, and the valuable lessons I'd learned in my sales career over the past few years.

Eventually, I was ready to make another call to Victoria's. I asked for a meeting with the owner, but it seemed that he was far too busy, planning a special lunch for the official opening. Having got more details of this event, I finalised what was effectively my sales plan.

The day of the opening eventually arrived; and to my delight, the weather was fine, an important factor in my strategy. My research had shown that the lunch that had been planned would be an impressive affair, with invitations going out to a long list of influential business figures from the region. The pre-lunch reception was due to start at 12:30 p.m.

At precisely 12:20, I drove my Xerox Ford Escort into the large car-parking area in front of the club. Apart from half a dozen cars, it was empty, and I got out to make sure that I was within the white lines. What I haven't mentioned up to now is that, attached to the Ford Escort was a trailer, on which a Formula Ford racing car was tethered. I'd literally borrowed it from the person who had advertised it for sale and who had agreed that I could use it as part of my sponsorship acquisition strategy, hopefully securing the sponsorship money that I needed to buy the car!

The car and trailer was now positioned slap bang in the middle of the car park. I looked at my watch, it was time to go. Dressed in a smart navy blue business suit, I walked across to reception, pushed open the door and went up to the main desk, where a young lady was standing laying out a number of name tags. I introduced myself and told her that I was there to meet Mr Jorkov. She asked me if I was a lunch guest. When I told that I wasn't, she frowned, but I quickly explained that I wanted to speak to him about an idea that I believed would help him sell a lot of membership subscriptions for the club. I then made a point of looking out of the window and saw that several cars were now arriving in the car park. To my delight, several guests were wandering over and looking at the Formula Ford. At that moment, the door from the club into reception suddenly flew open, and a massive individual, dressed in a suit, strode in. He must have been at least six foot eight, with the build of a weight lifter.

'Is that your f***ing car and trailer stuck in the middle of the car park?' He asked, in a raised voice. I confirmed nervously that it was.

'Then get it out of there NOW! I've got a huge number of guests arriving for lunch.'

I told him that I would, but quickly looked out of the window again and was relieved to see a lot of people now looking at the race car. I thought he was going to hit me, but I stood my ground. Nervously, I asked him to look at what was happening outside, which he did, but not in a positive way. I knew that I had one last chance.

'Look at the number of people walking across to look at the race car. Imagine that car, painted in Victoria's distinctive gold and maroon livery, on display in the main shopping centres in Maidstone on a Saturday morning. A sales promotional person selling Victoria's membership subscriptions would do really well, I'm sure.'

There was silence. He looked once more at the car park, and luckily for me, there were still several people gathered around the race car. He didn't say another word but put his hand in his pocket and took out, not a gun as I feared, but a business card instead.

'Give me a call in the week, but get that f*****g car out of the way.'

Two weeks later, we agreed a 12-month sponsorship deal that was based on a not-insignificant fee, supplemented by the cost of painting the race car in Victoria's livery. The real earning potential for me was a commission on every subscription sold at the regular sales promotions that I'd proposed, as well as at Brands Hatch race weekends. The deal meant that I could buy the Crossle 20F Formula Ford, which the seller had kindly loaned to me for that opening day promotion. It also allowed me to pay a race mechanic on a race-by-race basis.

I really had proved that you don't have to be a champion to be a winner. I'd never raced a car, let alone won a race. The reaction from so many people to my Victoria's deal was to ask how I could possibly have got a motor racing sponsorship when I had absolutely no track record. It went against everything they believed sponsorship was about. Despite that, I was a winner inasmuch that I had secured a significant sponsorship deal.

Brian's first ever sponsorship deal (1974) was with Victoria's Nightclub in Kent. Significantly, he hadn't raced prior to this, demonstrating that you don't have to be a champion to get your share of sponsorship.

It was a lesson that I still pass on to so many young drivers who get in touch with me in respect of sponsorship acquisition. When it comes to evaluating sponsorship proposals, companies are concerned first and foremost with finding ways to increase market share or sell more products or services. The fact that a driver has won races, broken lap records and secured championships is only important to a potential sponsor if that success can be directly linked to selling more products or services in a measurable, sustainable way.

I was chuffed that just six years after the first ever sponsorship deal in motorsport had been completed in 1968, the Gold Leaf Team Lotus agreement, I had put together a significant sponsorship deal of my own.

It heralded the start of a 45-year career in motorsport and still counting!

Chapter 4
Brands Hatch, Formula Fords and a Man
on a Plane

Having put my first sponsorship deal together, it was time to plan my racing activities in a way that would allow me to fulfil my sponsorship promotional obligations, at the same time as continuing my role at Rank Xerox. I won't go so far as to say that I lost my concentration for selling Xerox machines, but the reality was that I was having to multitask a great deal. However, in a strange way, one could say that my motor racing activities that were partly responsible for a major development in my business career. Let me explain.

I had already developed a fascination for professional selling, particularly as taught by Rank Xerox. I was also very aware of the rapid growth and success of Xerox Learning Systems, the company that had been set up by Xerox to market its own sales training programmes. I came to realise that I was also extremely interested in the whole topic of sales training, and a thought entered my head that I might enjoy being involved in its delivery.

I was racing at Brands Hatch one weekend, in the regional Kent Messenger Championship, which was sponsored by the rapidly growing newspaper and media group. On the first lap of my Heat, I'd been caught up in a multi-vehicle pile-up, which badly damaged the front end of my Crossle race car. The race had been stopped, and the four cars involved, including mine, were pushed out of the way onto a part of the track that led from the Indy Circuit, on which we were competing, to the full Brands Hatch Grand Prix circuit.

The racing continued without any us. I sat in my cockpit, helmet off, staring at the badly damaged steering and wondering what it would cost to repair. At the end of the race, the tow truck came out, and two burly guys attached a tow rope from the rear of their truck to the roll bar above my head. I told them that the steering was badly affected by the damage, only to be told not to worry and to let them get on with what they did best! I obviously didn't get my message across, because the next thing I knew, they'd started the tow truck, put it into gear and steered left onto the track at what was then known as Clearways Corner. I knew instantly what was going to happen, and I was spot on. The race car's steering was jammed to the right. Instead of following the direction of the tow truck, the car was pulled sideways, then turned completely upside down. My head hit the track with a resounding thud, and I could sense and smell petrol dripping from the fuel tank, which worryingly formed part of the driver's seat.

I came around a few seconds later, being dragged upside down along the track, with my head still banging on the track. It was apparent that the driver and his mate were unaware of what was happening. Eventually, I guess they worked it out, thanks to the dozens of people in the crowd, who, I found out later, were pointing at my car and waving their arms about frantically. I heard a subsequent comment that they thought the crowd was cheering them!

That had happened on the Sunday, now it was Monday morning, and I was sitting in the reception of a company in Ashford, about to talk to them about possibly installing a Xerox 3600 Copier. I had a bandage around my head, a bad headache and was flicking through the *Sunday Times*. At the back of my mind was the likely cost of the accident damage to the race car.

Then I saw it; a quarter page recruitment advertisement inserted by the massive American conglomerate, ITT, looking to recruit a UK sales training manager for its TV and radio division, ITT Consumer Products, based at Foots Cray, not far from Brands Hatch.

ITT was a big name in the business world, owning companies such as ITT Sheraton Hotels, Avis Car Hire, Rimmel Cosmetics and Koni Shock Absorbers, amongst many others. My appetite for sales training had been whetted at Xerox, but the opportunity to spend time in that capacity at the Xerox training school had been thwarted by the three-day week issues that had hit the country hard. Maybe this was an opportunity that I should look into. I surreptitiously tore out the page in question and slid it into my briefcase just before the person I was meeting, walked into the reception area.

After discussing the opportunity with Melanie, I took the decision to apply for the position. This time, a house move wouldn't be necessary. Two very intense interviews followed. The more I was told about the job, the keener I became to be the lucky one. It was once again time to wait for the post to arrive. When an ITT-branded envelope finally dropped on the front doormat, I was nervous, but it proved to be positive news. I was going to move from sales into sales training, embarking on a new adventure in the process.

Excited as I was at the prospect of joining one of the world's largest corporations in a senior position, I had mixed emotions. I had so enjoyed my years working for Rank Xerox, and in the process, had learned more than I realised was possible about the world of professional selling. I'd made a lot of money and met some incredibly talented people within the company. If I hadn't joined Xerox, I knew for sure that I wouldn't be in a position where I was not only competing in Formula Ford, but had the belief that my sales skills would help me secure even more sponsorship.

As it turned out, there was a month's gap between leaving Xerox and starting my new role at ITT. It was by now late February, and I thought that a short vacation might be a good move. Unfortunately, Melanie was unable to take leave at that time, but suggested that I should take the opportunity to visit my parents, who had been living in Johannesburg since 1969. I'd never been to South Africa, and the chance to see them again, whilst at the same time getting away from an English winter, certainly appealed.

The airline deal, that best-suited my budget, involved flying Alitalia to Rome, then on down to South Africa. My folks were delighted when I rang them and told them of my imminent arrival. I think they were finding that South Africa was a lot further away from the UK than they had imagined, in respect of communication. For a start, they didn't have the luxury of technology, such as Skype, whilst phone calls to and from South Africa, particularly at Christmas time, had to be pre-booked. It really was a different world then.

A couple of days before I was due to fly, an airmail letter arrived from my dad, telling me that he had arranged for me to go to the South African F1 Grand Prix at the Kyalami Circuit near Johannesburg. I must admit that it hadn't occurred to me that the event would be taking place whilst I was out there. It seemed that a business friend of Ken's had a spare ticket and offered to take me as his guest. What an unexpected bonus.

Little did I know then that I would be sitting next to a passenger on the flight down, who would ultimately change the direction of my career.

Chapter 5
Kyalami, Braii's and Sunshine

I was lucky enough to get a window seat on the packed flight to Rome and was sitting reading a copy of *Autosport* magazine, as everybody in racing did in those days. The man in the seat next to me had been reading *The Times* newspaper; but when the stewardess arrived with some food, he put the paper down and started talking to me. He told me that he'd noticed the magazine that I was reading and asked me if I was a motor racing fan. When I told him that I was indeed a fan and had just started racing in Formula Ford, he smiled and wanted to know more. A few minutes later, he asked me where I was heading. On learning that I would be going to the Grand Prix in South Africa, he passed across a business card and suggested that I should meet up with him in the F1 Paddock at the track.

That was how I first met Max Mosley, who was not only a director of the March F1 Team, which would competing in the South African Grand Prix, but the letter M for Mosley, together with the first letters of the other directors names, formed the word MARCH. He would go on to become president of the FIA.

That chance meeting on the Alitalia flight was to be very fortuitous. Not only did I meet Max in the Paddock at the South African Grand Prix, as he had suggested, but a few years later, our paths would cross again, and he would help me secure a career development opportunity that I could never have dreamed of.

My 1975 visit to South Africa was memorable in so many ways. The incredible blue skies and almost constant sunshine were in marked contrast to the grey, cold, rainy weather that I'd left behind. The sheer scale of everything was quite different. In a country with so much land available for building, properties sat on huge plots, with lush gardens and swimming pools being commonplace. Although I didn't have time to head up to the Kruger Park to enjoy some of the country's famous wildlife, I did get to a smaller reserve and found the sun drenched terrain so different to anything I'd come across in Europe.

The South African Grand Prix was an extraordinary event, especially for someone who had only been to British races. My dad's business colleague picked me up on the morning of the race really early. He was driving a Rambler Estate, an American style V8 which had a stack of strange-looking gear in the back. It didn't take long to understand what it was for, as we drove through the gates of the famous Kyalami Grand Prix Circuit, situated nearly halfway between Johannesburg and Pretoria. All around the fenced perimeters of the race circuit, hundreds of cars, pick-up trucks and vans had parked, most of which were facing the circuit with the frontend right up against the wire-fencing. Coming from English race tracks, such as Silverstone, which traditionally offer parking and a long walk, this was a revelation. Not only were the cars parked so close to the track, but alongside, a high percentage of the occupants had constructed towers made of scaffolding and planks. The resulting platforms provided superb viewing facilities, and most of them were alongside portable barbeques or *braiis,* as the South Africans call them.

As we drove around the dirt roads around the exterior of the track itself, heading to Clubhouse Corner, where Joe had a reserved space for his vehicle, he brought me up to speed on this phenomenon. He explained that about 50% of the expected 70,000 spectators would probably have driven to the track from Durban, Cape Town, Port Elizabeth and Bloemfontein much earlier in the week. They would have then chosen their preferred viewing spot prior to building a scaffolding stand. Once settled in, they would set about the task of cooking and consuming vast amounts of traditional boerewors (spicy beef sausage), accompanied by varying quantities of brandy and Coca Cola, lagers and wine, all of which could be purchased at ridiculously low cost, particularly compared to the UK.

It was expected that temperatures would rise to 30 degrees Celsius, or more, with the African sun beating down on some very tender-looking exposed skins! Johannesburg is 1800 meters above sea level, and the air is quite rarefied. I was reliably told that it takes a minute longer to boil an egg in Johannesburg than it does in Cape Town, situated at sea level.

As the week went by, the crowds would increase, finding innovative ways of keeping themselves amused until the Thursday or Friday when the first F1 cars would take to the circuit. The atmosphere generated in this way was totally different to a British Grand Prix.

Joe eventually found our place at Clubhouse, and we unloaded all of the equipment from the back of the Rambler. Some temporary small stands, open to the sun, had been erected by the circuit owners; and right on the very front row, probably some ten meters from the track barriers, some spaces had been covered in red and white plastic tape, embossed with the word "Reserved". Joe explained that one of his workmen had been there the day before to reserve the places, sleeping overnight in a sleeping bag, to ensure that no one hi-jacked them. The equipment that Joe unloaded included enough Castle Lagers to keep a cricket team in beer for an entire test match! The mandatory *braii* was now in place, and everything was ready for what we hoped was going to be a cracking Grand Prix.

It proved to be a great spectacle, and we were in prime position to see the cars, many of them sliding in opposite lock fashion through the 90 degree left-hander. Tom Pryce, in his Shadow, was the most sideways of all, and he would get a huge cheer every lap from the thousands around us.

Suffice to say, with victory ultimately going to the local boy, Jody Scheckter, in his Tyrell, the crowd's reaction at the end of the day's racing was something to behold. All in all, the experience was one I'll never forget.

My two weeks in South Africa flew by, and I enjoyed some quality time with my folks. However, a new job awaited me in the UK, and it was time to leave the sunshine, and some of the most wonderful scenery I'd ever seen, and head back to my wife, to ITT and to a new season of racing.

Chapter 6
Training, Egg-Packers and a Hawke

ITT's UK headquarters was located in Foots Cray, Kent, within easy travelling distance of our house. Melanie was working at the Maidstone Eye Hospital, and between us, we were now earning good money. Life was treating us well.

My new role as UK sales training manager for ITT consumer products started well. Malcolm McCarthy, the company's sales training director and my boss, was not only extremely good at his job, but I found him to be friendly, highly enthusiastic and extremely helpful. This division of ITT designed and manufactured a range of electrical products, which could easily be classified as white goods and brown goods. In the first category were items such as fridge, freezers, washing machines and similar items, whereas the brown goods included radios, televisions, music centres and tape cassette players.

One of the major retail distributors for ITT was the Curry's Group, then an independent chain in its own right. My first task was to embark upon a national tour of Curry's city centre branches, staging product sales training classes for their retail sales staff. I would accompany my boss for the first three events, after which I was on my own. The thinking behind these courses, which were funded by ITT, was very simple. With a range of competitive brands on offer in Curry's shops, it stood to reason that the staff, when facing a potential customer, would feel more confident about demonstrating a product about which they knew the most. ITT wanted to make sure that it was their products, rather than a competitor's, that they felt most comfortable talking about. My job was to provide them with the product knowledge that would give them that confidence.

I learned a great deal in the process of running these training sessions, which lasted in total for about eight weeks and took me all over the UK. They normally started at 5:30 p.m., shop closing time and lasted for about 90 minutes. I met some real characters during my travels to different stores. On one occasion, in Diss, a small town in Norfolk, I recall asking the 15 or so trainees to introduce themselves to me, one by one. I'd noticed a young guy, about 20 years old, with his arm firmly around a much younger girl sitting next to him. When it came to the introduction, he told me that he was van driver for the branch, but was hoping to move into sales. I then asked the girl what she did at Curry's. In a broad Norfolk accent, she explained why she was there. "Oi don't do nuffing for Curry's. Oi'm an egg-packer at the local farm, but oi'm his girl, and where he goes, oi go!"

The more training sessions that I ran, the more feedback I received from within Curry's, as to the difference it was making to performance levels in-store around the UK. Having seen the success of the concept, Malcom McCarthy asked me if I would like to offer a similar course to one or two other retail chains. This meant that I would be doing a lot of driving, which I didn't mind. Traffic volumes in the 1970s were very different to the nightmare scenario that we have to endure today. For a start, we didn't have the M25, which only fully opened in 1986, whilst the M40 was built in stages and completed only in 1983. As long as you avoided what was commonly known as the "rush-hour", you could normally travel without too many hold-ups. Today, I find that rush-hours are a thing of the past. I often use the A3 or the M3 early in the morning at around 5:45; and the traffic density is much the same then as in the daytime or evening. Wherever you seem to go, it's the same old story, with constant streams of trucks, vans and cars, very little policing, and a level of lawlessness that is quite extraordinary.

Having learned a great deal about retail selling in my new role, I was starting to grow in confidence. I was also gaining a lot of pleasure from training people, as I had hoped I would. What I found particularly interesting was that training salespeople, who worked in the retail environment, required a very different type of training to that which I had gone through with Xerox. In the process, I was starting to spend a lot more time looking at how I could present sales training in a more entertaining and relevant way, and how best to deal with the specific challenges that retail and business-to-business selling presented.

My working relationship with Malcolm McCarthy continued to motivate me, helped greatly by his high level of enthusiasm. Then one morning, he invited me to the canteen for a coffee and a chat. It seemed that he wanted to throw me in at the deep end once again. He told me that a new exhibition centre had just opened (Feb 1976) close to Birmingham Airport, the National Exhibition Centre (NEC). One of the very first exhibitions to be held at the new venue would be the Radio and TV Show, at which ITT would have a large stand. I wasn't sure what was coming next.

Malcolm explained that he and I would be teaming up to design and deliver a training programme for the company's sales force and also for its management team members who would be attending the NEC. The purpose was to help them adjust from their normal style of selling, as sales representatives out on their own visiting their customers to the very different style of selling from an exhibition stand. Another difference would be the presence of the general public, always an underestimated factor at exhibitions.

ITT consumer products' 16 individual sales reps, each had their own geographic territories; and throughout the year, I would visit the high number of independent retail shops which specialised in selling radios, TVs, music centres and other similar products that were the norm in that era. Their aim was to take orders for new and replacement products. ITT Music Centres were extremely popular at that time, comprising a turn-table, a radio and a tape cassette player, all built into one quite flat, long unit that had a clear plastic lid, which opened upwards.

In my first year, along with delivering the retail training programmes that I've described, I'd spent time travelling with each one of these 16 sales reps. What I discovered was that most of these men weren't what I would call professional sales personnel but rather order-takers, or commercial travellers, as they used to be known. They could hardly be called pro-active business development sales exponents of the type I met at Xerox.

Their average age must have been early 50s, and many of them had known their customers for a long time. As a result, their "sales-calls" comprised a good chat, a cup of coffee, and the question 'Right Charlie, what you would like me to send you on the next delivery?'

I'm not criticising at all. That's how they saw the job. What I had come across was a sales force that was surviving the last few years of a drastically changing industry. You no longer find the types of privately owned shops or independently run regional chains that existed at that time. They were dedicated specifically to the sale of TVs and radios. Each shop would probably have its main agency range, such as Bush, Grundig, Cossor and ITT, but also stock a few other lesser-known brands. Nowadays, you would go to a superstore, or even a supermarket, where you are presented with a wide range of items; that is if you don't buy online. It was a different world then, in 1976. I discovered that many of ITT's sales force had been on-board for 20 odd years or so; and much as I might have thought that I could help them improve their performance, the reality was very different. They had developed their own style of selling, one which they believed worked well enough. Who was this young whipper-snapper to try to move with the times?

Nevertheless, they had to admit that selling on an exhibition stand, which is what they would be facing at the NEC, would be a different kettle of fish. To their credit, however, once Malcolm and I started the training courses that we had put together for them, they really entered into the spirit of it all, and we had some very enjoyable sessions with them. I was also on another learning curve; and although I didn't know it at the time, these training skills would prove very beneficial later in my career, but in way that I would never have expected.

Most people, including me, who were involved with the ITT's presence at the NEC in 1976, agreed that it was the highlight of their business year. They also added that it was one of the most tiring.

Enjoyable as it had been, I was glad to get back to my office in Foots Cray and be able to focus a bit more on my Formula Ford racing. Simply because I didn't have the budget, or the time, to do a lot of travelling to other race circuits around the country, my racing was restricted to Brands Hatch, with occasional forays to Castle Combe in Wiltshire and Lydden Hill in Kent. Much as I was enjoying my racing, I wasn't proving to be as competitive as I had hoped. As I saw it, there were two primary reasons for this. Firstly, my mechanic was trying to hold down a full-time job and simply didn't have a lot of time to prepare the car properly; and in addition, he had absolutely no experience of motor racing and was led by me in terms of set up and preparation. I suppose that the blind leading the blind was one way of describing it. The second reason was closer to home. I wasn't quick enough.

Unlike a lot of my fellow competitors, I hadn't raced karts or come up through 750 Motor Club racing. As a result, I had to learn as I went along. With no one to give me guidance in how to set up a car, I was reliant on a book on that topic by Brian Smith, which I still have incidentally. It was OK, very good in fact, but wasn't the same as having an experienced race mechanic working with me. I had to make some fairly major decisions if I was to continue with my aspirations of making it to the top of the sport.

Strangely, just as my Victoria's sponsorship deal began with noticing their new advertising sign when I was driving my company car, the solution to my mechanic issue presented itself when I stopped at a petrol station to fill up that same car on my way to a practice session at Brands Hatch. My mechanic couldn't attend, as he was working, so I was on my own. I spotted a Mobil petrol station in Bearstead, on the

A20, some three miles away from Victoria's Nightclub, which offered easy access to the pumps, an important factor when you're towing a trailer.

Whilst I was filling my Escort, one of the staff from the workshop section of the garage walked up and asked if he could look at the Formula Ford. We got chatting, and he asked me who prepared the car. I explained the current set-up and its inadequacies. As other cars were now heading in to the pumps, he suggested that I should park up beside the garage and have a chat with Bill Collier, the owner.

An hour later, I had a new sponsor to add to Victoria's Night Club. Collyer Engineering, plus a fuel and lubricant deal with Mobil. Most importantly, the race car could be stored at the garage and prepared by Alan Radcliffe, who Bill had assigned to become my race mechanic, with all the facilities at his disposal. Things were most certainly on the up. All I needed now was to get myself up to some proper speed.

Later that day when I'd finished practising at Brands Hatch, I sat chatting to one of the other Formula Ford regulars. Kenny Gray was a young South African, who'd won South Africa's *Driver to Europe Award* which entitled him to a fully paid season of Formula Ford racing in Britain. In a Van Diemen manufactured car, he went on to become one of the fastest and most successful drivers in the category, holding the lap record at several tracks. He then switched to the Royale Marque, as a works driver, where a fellow South African, Rory Byrne, was then a designer. Byrne eventually became the chief designer for Ferrari F1, designing the cars that won around 70 Grand Prix in the hands of Michael Schumacher. Sadly, Kenny's career, which on merit should have seen him go through the ranks to Formula 1, was ended at an early stage when he crashed at Silverstone and suffered a freak injury. One of the posts supporting the catch-fencing, then mandatory at British race tracks, hit Kenny across the front of his helmet, resulting in a serious head injury and a damaged eye. Kenny was one of the best. You'll hear more about the way our paths crossed some 12 years later, in his home country.

I told him of my concerns that I wasn't quick enough in a Formula Ford, and he took a look at my car. The advice that followed his inspection was that I should seriously consider trying to get a newer car. He felt that whilst my Crossle 20F had been good, in its day, mine was looking very "tired". That hadn't been helped by the accident I'd had last season. He told me that if I was going to continue racing, mainly at the short, undulating Brands Hatch circuit, it might be beneficial to look for a short-wheel-based car, ideally with a proven record at that track. I must admit that I was feeling more confident about increasing my spend on motor racing, now that I had the Collyer Engineering technical backing. Kenny assured me that he'd look out for some possibilities.

True to his word, Kenny phoned me a month or so later to tell me that the car that had won the previous year's British championship was for sale. The Hawke DL11 had a great record of success at Brands, in the hands of championship winner Syd Fox. Ironically, Syd was one of the instructors who I'd met at the racing school at Brands, a couple of years back. I discovered by phoning the Hawke factory in Ware, Hertfordshire that the car was being sold by Ken McKinstry, Syd Fox's patron, who owned it. If I was interested, I'd have to negotiate with him.

I got out my calculator and did the sums. Maybe I could secure some more sponsorship which would help fund the purchase. I spoke to my man at Victoria's to see if he would consider increasing his deal, but he told me that cash flow was a little difficult; and although he was happy with the sale of subscriptions generated by our sponsorship, he couldn't increase his payments. However, he did say that if I could find a new title sponsor, he'd be prepared to stand down and release me from my contract.

Then it came to me. ITT! Why not approach the company for whom I was working? Geoff Thomas was the head of communications for the consumer products division, and someone who had helped me a lot in the year since I joined. We set up a lunch time meeting, and my proposal was received quite well, followed by an offer from Geoff to see what could be done. Incidentally, Geoff mentioned that he was a good friend of a racing driver, Mike Wilds, who by then had gone through the Formula 3 ranks to secure a drive in F1, with the Stanley BRM Team F1. It seemed that Geoff was quite keen on motor racing. So far, so good. Now I had to wait!

At the launch of another major sponsorship, the American corporation ITT. Brian at the launch, together with Olympic Silver Medallist show jumper, Ann Moore, who would also go on to compete in motorsport.

A couple of days later, Geoff called me and asked to meet in the staff canteen for a coffee. He'd put together a very interesting change to the sponsorship proposal that I had put forward. What he proposed was that instead of being sponsored by ITT consumer products, as per my proposal, the sponsorship should be in the name of *ITT Focus*. This was the ITT group in-house magazine that was published monthly and went to the entire UK section of the ITT group. He felt that it would provide an

45

excellent platform for a range of staff motivation activities. He finished by saying that he could get a quick decision on this if I like the concept.

It was a no-brainer as far as I was concerned. It wasn't a big sponsorship, but would allow me to buy the new car, have it re-liveried professionally and provide a great opportunity to attract other potential sponsors; such was the prestige of the ITT brand.

One of the promotions that Geoff had proposed really grabbed my attention. Today, it would be deemed to be so politically incorrect that it would never see the light of day, but in 1976, the British population was renowned for its sense of humour. Where it has gone, I'm beginning to wonder? Geoff explained that ITT group held a national beauty contest for employees, with the final being in Hastings at the company's manufacturing centre. He explained that the judging panel for 1976 comprised Olympic silver medal winning show-jumper Ann Moore, 10,000 meters world record holder David Bedford and Team GB Olympic sprinter Brian Green. Quite an impressive group, I thought. Then he asked me if I would agree to join the panel! We would have the race car painted in the distinctive yellow, red, white and blue livery of the *ITT Focus* magazine and have it on display at the final of the contest.

I was keeping fingers crossed that Geoff would be able to get the approval he was seeking from the MD, Ronnie Russell. I needn't have worried, Geoff was as good as his word, and the sponsorship was rubber stamped. I would be getting a new car, one that had won the top Formula Ford Championship the previous season. No excuses now!

I set up a meeting with Ken McKinstry at the Hawke factory and negotiated a slight reduction in the asking price for the car. I'd put an advertisement in Autosport, hoping to quickly sell my Crossle, but hadn't received any interest so far. I had really enjoyed racing it, but it had never given me the confidence to throw it about in the way that the quick drivers were doing. It was probably my own fault, not really understanding how to set it up in the way that would suit my driving style. That would need to change if I was going to make my mark in Formula Ford.

Ken McKinstry took a small deposit and held the car for a couple of weeks whilst I tried to sell the Crossle. He was very understanding and told me that I shouldn't worry. He was right. I sold it the following week and was able to complete the purchase of the Hawke DL11.

We had a big in-company launch of the new race team, and the car looked really impressive in its new colour-scheme. Then it was time to arrange a practice session at Brands Hatch and find out if the new car had been worth the expenditure. I was instructed by Geoff Thomas not to "bend it" as we would be going down to the ITT factory in Hastings that weekend, with the car, for the final of the national Miss ITT competition.

I couldn't believe the difference. The Hawke DL11 felt so stable and confidence-inspiring around the one and a quarter mile IndyCar circuit. My times tumbled quickly, and I finished the afternoon nearly a second and a half quicker than I had ever gone in the Crossle. I was still about a half a second off the really quick guys, but it was early days. The car went back onto the trailer, and we dropped it off at its new home, the workshops in Bearsted.

Chapter 7
A Winning Formula, Rich Fathers and Diamond Mines

I should explain that throughout the 1970s and '80s, Formula Ford 1600 was undoubtedly the most popular and successful motor racing category by far, in both Britain and Europe. It was relatively inexpensive, mainly due to the fact that the cars could be raced by private individuals, preparing them themselves, without the need to pay a professional team to do so. By comparison today, the entry level Formula 4 series, also powered by Ford, can in reality only be run through a professional team and requires a budget in the region of £150,000 to £200,000, for a season's racing. Lando Norris, now an F1 driver with McLaren, raced in that series, and it is rumoured that his father spent well over double that amount. In addition, he was taken to Australia and New Zealand during the off-season in Britain, allowing him to carry on racing there, giving him even more of an advantage the following season. But that's the way that motorsport has been allowed to go. There is no way that a driver can just prepare the car, stick it on a trailer and go racing, as regularly happened with Formula Ford 1600. The complex electronic engine management systems alone put paid to that!

Brian finishing 2nd in a Championship Final at Brands Hatch in 1978, driving an Image Mk 4 Formula Ford 1600.

The proof of what I am saying about the success of Formula Ford 1600 can be seen in the fact that in the 1975/76/77 era, fourteen of the drivers I was competing with, including Nigel Mansell and Derek Warwick, went on to race in F1, albeit that not all of them stayed there for more than a few races. Very few had wealthy fathers supporting them. With one F1 father now paying up to $80 million for his son to compete for a season's racing at that level, it puts matters into perspective. In my opinion, Motorsport, not just F1, is becoming increasingly elitist and needs sorting out.

To give you an idea of how competitive the Formula Ford category was, in 1975, there were three major FF1600 championships:

- National Organs Formula Ford Championship
- British Air Ferries Formula Ford Championship
- Brush Fusegear Formula Ford Championship

In addition, each race circuit ran its own regional FF1600 championship.

Geoff Lees, one of the fourteen drivers, who would go on to race in F1, won all three major championships in 1975. From 40 starts, he won 32 races and then went on to win the prestigious Formula Ford Festival.

I was feeling very much more confident in my own ability to compete, as the new season arrived. I wish I could say that I won my first race in the new car, but I didn't. In fact, I didn't win at all that season. The big difference, however, was that with there being three Heats, each with a grid of between 24 and 30 cars depending on the individual circuit, followed by a final, I was now able to make the final on most occasions. Then, more often than not, I'd finish in the top ten.

Being brutally honest about my own performance, although I was reasonably quick, I lacked the sheer natural speed that the top drivers such as Mansell, Warwick and Daly were achieving. Would my ability to secure sponsorship help me get to F1? That was the big question I had to ask myself. My age was against me for a start, I was by now 30, and although drivers were then starting their careers later than they do today, it was still a disadvantage. Secondly, a lot of the top FF1600 drivers were effectively professional, doing little other than race week-in week-out. Some would compete in all three major championships, racing up to 60 times a season.

Another question I needed to ask myself was whether or not I had the level of determination that it would take to make it in this fiercely competitive sport. I recall that David Kennedy and Derek Daly, both very quick Irish Formula Ford racers in the mid-1970s, went to Australia in the off-season and worked in the diamond mines for a few months to secure the funding to compete next season. Both would eventually make it to F1.

In the meantime, I carried on racing my Hawke DL11, a car that was built in 1974, and I was really enjoying the experience. In 1975, the Hawke DL11 was replaced by the DL12, a car that didn't prove very successful, but in 1976, the DL15 was a winner in the hands of some talented drivers including Derek Daly, Bernard Devaney and Derek Warwick. In my opinion, it was the most successful car that Hawke Race Cars ever produced. At the end of 1976, Hawke introduced a supposedly ground-breaking Formula, the Hawke DL17.

The competition between Formula Ford constructors was immense. Crossle, Van Diemen, Hawke, Elden, Ray, Merlyn, Jamun and Royale were just a few of the names that were all making good money out of the category. The annual, end of season Formula Ford Festival at Brands Hatch was the most competitive event on the calendar, attracting around 150 entries from all over the world. In 1976, Hawke's finished 1-2-3 in the final, with one DL15 and two DL17s. It was to be the company's finest hour, as you'll find out later. It was an event at which the constructors all showed off their new designs for the following season. A win at the festival usually resulted in a significant increase in advance orders for the winning constructor.

Looking back at the Formula Ford Festival during the mid-1970s, I think that once it moved to Brands Hatch, from Snetterton, it featured some of the most competitive, exciting and dramatic racing that I've witnessed throughout my career. When I look at Formula 4 today, with grids of around 14 cars, I really do believe that there needs to be a huge re-think in the way that the junior categories of racing are managed.

Chapter 8
SodaStream, Relocation and Thruxton

It came as a major surprise to most of us at ITT when my boss, Malcolm McCarthy, resigned. He was extremely popular and had done a great job in raising the professionalism of the sales division. I'd learnt a tremendous amount from him and was disappointed when he told me that he was leaving. I wasn't afraid of change, but like most of the staff, I was a little nervous as to what would happen. I was asked to temporarily take on Malcolm's role whilst decisions were being made as to his replacement.

What we didn't know at the time was that Malcolm's departure would be just the first of many changes that would be announced later in the year. These would, in the process, affect everyone in the company. In the meantime, I knuckled down and got on with the on-going programme of sales and product training sessions for some of our major customers. Since completing the round of courses at Curry's branches, we had many other requests coming in for a similar programme.

I was on my way home from Foots Cray one evening when I decided to call in to the petrol station where my car was being prepared for that weekend's race meeting. Alan Radcliffe, my mechanic, was finalising some suspension changes when I walked in. He asked me if I'd help him push the car out onto the forecourt whilst he cleared everything away. I waited with the race car, watching a middle-aged man in a business suit filling-up at the pumps. After he'd paid at the till, he strolled across to the race car. As was so often the case, he asked what sort of car it was. This led to a short conversation, and I eventually asked him what he did. It turned out that he was sales manager within the Kenwood Group of Companies. I knew a little about them, as Melanie had recently bought a Kenwood food mixer. He told me that he was a regular customer at Bill Collyer's garage, and that he lived locally. I asked him if he had a business card. It showed that his name was Don Philpott.

You can probably guess what was already going through my mind! A couple of days later, I called Don and asked him if he'd like to come to Brands Hatch as my guest. He couldn't make it, but what he suggested was that we should get together for a chat over a coffee at some stage.

The subsequent chat, which was at the Great Danes Hotel, on the A20, was very educational for me. Don explained that he was involved in a proposed management buy-out from Kenwood, in respect of a specific product brand called SodaStream.

I told him that I'd heard of SodaStream, but had never used one. He explained that it was primarily a machine for carbonating water and soft-drink concentrate to produce fizzy drinks at home, for a fraction of the cost of buying canned drinks, such as 7-Up, Pepsi and the vast assortment of other well-known brands. He went on to tell me that the brand was proving very popular with families, conscious of the increasing costs of buying canned drinks for their kids.

Over coffee, I asked Don to tell me more about the buy-out, and how it would work. In particular, I wanted to know what the major issues would be that faced the management buy-out team. Looking back, I was probably a bit pushy in trying to get all of this information, but Don was a very relaxed individual and explained in some depth how much pressure there would be on the team of individuals, including himself. Selling a product with the backing of a giant corporation, like Kenwood, was one thing; but being out there on your own, with a brand that wasn't that well-known, was another.

He went on to tell me that production of SodaStream machines was about to be switched to a new factory in Peterborough. It would then be sold direct to major store groups, as well as through wholesale distributors to smaller retail outlets. Don then looked at his watch and told me he had to head off to a meeting. We hadn't even mentioned the word sponsorship, but as we walked out to our cars, I asked Don if he'd mind me contacting him again if I had any thoughts about ways in which I could help them increase sales and awareness of their new brand. In our earlier conversation, I'd mentioned that I was working for ITT Consumer Products and was involved in retail sales training, which seemed to interest him. Before getting into his car, asked me quite a few more questions about my work.

It had been an informative conversation. My mind was in overdrive, recognising the potential that the information I'd gathered now offered. I knew that it was time for some serious research and planning if I was to put forward a proposal as to how a motorsport involvement might help the new management buy-out team to hit their sales targets. It would have to be based on the experience I'd gained in my relatively short but successful business career, rather than on anything to do with motor racing itself. I was learning fast!

It took a while, but I was able to put together what I thought might be a relevant strategy for SodaStream, based on the limited knowledge that I'd gained from my chat with Don Philpott, and the research that I carried out. Remember, this was in the era before PCs and social media. Research was either done at the library or from personal contact.

My research confirmed that the biggest factor in a person deciding against a SodaStream machine was the assumed perception that the range of concentrate flavours wouldn't be as good as the well-known canned-drink brands. I had also realised from my conversation with Don, that just as desktop printer manufacturers make their money from the sale of cartridges and not the printer itself, in the same way, SodaStream made its money from the sale of concentrates and other consumables as opposed to the actual machines. It was key element in my sponsorship strategy.

I felt that I was ready for another meeting with Don Philpott. In my subsequent phone call to him, I explained that I'd given some thought to ways in which I might be able to help the company increase sales, of both the machines and consumables, through an innovative motorsport programme. He chuckled and told me that he had been expecting my call.

We met in Woburn, which would make it easier for his CEO to attend. Things were getting interesting! It turned out to be a very worthwhile meeting. Don seemed really enthused, and his CEO seemed to find it infectious. They seemed impressed with the work that I'd done in advance of the meeting. Roger, the CEO, admitted to me that his impression of sponsorship in motor racing was that it involved covering the car in stickers and hoping that it would encourage spectators into buying or at least trying the product. When I showed him the outline document that I'd brought with me, indicating that the objective of my proposed sponsorship would be selling high levels of consumables, in particular the bottles of various flavour concentrates, his mind went into overdrive. He particularly liked my thoughts about capturing the personal details of the people buying the concentrate. This would be invaluable of setting up a database, allowing direct contact in respect of special offers and the like.

We sat there for about two hours before I eventually left with a list of all the objectives that Roger and Don has confirmed would be key to the future success of SodaStream as a stand-alone brand. We agreed that I'd work on finding ways that my motorsport programme could deliver ways of helping achieve these objectives. Roger asked me to then submit a detailed proposal, which he would ask the board to consider. Wow! I don't mind admitting that I was mentally exhausted after this in-depth meeting. Did I have some work to do?

A month later, I was sitting in the office of David Lazenby, the boss of Hawke Racing Cars, which was based on the industrial estate of Southend Airport. David had been Jim Clark's mechanic when he was driving for Lotus F1 and also competing in the Indy 500 in America. Sitting next to me were Roger and Don from SodaStream. I kept pinching myself to be sure that this was really happening. The sponsorship proposal that I'd put forward had been accepted in its entirety, and we were in the process of negotiating to buy the new Hawke DL 17 that, in prototype format, had won the prestigious Formula Ford Festival at Brands Hatch earlier that month; driven by Derek Warwick, who would go on to drive in F1, initially with Toleman, then with Renault.

I wasn't as clever as I thought I was. Instead of pinching myself, I should have been kicking myself. We'd chosen the Hawke as the car to go for, based on the successful performance of the DL15 in 1976, and then Warwick's victory at Brands in the festival. We'd been to see Alan Cornock at Royale and Ralph Firman at Van Diemen International, both of whom had new designs for their 1977 models. They were both keen to sell us a car, but finally we'd settled on the Hawke. Lazenby had enthused us with his new design, which moved the driver six inches forward in the car by splitting the engine and gearbox with a spacer. In this way, it would improve the weight transference and driveability, he assured us. Looking back, I should have been more sceptical, but I didn't have the experience that I have now. After all, the car had won the Festival. I now know that Derek Warwick would probably have won the Festival in just about any Formula Ford, he was that good. My problem was that I wasn't Derek Warwick!

Joining us in the meeting was Vic Holman, Hawke's sales manager, who would shortly leave the company and set up a rival Formula Ford manufacturer, PRS. I could see that they were both impressing Don and Roger, and it didn't come as a surprise that we left the factory as the owners of a brand new Hawke DL17.

Of course, at that time I was so excited that I didn't ask the in-depth questions that I should have done. This was my big opportunity, after all, despite a realisation in the back of mind that I wasn't good enough to get to the top level of the sport. I wanted to believe that I could be successful, and this new, ground-breaking race car would be way of hitting the headlines. If I could do well in 1977, with the backing that I now had, there were other categories to aim at, maybe sports cars even. As we headed off to a local restaurant for a quick lunch together, I was fully aware that thanks to Don Philpott and SodaStream, not only was I getting a chance to show my racing skills, but that I was now developing a reputation as a driver with the unusual ability to acquire sponsorship, lots of it. If I could have bottled the way that I was feeling right then, I'd have made a fortune.

It was agreed that I would compete in the 1977 Townsend Thoresen Championship, which was effectively the British Formula Ford Championship, with rounds at virtually all of the major tracks. Sadly, we also came to the conclusion that Alan Radcliffe wouldn't be able to stay on as our mechanic, short of giving up his job at the garage, which he felt he couldn't do. We opted to use one of the professional race car preparation companies that were starting to emerge within Formula Ford. We chose a company called Race Care, owned by fellow Formula Ford racer David McPherson and race engineer Marc Julyan, which was conveniently based at Brise Yard, Dartford. A transporter was then acquired and fully painted in the stunning red, black and white SodaStream livery to match the race car, incorporating their Guardsman logo. I should add that the transporter was one of the first to appear in the series, as most cars were either towed on a trailer behind a road car or transit van. Maybe that's not something to be proud of, as it was elevating the costs of competing, once other people felt they needed one.

The final decision that had to be made was a critical one and could only be made by me and, of course, Melanie. How was I going to fit in a season's racing, with all the testing that was necessary to be competitive, into my business schedule at ITT?

Another issue also loomed large. As part of the sponsorship deal, I'd proposed that we put the race car on display in selected retail outlets, mainly departmental stores, such as Barkers of Kensington, with a SodaStream sales person in attendance. I'd suggested that as parents came into the store with children, the youngsters would be attracted to look at the race car, and we would offer them the chance to sit in the cockpit and have their photograph taken. Whilst this was happening, the salesperson would offer the parents sample drinks of the various concentrate flavours, before offering a special discount on a machine purchase.

Roger and Don had liked this idea very much, but felt that it would add value if I could also be there, in my race suit, to sign autographs and talk to potential customers. My immediate response was that it wouldn't be possible from a time point of view. This discussion about this was still going on between us all.

As this was happening, ITT made public the dramatic changes that we had been awaiting. In the announcement, to all the staff at Foots Cray, we were informed that the company would be closing its Kent-based UK headquarters. It went on to state that the entire Consumer Products division would be relocated to a new site, close to Basildon in Essex. I don't think I'm exaggerating when I say that the decision went down like a lead balloon amongst a high number of staff, most of who lived in Kent. It certainly wasn't a popular choice, as it offered either a long drive from Kent via the Dartford Tunnel or possible re-location to the Basildon area.

Like most people, Melanie and I were quite gutted when we read the announcement. It didn't take long to agree that neither of us wanted to move to Basildon. Melanie had a very good job at the eye hospital in Maidstone and thoroughly enjoyed her work, whilst I have to admit that a move to Basildon just didn't do much for me. As we considered our options, I was aware that I still hadn't heard who would be filling Malcolm McCarthy's shoes, although I was now being referred to as the training director within the company.

It seemed to me that this massive change might be happening for a reason. Maybe it was the right time for me to hand in my notice to ITT and take the big step of focussing totally on my racing career. In other words, I would turn professional. The deal that I had negotiated with Roger and Don was a good one, but it didn't take into account the fact that they wanted me to spend time with the car on promotional duties. I needed to have another chat with them.

I spent some time running through my sponsorship budget and put together a proposal that would increase it quite considerably. It was based on the suggestion that it would be in their interests to have me available on-tap in order to ferry the car to display promotions, as well as personally attending such events. It didn't take long to gain their agreement.

I now felt ready to tell my boss at ITT that I would be leaving. I'd enjoyed my time with this huge organisation, and once again, had learned some extremely valuable lessons that would benefit me later in my motorsport career.

Funnily enough, just after I had re-negotiated my sponsorship deal with SodaStream, another opportunity to generate revenue came my way. A new motor racing school was opening at the Thruxton Motor Racing Circuit in Hampshire, started by someone I'd known for a couple of years; Mike Eastick. He had been successfully running what was then called a race-hire business, Scorpion Racing. It was effectively the pre-cursor to professional teams, such as Carlin and Fortec.

Mike rang me one evening and asked if I would be interested in becoming a professional instructor at the new school. I'd be joining Derek Daly, Rob Wilson and my South African friend, Kenny Gray, in teaching people how to drive Formula Fords. James Weaver, who would go onto become a successful sports car driver in America, was then employed as a mechanic at the school. Mike explained that I'd be paid on a daily basis as required, which would be an ideal arrangement for me.

Suddenly, my life was heading in a totally different direction. I was leaving the corporate world behind me, together with regular salary cheques, pension contributions, sick leave and paid holidays. It was a decision that we both supported, helped by the fact that Melanie was earning good money. Nevertheless, I admit to feeling some serious trepidation on more than one occasion.

That wasn't all. With a major sponsorship, the pressures of motor racing would change dramatically. Results on the track now mattered, although I felt very confident that I would be able to deliver the results that mattered even more for my sponsors, an increase in the sales of SodaStream machines and consumables. That said, with several factory visits to the races planned for SodaStream staff, no one wanted to see the Hawke lagging around at the back of the pack. The days had gone when I could wake up on a Saturday morning and decide that I didn't feel like racing. I was now fully committed to being on the grid.

I thought about the level of fitness that would be required, although I must point out that at that time, there wasn't the obsession with fitness, diet and mental attitude displayed by youngsters competing in categories like Formula 4 today. We all kept ourselves as fit as you needed to be to compete in 10 or 12 lap races. It's now all become a bit over the top, in my opinion. As we see in so many sports, kids at the age of 14 or 15 ape the stars that they see competing at the top level. The way that Premier League footballers celebrate a goal can be seen copied on the park pitches on a Sunday morning. The same in motor racing; what you see happening on your TV screen at the Grand Prix, maybe a driver drinking champagne out of his racing boot, so you see the youngsters on the Podium in junior categories, such as karting, trying the same thing, although probably not with champagne!

I recall watching a Formula 4 championship round at Brands Hatch back in 2015. One of the favourites for the title was strutting around the paddock, with an entourage of followers, one was carrying his helmet, another the trophy that he'd just won, another was apparently his dietician and another his trainer. He was racing for the top team in the series. I commented to a colleague alongside me that he looked as though he should be on a film set. There was a nod of agreement. We both knew that it was Daddy's money that was paying for everything.

Melanie and I then brought a new house. We had gone to Thruxton to meet with Mike Eastick and learn more about his racing school and decide when I was going to start my job as an instructor. On the way back, we drove through a local village called Shrewton, very close to Stonehenge, right in the middle of Salisbury Plain. We popped into the local pub, the Plume of Feathers, and spent hours or so chatting to some of the locals. We then took a short stroll around the village and saw some new bungalows being built in a prime site, overlooking a stream that meandered through the village.

That evening, Melanie asked me what I thought of the village and whether it would be convenient for me in respect of working at the Thruxton Circuit. It transpired that she rather liked the new bungalows and the pub, but as I pointed out, it would mean one hell of trek for her from Shrewton to Maidstone, where she worked at Maidstone Eye Hospital. She told me that she could probably get a job at Salisbury Hospital, so that wouldn't necessarily be an issue. On the Saturday morning, we went to look at the bungalows and liked what we saw. We went back to the Plume of Feathers for lunch and talked ourselves into moving to Shrewton.

There had been a lot of change in my life, of late, but I was now ready to take on the challenge of becoming a professional race driver and having a major sponsor to keep happy. I was also going to teach at a race driver school, and I remembered my vow to not treat a pupil in the way that I had been that day at Brands Hatch, however, poor they might be as a driver. I could still remember their stinging comment that I would never make a racing driver. I might not have the talent to get to the very top, I reflected, but I wasn't doing too badly, and I was thoroughly enjoying myself.

Chapter 9
Football Hooligans, Rogue Race Cars and a Scary Farmer

My first big event in 1977 was the official launch of SodaStream Team Racing, which was to be held at the Tara Hotel in Kensington. There was a big turnout, and we generated some excellent media coverage. The following day, SodaStream's PR agency organised a special PR activity, with the aim of securing some worthwhile TV coverage. The new factory was positioned fairly close to Peterborough United Football Club's ground, and the agency had arranged for me to drive the race car around the edge of the pitch at half-time, during what was then a third-division fixture. The ITV regional news cameras were there and seemed keen to film the car. I had my race suit on but no helmet. Just as I was about to start the car, a policemen approached me and kindly suggested that I put my helmet on. When I replied that I wouldn't be doing more than about 20 mph, he smiled and told me that it had nothing to do with my driving but rather to protect me from beer cans and other items that might be thrown at me from both sets of supporters. Nice!

I'm glad that I took his advice. I did get hit by a couple of plastic bottles and a toilet roll, but more disturbingly, when I took my helmet off, I discovered that it was covered in what can best be described as "spit". I think football crowds are much better controlled these days, but I must admit to feeling quite sick as we rolled the car back into the transporter prior to my taking my helmet to the Gents to wash it clean. Still, the good news was that we made it onto the regional news that evening, which pleased Roger and Don, who had both worked hard to help me put this sponsorship deal together.

I didn't mention that one of the proposals Roger had come up with to generate interest amongst the public, was a national competition. It was open to anyone who brought a bottle of SodaStream concentrate at a retail outlet. As per my proposal, the bottles had been fitted with colourful cardboard collars, promoting SodaStream Team Racing. Each collar incorporated a coupon, which could be filled out with the purchaser's name and address. By returning the coupon to SodaStream, together with what I think was £1, the customer would be sent a team pack, comprising a large colour poster of the car and driver, a sticker, a team T-Shirt and entry into a competition. It was a great way of capturing data at a time when e-mails were unheard of, which was a key part of my proposal. I had to congratulate Roger and Don for coming up with a highly innovative prize for the winner of the competition.

The announcement of the competition prize generated a great buzz of reaction at the launch in London. The winner of the draw, into which all of the returned coupons would be entered at the end of the season, would receive as their prize the actual SodaStream Hawke DL17 race car, together with a full course of lessons at the Jim Russell Racing Driver School. The announcement resulted in a high level of media coverage.

Brian's big break came in 1977, with a substantial sponsorship from SodaStream. The budget allowed him to give up the day job and start racing professionally. The Launch, at the Tara Hotel in London, featured the infamous Hawke DL17 car, which looked good on the stage but caused many issues on track.

Once the official launch was a done and dusted with, it was time for me to head off to Thruxton and the racing school. Mike Eastick had put it together in a very professional way. The single-seater Formula Ford race cars that would be used for instruction were Royale RP21s, whilst four Ford Escort Mexico's provided the chance for the instructors to either drive the pupils around the circuit at speed to show them how it's done, or else to accompany them when they took over the wheel.

The cars were all stored in the new workshops that Mike had organised in nearby Amesbury. Together with his lovely wife, Jenny, he'd moved from Saffron Walden in Essex, where the race car hire business had originally been based. Business at the new racing school was brisk from the start, and we were kept busy taking pupils on "hot laps" in the Escorts before they took over the wheel and drove us around the wide and very fast Thruxton circuit, via the cones that showed them where to brake, change gear and apex the corner. I can't say that I really enjoyed being driven around, at speed, by all and sundry, as it gets very hairy sometimes. Everyone seems to think that because they can break the speed limit in their road car, on a straight dual carriageway, they can drive at speed around a race circuit.

I quickly found out what the expression "white knuckle rides" meant.

As instructors, we would meet up with Mike, early in the morning, at what was best called a "greasy spoon" café, just off the A303 in Andover, and there we'd be given our schedules. The school didn't operate every day of the week, and I seem to recall that we worked about eight to ten days a month. It was a great time for me, totally different to anything that I'd done before. Together with Kenny Gray, Rob Wilson, Derek Daly, Jim Weaver and, of course, Mike himself, we had some great experiences.

I remember on one particular day, Mike came over to me at the track, together with someone who looked like an elderly farmer, wearing a tweed jacket and a matching brimmed hat. Mike introduced him to me as indeed being a local farmer who had heard the cars going around the track and had popped in to see what was happening. He went on to ask me if I would look after the gentleman and take him on some hot laps before letting him do three laps behind the wheel. We'd added a couple of Triumph TR7 sports cars to the school fleet by then, and I was given the keys to one by Mike.

As I explained, we positioned traffic cones around the track to help pupils learn the racing lines. Thruxton is a difficult circuit to race on but very easy to drive around. It comprises almost one long curve, interrupted by a short right, left, right complex and a chicane as you enter onto the pit straight. It's not that difficult to drive around quite quickly, but to go very quickly can be extremely hazardous.

We jumped into the TR7, both with our helmets on. I took him for three fairly quick laps, showing how the lines actually flow, the faster you go. I explained that the slower you go, the more difficult it is to follow the lines. Then, it was time to swap seats.

The first lap was slow, very slow. I don't think we exceeded 50 mph. There were other cars on the track, and I had to keep a good check on where they were. Lap 2 was no quicker. We were driving slowly from cone to cone, and it was very difficult to get any rhythm going. We then pulled into the pits, and I explained to the farmer why he needed to put his foot down a little more, to allow the car to naturally follow the racing lines.

On the third and final lap, we exited the complex, and he managed to get the speed up to around 70 mph. With a little more encouragement, we hit 85 mph. We were in top gear and heading along the back straight towards, what for pupils was, a 2nd gear chicane. As we approached the first cone, I told the farmer to take off some speed. Nothing happened, so I repeated it, telling him to brake and drop down a gear. As he looked down at his feet to find the brake pedal, he almost knocked the car out of gear; then the engine suddenly started revving, and the brakes went on. He'd jammed his foot hard on the accelerator and brake pedal at the same time before slamming the car into second gear, with the revs shooting even higher.

I could see what was coming; the steel Armco barriers around the chicane, head on! That's the last thing we needed, so I leaned across, grabbed the wheel, and we spun. Amazingly, and with no skill on my part, we missed hitting anything and ended up on the grass inside of the track. I admit to shaking a little. We both climbed out of the car and took our helmets off. I leaned in and turned the ignition off. When I turned around, this gentle farmer was taking a pipe out of his jacket pocket with one hand and a box of Swan Vesta matches from the other pocket.

He carefully lit the pipe, puffed until the smoke bellowed out and then grabbed my arm.

'I can see why you young guys like this racing lark. It's bloody great fun, isn't,' he chuckled, in a Hampshire accent!

By early February, I was feeling impatient for the racing season to start. The weather in the UK was pretty awful, and I yearned for some sunshine, but there was no chance of repeating my previous year's visit down to Johannesburg. Looking back, I think that I was getting a little bored and missing the cut and thrust of work that I had been involved in for nearly ten years. The days at the racing school were OK, but after a while, became somewhat tedious. There seemed to be a lot of hanging around, which is not much fun in the middle of Salisbury Plain in February. We obviously had some testing to do, and therein lay a problem.

My first test session the previous year, with the DL11 car, had gone well. I had immediately taken to the car and was quick from the start, but the new SodaStream DL17 was just the opposite. Despite it having been professionally set up for me, it just didn't feel right. I knew the circuit inside out, and that hadn't changed, but the car gave me no confidence whatsoever. One corner in particular where there was a problem was after Druids, the second gear hairpin at the top of the hill. In the DL11, I didn't have to lift off the accelerator, in third gear, as I accelerated hard down the hill into the left hander called Bottom Bend. In the DL17, I was actually getting wheel-spin as I steered left, and no way could it be taken without a slight lift. It was a bit worrying, but I assumed that we'd set it up incorrectly. Then another DL17 driver on the day, Rob Coates, came up to me and asked what times I was doing. It transpired that we were both around three quarters of a second off our normal times. He confirmed the same lack of confidence in the car. We looked at one another and shrugged our shoulders.

We called David Lazenby at Hawke and asked him what could be the problem. He mumbled some comment about it probably being the driver, but I explained that several other drivers were having the same problem. All that did was to generate a response that we should change the set up on the car. Quite frankly, there didn't seem to be a real desire to help. I fully accepted that I wasn't one of his works drivers and not in the Derek Warwick or Derek Daly category of drivers who would almost certainly go on to F1, but, with SodaStream's help, I had spent what was a lot of money in those days and expected a far better service.

With help from the guys at Race Care, we played around with settings and found a little bit more speed, but when it was time to head off to the first round of the championship at Oulton Park, near Chester, I can't say that I was feeling very buoyant.

Quite a few drivers had decided to buy the DL17, based mainly on the tremendous results of the previous year's model. One of them was quite a character in his own right, who shot to fame in 1963. It was the year of the Great Train Robbery.

Whilst a £2.6 million robbery might not seem much now, the audacity of this crime, which took place on 8 August on the West Coast mainline and involved the Glasgow to London Royal Mail train, was such that it became headline news in every newspaper and on every TV and Radio news broadcast. Photos of the leading gang members appeared everywhere, particularly Bruce Reynolds, Buster Edwards and Ronnie Biggs.

Roy James, nicknamed The Weasel, was one of the robbers, and prior to the crime, he had been involved in motor racing, competing in the Formula Junior category. Roy drove the getaway car but was eventually arrested and handed a 30-year sentence, of which he served 13 years. Interestingly, he was a silversmith by profession and whilst in jail, made several motor racing trophies for the sport. Upon his release, he expressed a desire to get back to racing, and I believe that it was Bernie Ecclestone who helped him secure a drive in a Formula Atlantic car. Unfortunately, whilst testing the car, he crashed and broke his arm. The decision was then made to drop down a category to Formula Ford 1600, and a Hawke DL17 was purchased. As you might expect, the joke in the Paddock was that he'd secured big sponsorship from British Rail. I spoke to him on several occasions and found him polite but fairly non-communicative, which is probably not surprising. I distinctly remember talking to Roy a little later in the season, at the Snetterton Circuit in Norfolk, where nearly all of the DL17s were about two seconds off the pace. It was one of the rare occasions when he opened up and told a few of us just how pissed off he had become with the car.

Other drivers who chose a DL17 included James Weaver, who had been the mechanic at the Thruxton Racing School and went on to be a very successful sports car racer, Bernard Devaney, a top Irish Formula Ford driver and Rob Coates, with whom I had enjoyed several battles in my DL11. For all of us that season, it proved to be the wrong choice of car.

Returning to the events at Oulton Park on that opening day of the season, I had another reason to remember the occasion. The hotel, at which Melanie and I chose to stay that weekend, was called The Wild Boar and was a Tudor-beamed, country hotel in its own grounds, quite close to the race track. Our room had a large bay window, with heavy velvet curtains on a high-curved runner. That night, not for the first, or last, time in my life, I started sleep-walking. In the process, I managed to head for the window, and I can only think that in my dream I wanted to pull open the curtains. What happened was that I woke up with a start, with the curtains and curtain rail all pulled to the ground, dust and dead flies everywhere, and a startled wife sitting up in bed wondering what the hell was going on. As you can probably imagine, it was rather embarrassing to have to explain to the woman on reception duty the following morning that the curtain rail had pulled out as I tried closing the curtains. I'm not sure that she believed me, but short of calling me a liar had little choice but to simply apologise and hand me my bill. I was too embarrassed to ever stay there again.

As far as the race was concerned, although I had qualified better than I expected, I found that the handling of the car was still far from what I wanted. It seemed to switch from understeer to oversteer in the corner; and no matter what we did, it made no difference. Not being an engineer, I guess that my feedback to the Race Care guys wasn't particularly helpful, but I did mention that I had a strange feeling the chassis was flexing in corners. To say that the car wasn't confidence-inspiring would be an understatement. I wasn't too unhappy, however, as I'd qualified two places behind Nigel Mansell, but we were both some way off the pole position time of Brazilian Chico Serra. He would go on to win the championship that season, in his Van Diemen RF77, built by Ralph Firman's company. Ralph's son, you may remember, eventually raced in F1 for Eddie Jordan but for just one season.

Then the big moment arrived. To this day, I can still remember sitting in the SodaStream car on the grid, nervously waiting for the race to start. I knew that I had to get a good start, but I must admit that in practice, we'd been so focussed on sorting out the handling issues that I hadn't given much thought to the start procedure.

It seemed to take an age, but eventually, the starter waved us away, and we headed for the first bend, Old Hall. Apologies! I should have said that everyone else was away. The Hawke just dribbled forward a few yards and stopped with a blown clutch. It wasn't the best way to launch my professional career, but was out of my control. What was embarrassing was that there were quite a few people from SodaStream there on the day of the race.

I'm not going to bore you with all the details of my next few races. They were average, no better than that. I just couldn't get this wretched car to handle as I wanted. We also blew three clutches. By this time, there was a consensus of opinion amongst several Hawke DL17 owners that the chassis was flexing, as I'd mentioned, with the cause possibly linked to the spacer that had been inserted between the engine and gearbox, to move the driver forward in the car by six inches. Whether that was the problem, I never really knew, because I found the Hawke response very unprofessional. It got to the stage where I sat down with Don Philpott, from SodaStream, and suggested that we look at selling the car and doing a deal with Hawkes' competitors, with either Alan Cornock at Royale or Ralph Firman at Van Diemen. Don was a real star. He so wanted me to do well, for many reasons obviously, but one of them was that he could see how frustrated I'd become and knew that I was a better driver than he was seeing. He promised that he would talk to Roger, the CEO.

I wasn't surprised when the answer that came back was a firm "no change". Roger was aware that all of the promotional material that had been produced, including the T-shirts, colour posters of the car, competition entry forms and in-store merchandising material would have to be replaced and quite openly said that he didn't have an appetite for that. What he did suggest, however, was that he would set up a meeting with David Lazenby and Vic Holman at Hawke and demand that something be done about the car.

I didn't attend that meeting, which also included Don Philpott, but what I heard from them on their return was that the race car would be sent to the Southend factory, and that they would make some minor updates. It was better than nothing, but my suggestion, that Hawke takes the DL17 back and replaces it with a DL15 from the previous season, fell on deaf ears. It seemed that I would have no choice but to persevere with what I'd got.

What really puzzled me with the problems I was enduring with the DL17 was that, in both of my previous seasons, I'd always been quick in wet conditions, particularly with the DL11. However, I got to the stage in 1977 with the new car that I dreaded rain. The car just became so unpredictable that I lost so much of the confidence I'd previously built up.

To make up for the disappointment on the track, I worked my butt off at in-store promotions, desperate to show that the sponsorship itself was delivering the results that I'd forecast; in other words, increased sales. I visited the factory at Peterborough on several occasions to talk to the staff and found them really supportive, but when I wanted to sit down with Roger and Don and start talking about plans for 1978, there was a distinct lack of enthusiasm.

It transpired that they had been in discussion with John Webb, managing director of the Brands Hatch Circuit in Kent, about a new series that John was launching in 1978. It was to be called Sports 2000 and featured a Brands new design of sports car but based on the highly successful Formula Ford concept. To my disappointment, but not to my surprise, a deal was struck whereby SodaStream would become the title sponsor of the new series in 2018. I could see the benefits of the company being a series sponsor as opposed to sponsoring an individual driver, particularly after the issues with Hawke, but I was still devastated. Nevertheless, the decision had been made, and I learnt a big lesson that year in respect of managing a major sponsorship.

I often think back to 1977 and wonder what might have happened to my racing career if I'd chosen a Van Diemen instead of a Hawke race car, but I didn't and that's that. I was offered the chance to race in the new Sports 2000 series but not fully sponsored as I had been, but it wasn't what I wanted at that stage of my career. I wanted to stay in single-seater racing and switching to sports cars didn't appeal. I think that it was probably a big mistake and that I could have done well in another category, but as they say, hindsight is a valuable commodity.

The decision from SodaStream came towards the end of the 1977 season, and I still had the last race to complete. It was to be held on the full F1 Grand Prix Circuit at Brands Hatch as opposed to the short Indy Circuit on which most national racing took place. I'd never raced or even practised on this circuit before, and so I was a little bit apprehensive about learning it in a car in which I had little confidence.

For some reason, although the car still didn't feel brilliant, I was able to qualify quite well and actually enjoyed the undulating nature of this track that was still being used for the British Grand Prix, alternating every other year with Silverstone. Race day was clear and sunny. I realised that this would be my last appearance in the SodaStream car and was determined to give the large contingent of factory workers and their families something to cheer about.

I can't remember how many laps we had to complete, but to my amazement, when it came to the start of the last lap, as we streamed past the pits and into Paddock Hill Bend, I found myself in 7th place. There was a small gaggle of cars right on my tail as we raced down the fairly steep hill that led to Pilgrim's drop and then uphill to Hawthorn Bend. I recognised the all black Crossle of American driver Pete Argentsinger. As we headed back on to the Indy Circuit at Clearways, the camber of the track changed, and I prepared myself to hold a fairly tight line. I could see that Pete was trying to squeeze through on the inside, at the approach to the right hand bend leading onto the Pit Straight. The next thing I knew, I flying sideways through the air a few feet off the ground, out of control and heading across the short expanse of grass that ran around the outer edge of the race track. What happened next, hurt. I was knocked unconscious as the Hawke slammed into the metal Armco barriers on the edge of the track sideways on.

Brian is seen leading a gaggle of Stannic Group N cars at Club House bend, on the famous Kyalami Grand Prix track.

I came around, lying in the back of the ambulance being taken to the Brands Hatch Medical Centre, a white-faced Melanie sitting beside me. I immediately felt a lot of pain from my right leg below the knee, but otherwise, everything seemed to be OK. The staff in the Centre checked me out for a short while; and apart from very bad bruising where the inboard front spring and shock absorber had impaled itself against my leg and my ankle, I had got away very lightly.

The next thought that went through my mind was that this was the last round of the championship and the race car was going to be given as the prize in the SodaStream consumer competition. I immediately asked Melanie what state the car was in. 'Not too good,' she whispered. Now what?

After the race meeting, the car was taken back to Race Care, where a subsequent examination showed us that there was quite a lot of damage to the right side of the car, which confirmed what a couple of people had told me, inasmuch that I must have completely spun around in mid-air and heading backwards towards the pits straight as I hit the barriers.

All in all, I was very lucky, not just on that specific day at Brands Hatch, but in having survived a season's racing in a car that I came to dislike very much. It could have ended in a far more unpleasant way.

I'm sure you'd like to hear about the competition and who was the lucky (or maybe unlucky) person who won the car. Well, there's a story there as well. The young guy who won the competition had recently got married and decided that he would rather have the money than a race car, even with the course of lessons that had been thrown in.

A couple of months later, he had a big win on the football pools. Some people are certainly born lucky.

The burning question for me was what should I do now? I'd lost my sponsorship for 1978, I had given up a very good job at ITT, I'd bought a house, and I had no spare money to invest in my racing. There was only one answer. I would have to get cracking and find a new sponsor for next year. The problem was I'd left it a bit late; most companies signed off their marketing budgets by November or December latest. It was now October. There was no time to lose.

I realised that I'd also need to spend as much time as possible at the race driver school, ensuring that we had some income, in addition to the funds coming in from Melanie's major contribution.

Chapter 10
A BBC News Reader, Chrome Polish and a Successful Image

As we often did, Melanie and I were chatting with a couple of our friends one evening in the Plume of Feathers in Shrewton. Joe and Rosie Maws also lived in the village, quite close to us. Joe was in the Royal Air Force, a radar operator on Nimrods, based at nearby RAF Brize Norton. On one occasion, he confided to me that was very much the black sheep of his family and had turned down a very good job working in the family business. I must have looked a bit dim, until Melanie pointed out to me that Maws baby food products were famous all over the world.

They were a fun couple, and whenever we spent time with them, we found ourselves getting into some fascinating conversations. On one occasion, Joe told us about his interest in Ley Lines. Being a radar operator on an aircraft gave him an inside knowledge into this much debated topic. He explained that Ley lines are ancient, straight "paths" or routes in the landscape which are believed to have spiritual significance. His thoughts were based on research that he'd been able to carry out, and with his vast knowledge of the subject, he could be very convincing.

On this particular evening, we were discussing what I should do to secure funding for the 1978 season. It was Rosie who came up with an idea. She suggested that with my sales background, and specifically in sales training, why didn't I offer to train sales people in the corporate world? Joe chipped in with his view that it made a lot of sense. I could fit the training into my racing schedule, whatever that might be, and it would probably pay quite well.

The next morning, I was on the case. I found out where I could hire a video camera and began outlining the basis of a two-day course. Melanie helped me by compiling a list of companies that were within reasonable geographic distance, and that met the criteria we'd selected. I decided that the topic that I could best deliver would be sales presentation skills.

To our astonishment, the very first company that I called immediately displayed an interest and set up a meeting with me the following week. It gave me time to put a short presentation together. I should point out that we had no computers at that time, and of course, PowerPoint was unheard of. What sufficed was basically a typed A4, detailing what we were offering within the course. I looked at it and realised that we didn't have a USP, something that would make the decision-makers sit up and take notice. I couldn't think what that might be. Then it came to me. We needed a celebrity on board, someone who would immediately add interest value but also could add to the skills being taught.

We sat for quite a while, in the Plume of Feathers of course, looking through magazines and jotting down names. It didn't take us long. I wanted to find a person who everyone had heard of, but, more importantly, who was a skilled presenter. When I thought of voice, it became easier. The name starred out at us. David Jacobs. He was an incredibly popular broadcaster at that time and had fronted a lot of BBC programmes, including the never to be forgotten *Juke Box Jury*. Jacobs also chaired the long running BBC Radio 4 topical forum *Any Questions?*

A call to the BBC gave us his agent's name, and within an hour or so, we had confirmation that subject to availability, David would be happy to run a short session within our two day course. The next job was to convince the company that had shown some initial interest that we could deliver something that was not only professional but highly effective.

That company was Fiat, based in Brentford, and they committed four delegates to the course.

I have to admit that I was so nervous about the prospect of delivering my first ever course on this particular topic to such a prestigious company, that I hardly slept the night before the big day. Nevertheless, the four delegates were all what you would call "middle" managers in the organisation and seemed to be looking forward to a break from their normal routine. Once we'd got through the first half an hour or so, everyone was relaxed, including me; and by the time David Jacobs arrived for lunch and his subsequent 1-hour session, I was actually enjoying myself.

The cheque arrived a week later and with it came a request for a further course, the following month. This was a good way of making some money. I was told that his next course would be for four Italian managers who were now based with Fiat UK, but all spoke good English.

I decided to try another personality presenter and was delighted when his agent proposed a very reasonable fee. Richard Baker OBE was a BBC TV newsreader from 1954 to 1982 and one of the best-known faces on TV back in the late 1970s. I met with him in London for an initial discussion as to what I required of him. He immediately came across as a relaxed, friendly and humorous individual and quickly grasped what I expected of him.

Brian worked with BBC News-Reader Richard Baker, on a sales training course and invited him with his two sons to drive Formula Ford race cars at the Thruxton based racing school where Brian instructed. In return, Richard hosted the Launch of yet another major sponsorship as a "thank you" to Brian.

On the first day of the course, the Fiat managers arrived at the London hotel where we'd booked a meeting room and strode into reception. They looked like actors in a film, with dark, neatly cut hair, swarthy skins and were immaculately attired in dark blue pinstripe suits, white shirts and, what I assumed were Fiat ties. All that was missing were the black violin cases under their arm.

Too say they were uptight would have been an understatement. Not a smile flickered across any of their faces. This was going to be hard work, I remember thinking. We got through the first day, but I can't say that it was particularly enjoyable. My inexperience was evident as I tried to get these guys to relax when they were standing up and delivering their presentations. I hoped that by the second day, they might have unwound slightly, and I did at least get a smile from them all when they arrived. Richard Baker was due to arrive at the mid-morning coffee break, and as far as I was concerned, it couldn't come too soon.

I had the chance to chat to him when he arrived and explained the problems I was having in getting the delegates to relax. He smiled at me and patted a leather brief case he had brought in with him. He told me not to worry; it's a common problem, he added.

We headed back into the room, and I introduced Richard. They were obviously delighted to meet the famous man, my having earlier shown them a video of him reading the BBC News and he shook hands with each one. They were about to sit down when Richard asked them to take off their suit jackets and loosen their ties. He then handed each of them a colour magazine, of the *Vogue* or *Tatler* variety, and tossed a small roll of Sellotape onto the desk. When he told them to roll the magazines into tube-like coshes and wind tape around them, the looks he got suggested that he had completely lost the plot.

The next instruction was for them to lie down on the carpet, on their backs, alongside each other with the rolled-up magazine in the right hand. What then followed was extraordinary to watch. Richard told them that he would shout out each line of a short "poem". They were then to shout out that line back to him, as loud as they could, whilst slamming the rolled-up magazine as hard as they could in time with each word they were shouting.

The look on these delegates' faces was a picture as Richard started to call out:

Fuzzy Wuzzy was a bear…
Fuzzy Wuzzy had no hair…
So Fuzzy Wuzzy wasn't fuzzy, wuz he!

He repeated this about six times, constantly telling then each time to shout louder and to bang their magazines harder on the floor.

It worked, and the difference was amazing. We now had four very-relaxed Italians. The rest of the course ran incredibly well; and the feedback at the end, both from the delegates and subsequently from their boss, made it all worthwhile.

Over lunch, Richard asked me if I ran many training courses of this kind and was surprised when I told him it was my second such course. I eventually explained that I was actually doing this to generate income to help with my racing programme. He was genuinely interested in my racing activities and told me it was a shame his two boys weren't there, as they both loved motorsport. We then chatted for a while about the course, and he gave me a few tips, which, coming from such a top professional, were really welcome. Before we headed off to the meeting room, I told him about my role as an instructor at the Thruxton Racing School, suggesting that he might like to send his sons down for a free trial lesson. He asked me if I was serious; and when I confirmed that I was, he asked if he could join them.

I rang Mike Eastick, the schools' owner, to tell him what I'd done. He was really chuffed and promised to immediately send off some available dates to Richard and his two boys. A couple of months later, the Bakers arrived at the track, and we kitted them up with helmets, before enjoying three or four hours together on the track. They started in the Escort Mexicos and then had sessions in the Royale Formula Fords. Our biggest problem was getting the wide grins off their faces! They all loved it; and when it was time to go, I think that they were genuinely sad to leave.

Then a week later, I had a very pleasant surprise. A small package arrived in the post, containing three handwritten letters, one each from Richard and the two boys, thanking me and the racing school instructors for what they described as one of the most fun days they'd experienced.

Having dealt with a lot of so called "celebrities", many of whom seem to think that they are far too important to say thank you, the Bakers Family response came as a real breath of fresh air. It didn't stop there!

The following season, I acquired another major sponsor, Perivan Colour Print, a fairly large business based in Southend. We were planning a high-profile launch of the sponsorship at their head office, and so I thought it might be beneficial to recruit a celebrity to compère the event. Richard's name immediately came to mind. I phoned his agent, and he quoted a reasonable fee.

That evening, I received a call at home from Richard. He told me that he'd heard about the booking from his agent and would be delighted to attend the function as requested. Then he went on to tell me that he and his sons still talked about their great day at Thruxton, and how much they'd enjoyed it. Richard then insisted that as a way of saying thank you for those memories, he wouldn't dream of charging me for attending the proposed sponsorship launch.

True to his word, this great professional arrived at the event early and then spent most of the day there, combining his presenting duties with talking to staff, their families and the local media and TV. I was just over the moon and have nothing but admiration for Richard Baker for his attitude and commitment. Far from the norm, that's for sure. Richard is now 92 years of age.

I haven't mentioned much about my racing activities in 1978. The previous season, with the SodaStream Hawke DL17, had done little for my confidence. On the one hand, I had just about come to terms with the reality that I wasn't good enough to compete with the really quick guys, and that F1 was just a pipe dream. On the other hand, I still enjoyed racing and wanted to continue as long as finances would allow. The Perivan sponsorship was quite substantial and allowed me to secure a worthwhile drive with a Formula Ford constructor called Image. The company was owned by Alan Langridge and started life in 1974 at Tangmere in West Sussex, a couple of miles from where I now live, before moving to the Shell Building at the Goodwood Circuit. Alan was an extremely innovative designer, and the Image FF1 was effectively a kit car that could be built in someone's garage. Whilst the first Image car wasn't very competitive, its successor, the follow-up FF2, driven by Frank Bayes, won a lot of races.

I opted for what was then the latest FF4 and in my initial testing at Oulton Park, found the car to be very quick and a delight to drive. A new race team had just been established, and Alan Langridge introduced me to the owner of the team. His father ran a major truck and coach manufacturing business, and had financed his son and a friend, to set up the race team. With my Perivan sponsorship, I was able to negotiate a good deal for the season, which saw the team buying the Image FF4 and running it for me throughout the year.

The first race of the campaign was at Silverstone, and as the car was rolled out of the transporter, which was a professionally converted 36-seater coach, it attracted a lot of attention. The Image had a very aerodynamic bodywork, with the predominant colour being bright orange, with white Perivan livery. The car looked quick, which is not as silly as it sounds.

As official practice commenced, I drove out of the garage and down the pit lane to join the queue of about 30 other Formula Fords, waiting for the signal to go onto the track. As I braked to bring the car to a halt, nothing happened! I had to swerve quickly into the narrow amount of space between the row of cars and the pit wall and hoped the car came to a halt without making contact with anything. It wasn't the best of starts. I jumped out of the car and went to the back of the car to look at the inboard brake discs. I could see and smell what had happened. The race team duo ran to the car, and I asked them if they'd polished the discs with chrome polish. Yes, they confirmed, the discs had looked a bit rusty!

The season with the Image did one important thing for me; it allowed me to get my confidence back. By the time the last race had arrived, at Brands Hatch, I was feeling as good about the Image as I had about my first Hawke, the DL11. A large number of Perivan staff had been bussed in to the circuit to watch their car perform. I knew that with all of my Brands Hatch experience, I should get a good grid position, but I hadn't bargained on a clutch failure as I left the pits for official practice and qualifying. This meant that I would have to start the main race from the back of the grid in 24th place, which is not what I wanted the Perivan fans to witness. On top of that, it started raining as the start time approached. This in itself didn't worry me. I knew that the car handled well in wet conditions, but I felt for the spectators with their families.

The car was a pleasure to drive. One by one, I was able to overtake most of the field, but the race was one lap too short for me. I finished a close second, which in the circumstances wasn't too bad and kept the staff happy. They gave me a welcome ovation as I joined the winner on the podium, followed by a lap on the back of the safety car.

All in all it had been a good season, but I had come to the conclusion it would be my last in that category. I needed a new challenge. My intention was to secure a major sponsorship, hopefully with Perivan again, but I felt it was time to move up a category into Formula Ford 2000, where the cars raced on slicks and were equipped with aerodynamic front and rear wings.

Now that the racing season was over, it seemed a good time to take a holiday. After some careful examination of our finances, Melanie and I decided to head off to South Africa for a couple of weeks of sunshine, staying with my folks in Johannesburg. My sponsorship and plans for 1979 would have to wait until we got back.

Chapter 11
David Croft, a BBC Sit-Com and Monty Python

The time we spent in South Africa did us both the world of good, in the way that predictable blue skies and sunshine always seem to. We weren't able to get down to Cape Town, unfortunately, but did manage to visit Durban this time. I remember that we both kept remarking just how much space there seemed to be in South Africa, and driving on the excellent road network was an absolute joy, with very low traffic levels. The scenery really was breathtaking, and as we headed in the direction of Natal Province, we could see the Drakensburg Mountains in the far distance. One day, we decided, we would definitely head back and hopefully explore that region.

We must have enjoyed ourselves, because the two weeks sped by, and it was soon time to start thinking of the journey home. Something that I have always found rather depressing, after being in South Africa, is flying back into Heathrow. After the beauty and sheer space of South Africa, London and its suburbs always seems to be so incredibly congested. More often than not, the grey skies add to that feeling.

There was no time to reflect on this, however, as I was very aware that I had a lot of work to do back in England, preparing for what I hoped would be a fun season of racing. During my 12-hour flight from Johannesburg, I tried to think about the way forward commercially, but it was tough. Visions of Durban's beautiful sandy beaches and constant blue skies kept running through my mind, as did buying wine at less than a pound a bottle, eating succulent steaks outside in the warm evenings, and most of all, that feeling of extraordinary space. An announcement from the flight deck informed us that we were approaching Heathrow, and I realised that I hadn't done anything like the amount of planning that I had intended.

So confused was I becoming, that I even gave some thought to the idea of going back into the business world in some capacity and looking upon motor racing as a pastime rather than a job. In particular, I became aware that I missed the sales training courses that I'd been involved with at ITT, as well as the presentation training that I had delivered to Fiat. I have to admit, I didn't know quite what I wanted to do.

Then one Saturday morning, as I was walking through Salisbury town centre on my way to the bank, I was approached by a rather attractive woman, who asked me if I owned a house. I couldn't see the point of the question, until I saw that she was in a uniform representing Anglian Windows. Further on in the square was a promotional vehicle, comprising a medium-sized van, painted and sign written to look like a small house. She tried to interest me in double glazing, which was the big thing at that time, but eventually tired of me, once I explained that I had a brand new house. I wasn't done with her, however, and to her slight annoyance, I continued the conversation, asking where her regional offices were and who her regional manager was. In an effort to get rid of me, she dug a business card out of her handbag and handed it to me, before turning away and pouncing on what she hoped would be a less troublesome shopper.

My persistence paid dividends and a couple of months later, I was standing in the Paddock at Thruxton race circuit, next to a navy blue Van Diemen RF78 Formula Ford race car, that was branded in very distinctive Anglian Windows livery. Behind the car was a truck, painted to look like a house! A uniformed, promotional woman stood talking to a number of people who were grabbing brochures from her stand.

A high-profile sponsorship with Anglian Windows saw Brian in a Van Diemen RF78 at the Thruxton Circuit in Hampshire. Even more sponsors adorned his race-suit.

The deal that I had proposed, and which they liked, reminded me very much of the one I'd secured with Victoria's Night Club, my first sponsorship, back in 1974. In the same way that I had constructed the deal to help them sell more membership subscriptions, so the Anglian Windows deal had been structured to secure more sales enquiries. It's not rocket science. As I keep saying, companies are always keen to find ways of increasing sales. It was a platform on which I would acquire a lot more sponsorship throughout my career.

Although I was delighted to be back racing albeit in Formula Ford once again, which hadn't really been the plan, I needed something more in my life. I had come to know a lot of racing drivers in those early days, and I could see the ones that would make it to the top echelons of the sport. It wasn't just because they were faster than anyone else, but they were more determined to give up everything to get there. Throughout my career, I've realised that talent alone is rarely enough, and I'm not just talking about motor racing. An intense level of determination, added to a high skill base, can very often prove to be an unstoppable force.

I came to the conclusion that I didn't have that same determination to give up everything for motor racing; there would always be other interests in my life. I must say that some of these incredibly focused drivers were actually quite boring individuals in many ways; there was nothing else they could talk about. But who am I to criticise? That was their choice. Having admitted that I lacked that 100 per cent

70

dedication necessary to be winner on the track, I also accepted that neither did I have the levels of skills to get to the very top. This didn't mean that I wasn't trying hard to win races, far from it. It was just that I was now able to recognise that I couldn't eat, drink and sleep motor racing.

I mentioned the enthusiasm that I had generated for training sales people. I can honestly say that it's never gone away, and as a result, I often find that when I'm out shopping or perhaps speaking to a sales person on the phone, I find myself analysing their performance. Sometimes I'll be really impressed, but all too often, I reflect on how poorly they have managed the sales process.

For me, one of the worst categories, in respect of unacceptable selling technique, has always been the retail motor trade. So often, I've walked into a show room, with the desire to buy a car, only to come to the conclusion that I must have an innate ability to become invisible. It's amazing how the sales staff suddenly realise that they have a phone call to make, or perhaps they bury themselves in their admin paperwork. Some even get up and walk through to another department, trying to looking oh so busy! Then, if and when you find one who agrees to talk to you, they have an uncanny ability to look at the vehicle you want to trade in and convince you that it's the least popular car ever to be manufactured, in the wrong colour, with an unpopular interior material, De Luxe not the De Luxe Mk2 model, manual not automatic and so on; in other words, it's the wrong everything. I find the way the process is handled so often totally negative.

My absolute worst is when a salesperson looks at you, a rare occurrence in itself I admit, and then instead of greeting you with a good morning or hello, tosses the meaningless words at you, like "You alright?" This expression is becoming more and more prevalent in shops, and it really bugs me.

I remember going into a photographic shop in Salisbury on one occasion. Melanie and I were going off to Italy for a week, and I decided to buy a camera, one that was light and took up little space. I was greeted by a young man who told me his name was Scott. He asked how he could help me. A good start perhaps, but it went downhill from there. He couldn't answer any of my product questions, miserably failed to demonstrate one particular camera and kept up a running conversation with another one of his colleagues. I left the store without a camera.

Eventually, we came across a woman in a small independent camera shop, and the difference was quite marked. I felt that I had bought a camera rather than being sold to. She knew her products, was a good demonstrator and listened to all of my questions.

As we came out of the shop, I remember joking to Melanie that the woman must have been on one of my ITT sales training courses. She agreed totally with me, then made the suggestion that perhaps I should look at running some training courses for shop owners and their staff. Her idea was a good one and got me thinking about ways in which we might set up some courses in the same way as we had with Fiat. One obvious problem, however, was the fact that the courses would have to be paid for by the retailers, and I knew from experience that they didn't spend much on training, in those days. Another was that it would be difficult to find a celebrity, as we had done previously, who would add credibility and interest. Dealing with shop owners would be very different to approaching a large corporate, such as Fiat.

I didn't think any more about the idea, until a few days later when I switched on our TV and found myself in the middle of an extremely popular BBC sit-com, *Are*

You Being Served? It was set in a fictitious departmental store called Grace Brothers and written by the highly talented David Croft, who together with Jimmy Perry had created *Dad's Army.* The weekly plot involved the interaction between the sales assistants in the men's clothing department and the women's lingerie sales staff, who worked on the same floor.

I found out that Actor Jeremy Lloyd, Joanna Lumley's ex-husband, had worked as a salesman in the men's clothing department at Simpsons in the Strand during his early career. He joined forces with Croft and used his experiences as the basis for *Are You Being Served?* The cast included Mollie Sugden, Trevor Bannister, John Inman, Frank Thornton and Wendy Richards, who went on to play Peggy Mitchell in the soap opera *East Enders.*

The more episodes of the sit-com I watched, the more convinced I became that this had the potential to add huge value to a conventional training course, just as the involvement of Richard Baker and David Jacobs had in the case of Fiat. I started to plan the best way of creating something that would meet the specific needs of the retail sector.

From the work I'd done with Curry's sales staff, whilst at ITT, I knew that most existing retail sales training was simplistic and very restricted time-wise, to say the least, with sales personnel not considered as being very skilled. They were generally paid quite poorly, and many stores and shops had a high turnover of staff. The question was, how could I best deliver training to these shop staff? I realised that unless I had a team of trainers, it just wouldn't be practical or economical.

I thought back to my ITT days and remembered a company with which I'd worked in respect of conference event management. Commercial Presentations was a small company, Covent Garden in London. It specialised in staging elaborate product launches for companies, such as JCB and Citroen, as well as large-scale sales conferences both in the UK and internationally. Another project that I clearly recall, involved them creating a powerful audio visual presentation, targeted at theatrical impresarios who were capable of funding the launch of the musical *Evita.* I wasn't aware that *Evita* had originally been launched in 1976, purely as a sound track album, comprising music by Andrew Lloyd Webber and lyrics by Tim Rice. They were then looking for commercial investment to take *Evita* to the London stage, as a fully blown musical, and then on to Broadway.

Commercial Presentations staged this investment-seeking presentation at a London theatre in 1977, and it served its purpose well. Evita eventually opened at the Edward Theatre in London on 21 June 1978 before closing after 3176 performances. It opened on Broadway on 25 September 1979, where it ran for 1567 performances.

I knew that the two guys who owned Commercial Presentations had a very impressive pedigree, and I decided to try and arrange a meeting with them. Stephen Batiste and Bob Scott did indeed remember me from their work with ITT and were happy to meet. Our initial meeting was at their offices and studio in Neal's Yard and went reasonably well. I outlined my thoughts to them as to how we might be able to create something that would appeal to retail groups, store groups and so on, using the TV series *Are You Being Served?* Whilst they saw the commercial potential, they expressed serious doubts about my being able to secure some form of licensing deal with the BBC, especially one that was affordable. We continued chatting for a while about possible ways of putting a marketable product together, one which would appeal to the retail sector, before agreeing to get back together, once I had spoken to the BBC. I'm sure that they believed it was the last they would see of me.

My next step was going to be tough. I would have to approach the BBC and find out who would be the best person to talk to about licensing deals. Then I would have to convince them that I was worth-seeing, and if so, how we could best structure a deal.

I was at the local library, doing some research on David Croft, when an idea came to me. I saw that David and his wife Ann had seven children, one of whom was named Penny. For some reason, the name Penny Croft rang a bell. Where did I know it from? Yet again, I must remind you that Google was still just a fantasy at that time. All I knew that somehow I had to find out about Penny Croft.

As so often happens, the answer came to me when I was thinking about something totally different. I was looking at an out-of-date South African newspaper that my dad had sent to me, as it contained an article about a South African racing driver he thought I might know. I flicked through the paper, out of interest, and saw a number of display advertisements promoting entertainment venues. Then I saw the name Penny Croft. The advert told me that she was appearing at a venue in Cape Town, where she'd be singing her hit song Count the Red Cars. That's where I knew the name. I'd heard the song when I was living there. From that, it was easy to find out that she had spent several years in South Africa, but she was now living back in London. A little detective work and we were in touch.

The South African link helped when I spoke to her, and I explained that I needed her advice on a project linked to AYBS. Her first reaction was to suggest I call the BBC, but she eventually agreed to meet me and invited me to an address in Wimbledon, where, she told me, a friend of hers lived. When I got there, I met him and discovered that he was a massive tennis fan. The lounge of his house was full of shelves. All were packed with VHS videos. They were neatly labelled, and I saw that they all related to tennis matches. His name was Mike Hawker, and Penny later explained to me that he had made a lot of money writing two songs, one of which had made him a small fortune and allowed him to retire. It was the song that launched the solo career of Dusty Springfield: *I Only Want to Be with You*. He had also composed Helen Shapiro's huge 1962 hit: *Walking Back to Happiness*. I could have sat and talked to him for ages, but I was there for a purpose.

I took an instant liking to Penny, finding her both relaxed and friendly, and when I explained why I was trying to set up a meeting with the BBC, she sounded very interested. We also talked a lot about our times in South Africa, her singing and my motor racing, as well as the fact that she had won the prestigious *Golden Microphone Award* for South Africa's best female vocalist. Then she told me a lot about her dad, including the fact that he was busy writing a new comedy series for the BBC, based on a 1950s holiday camp; *Hi-de-Hi!*

We sat talking and drinking coffee for a couple of hours before I asked for her opinion as to the best way to get into the BBC to talk about a licensing deal. She was quiet for a few moments and then told me that the best person to meet, the one who could make a quick decision as to the merits of what I was proposing, would be David Croft himself.

To my astonishment, she then offered to phone her father and arrange a meeting for me.

The subsequent meeting was even more astonishing. Arriving at the BBC Television Centre in West London, London, I was escorted by a lady up to David's personal office, very aware from her attitude that he was one of the VIPs. I don't mind admitting that I was very nervous as the door was opened, and I met the great man. He organised coffee and biscuits and, just as his daughter had done, chatted with me about my AYBS concept, as though we'd been friends for a long time. He then asked me a lot of question about the way in which I wanted to utilise the cast members of the series, including where we would be recording, then he moved on to the potential revenue generation and asked what royalty payment I would agree to. Finally, he promised to talk to all of the actors involved and get their thoughts on the proposed deal. My concern was that he hadn't yet mentioned an up-front payment. I made it very clear that this was quite a gamble. I didn't know what the buy-in would be from the retail sector, but he told me not to worry. His view was that it would probably take up so little time of anyone involved that that it wouldn't be a problem; and that if it made us all some money, great, but if it didn't, so be it.

I thanked him, and he told me that he would get back to me in due course. I left his office and don't remember much about getting to my car. I was dumbstruck that there was a possibility that this might work and couldn't wait to tell Stephen and Bob Scott.

In an innovative step to generate more income for his racing, Brian approached the BBC and secured the Rights to produce sales training programmes, using the cast of the popular sitcom, Are You Being Served?

The format that I'd worked out, and which I presented to David Croft as being the most appropriate, was to produce tape cassettes, accompanied by training books, containing strip cartoons and explanatory text. In the days before laptops, DVDs, PowerPoint, PCs and the myriad of other technological communication methods available today, the tape cassette and the small portable cassette players were then *de rigueur* for shop or department managers to run training courses.

With Bob Scoot's help, we found a brilliant cartoonist who faithfully created the AYBS characters whilst I wrote the scripts and the text. Each pack would deal with a different aspect of the retail selling process, including:

- How to Open the Sale
- How to Establish the Customer's Needs
- How to Deal with Objections

A week went by, and I hadn't heard from David Croft. Then one evening, he phoned me. 'Brian,' he said, 'the deal is on.' I didn't know what to say. Then he added that I should contact him when we were ready to start production. Wow! I couldn't believe what I had achieved. I also couldn't believe that it had been so relatively simple. David Croft's view had been that we didn't need to have reams of legal papers to sign. If it was going to work, he said, we all knew who would be paid what. If it didn't work, then let's all get on with something that does. He was a remarkable man.

To record the soundtrack of the various episodes, we chose the studios right next to the London offices of Commercial Presentations Ltd in Neal's Yard. The Redwood Studios were owned by Monty Python's Michael Palin and managed by Andre Jacquemin, nowadays a partner in the business and one of world's leading film score composers.

We had a great deal of fun and entertainment in the process of recording these scripts. Every cast member was a consummate professional and, despite the fact that they weren't getting paid for this, other than by a share of royalties on future sales, had rehearsed their lines as for any professional role.

Andre was also a real star and vindicated our decision to use a top-end recording company. Working with a group of professionals in this way, we were able to get through the entire set of recordings in a much quicker time than we had estimated, saving us a not-inconsiderable chunk of budget for studio hire. During the course of the recordings, I got to know the cast quite well. What I very much appreciated was the fact that everyone displayed a determination to create the best product that they could. On several occasions, we over-ran allocated times, but they willingly stayed on to make a section work to all our satisfaction. On one occasion, we finished late, and as I was staying up in London that night, I asked Andre where a good place to eat would be. Wendy Richard overheard us talking and told me that there was a good French bistro that she often used. She looked at her watch and asked me if I'd like to join her that evening, as she was meeting some friends later on to go to some club or other.

There I was sitting with Miss Brahms from *Are You Being Served?*, the same Wendy Richard who had been the girl's voice on Mike Sarne's number one hit single Come Outside and who went on to play Peggy Fowler in *East Enders*. She was a fascinating woman, and we enjoyed some interesting conversation about her life with the BBC and other theatrical work. I remember thinking that this was a very different world from driving race cars, but that had it not been for racing, I doubt if I'd have ever thought about creating this AYBS sales training concept and certainly wouldn't be able to boast that I had dinner with Wendy Richards. Life can take you in some strange directions!

With Stephen Batiste's and Bob Scott's much appreciated help and funding, the time came to launch the AYBS course. We held the media event on one of the beautifully restored Thames sailing barges, moored as a visitor attraction in St Katherine's Dock, adjacent to Tower Bridge. Wendy Richard agreed to be there, although David Croft couldn't attend. Reaction was very positive. My first sale was into Selfridges. Then it was on to Boots in Nottingham, where I was invited to address the audience at what I recall was a regional conference.

I remember that on the day of our last recording session with the AYBS cast, Andre, the studio manager, asked me if I would like to meet some of the Monty Python team who were busy in the upstairs studio, recording the sound track for their new movie. We walked up the stairs, and he held open the door for me. There in the middle of the room were four Pythons, one of whom was sitting at a keyboard whilst the others were watching intently. 'Gentlemen,' shouted Andre, 'meet Brian.' As one, they looked across at me, and in unison, replied, ''Ello Bri-ern,' in their usual comic style. Andre hadn't told me that the movie on which they were working was *The Life of Brian!*

John Cleese was one of the quartet. After I'd been introduced to each one of them, he asked me if we could possibly set up a meeting at some stage. He told me that his highly successful film production company, Video Arts, made a lot of business training films, which I did know and had seen many of them. Having been told by Andre about my background in training, he felt that I might be able to help him with a new project on which he was working.

Our meeting took place a week later at the offices of Commercial Presentations, next door to the Redwood Studios. It was a converted old warehouse and had quite low door frames. When John arrived, on a very cold winter morning, he was wearing a long overcoat, with a scarf wound around his neck. I hadn't realised how tall he is. Instead of lowering his head, as most tall people tend to do when entering our office, John leaned right back and strode in. It was so close to his famous *Ministry of Silly Walks* posture that I battled not to smile.

As a result of our meeting, I was commissioned to write the script for a sound cassette, based on teaching sales people, who will be working on an exhibition stand, how to improve their sales performance.

We managed to generate a lot of publicity for the *Are You Being Served?* training courses, but, to be honest, although the trials seemed to be going well, there was also a lot of apathy when we contacted other retail groups. Despite considerable evidence to the contrary, a lot of contacts told us that they were quite capable of delivering their own training. The original objective of making enough money to feed my motor racing habit seemed a long way off. Stephen and Bob were incredibly supportive, but understandably had other priorities. These included designing and managing spectacular product launches for several clients, as well as dealing with the influx of enquiries for audio-visual presentations, based on the great success of their *Evita* project. As a result of their rapid growth, they were unable to spare any more significant time working on a project which reluctantly they saw very much as a sideline for the company.

One of their new projects was to design and create another "trailer" for promoting a potential stage musical. This one was based on the topic of a weekly magazine's Agony Aunt and was called *Dear Anyone*. As with the *Evita* project, the creators of *Dear Anyone* had written and released its musical score as an LP, featuring Elaine Stritch, prior to then launching the concept as a stage musical, subject to the required investment being secured.

One of the singles from the album, "I'll Put You Together Again", was recorded by Hot Chocolate, becoming a Top-20 hit single. As far as investment was concerned, it eventually came together; and in 1983, *Dear Anyone* eventually opened at the Cambridge Theatre in London's West End.

During the time that I was working on the AYBS project, I was able to watch Stephen and Bob at work, creating dynamic presentations, whether for a product launch, or for investment purposes as was the case with both Evita and Dear Anyone. Much of what I saw came as a revelation to me and I carefully stored the information in the memory banks for future use. I subsequently referred to it in various ways, as my career developed. Looking back, I realise that I was absorbing information in those days like a sponge.

Although I was gaining valuable experience, I wasn't making the levels of money that I needed to plan a serious racing programme. The fact that I'd so enjoyed creating the new training programme showed me that I really didn't have the total dedication to give everything up for a career driving race cars. Yes, I missed the adrenalin and pleasure of racing, but I knew deep down that I also demanded a level of variety in my life. It was time to take stock.

Many questions ran through my head. Could I make my mark in another category of racing? Was I happy to stay in Britain? Was it time to pull the plug on race-driving? Then there was the question of children. Melanie and I had talked about the possibility, but that was a while ago. What did she think about it right now? Should I look at trying to make a lot of money and stop being so selfish, which, I had to admit, motorsport had made me become. I knew that if I decided to continue in the sport, I somehow had to combine motor racing with satisfying the emerging, creative side of my personality.

Many discussions later, Melanie and I both came to the conclusion that it might be good for us to leave Britain and head overseas. We realised, however, that this wouldn't be as easy as it sounded. We didn't have a lot of money and whilst Melanie might get a job working in a hospital, as she had been for some years, I would find it more difficult without any qualifications. We came to the conclusion that if we did want to work overseas, it would have to be in an English-speaking country. America seemed a strong possibility, as I had now worked for Goodyear, Xerox and ITT, all major American corporations and had built a good reputation in sales and sales training. Then we considered Australia, but decided it was too far away. At that time, the Middle East wasn't even an option. Then, of course, there was South Africa, where I had family. We made a lot of enquiries and came to the conclusion that a move there would make the most sense. The problem was that when I made contact with South Africa House in London, I was informed that if we wanted to stay for a reasonable amount of time, I would need to have a job to go to, despite the fact that my mother and father had Permanent Residence status and were living in Johannesburg. This meant that they didn't have South African citizenship, but could work and live for an unspecified time in the country. We would have to go the same route, it seemed.

I made some enquiries in the automotive and the motorsport sector in South Africa but with little joy. There had to be a better way, I kept thinking. It turned out that there was.

I talked to several UK recruitment agencies and asked if they offered overseas recruitment. After several dead ends, I eventually spoke to a young guy who told me that he was looking for senior staff for an American computer company, Control Data Corporation. The company ran training institutes in the US and an increasing number in the UK, offering skills training in computer programming, which in those days meant learning languages such as Fortran and COBOL. These were the pioneer days of computing, and it offered an exciting future for so many young people.

One of Control Data's UK-based institutes (CDI) was in Southampton, and the consultant informed me that that they were currently looking for an institute manager. I think he could see from my reaction that I wasn't particularly interested. For a start, I knew sweet nothing about computing; and secondly, I was looking to work overseas, not in the UK.

I shouldn't have been so impatient. Luckily, for me, he hung in and suggested there might be something of interest related to the Southampton vacancy. He suggested that it would be a good idea if we could meet there and take a look at a typical CD institute. In that way, he told me, I would better understand what he had in the back of his mind.

It made sense; and as we were living in Shrewton, not that far from Southampton, I agreed to meet him there the next day. Situated in Clifford House, right on the perimeter of the Seven Dials Roundabout in the heart of the city, the Control Data Institute was on the top floor, offering quite good views across the city and docks. We wandered around the large classrooms, which had more than 20 computer terminals positioned on wooden desks. A wide assortment of students sat working at these, ranging in age from around 18 to 60+.

A move to South Africa beckoned in 1980 and Brian spent a year working for the American Control Data Institute, as Manager of its Cape Town training school. Whilst there, he secured a sponsorship deal with the company, allowing to him to get back to race-driving.

The agency man explained that in the UK, Control Data had a 5-year government contract in place to deliver computer training courses, with a view to the students securing employment at the end of the course. There was a selection process to identify appropriate students to enrol on the course; and once a student was selected, there would be no fees involved. In other words, the UK government picked up the tab. It seemed a very good scheme and was proving extremely popular now that the IT industry, as we refer to it today, was predicted to be on a huge growth path. How right those predictions were.

The recruitment consultant then suggested we went into the manager's office and had a coffee, whilst he told me more about the vacancy. I explained for the umpteenth time that I was looking for a job overseas, but he persevered, and what he subsequently outlined to me certainly grabbed my attention.

It seemed that Control Data Corporation was opening new institutes in many countries and were planning to one in Johannesburg, South Africa. He went on to suggest that if I were to initially get a job here in the UK with CDI, it would be a reasonable expectation that I might be able to get a transfer to South Africa in due course. Now this certainly sounded more interesting.

When he outlined the outstanding remuneration package that the Southampton job offered, I confirmed that I would most definitely like to put forward an application. I didn't have long to wait before being offered a formal interview. I started to worry that perhaps my motor racing background wasn't quite what was wanted. I would have to stress my level of management experience with Goodyear, Xerox and ITT as being more relevant. Mention of those three powerful brands obviously did the trick, because I received a phone call the very next day, offering me the job as manager of the Control Data Institute in Southampton.

The government supported student selection process had been mentioned but not in much detail. I hadn't realised quite what it involved until I was invited to one in Southampton, prior to my start date with the company. It transpired that the interview process involved a detailed application form, followed by a face-to-face meeting with the manager (me!) often accompanied by a representative from the regional government department, which would be coughing up the budget.

It took me a while to get the hang of this, with a very diverse range of applicants occupying the chair in front of my desk. Nevertheless, within a couple of months, I was really enjoying my new role. Working with so many people from such a diverse range of backgrounds was something I hadn't done to such a degree before, and I grew into it with increasing enthusiasm.

The journey to Southampton from Shrewton didn't bother me. In fact, it was quite enjoyable heading off in the morning across Salisbury Plain and down through the Hampshire countryside. I should point out that traffic volumes in 1979 were very different to what they are in 2018.

When a call came in about ten months later from the UK personnel manager of Control Data, asking me if I was still interested in a possible move to South Africa, I have to admit that I had put that option to the back of my mind. The reality came as somewhat of a shock. On my application form, when I joined CDI, I'd filled in an appropriate box which asked me if I would be interested in job opportunities in other countries. I'd ticked South Africa. It transpired that such an opportunity had arisen at the soon-to-open Johannesburg CDI. Now Melanie and I really would have a major decision to make.

Chapter 12
Johannesburg, High Altitude Balls and Skiing

Moving country is a big step for most people at any time, but nearly 40 years ago, it was even more so. Today, South Africa is a very popular holiday destination, but that wasn't the case back in 1980. Communication channels were far more antiquated; and whereas today, international travel is commonplace, in those days, it was quite a daunting prospect. Then there was the political scenario, with the Afrikaner-dominated Nationalist Party in power. Apartheid was still in place, and I'd witnessed its presence in many ways during my two holidays in the country. I'd obviously spoken to my folks about the politics when I'd been staying with them there. My father worked for a company involved in gold-mining and saw many of the evil aspects of the system which divided people by colour. His view was that by leaving South Africa he wasn't going to change the politics, but by being there, he could do more to bringing about change. Besides which, he hadn't been able to find employment at his age in the UK.

Many people, far more learned than I am on the subject, have written books and papers on the politics of South Africa, and I am not going to talk about the rights and wrongs of the policies of the RSA government, but what I will say that Melanie and I thought long and hard about the pros and cons of living there. For personal reasons, we took the decision to pursue the opportunity that was being presented to us in one of the most fascinating continents on the planet.

The selection process for the South Africa position meant a one-week trip to Johannesburg, for both Melanie and me. As I had been shortlisted for the position, the company paid for this. I was to be interviewed by Jim Miller, CEO of Control Data in South Africa.

Everything went smoothly, and I liked what I saw, as Jim Miller obviously did, because he offered me the job within a day of my interview. The new institute was situated in the centre of Johannesburg, which was then a very vibrant place to work. It seemed totally safe, unlike the crime-ridden area it has subsequently become. We then checked out rental accommodation in the area and found it to be both attractive and affordable. The package that we'd been offered to relocate to RSA was quite substantial, and we felt confident that we could enjoy a good standard of living if we were accepted.

It was time to our farewells to my parents, with whom we had stayed for most of the trip. I had deliberately avoided telling them the real reason we were there, why we were there, simply explaining that it was a business trip on behalf of Control Data in the UK and left it at that. I knew that if I told them about the possibility of my working in South Africa, they would have been so excited, but didn't want to then disappoint them if things failed to work out. Once I had received and formally accepted the verbal offer that had been made, there would be plenty of time to tell them the news.

We flew back home and started planning our move, which wasn't going to be that easy. The reality struck home that we were actually emigrating, and we had been warned by Jim Miller that there would be a lot of SA Government red-tape involved. He then added that Heather Morris, the company's HR Manager, based in the same Johannesburg office, would help me sort it all out if things were agreed.

Brian in his Johannesburg home office, doing what he does best, on the phone endeavouring to secure yet more sponsorship.

Within days of arriving back in Shrewton, my letter of appointment duly arrived, confirming everything that he had verbally promised. I sent my acceptance by return. No looking back now, the deal was done.

Melanie and I eventually came to the conclusion that I should initially head back to South Africa on my own, to sort out the emigration administration; and at the same time, look at potential properties to rent. It made sense to do this, rather than buy, until we knew the area a lot better. It also gave Melanie the chance to put our Shrewton house on the market before heading down to South Africa to join me.

As I explained at the beginning of the book, I'd left home in 1964 at the age of 17 to live in Southampton and take up my first job. I'd met Melanie in 1966, and we started dating. In 1969, we married and had now been together for ten years. I got on famously with her family and had been quite happy for most of the ten years. Now we were heading 6000 miles to South Africa.

I felt extremely emotional as I waved to Melanie and drove away from our Shrewton house, on route to London. There, I would hand back my company car and head to Heathrow for the flight to Jo'burg. Something was worrying me, but it would take me a while to realise what it was.

I hadn't let my folks know that I was flying down, deciding to surprise them once I'd landed. Having hired a car at the airport, I drove from Jan Smuts Airport (renamed Oliver Tambo) to the Holiday Inn that I'd booked in at Mill Park, close to the city centre. Once there, I dialled my parents' number. My mother answered and assumed that I was calling from the UK. We chatted briefly about the usual things, such as the weather in the UK, and how we were both keeping. I then made a comment that it had been very hot driving from Jan Smuts Airport to the Holiday Inn. There was a short silence, followed by, 'What do you mean?' I told her where I was, and she immediately assumed I was on another business trip, telling me that they'd be with me in an hour. When they arrived, we went into the bar where I was able to explain that we were coming to live in South Africa. Once the tears had stopped, she told me to book out of the hotel the next morning and come back to their house to stay for a while. You could say that they were rather excited about the prospect of my living there!

My first week in Johannesburg went quickly, with so much to do. Not least of all, there was the paperwork required to secure my permanent residence permit, without which it would be impossible to work in South Africa, let alone be paid. The Afrikaner-led government was renowned for its crippling bureaucracy, and it seemed determined not to disappoint me. Thank goodness for Heather Morris, who had a wealth of experience in HR matters and knew who to contact, and how to pull strings.

In the process, also she helped me settle in, by inviting me to supper with her family. I liked Julian, her six-foot-two-inch tall husband, and we hit it off straightaway. For a start, he loved motorsport, and he also played tennis at quite a high level. I was immediately invited to join a group of his friends who played floodlit tennis at one or other of their houses, a couple of evenings a week.

I had taken up my mother's invitation to stay at their apartment, close to the Sandton suburb of Johannesburg, whilst I looked around for somewhere to rent. My folks were so delighted that I was there, and they didn't tire of showing me their favourite steak house and restaurants. Then Heather Morris arranged to take me into the centre of the city to see the Control Data Institute, where would be based, and also to meet the staff and my boss, Eric de Villiers. All of this was happening under beautiful blue skies, and I loved every minute of it; having said that, the weather did take some getting used to. Johannesburg is 1800 meters above sea level, and until you acclimatise, it's very easy to become breathless. The winters there are very special, with blue skies most of the time, very little rain, if any at all, and cold nights which contrasted with midday temperature of around 23 or 24 degrees centigrade. In the summer, it's all about blue skies and heat, with frequent electric storms bringing torrential afternoon rain during January and February.

I eventually found the most incredible apartment, about a mile out of the city centre. It was in an area called Zoo Lake, named partly because of its close proximity to Johannesburg Zoo and partly because of an enormous lake that was surrounded by parkland. The apartment was a huge self-contained unit within a massive detached house, which had been built around 1935 and boasted two acres of garden, with beautiful rose gardens, mature trees and two swimming pools. Originally it belonged to one of the many gold-mining magnates who lived in Johannesburg in that era. I had my own pool, pool-house with bar, and a wide balcony overlooking the gardens. All this for 350 South African Rand per month, fully furnished. That equated in 1980 to £196 per month.

One amusing aspect of living so close to the zoo was that you could often hear the roaring of lions, amongst many other strange sounds. I remember being on the phone to my uncle in England on one occasion, and he asked what the strange roaring sounds were. I told him that it was a lion but failed to mention that I was living next door to a zoo. I'm sure he thought that we had wild animals on the loose in Johannesburg!

Socially, I was being well-looked-after and often invited to parties, tennis events and sightseeing tours. I spoke earlier of getting breathless quite quickly. I soon found out another side-effect of the high altitude. It has a big impact when you play tennis or football, which I did quite a lot. My work colleagues told me that if I bought tennis balls in a shop, to make sure that I asked for "high-altitude balls". I thought they were taking the mickey, but they weren't. In Cape Town, you played with ordinary tennis balls, but at 1800 meters above sea level, the speed of the ball through the air and its subsequent bounce at was totally different, hence the need for special tennis balls.

Later, I was to discover that in motor racing, cars had to be re-tuned when going to the Cape or Port Elizabeth to compete. Being at sea level produced a 17.5% increase in power when the car was put onto a dyno.

I'd been in South Africa for about six weeks when I began to realise that something had happened to me. I was feeling incredibly liberated and relaxed. I couldn't remember feeling that way for some years. I'd been happily married and very much loved all of Melanie's family, particularly her youngest brother Royston, who seemed to get on so well with me because he loved motor racing and coming to watch me compete. I missed our regular games of Subbuteo!

I loved Melanie, that I knew, but there were several occasions when I had felt that we had got married too young. I'd left home at a young age, struggled to look after myself financially. I'd missed out on socialising with all of my former school friends, having moved away from Isleworth down to Southampton, and then I had to look after myself, from living in a shared room in digs to bedsits and then, eventually, rental apartments.

Now I was in South Africa, enjoying a great social life and feeling that I really belonged there. I think it all went to my head. I'm not going into detail about how it happened, but I had this feeling that I didn't want to be a married any longer. Through a mutual business colleague, I met a German girl who had recently arrived in South Africa, and we went to a lot of parties together, although I knew that it was never going to be a serious relationship.

It was soon time for Melanie to arrive, and I had come to a conclusion as to what I should tell her when I met her at the airport. There is no easy way to bring a marriage to an end, and I know now that I could have handled matters in a better way. The reality I believe, looking back, was that we had both got married too young, coupled with my leaving home so early in my life. There was hurt on both sides. Melanie had done nothing wrong, and we had been happy in many ways; but the moment I arrived in South Africa, I became a different person, that's the truth of the matter. I often wonder if I hadn't gone to South Africa, whether our marriage would have survived. Looking back on it, I sadly feel that it might have done so for a while longer, but that it was inevitable that my feelings eventually came to the surface. We'd had some great times together, and I will always feel bad about the hurt that was inevitably caused. As I will explain further on, I did re-marry, and that has lasted nearly 32 years and is still as strong as ever. I hope that it will indicate that it wasn't a case of wanting to live a playboy existence that overcame me, but rather just a feeling that I need to enjoy living free of responsibility for a while. I'm sure Melanie would see it differently, and I wouldn't blame her, but that's all I am going to say on the matter.

The first few weeks of my new job went well, and I really enjoyed the variety that it offered. It was similar in some ways to what I'd been doing for the company in Southampton. However, there was a major difference between the ways that the company operated in South Africa to that in the United Kingdom. The South African government did not fund the applicants who wanted to do the full programming course, in the way that UK government had. What this meant was that anyone who applied would have to fund themselves. This was helped by a very low interest rate loan, offered by Control Data. This also applied in South Africa to university education at that time, as well as a lot of schooling. From a health point of view, people also had to look after themselves by taking out medical insurance, as has always been the case in the USA. There was no safety net in South Africa. What I mean by that is that you have to take full responsibility for your future well-being. You can't rely on anyone else.

Another notable difference between my new place of work and the Southampton Control Data Institute was the average age of the students. As I'd mentioned, there were quite a few mature students who'd been encouraged to learn new skills, whereas in South Africa, they were mainly within the 18–25 age group. The student selection process was also totally different. In the UK, the emphasis was on more people applying for government grants than there were places available. In Johannesburg, it was a structured sales process, aimed at persuading potential students to part with the cost of the course.

As part of this sales process, I would be expected to run evening sales presentations, in a nearby hotel, on a weekly basis, open to the public. It was my job to enthuse them about the demand for programmers, and the level of salary that could be attained on successful completion of the course. The institute also employed a couple of women whose role was to help students to subsequently secure employment. This is where my sales training experience would stand me in good stead, and it was something I was looking forward to.

Eric de Villiers, the manager of the institute, and I got on well together straightaway. Most days, we'd head off for a lunchtime sandwich at lone of the local cafés in downtown Johannesburg. It was during one of these sessions that he told me about his passion for wildlife exploration. A while back, he had bought a 25% share in a private plane and spent a lot of weekends flying with three friends from Johannesburg to the Okavango Delta, which is a vast inland river delta in Northern Botswana. He described the region as comprising of sprawling grassy plains that flood each season into a lush animal habitat. He enthused about the way that he and his mates used wooden dugout canoes to and paddle upriver, passing hippos, elephants and terrifying crocodiles before setting up camp. It sounded divine, and I stored the destination firmly in my memory bank.

As the weeks went by, I came to realise that living in South Africa was totally different to the UK in so many ways. Yes, English was the primary language, and you drove on the left-hand side of the roads, but that's where it stopped. For a start, the cost of living was so different. I regularly went out for an evening meal in one of many superb steak houses. For what was the equivalent of less than a fiver, I could enjoy a succulent fat sirloin steak and a bottle of South African red wine, followed by an ice cream and a coffee. I found myself starting to become accustomed to this new life style, living in a country that delivered those amazing blue skies, virtually every morning.

Working with so many youngsters, as I was at the institute, was good for me; and just as I had in Southampton, I thoroughly enjoyed my role. My sales figures were well above target, and I was enjoying a relaxed social life. I mentioned a German girl, Angelika, whom I'd met; and one day she told me that her parents, who lived in Duisberg in the Ruhr, also owned a ski-chalet in the Dolomite Mountains. It transpired that in December, she was joining her brother and folks for a week's skiing and asked if I'd like to join her. I'd never ski-ed before, but it was something I really fancied. Here was a golden opportunity to receive expert tuition and enjoy some excellent company at the same time. I told her I was up for it.

Brian and Liz take a ride during a ski-ing holiday in the Dolomite Mountains.

By the time we caught the flight to Luxemburg, where we would be met by Angelika's brother, I was really looking forward to what would be another totally different experience.

Thanks to a few liberal swigs of Jägermeister on a regular basis, it didn't take me long to be able to stay on my skis and tackle some of the Blue designated gradients. In the evenings, the *après*-ski was fantastic. I was a having a ball, and without realising it, getting fit, which was something that I had rather ignored during my short time in South Africa.

Both Angelika and her brother proved to be useful skiers and excellent instructors. They kept telling me that as a racing driver, I should be used to high speeds and bit of danger. They would accept no excuses; and on the last day of our stay, took me with them onto a Black gradient. I recall them standing on the edge of

85

what seemed like a 45° sheet of ice, and in turn showing me how I should "tack" my way across, first left and then right. They waited at the bottom of the slope for me, as I closed my eyes and went for it. The first two "tacks" went to plan; then it got beyond me, and I headed straight down the slope, picking up speed as I hurtled along. Crouched low over the skis, with a fixed grimace on my face, I passed my two companions at high speed, realising that there was a small jump ahead of me, careered over that before heading uphill. After 30 or 40 metres, I came to a halt as the gradient increased. Phew! I was quite proud of myself, but you know what they say about pride! I forgot to turn my skis and, gathering speed, went backwards down the slope, hit the jump from the wrong direction and cart-wheeled through the air, landing in a heap right next to Angelika and her brother, who were both roaring with laughter, tears streaming down their faces.

It didn't matter; I believed that I was now a skier!

A week later, we were back in South Africa, a very hot South Africa. Temperatures in summer can vary greatly, with highs of 40°C not uncommon. For me, the ideal was around 25°. In Johannesburg, being at altitude, it's very easy to get sunburned, and I learned very quickly that the African sun is very different to that orange ball that every now and again appears in the UK skies.

Even back in 1980, most South African cars had air conditioning, and as I headed into the city centre on the Monday morning, I was really glad that my new Ford Cortina had it as standard equipment. Sitting in a traffic jam, as I got near to the Queen Elizabeth the Second Bridge, I switched on the radio to catch up with the news. At the tail end of the local bulletin, my ears pricked up when I heard the name Kyalami being mentioned.

As I've already explained, Kyalami was, at that time, an F1 motor racing circuit that was home of the South African Grand Prix. The news snippet about the circuit was very short, simply stating that Kyalami was at the heart of a possible purchase by a business consortium. Why would that be of any interest to me, happily ensconced in a new job, I couldn't imagine!

I couldn't help myself. Later that day, I put in a call to Max Mosley in his London office.

Chapter 13

An F1 Dream Shattered, a Tractor Race and a Letter from James Hunt

I hadn't spoken to Max since sitting next to him on the Alitalia flight some five years earlier, and I wondered if he would remember me. Luckily, he did. After a couple of minutes of general chat, I raised the subject of Kyalami and asked him if he knew anything about the news of the impending sale. He confirmed that he was aware of it, then added that as far as he knew, the sale at auction had gone through, with no competition, and that it had been sold for R1.4 million (then about £6, 75,000). He then asked me why I wanted to know. I replied that as I was now living in RSA, I'd be interested to find out what was happening at the track, and whether there were any ways in which it might help me get back into a racing car.

Max asked if I could leave it with him and told me he'd get back to me if he heard any news that might be of interest. I was later to find out that back in 1978, it was rumoured in South Africa that Max and Bernie Ecclestone had failed in a bid to buy the famous race circuit from SAMRAC. Now there were rumours flying around that they were somehow involved in the new consortium that had taken control, with a certain Bobby Hartslief at the helm.

The next morning, I received a surprise phone call. It was from Bobby Hartslief, telling me that he had been contacted by Max Mosley the previous afternoon. Max had suggested that it might be helpful to meet up with me. I got the feeling that he wasn't too pleased at being told to do anything, let alone to ring some UK character that he had never heard of and then invite him to meet for a coffee. Nevertheless, Bobby invited me to a quick meeting at Kyalami Ranch Hotel, which was situated in a river valley about 800 metres from the entrance to the race circuit. He added that he was meeting his lawyer and accountant there a little earlier, so it was convenient for him. I made an excuse to leave the institute early that day, and at five minutes to four, I drove into the hotel car park.

I was astonished to find that at about six o'clock, that same afternoon, I was walking back to my car as the new manager of the Kyalami Grand Prix Circuit, subject to being released from my contract with Control Data Institute, which still had less than six weeks to run.

When I sat down with Eric de Villiers and told him what had happened, I wasn't sure how he'd react, but to my delight, he immediately stood up from his desk, walked over and shook my hand, telling me how chuffed he was for me, and that I shouldn't even hesitate about accepting the offer I'd been made. He then added that, of course, it was subject to half a dozen passes for the next South African F1 Grand Prix!

I had mixed feelings, I have to admit. I'd enjoyed my six month role with CDI in Johannesburg and knew that if I had continued, I could have done really well for myself within such a large international organisation. On the other hand, my passion was motorsport; and although I had accepted the fact that I would never become a Formula 1 driver, my ambition of one day working in F1 was still burning bright. Becoming the manager of a Formula 1 race circuit was something I had never thought about, but I knew I'd never forgive myself if I didn't grab the opportunity with both hands.

The next day, I called Bobby Hartslief, who was once again in a meeting with his lawyer Mervyn Key and his accountant Laurie McIntosh and told them I would gladly accept their offer. One of the first things they mentioned was that I should go out and buy a company car. I'd had no complaints with the Ford Cortina that I'd been driving, but that belonged to CDI, so I needed to choose something a little sportier and in keeping with my new role. I found a second-hand Lotus Eclat in a showroom near to the track that seemed to fit the bill.

Things were happening fast. The South African media wanted to know who this new kid on the block was, who'd been appointed by Bobby Hartslief to run the track. I was still living in the Zoo Lake apartment, and someone had obviously found this out, because a few journalists shortly arrived to interview me. It was a strange feeling suddenly being thrust into the spotlight, albeit for a very short time. Many of the headlines gave me a new title, Kyalami Kid, which I thought a bit rich seeing that I was by then 34 years of age.

There was a highly embarrassing incident, however, which I didn't enjoy and made me feel very embarrassed. The man who had been in control of the track was Alex Blignault, and he'd been at the helm for many years. The more people I spoke to about him, the more I understood that he was held in high esteem by many people within the sport. With a very limited budget, he had been a wheeler dealer par excellence, bringing some of the biggest names in the sport to race at Kyalami in a variety of race cars and motorbikes, including Formula 1. He had a reputation for knowing a high number of people within the sport, all over the world, and had a contact book that was probably worth a lot of money.

One morning, Bobby and his team of McIntosh and Key invited me to see my new office at the circuit. As we walked in, Alex Blignault was sitting at his desk, with two female assistants sat opposite him on the other side of the room.

Without any hesitation, Hartslief shook hands with Blignault and told him that he'd like to introduce the person who was going to replace him, waving me over as he spoke. I have never been lost for words, but I have to admit to feeling completely tongue-tied on this occasion; but that was Bobby Hartslief, as I was to find out on many more occasions. He'd been head boy at King Edwards Grammar School in Johannesburg, and I think one could accurately describe him as being rather full of himself.

I'll never forget my first morning as the manager of Kyalami. I walked into my office and said hello to the two secretaries, who had worked for Alex. I explained that I wanted to meet the live-in work force. I knew that there were about 16 or so workmen, who carried out all of the maintenance of the track, including grass cutting, painting and cleaning. They had a residential site in the middle of the race circuit. The track itself was 4.1 kms in length and was positioned on a highland, providing a magnificent view of the Johannesburg skyline, some 25 kms away. In the other direction was Pretoria, the administrative capital of South Africa.

Cunera and Gaynor both looked at one another and smiled knowingly. The usual place, they told me, rather smugly. I didn't want to start my working relationship with them in the wrong way, so I played along with them. It eventually transpired that the staff were under arrest at the nearby Mid-Rand Police Station, all sixteen.

I got in my car and drove the couple of miles to Halfway House, the collection of shops, houses and small business that sat alongside the N1 motorway between Johannesburg and Pretoria. Walking into the police station reception office, I was greeted by a massive individual in a uniform, comprising a light blue safari suit, with shorts and long socks. A military style cap was perched on his head. He must have been well over six foot in height and over a 100 kilos in weight.

He greeted me with the normal Afrikaans, '*Qoeie more, meneer.*' I replied in English to his 'Good morning, Sir' by introducing myself and explained that I was looking for my workforce. Without a smile or comment, he turned his back on me and walked through the door at the back of the office area, then disappeared. He returned after a few minutes with a clip-board in his hand, which he thrust in front of me. He told me to sign the form at the bottom. I looked at and found it was in Afrikaans, one of the country's two official languages at that time (the other was English), then turned it over and saw an English translation. It was basically a release form, confirming that I would take responsibility for the 16 miscreants. I asked the police officer what they had done wrong. He could barely speak English, but I came to the conclusion that our workman had invited some girls into their work camp on the Saturday evening, which was apparently against the law. I couldn't get any more information from him. So now what? He called out to the back office, and another uniformed officer stepped into the reception. 'Good morning,' he said, and asked if I was the new manager of Kyalami, whom he had seen on the SABCTV News. An English speaker, so maybe we could now get this matter sorted out. He explained that there would be a Notice of Fine notice, which would be sent to the Kyalami offices, but if I signed the form, I could take the 16 workmen with me right there and then. *Great,* I thought, *this should be fun with a Lotus Eclat.*

The English speaker walked out to have a look at the car, parked in front of the building and told me that he liked motor racing and often came to watch events at Kyalami. Things then relaxed a little, and I gave him my new card and suggested that if he wanted to come to a race meeting, give me a call. I still had the problem, however, of getting my workforce back to Kyalami. My new "buddy" solved the problem, offering to bring them in the police vehicle.

Half an hour later, I drove through the gates of Kyalami, followed by what, in South Africa, is called a bakkie or pick-up truck, driven by the police officer. In the back, amazingly, were stood all 16 workmen. I was to discover that this was quite a normal sight on South Africa's roads, with builders, farmers and a host of other businesses adopting what they obviously found to be a cost-effective means of transporting their work force.

As I parked the Lotus and headed for my office, it really dawned on me that I had a huge amount to learn about this complex country. But then again, I have always enjoyed a challenge.

With the 1981 South African Grand Prix scheduled for the 7th February, there was very little time to prepare, and a huge amount of work to be done. Maintaining a Formula 1 track is a little bit like painting the 2737-metre Golden Gate Bridge in San Francisco. You no sooner finish painting the entire span, than it's time to start all over again because the paint is now flaking at the beginning. With our Kyalami track, the grass cutting could be equated to the painting, as soon as you finish cutting the massive expanses of grass; it's time to start again.

Looking around the area that actually belonged to Kyalami, and then the high density of commercial units that surrounded the perimeter fences, it was easy to see the potential for the Grand Prix circuit to be sold for commercial or industrial development. Maybe that was the thinking behind the purchase by the new consortium, who knows?

I haven't mentioned that in line with my change of job, I had left my Zoo Lake apartment and moved to a new, single-storey house in a small development called Vorna Valley, situated right opposite the Grand Prix Circuit. It was ideally located for me, as I was spending a lot of hours at the track and to have less than half a mile's drive home in the evenings was a bonus.

It also provided me with a new source of entertainment. The Kyalami Ranch Hotel, as I've previously explained, was situated on the perimeter of the Grand Prix Circuit and was built in an African style, spread over a few acres. A number of thatched chalets provided the bulk of the guest accommodation, many of which were situated around the outside of the large swimming pool. Thatched umbrellas covered all of the tables and chairs, spread liberally around the grounds of the hotel, and added to its attraction. The large clubhouse building housed more bedrooms, a coffee shop and a large restaurant which featured a stage, where shows were regularly presented. Another feature of the Kyalami Ranch Hotel was the Grand Prix bar, in which a host of F1 and other racing memorabilia hung from the walls and ceiling, whilst photographs and autographs could be seen in great abundance.

What I haven't mentioned is that four international airlines used the hotel on a regular basis. It provided excellent accommodation for crew stopovers on long haul flights and was highly popular because of its beautiful location, thatched style of cottages, a nightclub, a swimming pool and tennis courts. In the 1980s, airlines' stopovers were a lot longer than today, and South Africa was a very popular destination for that reason. Alitalia, Lufthansa and Swissair were three of the most regular aircrews to be seen at the hotel.

Living just across the road from the circuit and the hotel, I used the pool facility at the hotel on a regular basis. In the process, I got to know many of the crew members who stayed there. In particular, several Lufthansa pilots would ask if they could come up to the circuit and drive around in a hire car. The previous management hadn't exploited this opportunity, which was rather surprising. It struck me that there as a genuine commercial opportunity in this respect. However, it wasn't something to worry about right then, as we had the 1981 F1 Grand Prix to prepare for.

Kyalami Enterprises, now the name of the new owners of the track, negotiated a title sponsorship deal with Nashua for the Grand Prix. The company had a significant presence in South Africa. Accordingly, the track barriers, buildings and everything else that didn't move was to be painted in their corporate colours.

A huge number of activities had to be put in place in readiness for the Grand Prix, including the logistics of getting the race cars from the airport when they landed, preparation of the pits and large-scale catering activities. In those days, we didn't have the F1 Paddock Club to cater for most of the teams' hospitality requirements. When hospitality was needed, it was usually organised by hiring in individual marquees, so that had to be sorted. Another headache was always parking and traffic control, involving liaison with the Traffic Police. Unlike modern F1 circuits, spectators could bring their cars into the circuit and park up close to the barriers, constructing their own scaffolding as viewing stands, often based in the back of their *bakkies*. It added to the atmosphere of the event, but took some careful policing.

Then in December 1980, just weeks from the Grand Prix, a communication arrived from FISA, then the governing body under the presidency of Jean-Marie Balestre. Its content came as quite a shock. He was asking us to change the date of the South African Grand Prix, from 7 February to 11 April.

The reason could be traced back to some political manoeuvring that had been developing in Europe throughout the 1980 season, between Balestre and Bernie Ecclestone. It was effectively a power struggle between the two men. On one hand was FISA; on the other, a relatively new organisation, FOCA, set up by Bernie. The Formula One Constructors Association was unhappy about FISA introducing a ban on "sliding skirts" on the sides of the race cars. Bernie even threatened a new breakaway F1 series. Matters deteriorated when FISA announced the calendar for the 1981 season, with the non-British teams, namely Renault, Ferrari, Ligier, Osella and Alfa Romeo supported FISA, whilst the remainder including Williams, McLaren, Brabham, March and Tyrell sided with Bernie.

The first scheduled race of the 1981 F1 calendar was meant to be the Argentinian Grand prix, but due to the arguments and delays, that was cancelled. It was then agreed that the Kyalami race would also have to be delayed.

As you can imagine, this went down like a lead balloon with the new owners of the track. For a start, April was notorious as being the start of the rainy season. In addition, tickets and promotional materials had been designed and produced, sales were well under way, Nashua had committed to a high level of hospitality, and finally, the new owners had signed a contract with FOCA. How could we be expected to change the date of the event, at such short notice? Mervyn Key, our lawyer, explained that it would be virtually impossible to change the date, to which the FISA response was to inform him that the race could go ahead but not as a round of the F1 World Championship. It would be run as a Formula Libre Race, without world championship points being awarded.

As if that wasn't bad enough, FISA then added that the FISA aligned teams would not attend the race. Notwithstanding this, our directors decided that they would continue with the race being held on 7 February. I think they were seriously worried about being sued by Bernie and FOCA if they broke the terms of the signed contract with him.

It dawned on me that my F1 debut, as it would have been, wouldn't now happen. I was disappointed, but what could I do? The answer was very simple, I had to play a role in promoting the race in its new format and make sure that everyone who'd brought a ticket or who was still considering doing so, still had a great day's entertainment. I came up with some innovative ideas. The first was to plan some entertainment on the morning of the race. We had already decided on some support races, but we needed something a bit different, something that would create a lot of publicity and media coverage. This was as much for Nashua and other sponsors, as it was for us as circuit owners.

Where the idea came from, I don't know. Maybe it was the way that I'd taught my brain to work, in terms of securing the sponsorship deals that I'd put together up to that point in my career. All I knew was that I needed 24 tractors. I had to do some quick research.

The German tractor manufacturer, Deutz, had a major operation within South Africa, and their head office was in Johannesburg. I made an appointment to meet their marketing director and presented him with my idea. It involved staging a two-lap tractor race around the Kyalami Grand Prix Circuit on the morning of the "Grand Prix". I envisaged that the starting grid would comprise eight of the F1 drivers, seven cast members of the SABC TV soap opera, *The Villagers*, and eight members of the British Speedway Team that was touring South Africa at that time. I also planned to sign up another personality, but more of that later. The 24 competitors would race to raise funds for a charity.

To my surprise, Deutz immediately told me they liked the concept and would arrange for 24 brand new tractors to be delivered to the circuit the day before the race. Can you imagine such an event happening in F1 today? Then something quite extraordinary happened, involving me in having to go back to Deutz, with a further proposal.

Desire Wilson was a South African woman who had made quite a name for herself in motorsport, initially in her own country and then internationally. In Britain, she competed in the Aurora AFX F1 Series, also known as the British F1 Championship, which featured pre-owned Grand Prix cars. In 1980, Desire became the only woman to win a Formula 1 race, at Brands Hatch, in a Wolf F1 car.

Up to that time in F1, it wasn't unusual for some of the less well-financed F1 teams to offer a drive to a local driver, obviously of an acceptable competence level, to drive their second car. It was, of course, subject to them bringing a significant sponsorship package with them. That year at Kyalami, Ken Tyrrell, boss of the British-based Tyrrell Grand Prix team, offered such a drive to Desire Wilson. There wasn't much time to find the thousands of pounds that he demanded, and I was asked by Bobby Hartslief if I would introduce the opportunity to my contact at Deutz. I made the appropriate phone call, and within a very short space of time, a deal was struck. It would allow one of the two dark blue Tyrrells entered in the South African Grand Prix to be branded in the white livery of Deutz, with the name Desire Wilson clearly shown on the side of the cockpit.

She would go on to qualify the car in 16th place on the grid; and in the wet conditions in which the race was run, drive a good race after stalling at the start. Her race sadly came to an end when she brushed the wall whilst being overtaken by another car. She certainly didn't disgrace herself, especially considering how little time she had to prepare for her Grand Prix debut.

Let's get back to the other Deutz involvement in the Grand Prix; their sponsorship of the Tractor Race. I explained how I had decided upon 23 of the 24 drivers, but didn't tell you who I had in mind for the final spot. I wanted somebody really high profile and a former F1 World Champion would certainly fit the bill. The person I wanted to race against some of his former competitors was none other than James Hunt.

When I contacted him, via the BBC for whom he had just started commentating on F1 in partnership with Murray Walker, and invited him to race a tractor, James was only too pleased to oblige. Cheekily, I also took the opportunity to invite him to a party at my house, opposite the Kyalami Circuit on the Thursday night, prior to Saturday's race.

On the Wednesday before the race, I received a phone call, which I certainly hadn't expected. It was from Nigel Mansell, inviting me to dinner with him at the Kyalami Ranch Hotel that evening, together with his wife Roseanne. When I got there, we were sitting at the very next table to Lotus F1 boss, Colin Chapman, for whom Nigel was driving in his first season of F1. It was quite strange for me, as the last time I'd met Nigel, he was a Formula Ford driver back in England; now here he was a full-fledged F1 Grand Prix driver, and I was running a Grand Prix circuit in South Africa. Life moves in mysterious ways, as I have found on so many occasions throughout my life.

James Hunt

85 Lillie Road, London SW6 1UD.
Telephone: 01-381 5166
Telex: 8814596 Norman G.

Brian Simms Esq
Kyalami Motor Racing Circuit
Bergviei Bet
Johannesburg
South Africa   11 February 1981

Dear Brian

With my tail firmly between my legs, I write to apologise for letting you down so badly on Saturday by missing the charity tractor race. To make it even worse, the best excuse I can offer is that I purely and simply overslept and arrived at the track just as the tractor race was finishing. I realise that my failure to appear would have upset the organisers of the race, the charities involved and the public who came to see the race, and I should be very grateful if you would extend my apologies to the organisers and the charities. The only loser as far as the public is concerned is me, but I do hope that the very exciting motor race in the afternoon gave all your spectators a good day out.

Your decision to go ahead with the race despite all the aggravation from FISA was a very brave one, and I hope that it was financially successful.

Once again, my sincere apologies for my bad manners.

Yours sincerely

James Hunt

Brian organised a Deutz tractor race on the morning of the 1981 South African F1 GP, with eight F1 drivers competing against local TV celebrities, as well as James Hunt, who was by then the BBC TV presenter with Murray Walker. James failed to turn up for the race, but a few days later sent Brian this much-appreciated letter of apology.

I wasn't sure why Nigel had invited me, but it soon became quite clear, as the evening went on. He had the nous to realise that as I was now living in South Africa and spent most of my time at the track, there was a strong possibility that I might be able to give him some advantageous tips. Over dinner, Nigel wanted to know about the effects of altitude, what was recommended in terms of water consumption, whether salt tablets worked, what the circuit was like to drive in the wet and a lot more. In other words, he wanted to know everything that might just give him an edge. I was impressed.

During the meal, Nigel pointed to Colin Chapman at the next table and told me how incredibly grateful he was for the opportunity that Chapman had given him in terms of a F1 drive. He went on to tell me that no matter what it took, one day he was going to win the F1 World Championship. His tone of voice left me in no doubt whatsoever that he meant it. Sitting alongside him was his staunchest supporter, his wife. I'd known them both since we raced in the National Championship in 1977. Here he was, just 4 years later, contracted to one of the world's most famous F1 Teams, and Roseanne had played a massive role in helping him get there. Nigel and Roseanne were a great team themselves!

The party at my house the following evening started off quite slowly, but before long it was buzzing. I'd invited quite a lot of people, but had no idea who, or how many, would actually turn up, such was the nature of Formula 1, with changes to people's schedules happening all the time. One of the first to arrive was Geoff Lees, who was driving a Theodore in the Grand Prix. Geoff had been one of the most talented Formula Ford drivers, and you may remember my explaining how he had been the first ever driver to win all three different championships in one season, as well as the Formula Ford Festival. Sadly, Geoff never got the chance that his talent deserved in F1, starting only 5 Grand Prix, but went onto build a highly successful career, both in Europe and Japan, driving sports cars. An interesting historical note; each of Geoff's 5 GP starts were in a different car, namely Tyrrell, Shadow, Ensign, Theodore and Lotus.

The party was well under way when two more guests arrived. I had invited them both, but I didn't expect either to turn up. Max Mosely was standing at the front door with James Hunt beside him. I was really chuffed to meet James for the first time.

He commentated on Brian's first ever race at Brands Hatch back in 1974, before going on to become an F1 broadcasting legend. Murray Walker is seen here with Brian at the opening of the Motorsport Exhibition at Beaulieu Motor Museum in 2016.

As the evening rolled on, James slid further down the lounge wall that he was leaning against. I can still remember it, as if it was yesterday. I don't know what he was on, but it was certainly having the desired effect of relaxing him. I'd had a chance to chat with him about his new role as Murray Walker's companion in the BBC TV commentary box. He was looking forward to it, he told me, but I didn't get the impression that he would see it as a long-term activity. In reality, James stayed in the role until his untimely death in 1993. As you can read in Murray Walker's excellent autobiography, the pairing wasn't exactly made in heaven and was very much a case of chalk and cheese. I was delighted when some year later when Murray told me that by the end of their BBC relationship they had become quite good friends.

In my opinion, and those of a lot more viewers', the Walker/Hunt combination was the best motorsport commentary team we've ever had on TV. The two of them were so different, with James being at times viciously hard on some drivers, particularly wayward backmarkers, who didn't, in his opinion, use their mirrors and move out of the way of the leaders who were lapping them. Murray, by contrast, was incredibly enthusiastic and colourful, on several occasions coming out with some real "bloomers" which have been recorded in the annals of BBC history.

Murray continued in his role after James died, and the BBC tried several other former drivers, including Jonathan Palmer and Martin Brundle. Palmer wasn't to my taste, and although I thought that Brundle was OK, I personally found all of them to be far too deferential to everyone in F1. They came nowhere near the magic combination of Walker and Hunt. For a start, there was a definite lack of humour, which I believe is required to lighten some very tense and often quite boring track action. My complaint today about TV coverage of F1 is that both Sky's and Channel 4's commentaries are far too "anorakish" to attract new viewers. They get bogged down in endless detail and analysis that is not what makes for entertaining commentary.

I suppose those F1 fans who love the in-depth technicalities of the races don't mind paying a Sky subscription to get their style of presentation; but looking at it from the point of attracting new viewers to F1, it will never work. This will surely come from Free to Air TV coverage, currently Channel 4, but I don't think they are getting it right. I now hear that Sky will be the exclusive broadcaster from 2019 onwards. I personally think it's a big mistake.

The complaint that I hear from so many people I talk to is that Channel 4's coverage is all too cosy and incestuous. Mark Webber comes across well, but there is far too much bias towards Toto Wolff and Christian Horner. I personally think that David Coutlhard does a good job and feel that Ben Edwards is a talented commentator, but I much prefer the more laid back, slightly humorous style of BT Sport's coverage of Moto GP. In 2017, Julian Ryder and Keith Heuwen continued as a great pairing, rather in the Walker and Hunt style. Little wonder that TV viewing figures are Moto GP increasing. I must also mention the brilliant Suzi Perry, who adds a breath of fresh air to the rider interviews. Of course, broadcasting of F1 will be forced to change, with so many youngsters today not even watching television; such is the growth of streaming and other digital techniques for watching sport.

Heading back to 1981, and my party at the South African Grand Prix, it was at around ten o'clock that Max and James took their leave. As we walked to their car, James muttered to me that that he was really looking forward to racing the tractor on Saturday morning and thanked me for the invitation.

Alas, poor James never did get to race a tractor. When the 23 drivers, whom we'd selected to throw their Deutz beauties around the Kyalami Grand Prix circuit, gathered together in the race paddock, there was no sign of the 1976 World Champion. No one knew where he was, and all efforts to find him confirmed that he hadn't been seen that morning, either at his hotel or at the track. The organisers had no choice but to start the race without him.

It's always been a regret that I never got to watch the innovative promotional race that I had created and organised, but like everyone else who was involved in running the F1 race, we were being kept busy with so many things to be attended to done before the start of the main race. The tractor race was won by Carlos Reutemann, the Argentinian F1 driver, who, I was led to believe, ran a vast ranch in his home country and spent a lot of his time piloting a tractor around the acres of paddocks.

In some ways, he was lucky to be on the track in a tractor, let alone in a Williams F1 in the main race. On the Friday, following considerable rain, Reutemann had a serious shunt when he ran wide at Sunset Bend and careered through layers of the catch fencing, which was the fashionable way of slowing out of control cars in that era. Carlos eventually came to a halt, trapped in his cockpit under layers of wire fencing. When this happened, I was on a motor bike that I was using as a quick way of getting anywhere I needed to around the circuit and could see that as the excellent Kyalami marshals freed the driver from the cockpit; it was obvious that he was in some discomfort from having his neck jarred in the incident.

The tractor race had proved popular with the large crowd that had spread themselves around the entire perimeter fencing. In true South African style, the catering started early on race day. The smoke and smell from thousands of *braais* drifted across the open expanses of the race track. The atmosphere was unique to Kyalami and one that I would soon be able to soak up again, this time as a competitor.

Whatever Reutemann's neck problem from practice had been, it certainly didn't stop the talented Argentinian putting his Williams FW07 on the front row of the grid for the main race of the day; sadly, of course, not a world championship point-scoring event but simply a Formula Libre Race. The weather on the Friday and Saturday of the event was not typical of the weather normally experienced on the Johannesburg Highveld at that time of the year. It was ironic that one of the reasons the Kyalami directors had refused to move the Grand Prix to 11 April was that they considered the risk of rain to be far greater in April than in February.

During the warm-up session before the race, the track was proving treacherous, with several cars spinning off. The most serious of these involved the Tyrrell of American driver Eddie Cheever, who lost control on the pit straight and ended up in a concrete wall in front of the main grandstand, badly damaging the front end of the car. Cheever himself suffered a badly cut foot, but was still ready for the start of the race.

With the rain literally chucking it down as the cars sat on the grid, Carlos Reutemann had obviously taken some advice from a "local" and gambled that the rain would soon stop, switching to slicks at the last moment. It was a gamble that paid off, and despite falling back in the initial stages, eventually benefitted from the dry tyres and won the race from Nelson Piquet in a Brabham and Elio de Angelis in a Lotus.

Geoff Lees ended the day in hospital. His Theodore suffered a front suspension failure when approaching Crowthorne Corner at very high speed and, in the ensuing coming together with the catch fencing, was hit on his head by one of the fencing posts and knocked unconscious. I remember visiting him in Sandton Clinic the next morning and loaning him a portable television for his short stay under supervision.

So ended the 1981 Nashua South African Grand Prix. Extraordinarily, it was still not 100% clear after the race whether or not Carlos Reutemann's points would count towards the 1981 F1 World Championship. One thing was certain; everyone agreed that the race itself had been worthy of a Grand Prix title, with or without the presence of the FISA supporting teams. We later heard that the race would most definitely not count for world championship points.

It had been an extraordinary experience for me, being a circuit manager for the first time in my life. I learned so much that weekend, watching the entire logistics operation involved in staging an international event.

It was at this race that I met Bernie Ecclestone for the first time. He was then owner of the Brabham F1 Team, with Charlie Whiting as team manager. I already knew Charlie quite well at that time, as I'll explain later. Another team member was Herbie Blash, who recently retired from his role as F1's Deputy Race Director. A testament to Bernie's loyalty to his own personnel is that so many members of his Brabham Team, from that time, carried on working with him in F1, albeit in differing roles, for several decades. Charlie is now the FIA Formula 1 Race Director and Head of the F1 Technical Department. I first met Charlie when I was looking to buy my first race car and visited All Car Equipe, a motor racing retail and race car preparation business, situated on the A20, right opposite the main to the famous Brands Hatch motor racing circuit.

The business was owned by the three Whiting brothers, Nick, Charlie and Andy. Nick was the boss or certainly appeared to be. He was a very talented race driver in his own right; and I watched him on many occasions win touring car races at the Kent track in his Kent Messenger-sponsored Ford Escort BDA. All Car Equipe sold just about everything you could want to go motor racing, whether it be wheels, tyres, race suits, helmets, carburettors, fire extinguisher systems, exhausts, steering wheels or even racing seats. I spent a lot of time there and probably quite a lot of money. Charlie's role was involved in preparing race and rally cars, whilst Andy, the youngest brother, worked in the retail shop, learning the ropes under the tutorage of Nick and Charlie.

When I first approached Charlie at Kyalami, on the day that the race cars had arrived in containers from the airport, he didn't recognise me. Then it dawned on him who I was, and, after answering his questions about my new role in South Africa, we enjoyed a good chat about things back at his business back in West Kingsdown.

Eventually the race weekend came to a close, the teams started packing up; and when I drove into the track on the Tuesday morning, there was little sign of the teams, cars or personnel. It was a strange feeling, witnessing the contrast from a hub of noise and activity on the Saturday to a deserted, bleak scene of emptiness, just a couple of days later. Some year later, when I came to watch the Steve McQueen film *Le Mans*, there was a scene in which he returns to the track the day after the race and sits in the stand, watching the litter blow around the open spaces of the Le Mans Paddock and Pits area, in total isolation. It so reminded me of that day back at Kyalami.

I hadn't seen anything more of my Celebrity Tractor pilot after his non-appearance on race day, but to my astonishment, a letter arrived in the post the following week.

It was from James Hunt, on his own personalised letterhead and personally signed by him. I will never forget its opening lines:

Dear Brian

With my tail firmly between my legs, I write to apologise for letting you down so badly on Saturday by missing the charity tractor race. To make it even worse, the best excuse that I can offer is that I purely and simply overslept and arrived at the track just as the tractor race was finishing...

James Hunt was an F1 World Champion, a huge name in sport, and one of most non-stereotypical sports personalities on the planet. I didn't expect him to send a letter at all, after all he must get invited to a stack of special events and missing one was no big deal for him, except that by taking the time to compose a letter, apologising and blaming nobody else but himself, takes a special type of person. It would have been so easy for him to simply make up an excuse, pass the buck and get someone else to contact me.

I would meet up again with James some 12 years later, also at Kyalami; and in the process, I would discover a very different James Hunt to what most people would expect; more about that later.

Much as I enjoyed my role at Kyalami, I was becoming very frustrated in one specific aspect of it. I wasn't being involved in any of the marketing activities associated with either this particular race or the circuit itself. Max had known that sponsorship acquisition was my primary skill, perhaps my only skill many people would say. I felt that whilst I was gaining tremendous experience in general about event management, the directors were wasting an opportunity to let me help on income-generating activities, such as sponsorship.

I had effectively secured two worthwhile sponsorship deals within the short time that I'd been there, although both were with the same company. In identifying and then approaching Deutz Tractors, I had shown that even within the tough environment of F1, I could still very much hold my own. I was by now busting a gut to be given the chance to start working on next year's Grand Prix, hopefully an official FIA event this time. The signs weren't too promising, however. Bobby Hartslief, Lawrie McIntosh and Mervyn Key had now been joined by another former school friend Andre Bruyns. He had been a Western Province cricketer and was now trying to build a career in sports marketing. They really did operate as little clique, and I definitely wasn't included. However, to my surprise, an opportunity arose, not directly involved with the circuit, which would once again test my sponsorship acquisition skills, as well as my race driving ability.

Chapter 14
More Sponsorship, Racing and Circuit Politics

My father was a project manager for a company that manufactured equipment, such as conveyor belting for South Africa's gold-mining industry. As fathers tend to do, he had spoken to his colleagues about my race-driving activities in the UK and also about my sponsorship skills. One of his work colleagues, with whom he got on really well despite a sizeable age gap, was John Banks. When John heard Ken talk about me, he immediately asked Ken if he could arrange for him to meet me. It transpired that John raced a Lotus 23B in historic club racing, but because of the unique history of the car, had been invited by the race organisers to enter it into the forthcoming Castrol 9 Hours, a famous international sports car event that took place annually at Kyalami, attracting some of the world's leading sports professional drivers.

In 1981, Brian received an invitation to race a Lotus 23b in the prestigious Castrol 9-Hour International at the Kyalami F1 Grand Prix Circuit, subject to bringing significant sponsorship deal which, not surprisingly, he was able to achieve with a national recruitment agency, Churchill Personnel.

I met John and the full story emerged. The car had originally belonged to a famous South African race driver and race car constructor, Doug Serrurier, who had raced in three F1 Grand prix in the 1960s, all at Kyalami. The organisers of the event were running a story about Doug as part of the build up to the 9-Hours, hence the invitation for John Banks to enter Doug's old car. All John had to do was find a sponsor to cover the not insignificant costs of running the car in such a prestigious event, as well as finding someone to share the driving throughout the nine hours. In me, John saw a one-stop solution. It wasn't a challenge that I could turn down.

My research indicated a potential, specific business sector; recruitment agencies. I managed to secure a meeting with the CEO, Colin Christie, of one of the most high-profile of these, Churchill Personnel, a company with branches in all the major cities in South Africa.

My meeting with Colin was fascinating. He was very interested in the proposal that I put forward, which was not based on brand awareness but rather on using the race programme as the platform for a sales competition amongst all of the company's internal and external sales personnel. I felt that we were heading towards a positive outcome, until he stopped the conversation. He then explained to me that the company turnover had been down on last year's figures, and, as a consequence, he had put a stop to the annual salary increase for the 160+ staff. Going motor racing in those circumstances, he told me, might not go down too well! Just as I was waiting for the expected "no" to my proposal, he surprised me by issuing a challenge that would test my sponsorship acquisition skills to their fullest.

On Saturday morning, he explained that Churchill Personnel had arranged a national sales meeting in Johannesburg. Every branch manager would be attending. There would be about 60 such personnel, who would be discussing many key issues. The challenge that he outlined was this; he would give me a 30 minute slot on the meeting agenda. I could present my sponsorship opportunity; and if the branch managers liked what I proposed, he would issue a cheque, literally right then and there. If the majority of the managers didn't like it, I would be heading home empty-handed.

Facing an audience of 60 female branch managers, all of whom had recently informed their staff that there would be no salary increase that year, was quite a daunting task. However, the presentation went well, and they could see how it might incentivise their staff to win a range of prizes, the top one being an expenses-paid VIP weekend for two at a five-star hotel in Sandton, tickets to watch the race at Kyalami, followed by three days at a luxury game camp. The awards were based on sales performance over a six-week period. Its success could be measured by comparing it to the same period last year.

I stayed for lunch with the managers before being asked by Colin Christie to leave the room for ten minutes whilst they discussed the opportunity that I'd presented. It was a long ten minutes before I was invited back, but to my delight, I was then told that Churchill Personnel would be sponsoring my drive in the Castrol 9-Hour on 7 November. True to his word, Colin handed me a cheque covering the total sponsorship amount.

So once again, my one and only skill, the ability to secure sponsorship, had stood up to a tough test.

It was good to know that I would be back in a racing car again. However, I realised that I would have to get some serious testing under my belt, as I had never driven on the famous Kyalami Circuit, other than taking a considerable number of aircrew around the track in my Lotus. I came to the conclusion that the easiest way to achieve this would be to put a few small sponsorship deals together to allow me to run a Formula Ford in some race meetings at the circuit.

Kyalami was a superb track. On my first time out in the Formula Ford race car that I'd purchased, thanks to another sponsorship deal, I seemed to immediately acclimatise to its undulating combination of fast bends and long straight. The races that I took part in went well; and although I didn't win any of them, I was always near the front. It took some time to get used to the different tyres that Formula Fords ran in South Africa, being radial road tyres, as opposed to the CR65 race tyres we used in the UK. The time that I was able to spend on the track was well-worth the effort that I had put into securing sponsorship. I was now looking forward to the race in November, as the dry Highveld winter came to an end, and spring arrived.

My role at Kyalami was keeping me busy if not fulfilled. We were already starting to alienate more than a few local residents, who had put up with years of race meetings at the famous circuit; but now took exception to a new MotoX track, that Bobby Hartslief had authorised. This had been built very close to the circuit perimeter fence, behind which were many houses, each one mostly set up as a small-holding with cattle and sheep. The surrounding areas also included stables and paddocks for a large number of valuable race and equestrian horses. However, when rumours started spreading that a large pop festival was being organised at the track, the level of anger amongst the mid-rand residents reached new heights. It became obvious that we were heading for a major confrontation. I now knew that Bobby Hartslief wasn't a person who understood compromise. It was either his way or not at all!

Surprisingly, however, he agreed to my suggestion that I should address the Mid-Rand Residents Association and try to explain them what we were trying to do with the circuit and to seek some form of compromise.

At the same time, we were building a speedway track high up on the area furthest away from residents. I have long enjoyed speedway racing, having been taken to Wembley Stadium back in the 1950s by my mother and father to watch Wembley Lions race in the British League. Speedway motor bikes use a 500cc single cylinder engine, capable of reaching 0-60 mph in less than three seconds. Importantly, they have no brakes and only one gear. It was popular in South Africa at that time, and I believed that it could be quite a good money spinner at Kyalami. Unlike MotoX, a typical speedway meeting comprises 15 races, each of four laps in duration and one minute in total. Noise levels can be kept to a minimum with silencers, and the track was being constructed well away from the perimeter of the circuit. In addition, there would only be one meeting per week.

At my first appearance in front of the Mid Rand Residents Association, I explained the plans for making sure that Kyalami paid for itself, seven days a week. There were quite a few local business people involved, and they told me that they weren't anti-Kyalami. They saw the prestige of living and working close to a world famous Grand Prix circuit being financially beneficial. The more we spoke, the more I found out about their concerns. It was clear that their main issues were with the incredibly noisy MotoX facility, which ran all day and every day, as well as the rumoured music festival.

When I explained about the speedway track, they had some initial concerns, but once I explained what it involved, they were happy to wait and see, as they put it to me. I found them to be reasonable people and promised to convey their feelings to the Kyalami directors. I kept to my word, but I can't say that it made any real impression when I expressed my views. I told them that in my opinion, if we gave way on the Pop Festival and the MotoX track, we would most likely be able to increase the usage of the race track, build the speedway circuit and open the circuit for cycling, which was beginning to become a popular sport in South Africa.

Sadly, this wasn't to be the last we would hear of the matter from local residents. In April 1981, the Pretoria Supreme Court granted a final order against Kyalami Entertainment Enterprises (Pvt) Ltd after they had breached a temporary interdict made by the Court on 15 April 15. This had been taken out by a couple living near the Kyalami Circuit, who had complained about "the constant assault on their senses" caused by MotoX riders. The judge ordered that Kyalami Enterprises would not be permitted to use the area of Kyalami Circuit outside the permission granted originally, back in 1961. This meant that that no more than five race meetings a year would be allowed, all of which had to finish by 1830 hrs, and one meeting which would last until 23:30 hours. No use of the track on a Sunday was allowed, and no "dust nuisance" was to be created at any time. The ruling also stipulated that only invited club members would be permitted at any of these race meetings.

To say that the relationship between Kyalami and the local residents was going downhill fast would be an understatement.

To make matters worse, the 12-year-old son of one of the local residents, who was vociferous in his condemnation of Kyalami, managed to shoot himself, after gaining access to his father's gun safe. Stories circulated at the time that he had been stressed by the noise coming from the circuit. How true that was I don't know, and the stories eventually ceased.

Kyalami owners get hush-hush order

Own Correspondent

A couple living near Kyalami racetrack have finally been given peace of mind by the Pretoria Supreme Court.

Mr Justice D J Curlewis granted the final order against Kyalami Entertainment Enterprises (Pty) Ltd after they had breached a temporary interdict made by the Pretoria Supreme Court on

April 15.

A return date had been set for May 27 for the respondents to reply to the affidavits of Mrs Thora Mildred Theresa Wright and her husband, Mr Trevor James Wright of Plot Number 1, Barbeque Agriculture Holdings, Verwoerddourg District.

Because the temporary interdict had been breached the case retur-

ned to court for a final order.

The Wrights had complained about the "constant assault on our senses" by scramblers and motorcycles.

Mr Curlewis ordered that Kyalami Entertainment Enterprises, as the registered owners of Plot 39, Bothasfontein, where the Kyalami racing circuit is situated, and certain

motocross and speedway tracks, will not be permitted to use the area outside the permission granted by the Transvaal Board for the Development of Peri-Urban Areas on November 27 1961.

This includes:

● No more than five race meetings ending not later than 6.30 pm.

● No more than one race meeting ending not

later than 11.30 pm.

● No more than four race meetings ending not later than 6 pm.

● Only invited club members to be permitted.

The track may not be used on Sundays and no dust nuisance may be created at any time.

Club events other than race meetings will be restricted to club members.

P. 5. 81

As Manager of the Kyalami Grand Prix circuit, Brian faced a lot of opposition from local residents in terms of the noise issues that the track activities generated. It eventually led to a Court Injunction being imposed, as a headline from that time confirms.

I remember another incident which the headlines around that time. One of the leading motor magazines wanted to do a photoshoot of a new Porsche. The Kyalami directors were of the opinion that this wouldn't break the injunction that was currently in place, prohibiting mid-week use of the track, as long as no cars were actually driven on the track. They were proved wrong, and a complaint was upheld by the court.

I could see both points of view, but felt that the entire scenario was getting out of hand. The identified issues could have been sorted, in my opinion, but what was now happening was that people who didn't even live close to the track were supporting the residents' complaints.

As time moved on, it became increasingly apparent that my views on the way in which we should be continuing to work closely with the Mid Rand Council and the Residents Association were surplus to requirement.

On a positive note, I had the Castrol 9-Hour race to look forward to, in which I would compete with Churchill Personnel sponsorship. Then there was the likelihood of working at my F1 World Championship Grand Prix, which was scheduled for 23 January 1982. Hopefully nothing could go wrong this time around, unlike the debacle of the 1981 event.

November arrived, and it was time for me to get seriously fit for what was going to be a tough endurance race. The Castrol 9-Hours started at 2:30 p.m. and ended at 11:30 p.m. Bearing in mind that it gets dark in Johannesburg at about 7:00 p.m., it would be quite a daunting challenge, never having raced at night before. Through an introduction from some friends, I met the former Fulham and England Under-23 footballer, Tony Macedo, a goalkeeper who had played 346 games in his career for Fulham. Sadly, due to injuries, he had been forced to retire from professional football in England; and in 1968, he moved to South Africa, where he played for Durban City and also did a lot of coaching. When I first met him, he was also training young tennis players and ran a gymnasium in Jeppe Street, Johannesburg. I spent some time working with him to get fit; and by the time the race arrived, I was feeling good.

John Banks, my team mate in the Lotus 23B, had been looking for a team manager to help us during the event. It was easier said than done. Running a motor racing team in an international endurance race is not the easiest task. Decisions have to be made throughout the nine hours, whether it be tyre issues, technical gremlins, race strategy implementation and even crisis management, such as dealing with a bad accident. All of these responsibilities were down to the team manager. Eventually, the answer to this problem came to us.

You may recall that Julian Morris, with whom I played a lot of tennis, was the husband of the Control Data HR manager, Heather. In the course of these social matches, I learned that he had done quite a lot of rallying during the past few years. One evening, out of the blue, I answered the phone and heard Julian's voice. He wanted to know how preparations were going for the big race. In the process of telling him, I happened to mention that we still looking for a team manager. Without any hesitation, Julian told me that he'd be only too pleased to take on that role. In the absence of there being anyone else on the radar, I promised to call John Banks and see what he thought.

We all met up for a chat. Both John and I were highly impressed with the amount of planning that Julian had already done, working on the assumption he would get the job. He was a very bright guy, and at six feet two inches would be quite a commanding figure in the pit garage. Right then and there, we shook hands. We now had a team manager.

The week leading up to the race was a busy one for us all. The race was almost as popular in South Africa as the Grand Prix and attracted a similar size crowd. As usual, spectators started arriving on the Monday prior to Saturday's race, ensuring that they found a good position to set up camp. Then the race cars were transported in from the airport, mainly from Germany, joining the local cars and a few that had been shipped in from elsewhere. The list of drivers was impressive and included Jochen Mass, Derek Bell, Hans Stuck and Marc Surer, to name just a few. The entry list comprised 49 cars. They ranged from the Porsche 936 of Joest Racing to BMW M1s, Lancia Monte Carlos and a host of South African-entered Alfa Romeos, Mazdas and BMWs, together with one very small Lotus 23B.

We found ourselves in the top category of the race, which was quite surprising. After all, our car was getting on for 20 years old, albeit now powered by a 2.5 litre Alfa Romeo race engine. Nevertheless, it was confirmed that we would be running in the sports car category. This is where nearly all of the many F1 drivers were listed. We were quite surprised that we eventually managed to qualify 20th overall on the grid. No mean performance.

As the cars left the paddock and went out on a warm-up lap, the atmosphere was electric. Well over 60,000 spectators had come to watch this famous endurance race; and by the time the grid had assembled again, many in the crowd had filled themselves with boerewors, brandy, coke and biltong. How much notice they would take of the track action, I'm not sure. John was going to take the first stint in the race and was sitting patiently in the Churchill Personnel branded Lotus. I was feeling nervous standing in the pit lane, so what John was feeling I can't imagine. The 9-Hour was a huge event in South Africa; and as I've explained, attracted some of the top drivers in the world. There was this little, open-topped Lotus, built back in the 1960s, taking on the latest 540bhp Porsche 936. It was pure David and Goliath on four wheels.

The deal in 1987, with Mercedes Benz South Africa, resulted in Brian running a 2 car, factory supported team of Honda's in the Stannic Group N Championship. Brian chose local driver Mike O'Sullivan to be his team mate and to prepare the two race cars.

Through competing in this race, I met Mike O'Sullivan again. Mike and his brother Paddy had entered their modified Rover V8 3500 in the race, and they were in adjacent pits garages. I used the word "again" because I had previously met Mike whilst I was looking to buy a new Triumph TR7 sports car. At the time, Mike was employed as sales manager of the Elloff Leyland car showroom in Commissioner Street, Johannesburg. In the process of talking cars, we got onto the subject of motor racing and had chatted for quite a while. Now we were racing against each other. We would eventually end up as very close friends and even raced for the same team, later in our careers.

John Bank's start of the Castrol 9-Hour International went according to plan and he held his grid position as he reached Crowthorne Corner for the first time. Way up front, the Porsche 936 of Jochen Mass took off from the line and would go onto win the race outright.

When I took over the car for my second stint, at about 5:45 p.m., I found that the light was starting to deteriorate as we expected, but what I hadn't accounted for was the smoke that drifted slowly across the track from the thousands of *braais* that were burning within the crowd. There was virtually no wind, and so the smoke wasn't dispersing much. As I've described before, in the 1980s, the Kyalami Grand Prix Circuit was incredibly fast and boasted the longest straight in F1 racing. In particular, there was one section that was being seriously affected by the smoke. Following the third gear right-hander, Crowthorne, at the end of the kilometre long straight, you faced a fast right-hander called Barbecue, which in turn led into a quite scary and very quick left-hander, Jukskei. On your right-hand side, as you ran through this corner, there was a run-off area of no more than four or five metres. Worryingly, this was exactly where the smoke was settling as it drifted down from the spectator. Trying to describe what it felt like to approach this bend in smoke can best be compared to driving on the M1 in thick fog. You had to look out of the side of the car to find your turn-in point to the corner.

The first driver to fall foul of the poor visibility was the former F1 driver Hans Stuck, who I believed missed the all-important apex, due to lack of visibility, and careered almost head-on into the outside banking, ending up with a badly broken nose, which necessitated him being taken to hospital.

My troubles started about two hours from the end of the race, by which time, of course, it was pitch dark. As I approached the fast 90 degree right-hander, Sunset, in fourth gear, turning into the corner, the nearside rear wheel sheared off and bounced into the crowd, fortunately without causing injury to anyone. The Lotus suddenly veered right and headed straight for the unforgiving concrete wall that lined the inside of the corner. They say that accidents often seem to happen in slow motion, but I can assure you that this one didn't. In a flash, my headlights allowed me to see exactly what it was that I was about to hit. As I did so, the car literally split in two, with the front end spinning me for nearly 50 metres down the track and almost into the next corner, Clubhouse. Terrified of being hit by another car, I managed to undo my seat belts and stood up in the wrecked chassis, checked that the track was clear, then raced for the barriers which I clambered over before collapsing into the grass bank, surrounded by two Marshalls. An ambulance arrived, and I was off to the circuit's medical centre, a very lucky young man.

What I found out later was that, Julian Morris, our team manager, had been standing by the pit-wall when he heard the sirens going, and the ambulance hurtling out of its parking area. Next thing he heard was an announcement on the tannoy system that car number 12, driven by Brian Sims, had crashed badly. He told me later that his first thought was about having to phone my folks to tell them the news, so he leaped out of the pits, jumped a barrier and started running down through the spectator area. He bumped into someone who decided that he didn't like being bumped into and threw a punch at Julian, who promptly floored him and carried on running. By the time he arrived at the scene of the accident, I was on my way in the ambulance, so Julian turned around and ran all the way back to the medical centre, only to find me walking out of the Gents, stripped down to my Nomex long-Johns, with a urine sample in my hand, heading back to the doctor who was waiting for me.

I felt sorry for John Banks; the car was repairable but only just. The accident was nobody's fault, but motor racing can be very cruel. I seem to recall that we were amazingly running in the top 15 when the wheel came off. Looking back, I was really lucky to get away with bruised ribs and a very sore neck. It could have been a lot worse.

Colin Christie, from Churchill Personnel rang me next morning to find out if I was OK. He told me that it had been a great day out for many of the staff and that when they opened the *Sunday Times* newspaper to find a full colour photograph of the Churchill Personnel branded car, taken with myself and a model, prior to the accident, they all reckoned that it had been money well-spent.

It was now time to take my racing helmet off, in a manner of speaking, and put my business hat back on, as we prepared the Kyalami track for the forthcoming F1 Grand Prix, which was just a couple of months away. Much as I would like to have been involved in the sponsorship search for the event, my help wasn't required.

Chapter 15
Striking F1 Drivers, Super-Licences and a Big Decision

Some weeks before the Grand Prix, it was mandatory for an official track safety inspection to take place, on behalf of the FIA. In 1982, former World Champion Jody Scheckter had been selected for this task, and I was asked to collect him from the airport, bring him to the track and accompany him on his inspection tour. It was quite interesting to note how our two minds were working in differing directions. His mind was focussed on improving safety at the circuit, whilst mine was calculating the likely costs and feasibility of the requirements that he was freely listing. Crowthorne Corner, in particular, caused him a lot of concern. F1 cars approached this downhill at a terminal speed of around 320kph before braking and changing gear. Should there be a brake failure at that point, he told me, the car would continue into the run-off area which was probably about 50 metres in length from the edge of the track to the rear of the run-off. The big problem about extending this was that it was basically a rock surface, and the work involved in removing rock was immense. Dynamite was the only possible option.

Jody's report was submitted, but predictably, it wasn't feasible to extend the Crowthorne run-off area. A few other recommendations were adopted, however, and work started to get everything ready for January's race.

As 23 January approached, there was a high level of activity. The cars all had to be brought from Jan Smuts Airport, by truck to the track. They were all packed in containers, and I remember watching the customs officer, who was there to break open the seals on the doors of each container, go up to the first container with a pair of bolt croppers, cut the seal and then pull open the doors. The intensity of heat that came blasting out of the containers was extraordinary. By comparison with the garage layouts at modern F1 Grand Prix, what we had in the 1980s was very basic. No wall-liners, hospital-style flooring, hydraulic piping or banks of computers in those days.

Thursday was the first day of practice for the teams and was a far more relaxed process than it is nowadays. I was lucky enough to meet several of the drivers, some at the track and many others at the Kyalami Ranch Hotel. It's difficult to describe how the scene in the F1 Paddock was totally different to what it is at today's events. For a start, there were no motor homes, control centres, hospitality buildings or even PR girls walking two metres behind every driver, with a voice recorder just in case. God forbid, they should actually say something meaningful, or humorous, to the reporters who were wandering around quite freely.

Amongst the drivers I had the pleasure of talking to that day were Manfred Winkelhock (Team ATS), an extremely laid back, fun-loving German driver and

Derek Daly (Theodore), my fellow instructor back in the Thruxton Racing School days. I also met up again with the young Brazilian Chico Serra, against whom I had raced in the 1977 British Formula Ford Championship. Nigel Mansell was there, as was Derek Warwick, two more former Formula Ford racers.

I keep mentioning Formula Ford in the mid to late 1970s. Not only did this superb series propel no fewer than fourteen British drivers into Formula 1 with a four-year time span, but it also created a platform of business colleagues and friends with whom I would stay in touch with for the remainder of my career and beyond. Some carried on racing, some moved into the motorsport industry or the media, whilst others set up their own motorsport teams and businesses. Wherever I go in the world of motorsport, I can almost guarantee that I will meet someone from those incredible Formula Ford days.

Whilst we were getting on with preparations for the Grand Prix, some rumours of dissent amongst the drivers started spreading around the paddock. I knew that rumours were always abounding in F1 and still do, but this time there was even mention of, heavens forbid, a strike! Regrettably, it wasn't just a rumour. Matters came to a head on Thursday, the first day of practice when the drivers announced that were now on strike, led by Niki Lauda.

Brian at the Bahrain F1 Grand Prix 2015, chatting to Niki Lauda about the joys of winter testing in South Africa back in the 1980's. Kyalami was one of Niki's favourite tracks.

It seemed that the problem was centred around the contentious wording on a form that they were being asked to complete and sign in respect of the new Super Licenses that the FIA had introduced. From what I could find out, the drivers felt that the licenses were restrictive, being worded in such a way that a driver was committed to one team throughout a season. They also were unhappy at some of the personal financial information that was being requested. There may have been other issue as well, but I think that was the gist of what was upsetting them.

That Thursday morning, Niki positioned himself at the tunnel entrance to the paddock and as each driver arrived, he persuaded them all to climb into a coach that was parked there. He realised that it was important not only to project an image of solidarity but also to prevent their team bosses, and Bernie, getting to them individually. As you can imagine, Bernie and people like Frank Williams, John McDonald and Ken Tyrrell were far from happy, being only too aware of the potential for Breach of Contract law suits being instigated by their various sponsors, TV channels and other sources if they didn't deliver a Grand Prix, as they had contracted to do.

Of these people, one of the most incensed was John MacDonald, principal of the Rothmans March team, who took matters into his own hands and drove a VW Combi (minibus) across the front of the coach into which the drivers had by now locked themselves. I was later told that he had taken his race engineer, Adrian Reynard, to see if they could either persuade or force their Brazilian driver Raul Boesel out of the coach. It was to no avail.

Eventually, with a stalemate in place, French driver Jacques Laffite was allowed to slip out of the coach by Niki Lauda and head to the VW Combi to see if he could move it. There is a wonderful YouTube video clip of this entire scenario, showing the BBC TV News at the time. A very young presenter, John Simpson, introduced footage of Laffite jumping into the VW and trying to reverse it out of the way of the coach. At first he couldn't find reverse gear, which of course, being an F1 driver, resulted in a quip from the BBC commentator. Eventually, however, with all but one of the drivers aboard, the coach left the circuit and headed for the Sunnyside Park Hotel in Johannesburg, chased along the highway by the media and press photographers. The one driver who was missing was Boesel's team mate, German Jochen Mass.

It was reported that Mass had missed this entire saga by having slept in late, arriving at the circuit unaware of what was happening. He even got as far as completing a lap of practice in his Rothmans March before being advised against it.

In the meantime, we had our own problems. Unable to secure one large title sponsor for the Grand Prix, the Kyalami directors had taken on-board two much smaller companies, SA QuinDrink and a company called PointerWare. Apart from potential legal issues that might arise from a cancelled Grand Prix, there were the practicalities to deal with. Both companies had invited a lot of guests, and the worst factor would be uncertainty. Should they still come to Friday's practice and Saturday's race, or would it be cancelled? The circuit was expecting a minimum of 65,000 spectators, a high percentage of whom had already arrived and were camped at the track. There would be a huge demand for refunds, worryingly, from people well-oiled from wine, brandy and sun. As the pressure increased, tempers started to flare. I was busy on my motorcycle, as I had been the previous year, checking out hospitality facilities, marquees, track-safety installations, car parking and a host of non-glamorous tasks that need doing at a Grand Prix. It became apparent that should the race be scuppered, we could be in for some drama.

On Friday morning, we were hoping that the protagonists might have cooled down somewhat, having had the chance to sleep and relax. We got it wrong. Early in the day, the FIA issued an ultimatum to the strikers. Unless they went out to practice, their licenses would be suspended. Back came the response from the drivers' spokesman, Lauda. He agreed that they would take part in the practice session from mid-day, conditional upon the FIA agreeing to compromise on the wording of the license form after the event.

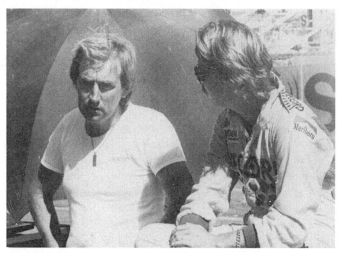

Brian was appointed a consultant by Unilever South Africa at the 1984 South African Grand Prix in respect of its Denim brand sponsorship of the Williams F1 team. He spent a lot of time with both Keke Rosberg, seen here, and Jacques Laffite, including a week with the team at the annual Goodyear tyre tests at Monza.

To everyone's amazement, the silence of the circuit was suddenly shattered by the firing up of a Formula 1 engine, then another. Suddenly it was bedlam, as they all fired up. There was still more drama to come, however. We learned that the police had been contacted a little earlier by Frank Williams, who claimed that his two drivers, Keke Rosberg and Carlos Reutemann, were being held against their will by the ring-leaders of the strike. A couple of police officers arrived in the paddock and then disappeared into the admin office. I never did find out what happened to this Williams-inspired initiative.

Everyone was now getting worried that this was all going to end in tears, with the race being cancelled. Lawyers were seen in the Paddock, easily identifiable by their tailored suits and expensive-looking brief cases! Mervyn Key, the Kyalami Enterprises lawyer, was in his element.

Then even more drama, with the FIA yet again upping the ante. In the process, they reneged on their earlier agreement to negotiate with the drivers after the Grand Prix. The FIA informed all of the drivers that their competition licenses would be suspended from the moment the chequered flag fell at the end of the Grand Prix. As you might imagine, this didn't go down too well with the likes of Lauda and co. It was back to the drawing board again.

I can't even begin to describe the total disruption this entire debacle was causing. The crowd didn't know if there would be a race, neither did the sponsors. The only people who were probably laughing all the way to the bank were the lawyers.

Then suddenly, they were all friends again. Some form of compromise had been reached. It was agreed by both parties that the matter would be discussed at an extraordinary meeting of the FIA and drivers in Paris, at a later date. It seemed that the race would go ahead after all. You could almost hear the sigh of relief that went around the circuit from spectators, sponsors, broadcasters, teams and drivers, as well as the FIA officials. Cancelling a Formula 1 race so close to the event threw up a massive number of issues, but nowhere near as many, one would imagine, as it would in the litigious era in which we now live.

On Saturday morning, the sun appeared in a beautiful blue sky. Was it to be a good omen? It turned out to be a real scorcher, that's for sure.

After all of the tension that had affected everyone for the Thursday and Friday, race day seemed remarkably relaxed, and, for the time being at least, their differences seemed to be left back in their hotel rooms, as drivers and teams focussed on putting a competitive car on the track. There was a race to be won.

A jubilant Alain Prost was the eventual winner of the 1982 South African Grand Prix, a race that nearly everyone at Kyalami doubted would actually take place. Alongside him on the podium was the Williams driver, Carlos Reutemann, with Prost's team mate Rene Arnoux third.

Looking back at the whole strike fiasco, I don't think that there were any real winners or losers. As I saw it, it was a political drama that no one, who'd had been involved, could be particularly proud of. Some argued that the global TV coverage that resulted from the strike action would be good for the sport. I personally don't believe the old adage that any publicity is good publicity. I'm not so sure that it was good for the sport. Having been there in person, I witnessed some very unsavoury scenes which highlighted the true character of a few of the protagonists. The one thing for me that came out of the three days was that it had delivered yet another learning curve about the world of Formula 1, a world in which I wanted to prove myself. The last people who seemed to matter were the 65,000 spectators!

Much as I had enjoyed working that close to Formula 1, I felt that I had a lot more to offer it than being a circuit manager. I wanted to operate at the top level and prove that I was just as capable of putting together significant sponsorship deals in Formula 1, as I had throughout my racing career up this point in time. The easy option for me would be to stay at Kyalami in my current role. I was well-paid, enjoying a great social life, making my folks happy and thriving in the superb climate of the Highveld. Why would I want to move on?

It didn't take me long, however, to come to the conclusion that it wouldn't be the right decision. Apart from anything else, I wanted to see a lot more of what I was discovering to be a wonderful country, albeit one of many contrasts. On the other hand, I was already thinking about the right time to head back to England and getting back into racing that way. In the meantime, it seemed a great shame to leave this amazing country before seeing some more of it.

Ever since I'd arrived in South Africa, people were telling me that I had to get down to the Western Cape. It seemed that whilst Johannesburg was the place to make a lot of money, for a better quality of life, there was only one place to go: Cape Town. From the photos I'd seen of the city in the tourist guides, it seemed hard to argue with them.

Apart from Johannesburg, the only other area of South Africa that I'd managed to visit was in Kwa-Zulu Natal Province. I'd seen the Drakensberg Mountain Range on my first ever drive down to Durban and always planned to go there to explore what looked a beautiful region. It was relatively close to Durban, but was considered a major tourist and holiday destination in its own right, with mountaineers, hikers and families all finding the place suited to their specific needs. I stayed at a wonderful hotel, Champagne Castle, which was built some 3,500 meters above sea level and took advantage of an opportunity to go up in small private plane to get an even better view of the region. It was quite scary, I must admit, being so close to some of the huge peaks as we banked around, but I wouldn't have missed it for the world. As we landed in a field close to the hotel, we scattered a herd of cows that were being driven into areas of new grass. Whilst we sat stationary, before disembarking, it was strange sensation having cows looking in curiously through the windows.

Driving to Cape Town, from Johannesburg, however, was a slightly more daunting proposition for a first-time tourist to South Africa, which I still considered myself. The distance between the two cities by road is about 950 miles and involves driving right through the Karoo. In 1982, the major concern was far more about vehicle breakdowns, and the possibility of falling asleep at the wheel, than it was about security. At that time, there was a government ruling that heavy goods should be transported by rail and not on the National Highways, such as the N1. As a result, traffic levels on these long highways were relatively light, with few trucks making the journey.

On a practical note, having made the decision to leave Kyalami, I realised that I would have to find an income stream. The chance of making a living from motorsport in South Africa was slim, but to move to Cape Town made it even tougher. I knew that there was a race track there, Killarney, but from what I gathered, it catered far more for club level racing, with the occasional national championship level meeting to bring in larger crowds.

It looked very much as though I would need to find a job. My first thought was to give Colin Christie at Churchill Personnel a call, but before I had time to do so, I happened to bump into Eric de Villiers, for whom I had worked at the Control Data Institute in Johannesburg. We met at a social function, and he was keen to hear about developments at Kyalami. Our conversation eventually led to my role at the circuit, and I told him that I was about to move to the Western Cape. Eric smiled when I told him, but didn't say anything more. We agreed to get together for lunch at some stage before I left for Cape Town.

I didn't expect it to be the very next day! Sitting in the sun at the Sunnyside Park Hotel, we chatted for a while about his latest trip to the Okavango Delta, and some of the wildlife that he and his mates had encountered. He suggested that I should seriously head up to the Kruger Park and stay overnight at one of their lodges. It would be a good way of starting to appreciate wildlife and also help me appreciate the sheer scale of the South African bush. He explained that the Kruger National Park equates with the size of Wales, which rather takes one's breath away.

Then the conversation changed direction, taking a surprising course. It started with Eric asking me if I was serious about heading to Cape Town. When I confirmed that I was, he came straight out with a question that really caught me by surprise. Would I like to become the manager of a new branch that Control Data would be opening in Cape Town?

My first thought was one of surprise; after all, I had left his Johannesburg operation to go to Kyalami. Although he had been very good about this at the time and had told me that he would have made the same decision in my shoes, I didn't expect him to take a second chance with me.

I raised that issue, and he told me not to worry about it, adding that although I would probably get bored with the job within a couple of years, that wasn't an issue for him. He explained that it was my skills at getting the place up and running that he wanted to utilise. Once it was generating a lot of fee-paying students, it was easy to find someone to maintain the status quo.

He then embarrassed me a little by telling me what a good job I'd done for CDI in the UK, from reports he had heard and then, in turn, for his Johannesburg institute. He went on to tell me a lot more about the new branch and the challenge that it presented. We discussed the financial package, and then he simply asked me if I would accept his offer.

What an opportunity, I thought. I would be making good money, getting the chance to see Cape Town and its environs, and hopefully being able to do some racing at the Killarney Circuit; and maybe even at the Aldo Scribante Circuit in Port Elizabeth, just a seven hour drive from Cape Town. What could I say but yes!

We agreed a start date, which would mean that I would be setting off for Cape Town in three weeks' time. In the meantime, I hoped that I might be able to move into my folks' apartment in Illovo, in the northern suburbs of Johannesburg. I didn't have to ask twice!

Chapter 16

A Naked Nun, a 950-MileDrive and
My First Sight of Cape Town

I'd been there a couple of days when Ken, my dad, came home from work one evening and told me that we'd been invited to visit their next-door neighbour's new weekend getaway. Reg and Peggy Milner had become friends of my parents as a result of the two men doing some business together. Reg was the managing director of a medium-sized steel foundry and had met Peggy just after she had left her vocation. For the previous 35 years, she had been a nun, living in a convent. It was an unlikely relationship, but they got on famously and shortly became husband and wife. My dad told me that he'd been quite shocked when Reg first told him about Peggy. To say that Reg enjoyed his wine, whisky and socialising would be an understatement. For some reason, their relationship flourished; and after they had married, they moved into the apartment opposite my parents.

Dad also told me that the Milners had bought some land in an area called Bronkhorstspruit, situated about 65 miles northeast of Johannesburg, and mostly comprising a huge natural reserve. They were building their own house there, literally. They got some help with deliveries, such as timber and bricks from some of Reg's employees; but once that had been done, he and Peggy would head out there every weekend and get on with the construction. They had an old caravan that they used as their base, but apparently quite often slept in the open overnight.

That weekend we drove out to Bronkhorstspruit, not to stay overnight but for lunch, which meant a *braii*. We hadn't appreciated that the last three or four miles of the journey was far more suited to being in 4x4 off-road vehicle than a 2.8 litre Chevy saloon. Nevertheless, we eventually made it, helped by the sight of smoke emanating from an old oil drum barrel that had been converted into a makeshift stove.

I think Ken was quite enjoying the challenge of coming out to such an unusual venue, but I got the distinct impression that my mother would much rather have met the Milners in the bar at the Wanderer's Country Club. Not a big lover of nature was Eileen, bless her! The food that Reg had prepared for us was basic but scrumptious. South African steak is really special, on a par with Argentinian meat. Sadly, being the allotted driver for the home journey, I had to refrain from adding some wonderful red wine to my lunch.

What I hadn't expected was the enormity of the land that Reg and Peggy had acquired. It literally was the entire side of a valley that stretched down to a river, meandering through open bush. I'm not very good at estimating the number of acres involved, but I guess the width of their plot was about half a mile, and the distance from the top of the valley down to the river about a quarter of a mile. You could see for miles in every direction, but whichever way you looked, there was not another property in sight. Reg informed us, much to Eileen's obvious concern, that leopards lived in the area, as did a number of snakes. In particular, Rinkhals, also known as ring-necked spitting cobras, were particularly dangerous and would live up to their name by spitting venom up to two metres, into the eyes of a horse, predator or sometimes a human. Not always fatal, their bites have, however, resulted in many limb amputations. Like many snakes, they are not aggressive to humans, but if disturbed, can become quite dangerous.

After a wonderful meal, Peggy said that she was going for a swim and asked if anyone would like to join her. I was the only taker! When I said that I couldn't see a pool and asked where she swam, she explained that she and Reg had dammed one of the tributaries of the river that ran through the valley and created a rock pool. It sounded divine and by then, after sitting around during lunch, I was feeling pretty hot. It was already up to about 30 degrees centigrade. Luckily, I'd brought some swim shorts with me. Peggy and I set off on the trek down the side of the valley about a quarter of an hour of stumbling over rocks and clambering down loose shale pathways, we could hear the sound of running water; and then between the trees, we could also see the light sparkling across its surface. The pool that they had created was stunning, with large slabs of natural rock laid out around its edges, providing perfect individual sun-bathing decks. The pool was about half the size of a tennis court and was incredibly clear. I put my hand in and found it cool but totally refreshing. I lay there on the warm rock slab, just admiring the scene in front of me. This was bliss, total bliss!

I turned around to talk to Peggy and to my astonishment was greeted by the sight of this former nun standing on another of the warm rock slabs, about to dive into the water, without a stitch of clothing on her. She saw me turn around and stood up straight, telling me to get my kit off and to dive in with her. There was a splash, and she was in the water. I walked over to the bag that I'd carried down with me and pulled out my swim-shorts. 'You won't need those,' Peggy shouted from the water, where she was floating on her back, and told me that she'd seen it all before and just to get in the water.

What else could I do? I stripped off and jumped in. It was the most incredible feeling to be in this cool moving water, with the African sun beating down on my head, and a view across the valley, through the trees. I really was falling in love with Africa.

We both climbed out after a few minutes and lay down on the sun-soaked rock slabs to dry off. We lay there chatting for about 30 minutes. She told me about her life as a nun and then some jokes that I couldn't believe I was hearing, in these circumstances. Eventually we both got dressed and headed across back to the pathway. Peggy then grabbed hold of my hand and told me to follow her, being very careful to watch out for any snakes in our path.

I didn't know where we were heading, but who cared? I was so enjoying my day.

We climbed up some quite difficult terrain before finding ourselves facing a sheer rock-face, covered in green climbing plants. There was a narrow footpath to the right which Peggy indicated I should follow. She tucked in close behind me; the rock face on our left as we sidled along. Suddenly, I came upon what can only be described as a huge open window in the rock face, about ten feet in width and six feet in height. I looked through this opening onto an extraordinary scene. To me, it looked like a tropical garden, dropping down about 50 or 60 metres to another river, flowing rapidly through the rocks below.

Peggy told me to climb up onto what could best be described as a rocky window ledge. We both sat there; our feet hanging down beneath me. She pointed out a shiny area of rock to her right-hand side on the same ledge, telling me that this is where the leopards spent a lot of their time, often with some small prey that they would be eating; hence, the shiny surface that resulted over many hundreds of years.

What I had experienced that day was to me like looking into another world. I'd never seen anything like it; and to this day, I have never forgotten it. The more I was seeing of South Africa, the more I was becoming hooked. I knew then that it would not be easy to leave the country within the two years that I had set myself.

Three weeks raced by, and it was time to say goodbye to my folks and head off to Cape Town. I'd finally bought myself a bright red Triumph TR7 sports car, which had a surprisingly large boot and allowed me to take my personal belongings with me. I felt capable of driving straight down to Cape Town, but the advice I received from quite a few friends and colleagues was that I should break the journey overnight. They advised this option for two reasons. Firstly because it was a very tiring drive, particularly in the draining heat of the Karoo; and secondly, if I wasn't in a rush, I would be able to stop when I wanted to and admire some of the amazing scenery.

In advance of the journey, I made a booking at a small hotel in Philipoulis, a small village, or in local terminology, a Dorp, located about halfway to my destination, off the national highway and which advertised a lovely swimming pool and a restaurant.

It was time to go … so I put down the soft top on my new TR7 down, put on a baseball cap, smothered my arms with sun lotion, waved goodbye to my folks and set off on the 950-mile journey.

The N1 motorway heads south towards the Orange Free State's major city of Bloemfontein, a distance of around 260 miles and compares with any motorway in Europe. The scenery is not spectacular, comprising acre after acre of flat fields in which mielies, soy bean, wheat, sunflowers and potatoes grow either side of the freeway. Once you get past Bloemfontein, you start heading across the Karoo, and the change in scenery is quite dramatic.

Today, South Africa has woken up to the potential of tourism, but when I first made that journey, there was little in the way of coffee shops, petrol stations with a Wimpy or equivalent or even hotels on the journey to Cape Town. You had to be very careful in planning your journey, as the last thing you wanted was to run out of fuel in the middle of the desert. The deficit of places to stop was made up for by the incredible scenery that appeared to your left and to your right. Every now and then, I came across a car or van that I had to either overtake or watch heading towards me on the other side of the two-lane road. It was all so different from driving in Britain.

There were times when I could have believed that I was driving through the set of an American-Western movie, in Arizona or Utah. The most extraordinary rock formations appeared with great regularity. By now, I was getting tired and, rather worryingly, very burnt. My arms were on fire, despite the sun lotion I'd used. It was time to stop, and when I eventually saw a sign post indicating the turn-off to Philipoulis, I was delighted. Images of a glorious blue swimming pool ran through my mind as I drove along a narrow, straight road. The hotel was easy to find, and I parked, put the roof back up and walked into the reception, where I was met by a middle-aged Afrikaans lady. I gave her my name, and she handed me a booking form, which I duly completed. I paid my money in cash and asked her where the pool was. In broken English, she explained that my chalet was close to the pool.

I quickly unpacked, put on my swim shorts, grabbed a towel and headed for the swim that I'd been dreaming of for the last hour or so. I found the pool, which was a surprisingly large one, lined with beautiful blue tiles. It was surrounded by colourful plants. Had there been any water in it, I would have dived in without delay. But there wasn't!

Back at reception, I asked the lady why she hadn't told me that the pool was empty. Her reply was a classic, 'Because you didn't ask,' she stuttered. Yes, I had a lot to learn about the antagonism between the English and Afrikaners.

After a cold shower, supper, sleep and a good breakfast, it was time to hit the road again. The scenery just got better and better as I reached the Hex River Valley, and the mountains that you have to cross before you can see the Western Cape coastline. On more than one occasion, I found myself thinking what it must have been like in 1836 and onwards for the Afrikaans settlers of the Western Cape, as they began what was known as the Great Trek through these mountains all the way from the Cape to the Highveld some 950-miles to the north. They certainly built them tough in those days!

The views that I experienced whilst traversing the mountains were quite spectacular. On one occasion, I pulled up at a parking area; and in the far distance, I could just see the outline of Table Mountain. Cape Town! I was nearly there.

The sun was by now starting to fall in the sky as I eventually reached the hotel where I would be staying for a week or two. I looked at my watch and remembered that in the Cape, it doesn't get dark until much later than up in Johannesburg. What a pleasure that would be, I never did get used to it being dark at 7:00 p.m., even in the summer.

I parked my car, walked into the foyer of the Greenmarket Square Hotel in the middle of Cape Town and was delighted to be greeted with an offer of a cold beer. I then went up to my room and had a wonderful cold shower before heading to the front terrace of the hotel. I suddenly found myself looking at the magnificent face of Table Mountain. The next morning, a healthy breakfast was served on the outside terrace, and it was at that moment I came to the conclusion that I was going to enjoy exploring this famous old city.

I had the whole day to myself, as I was only meeting Eric de Villiers the following morning. I decided to walk down the main street to find the location where I would be working for the next two years. The Nedbank Building was a modern office block, situated right on the foreshore, some 400 meters from the entrance to Cape Town Docks. As if emanating from the face of Table Mountain, the shop-lined Adderley Street headed due south towards the sea, before opening into a wide dual carriageway called Heerengracht. Standing outside the building where the new CDI would be located, looking north, I once again looked straight up at the mountain. What a place this would be to work.

One of my first tasks would be to find somewhere to live. The company would pay for me to stay at the hotel for a couple of weeks, but I needed to look around quickly at potential accommodation. It's not the easiest of tasks to do when you are not only in a strange country but also in a city that you have never seen in your life before.

The next day, I met Eric at the CDI offices and was delighted to see that this new, fully-equipped institute was something very special. It may sound old hat today, but this was the first time I had come across touch-sensitive computer screens. The large, open-planned space, which formed the student area, was set up to accommodate about 40 individuals, each with their own computer terminal. All around its perimeter, were the offices, each with a magnificent view of either the sea or Table Mountain.

I was given the corner office, which meant I had panoramic views of both. I couldn't have asked for anything better, it was a great place to come to work each day; that was for sure. We were due to open on the following Monday and had a lot of work to complete, prior to that.

I set about visiting some estate agents, searching for an apartment to rent. The one that I eventually selected was right next door to the world-famous Mount Nelson Hotel and diagonally opposite the famous Nelson's Eye Steak House. It had balconies that offered a magnificent view of Table Mountain, which at night was floodlit.

To get to my office, I had two choices. I could drive and park very close to the Nedbank Building, or I could walk. The latter entailed heading through the Company's Gardens, named after the Dutch West India Company that operated from Cape Town in the 1600s. The Gardens were created in 1650 to provide fresh produce to replenish ships rounding the Cape. Everywhere one went in Cape Town, it seemed that you were touching history.

The opening of the new institute went well and generated a great deal of publicity. On the same day, we staged our first "sales evening" in the Cape Town Hotel, next door to our office building. We were delighted to host a full-house, and the sign-up rate was exceptionally high. It seemed that we were in business.

Things went really well from that point on, and Eric one day told me that he'd made the right choice in getting me down to Cape Town. I was pleased he felt that way.

I'm sure you're wondering when I'm going to talk about motorsport again. Well, you won't be surprised to hear that during my first weekend off, I headed out to the Killarney Motor Racing Circuit. It was about a 15-minute drive from my apartment and was far more like a traditional British circuit, such as Mallory Park or Snetterton. There wasn't a race meeting on that weekend, but there were quite a lot of testing going on. I introduced myself to a few drivers and found a group of Formula Fords being worked on. I chatted to some of the drivers, and they seemed only too pleased to welcome me, especially when they found out my racing background in the UK.

Chapter 17
Kruger Park, F1 in Cape
Town and an F1 Neighbour

The Formula Ford that I'd bought when I was in Johannesburg, practising for the 9-Hour, was still there. I'd left it with Nino Venturi, a colourful Italian who traded in race cars and was the president of the South African Formula Ford Association. I called him, and he told me it still hadn't been sold. I asked him to take it off the market, I would come and collect it in due course.

The thought of doing some Formula Ford races quite appealed and would give me some valuable track experience at Killarney, whilst I investigated other opportunities. It also struck me that if I was racing, it would provide with a perfect chance to see a lot more of South Africa. In particular, by racing at the Port Elizabeth track, I could drive there right along the stunning Garden Route, which meant following the road that ran virtually alongside the Indian Ocean coastline. Life was looking good in many ways.

A month or so into my new role at CDI, I was sitting in my office, waiting to have a meeting with someone who'd made an appointment to talk about the training opportunities that existed. Normally, I would have suggested that she attended one of our sales evenings, but as the next one wouldn't be for another three weeks, I was happy to arrange an office meeting.

Gisela Gross, my German PA, knocked and opened my door, introducing Elizabeth Messaris, or Liz, as she told me she preferred to be called. She sat down and explained that she hadn't worked for a few years, having raised two children. She wanted to find a way of getting back into the commercial world and thought that computer programming might be just what she was looking for. I have to admit that although I was listening to what she was saying, I wasn't taking much on-board! Liz was a stunning-looking woman and made a huge impression on me. It wasn't just her looks, however, that did it. There was something else; maybe it was her personality, or maybe her voice, with its soft South African accent. All I knew that had she not been wearing a wedding ring, I would have made every effort to arrange a date with her. As it was, what I thought would be a 15-minute meeting, extended to over an hour. Then she was gone.

I have to admit that I was hoping the information that I'd given her would be enough for her to get back in contact and sign up for a course with CDI. She didn't despite my phoning her a couple of weeks later to follow-up on our meeting. I got the impression that her husband wasn't keen on her returning to work. I suggested a meeting to talk it over, but that wasn't going to happen.

I was thoroughly enjoying living in such a wonderful city. There was just so much to see. It seemed a world apart from my days back in England, and I revelled in heading out in my car to the wine valleys, the magnificent West Coast National Park and places such as Knysna, where I could sit on the beach, sampling the oysters for which the town is famous. I was going to make the most of my two years based here.

Then I met up with a South African racing driver, against whom I'd competed in the UK in Formula Ford. Roy Klomfass had subsequently returned to South Africa, getting as far up the single-seater ladder as the highly competitive South African Formula Atlantic Championship. He was a very talented driver, and in my opinion, never fulfilled his true potential. When he headed for England in 1973, he was accompanied by a South African friend, who had been helping him run his cars for quite a while. This was none other than Rory Byrne, who, having become the designer for Formula Ford-manufacturer Royale, went on to become chief designer for Benetton F1, then Ferrari F1, designing the cars that Michael Schumacher drove to his seven world titles.

Having arrived in the UK, in 1974, Roy Klomfass was offered a drive alongside Rupert Keegan in the Hawke DL11 works team. Rupert's father, Mike Keegan, owned British Air Ferries, a car transportation airline that operated out of Southend Airport. His son was already racing in Formula Ford but was building a reputation as being fast but excitable. Tired of writing out cheques to various Formula Ford companies for replacement parts due to accident damage, Mike Keegan eventually bought the Hawke Racing Cars business from David Lazenby, keeping him on as its MD. It was no surprise when Rupert became a works driver for Hawke in 1974.

Rupert was a talented racing driver and would eventually make it to Formula 1, but he will always be remembered for one particular photograph that was shown by several national newspapers, in the main body of the paper, not just the sports page. Rupert was racing at Brands Hatch, along with Roy Klomfass. Rupert was involved in a serious coming together with another car, resulting in his car hurtling high into the air, rolling over, then heading to earth from a height of around four metres, nose down, straight into the tarmac of the race circuit. It looked terrifying and could have been disastrous for Rupert. He escaped injury, fortunately.

The reason that this accident attracted so much national media coverage was very simple. In large clear letters along the side of the race car bodywork were the words "Fly British Air Ferries". It was hardly the best of advertisements for his father's airline business.

I happened to hear that Roy was back in South Africa, from one of the drivers I'd met at Killarney. Roy's mother ran a caravan park on the cliff tops of Knysna, about five hours' drive from Cape Town. When I phoned her and explained how I knew her son, she gave me his number. No mobile phones in those days, of course. He was surprised to hear that I was in South Africa; and we agreed that as soon as the opportunity arose, we'd get together.

Speaking to Roy reminded me that I needed to sort out my own Formula Ford race car that was still in Johannesburg. Going to fetch it was a major task, and I came up with the idea of phoning Nino Venturi and arranged with him for the car to be transported down when the teams next came to Cape Town for a round of the national championship.

Then I met Anelma. When the weather was good, which in a Cape Town summer meant most of the time, I would walk into the city, through the Gardens that I've described. On this particular morning, I decided to take the car for some reason. As

I drove from my garage to the road, a striking-looking girl was heading towards me along the pavement. I stopped to let her proceed and got a friendly smile in return. The next morning, I decided to walk, hoping that I might bump into her again. No such luck. However, the day after that we did bump into each other; maybe it had something to do with my getting up a little earlier and waiting until I could see her walking down the road towards me! She was heading into town, and we walked through the Gardens whilst she told me about herself.

Anelma worked for an Afrikaans publishing company, based in the city, and was the editor of the children's book division. Although most of her work involved the use of Afrikaans, she also spoke very good English. We started dating and before long planned a holiday together. I'd told her how much I wanted to go to the Kruger Park, and she did some homework on possible accommodation. We eventually spent a wonderful week in the Park, staying at one of the several small lodges that are state-owned and remarkably inexpensive. Olifants Camp overlooked the river that wound its way through the park, providing a superb view of the hippos that resided there, as well as a herd of elephants that would come to the river to drink later on the afternoon.

I had no idea what the Park would be like. The nearest that I had ever been to wild animals was when my folks took me to Whipsnade Zoo in Bedfordshire. The sensation that struck me at Kruger was just how huge it was, at two million hectares. As I mentioned earlier, it was about the size of Wales. We spent about three nights there and were lucky enough to see some great sightings. My only reservation was that you weren't allowed to drive off the dirt roads that traversed the park, meaning that you couldn't always get up close to creatures that you caught sight of. The camouflage of so many animals was extraordinary and made "spottings" quite tricky. The other thing I realised was that you need a great deal of patience if you want to see wild life.

When we eventually left the Kruger Park, we both decided that we would try to get to one of the privately owned safari camps at some stage, recognising that this would allow us to go out with a Ranger in a 4x4 and go off-road, where you could get really close to the animals. The only problem was going to be the high cost of staying at one of these camps.

On the way home, we stopped off for a night at my parents, where we got some bad news. Dad had lost his job at Jeffery Manufacturing, along with a number of other managers. It was quite a blow to his confidence; and he worried that at his age, it wouldn't be easy to find another job, particularly as the gold mining industry in general was going through some tough times. All I could do was to tell him that I'd give some thought to the problem and see what I could do to help.

On the 12-hour drive back to Cape Town, we talked about ways in which I could perhaps find Ken another job, but with little confidence that this was likely. I didn't have a huge contact base in the country and certainly not in Ken's field of work: my contacts were all in the motor-racing sector.

Then an idea came to me. Maybe they should leave Johannesburg and move down to Cape Town. For a start, it was a much nicer place to live, and secondly, I would be there, at least for the next couple of years, which meant that I could keep an eye on them, and maybe even find Ken something to do.

Suffice to say that after a couple of months, my father called me and told me that they liked the idea of moving to the Cape. Within six months, they had sold their house in Johannesburg and moved into a small bungalow in a very pleasant and ideally located area in the southern suburbs. There was, of course, one other inhabitant who came down with them; their very much loved German Shepherd, called Cheeky.

Another idea had come to mind which would hopefully provide a role for Ken and prevent him having to take a job which he didn't really enjoy, just to help financially. It was at this time that we fully understood the big difference about living in South Africa as opposed to the UK. As I've mentioned before, in South Africa, there is no safety net. By that, I mean that there was no NHS to rely upon, there was no "dole" money to claim if you lost your job, and trips to the doctor and dentist were normally costly expeditions. What most people did was to take out medical insurance, but that was becoming increasingly expensive. It was normal for employers to either fully provide such insurance or contribute a high percentage of the monthly fee. This was worrying for my parents with Ken's loss of employment. He could, of course, take over the premiums himself, but that was not feasible for very long.

The idea that I came up with was to open a shop in the City, which Ken and Eileen could run for me. There was an obvious choice as to what we could focus on selling. In South Africa, I had seen that there was a big following of motorsport, particularly F1. I decided to open a shop, selling everything from F1 team race jackets, F1 model cars, a range of motorsport videos, books, caps, umbrellas and a host of related merchandise. We found a suitable retail shop in a busy part of town and negotiated a decent rental. I sorted the stock through a range of different sources, including Charlie Whiting, who you may remember was at that time the team manager for Bernie Ecclestone's Brabham F1 Team.

Brian Sims' Formula 1 opened in blaze of publicity and provided Ken and Eileen with some much needed confidence. Anelma and I would pop in to see them during the week whenever we could; and for a short time, everything seemed to be going well. I had moved from my original apartment and was living in a magnificent house, high up on the side of the mountain overlooking Clifton Beach. One day, Anelma and I were talking about motor racing, which was of course a price she had to pay for going out with me! I mentioned that I'd read in a magazine that the German racing driver, Jochen Mass, was living in Cape Town with his South African wife. Anelma asked me what her name was. Jochen had been James Hunt's team mate at McLaren before moving into world championship sports car racing, with the prestigious Rothman's Porsche team. I looked for the magazine and found the article. When I told her that he had married a South African model, Este Mallete, she immediately told me that they had both attended the same university, Stellenbosch. She went on to say that although they hadn't been close, she knew her to talk to. I was suitably impressed!

It didn't take long for me to find out where Jochen and Este lived. By a strange coincidence, they owned a wonderful apartment, overlooking the Atlantic coast, just across the road from my house. I put a note in their post box and explained who I was and my Kyalami background, also mentioning Anelma and the university. I suggested it would be good to meet up, but I wasn't at all sure that it would happen. Jochen was a big name in motorsport, I wasn't!

Chapter 18
My New Role, Meeting the Shadows and Worrying News

An invitation arrived from Jochen Mass within a few days; and the following week we had supper with him and Este. I remember him telling me that he had just got back from testing the Rothman's Porsche at Hockenheim. In the process, he told us he'd watched the team trying out a new young German driver. Jochen went on to describe the youngster's performance as quite sensational, adding the comment that if this kid survived long enough, he would undoubtedly become a world champion. Stefan Belloff went on to drive in F1 for Tyrell, but he died in 1985 whilst driving a Group C car at the Spa Circuit in Belgium. He was trying to overtake Jacky Ickx, as they both headed into Eau Rouge, one of the fastest and most dangerous bends in the world.

I was to see a lot more of Jochen Mass over the next few years.

Anelma and I were still together and enjoying the experience. She was a very talented person; and in a country that wasn't exactly renowned for promoting the interests of woman in business, she had done incredibly well. Her father had been the headmaster of Panorama School, and I had some very pleasant lunches with her parents. Like me, Anelma was an only child. It seemed quite natural when I moved in to her new home, close to the Greenpoint Stadium, one of the 2010 World Cup venues.

I'd now been at Control Data Institute for my agreed two years. It had gone well, very well; and by exceeding my sales targets in the first and second years, I qualified to attend the company's international conference. This changed venue annually, but the one that I would be attending was being held in the Bahamas. I took the opportunity to travel down via New York, where I met some of my counterparts in the Control Data Global HQ. It was a great experience mixing in the Bahamas with so many of the company's top sales professionals, but strangely, it started me thinking about my career back in motorsport. CDI had been good to me, but I came to the conclusion that I needed a new challenge, one that might open doors into motorsport. It was time to think about going back to the UK.

Conveniently, my ticket allowed me a stopover in England, so it made sense to set up a few meetings with some motorsport contacts who might be able to help me. I stayed with my uncle and aunt in Kent, close to Brands Hatch, and one morning whilst flicking through a magazine, I spotted an advertisement for a UK Tour by the Shadows, Cliff Richard's former backing group, who had become a major name in their own right with a string of instrumental hits. As I mentioned earlier, I've always been a huge fan of the Shadows. Even my ringtone is Apache. Sad, you're probably thinking.

I knew that I had to get a ticket whilst I was there, but it turned out to be a lot more difficult than I'd imagined. All enquiries informed me that the Shadows tour was a complete sell-out. There had to be a way, I decided, and so I did a little research, not as easy as it sounds without the benefits of Google! I eventually found the phone number of their recording company and prepared to speak to a receptionist in the same way that usually happened when I first contacted a potential sponsor.

To my surprise, the man who answered the phone told me that he was the Shadows' manager, Brian Goode. I explained that I lived in South Africa and was in the UK for a few days, but couldn't get hold of a ticket for the tour. He put me on hold for minute or two then asked me if I could be in Bournemouth the following day. As I was staying in Kent, it was quite feasible. He suggested that I meet him at the Winter Gardens Theatre at 2:30 p.m., adding that he would have two tickets to the evenings Shadows evening concert for me. I couldn't believe my luck.

At 2:30 pm, I went up to the ticket office at the theatre and asked for Brian Goode. I was told that he had been delayed but had left a message, asking me to go inside and wait for him. She went on to say that the Shadows were sound testing on stage, and that I could sit in the stalls and wait for Brian Goode to arrive. An hour later, having had the pleasure of watching Hank Marvin, Bruce Welch and Brian Bennett run through many of their chart hits, Brian Goode arrived and handed me two front row tickets for the evening's show, before asking me if I'd like to meet the guys when they had finished their rehearsal in about 20 minutes' time. What a question! It was a memorable day, meeting my favourite group, watching them in concert and even being given a couple of complementary albums.

The next morning I was feeling really good as I headed up to Silverstone motor racing circuit where I had a couple of meetings arranged, neither of which turned out to be worthwhile, so it was back to Kent and another meeting at Brands Hatch before flying back to South Africa. If I wanted to get back into motorsport, it looked as though it would have to be in South Africa, at least for the next year or so.

Then in 1984, I got some news that would make leaving the country very difficult. My mother was diagnosed with lung cancer. As was the case with so many people of that age, she had been a heavy smoker in her early days. The diagnosis wasn't good, but her private doctor, Mike Mamacos, introduced her to a highly regarded surgeon, Mr Morgan. He was brutally honest with us, saying that in his opinion, the chances of surgery being the answer were very slim, but adding that he was prepared to take that chance if my mother was in full agreement. My mother respected his honesty, telling Ken and me that she had a good feeling about him. She gave him the thumbs up, and he set about the operation, which involved surgically removing one of her lungs. The procedure took a long time, and when we met Mr Morgan afterwards, he looked incredibly drained. He also looked very concerned, telling us that we should be prepared for my mother to perhaps only survive for about three months. We were naturally devastated, and I realised that I wouldn't be going anywhere until I found out what the next few months would bring.

Suddenly life didn't seem quite so good. I sat down with Eric de Villiers when he next visited Cape Town and told him what was happening. I explained that much as I had enjoyed my two year stint, I was going to move on, albeit not back to the UK at that particular time. As always, he was so relaxed and caring about my situation, offering an extension to my two year contract if it helped me. I will always appreciate Eric's friendship and was absolutely shocked when I later heard that he and his wife had been involved in a bad car accident which sadly took his wife's life. Eric survived unhurt, but it just goes to show how cruel life can be.

To everyone's surprise, my mother made good progress and demonstrated what a great job her surgeon had obviously done.

Chapter 19
Honda, a Championship and
Testing with an F1 Driver

During this period, I had been looking at a way of staying in the Cape. Eventually I saw a job advertised in the Cape Times which looked interesting, McCarthy Motor Group was one of South Africa's largest retail motor dealerships. Their flagship franchise was Mercedes Benz. Mercedes was huge in South Africa, with a large manufacturing plant situated in East London, between Port Elizabeth and Durban, right on the Indian Ocean coastline.

The advertisement explained that Mercedes had negotiated with Honda to import Honda passenger cars into South Africa, in what they called "knocked down car" format, or CKD as it's referred to within the motor industry. The cars would be assembled at the Mercedes factory and given Mercedes quality interiors and paintwork. The cars would be sold through Mercedes dealerships.

The job advertised by McCarthy Motors was for a Honda sales manager to work across their four showrooms within the region and to be based at their Strand Street HQ in the city centre. After convincing myself that this was a step nearer to motorsport, I sent in an application. I was invited to an interview with the group's HR manager. I was shown into his office and was pleased to find that he was from England. Then came the big surprise. It transpired that before coming to South Africa to live, Peter Groves he had been the HR manager for the Kent Messenger Newspaper Group, based in Ashford, Kent. The group sponsored a motor racing championship at Brands Hatch, which had been won more than once by Nick Whiting, brother of Charlie Whiting. That's not where the surprises ended. I used to visit the Kent Messenger Group when I was a Xerox salesman. In the process, I was dealing with the company's office manager, a lovely woman who was very helpful in my attempting to install Xerox machines in their HQ. I sometimes took her out to lunch. When I mentioned this to Peter, he laughed and said it must have been Audrey Shepherd, whom he had fancied for ages. What a small world, it was Audrey Shepherd!

We sat and talked about the role in question for some time; then, three days later, I was offered the position as Honda Sales Manager for the Western Cape.

It worked far better than I could ever have hoped for. I made a few changes in personnel; and within a very short space of time, the showrooms were buzzing. It had been a very smart move by Mercedes Benz South Africa to enter in this Honda deal, the only one of its kind anywhere in the world I believe. Within a fairly short period of time, the Honda Ballade, which was available with a choice in 1300 or 1500 cc motors and sold in Mercedes showrooms, took off in a big way. It eventually captured over 5% of the passenger car market in South Africa, no mean feat with just one model. Then the Honda Prelude was imported directly from Japan and again sold well, albeit as a prestige sports coupe. At the time, the Williams F1 team was achieving a lot of success with their Honda power units, and we were able to achieve a great deal off the back of this, sales-wise.

After a year or so, I sat down with Graham Damp, the group's CEO, and suggested that one specific problem was preventing even bigger sales of the Ballade. Statistics showed that it had appealed very much to a particular demographic, women in the 40 years of age bracket and above. There was resistance from young males when a company tried to introduce the car as a fleet model. As the company car was still a significant perk in South Africa, it meant that the likes of VW, Toyota and Nissan were very much the company cars of choice.

I made a suggestion as to how we might change this situation to our advantage. I proposed that we set up a McCarthy Dealer Team and enter a Honda Ballade in the first season of a new championship series called Stannic Group N. This could best be described as production saloon car racing, using standard road cars within different engine size categories. Street legal road tyres were compulsory, and there few changes that could be made to the suspension, other than fitment of competition shock absorbers, to make the car a lot stiffer. The cars could be fitted with roll cages and six-point seat harnesses. It was to become one of the most successful of South Africa's many racing series.

In 1985, Brian won the Class Championship in the inaugural Stannic Group N production touring car series in South Africa. He also won his Class in the Killarney 6-Hour Endurance race.

Graham really liked the idea and also suggested that it would be a real motivator for the company if it could be fully prepared in-house. To my surprise, he then made a call to the marketing director of Mercedes Benz, Peter Cleary, and asked him if

MBSA would supply McCarthy's with a new car for the purpose of entering it into the Stannic Group N Championship.

Spectators took to this new racing series like ducks to water. For a start, they could identify their road cars with many of the models being raced, giving them an instant connection with the series. On top of this was the racing itself. It was spectacular to watch, with cars that didn't look as though they were going around on rails, dicing three abreast sometime into corners, with tyres shrieking, and more than a few close contacts in the corners.

The team at McCarthy's Service Centre prepared a great car for me, and with ten Class wins and a couple of overall wins in the season, I was fortunate to clinch the Class Championship in what was undoubtedly the most competitive sector, 1400 to 1600 cc, involving Toyota versus Honda versus VW versus Nissan versus Ford versus Mazda. Having clinched the championship, we then entered the car into what was one of South Africa's most prestigious race meetings, The Killarney 6-Hour Endurance Race, held in December each year, when Cape Town was often at its hottest. The race was for production cars and comprised two drivers per team, each having to race one or two stints, dependent upon the fuel capacities of individual cars. It was always a tough race on what was very much a driver's circuit. The last part of the race was run in total darkness. In 1985, I chose as my team mate a young South African driver, Deon Joubert, who would go on to enjoy a successful professional career.

We were facing stiff competition from Toyota and VW in particular, both with full works entries. To our delight, we came out as winners of our Class, just pipping the highly competitive three-car Toyota works team. In addition, we finished second overall in the important "Index of Performance" classification. This is designed to allow the officials to compare the overall race performance of every driver in the race, by applying a set of technical formulae to balance out the cars, engine size, weight and a couple of other specifications. We lost out on winning the index by the closest possible of margins.

The media loved the story of how a small Dealer team, with just one car, beat the might of the full factory teams. Suddenly, the Honda was a car that the sales reps wanted, and we had fulfilled our objective of using motor racing to achieve entry into the lucrative fleet markets. Interestingly, the publicity that was generated opened up a fascinating opportunity to team up with a former Grand Prix driver on a project for South Africa's extremely popular *CAR Magazine.*

I received a phone call from the editor, asking me if I would be interested in taking part in a new feature that they were launching within CAR and subsequently running on an annual basis. It was a simple concept, calling for two professional race drivers to test what they described as South Africa's top 20 performance cars. The idea was that, over a period of two days, at the Killarney Motor Racing Circuit in Cape Town, we would each drive the full range of cars that they had decided upon and individually give our views on them as road cars. It seemed a no-brainer to me, and I was only too pleased to accept, asking who the other driver would be. The answer was Basil van Rooyen, who had been one of South Africa's most successful race drivers. During his career, he competed in two full seasons of Formula 1, in South Africa's own championship, as well as in two F1 World Championship Grands Prix, at Kyalami. He was good.

An indication of how highly van Rooyen was rated, came in 1969 when Jackie Stewart and Ken Tyrrell offered him a Matra works drive, replacing F1 driver Johnny Servoz Gavin, who had announced his retirement from the sport. Sadly, a couple of weeks before leaving for Europe, the South African was involved in a horrendous accident at Kyalami whilst testing for Dunlop in an F1 McLaren. It resulted in the driver being catapulted some 90 metres into the infield at Crowthorne, incredibly coming out of his 6-point safety harness. He was badly injured and took several months to recover from his injuries. His place at Tyrrell F1 was subsequently taken by Francois Cevert.

In 1970, Basil van Rooyen, with South African backing, was in discussion with Robin Herd of March to buy an F1 car. He had been competing in a Lola F5000 car in the South African F1 Championship to fully recover from his enforced lay-off. His performance in that car had been his exceptional, and he felt ready to try F1 again. He arranged to meet Herd at the Dutch Grand Prix in June.

Prior to that meeting, Basil was in Tokyo on an interim business trip when he heard that Bruce McLaren had been killed at Goodwood during a practice session. Bruce had been his idol, and the news upset him considerably as he flew from Tokyo to Holland to meet Robin Herd. As a guest of March F1, Basil was able to watch the Dutch Grand Prix from the pits. Tragically he witnessed the shocking crash and subsequent fire that claimed the life of Piers Courage. The trauma of these two deaths, in the short space of just 19 days, affected him a great deal, and he took the brave decision to pull out of his planned return to F1, announcing that he would return to South Africa and continue saloon and sports car racing. He was only 31, and with the statistics showing that a couple of F1 drivers were likely to die each season, it was probably a very wise decision.

I was really looking forward to meeting the man himself. I found him to be really likeable; very down to earth, with a good sense of humour. The *CAR Magazine* event went as planned, and we tested some exciting cars, including a Porsche 930 Turbo, BMW 535, Basil Green prepared Ford Escort Turbo and a Porsche 944 Turbo. Fortunately, the weather was good on the first of the two days, and we were able to get some good laps in. As we each got out of a car, so the *Car Magazine* guys would thrust a cassette recorder in front of us, to get our instant thoughts. It provided some interesting thoughts and critiques on the various models.

On the second morning, we were both due to drive the Porsche 930 Turbo. Sod's Law! It was chucking it down at Killarney when we arrived. I'm sure that I was a lot more nervous than Basil when it came to putting this extremely powerful motor car through its paces on the Killarney Circuit. He had far more experience than me, and he decided to take the first session. I was out on track at the same time in the BMW 535, in which I was having a ball. It handled like a dream and gave me a lot of confidence, even in the rain. A few months later, I would be offered a drive in the works BMW 535 in the Castrol 3-Hour race at Killarney, as team-mate to regular works driver Tony Viana, finishing a reasonable third overall.

Then it was time for me to climb into the white Porsche. What I can say, without any doubt, is that the car was quick. I recalled Basil's words of warning to me as he relinquished the car. He quietly mentioned that the car had an inherent understeer, meaning that at the end of the long fast straight leading into a tight 180 degree hairpin, the car didn't want to turn in; not a characteristic that you needed in the torrential rain.

Fortunately, the session went well, and I didn't embarrass myself. It had been a great privilege and a pleasure to share the track with such a very special racing driver. Basil now lives in Australia and runs a successful packaging business there.

Life in the Western Cape was proving to be very acceptable. I liked the relaxed lifestyle, which was noticeably slower than the hustle and bustle of Johannesburg. Then a chance meeting in Cape Town would change my life quite dramatically.

Chapter 20

An Amazing Coincidence, an Invitation from Mercedes and a Wedding

Things were going very well in my role at McCarthy Motors, where I was responsible for Honda sales across their four Cape Town branches. My office was in the main Mercedes/Honda showroom in Strand Street, right in the heart of Cape Town. One lunchtime, I nipped out for a quick lunch in a nearby coffee shop, one of many in the city. As I was sitting reading the Cape Times, three girls, who I would imagine must have been in their early 30s, came in and sat at my table, unavoidable because the place was nearly full. In such a situation, it's impossible not to overhear their conversation. They chatted about all manner of things for a few minutes, before one of them began telling the others how difficult they were finding it to get a job is sales. She told them something I knew to be true, that whenever she applied for a sales job, she was asked if she had previous experience. When she replied that she hadn't, she was turned down. She then asked her friends the obvious question as to how could she get sales experience, when no one would give her a sales job?

After a few minutes of this, I felt I had to tell them that I couldn't help overhearing their conversation about the difficulty in getting a sales job. I explained my own role in selling, before mentioning that my dad, who was still running the F1 shop on his own whilst my mother was still in hospital, had taken on a small agency for a portable printing machine. I knew that he was looking for a salesperson to help get this into small businesses in the city. I suggested that maybe it offered a chance for the person, such as this girl, who was looking to get into sales. She seemed very appreciative when I gave her my number and suggested that if she wanted to take it further, she could call me. I left them to finish their lunch.

A week or so went by, and I had completely forgotten about the conversation. Then I got a call at my office from the girl in question. She told me that she had at last found a full-time job, but she thanked me for my offer. I thought the call was at an end, but then she added that she had a friend who might be interested in talking to my dad about the sales role. I asked her to get the person to phone me.

She read out some contact details of the person she had in mind, telling me that if the person hadn't phoned within a week or so, to give her call; and she would chase it up for me. I looked back at my notebook, in which I had jotted down the information. The name seemed familiar. Then it came to me. Elizabeth Messaris was the woman who had made such an impression when she came to enquire about computer programming courses whilst I was at the Control Data Institute, some three year earlier.

I heard nothing for a few days, and then Liz called me about the sales opportunity. I reminded her of our first meeting and suggested that we should get together; so that I could bring her up to speed on what was involved. Ken was very distracted at the time, as was I, about my mother's condition. We met for a coffee in town, and I told her about the job. She quickly came to the conclusion that it wasn't quite what she was looking for. I have to admit that I was very disappointed when we went our own separate ways, but I promised to let her know if I heard of any other opportunities.

At that time in South Africa, National Service was still in force and would be until 1993. One of my Honda sales team was a young guy, Rob Frewen, who was proving to be a very good salesman and also had a high level of management potential. He had completed his full period of National Service, but was still eligible to attend the compulsory Reservist Camps for the next three year period. Employers, by law, had to release staff to attend these camps, which normally lasted six weeks and could entail going anywhere in South Africa. A few weeks after my initial meeting with Liz, Rob Frewen informed me that he would be heading off to one of these camps at the end of the following month. This meant that I would have to make a contingency plan and find a temporary replacement for him, which was never easy for such a short period of time.

Then I thought of Liz Messaris; it might be an ideal option for her. When I called her, she told me that a sales role in the retail motor industry wasn't something she had ever thought about, and that she needed time to consider it. The next day, she came to see me; and after a lengthy discussion, she accepted the role.

She fitted in well, with what was predominantly a very successful female sales team, and I could see her confidence growing as she dealt with potential customers. It had been a good appointment. There were many personal issues behind Liz looking for a job, and these came to light as the six weeks went by, and we got the chance to talk about it.

It quickly became obvious to both of us that there was something very special between us. I explained to Anelma how I felt, and we agreed to end our relationship. I was genuinely very, very fond of her and knew what a special person she was. So much so that Nelma, as she now prefers to be called, has become a great personal friend of Liz and mine, and whenever we visit South Africa, we always try to meet up with her.

I won't bore you with all the details, but suffice to say that Liz and I have now been married for 31 fabulous years, and we have had some great adventures together. Liz grew up in Cape Town, with her twin Peter and two brothers, John and Graham. As most South Africans seem to be, they were all into Rugby, so Liz has had to come to terms with my involvement with motor racing and the motorsport industry not an easy thing for anyone. Her brothers still wonder how on earth their sister got together with a Brit who, in their words, was "a man from the motor trade".

I can honestly say that without her, I would never have been able to achieve what I have done so far. We're so lucky to be able to spend as much time together as we do, with Liz invariably accompanying me on my business journeys. We really do operate as a team.

Motor racing never lets you rest on your laurels. It had been a great season for me with the Honda, having won the Stannic Group N Class Championship, in the most competitive category of the series, followed by our victory in the Castrol 6-Hour Race. No sooner had we collected our 6-Hour trophies at the Killarney-based prize-giving ceremony than it was time to start planning for next season. I had assumed that McCarthy Group would want me to continue in the Stannic Group N series, maybe with the new 1600i Honda that had just been launched. I wouldn't have had a problem with that, but I did have an ambition to race something a bit quicker, maybe even single-seaters again.

I remember sitting in my office in the Strand Street showroom when Graham Damp, the group's MD called me, asking if we could meet for a quick sandwich at lunchtime. After a catch-up on some business issues, he told me that Peter Cleary, marketing director of Mercedes Benz South Africa, had requested that I fly up to Pretoria for a meeting with him. I had no idea what this was about, and when I questioned him, Graham Damp just said it was something to do with my sales team's success, which made some sense, as we had been one of the top performing sales teams in the country.

A few days later, I stepped into Peter Cleary's office at the Mercedes HQ in Pretoria. He introduced me to a couple of people, one was Japie Coen, Mercedes' PR director, whilst the other was the company's technical director, Herman de Bryn. We talked for a while about our success in the 6-Hour, as well as in the Stannic Championship, and how best it could be developed to continue enhancing the Honda's brand image in South Africa, particularly in respect of broadening its market demographics. At this time, of course, Nigel Mansell was winning Grand Prix in his Williams Honda F1 car, so motorsport was playing a significant role in the global manufacturer's plans.

Then Peter told me that within MBSA, there was a feeling that it would be a natural step to enter a Honda Ballade in next season's national Stannic Group N Championship, to fully capitalise on the success that I'd enjoyed with the McCarthy Motors' motorsport programme. He then referred to my winning the regional championship and then the 6-Hour, which had included most of the national championship drivers and teams. He added, however, that it was not Mercedes Benz policy to become an entrant in its own right. I wondered what was coming.

I was asked whether I would like to race the new Ballade in 1987, in the national championship. What could I say but yes! Any other racing plans that I was considering would have to fit in somehow, or be put on ice. It was the next question that came as a total surprise. Peter then asked me if I would be prepared to set up and manage a two car Honda team, in what would effectively be an arm's length operation for Mercedes Benz South Africa. In other words, he explained, I would need to form a Pty company, which would be funded by Mercedes Benz South Africa.

Like most good news, there is usually a downside. It meant that I would have to move to Johannesburg. There was no way that such a team could practically operate from Cape Town, but I wasn't sure what Liz would feel about heading north! To a Capetonian, having to move to Johannesburg is one of their worst nightmares.

I spent another day at the MBSA HQ, checking out details of the proposed programme. This included selecting a second driver for the team, a technical manager, the financial aspects, the ideal location for the workshops and a host of other related matters. Then it was time to head back to Cape Town and sort out my employment situation; after all, I was still employed as the Honda Sales Manager for McCarthy Group.

After arriving back in Cape Town, I sat down with Graham Damp to discuss my situation. He congratulated me on the role that I'd been offered, having heard from

Peter Cleary about the proposals that he had put to me. He told me that he was sorry to lose such a successful sales manager, but fully understood that it wasn't an opportunity that I could turn down.

When I spoke to Liz, she told me that she was right behind me on the role that I'd been offered, even though she admitted that Johannesburg was far from being her ideal place to live. From a timing point of view, the move to Johannesburg brought forward our plans to get married. Two very good friends of Liz, Penny and Norman Lile, had a beautiful house in Constantia, in the southern suburbs of Cape Town, and they kindly offered to host the wedding and subsequent celebrations. On 21 February 1987, we exchanged our vows. Out best man was Julian Morris, who had been my team manager when I had raced, and crashed, in the Castrol 9-Hour race, back in 1981.

Brian met Liz whilst he racing for Honda in Cape Town. They married in 1987, before moving up to Kyalami, and setting up a new race team for Mercedes Benz SA.

We had travelled up to Johannesburg for a couple of weeks, prior to Christmas, to find somewhere to live and had chosen an amazing property situated about a mile from the Kyalami Circuit, where I had been employed as its manager. It occupied six acres of ground and included a dam and a swimming pool. The only thing that was missing was a tennis court.

Then we searched for a suitable place from which to run the race team. I also met a possible technical manager, Kevin McBride, whom I knew from my own racing, when I first arrived in South Africa. His problem was one of time, as he had

134

quite a lot of commitments with other drivers. He helped me find a suitable facility in the Wynberg district of Johannesburg. Now I needed to source a second driver. That wouldn't be so easy.

There would be lots of applicants, I'm sure, but how well would they fit into a team run by a British immigrant? It was an important consideration, as I'd already been on the wrong side of some predictable resentment, partly for winning the championship, but more often than not because I could secure sponsorship and that upset a lot of people.

As far as the second driver was concerned, I looked at several options. It was an attractive opportunity, and there was no shortage of people contacting me. After all, not everyone gets to race in a professional capacity and be paid by Mercedes Benz. Even fewer get to race in a Honda and be paid by Mercedes Benz!

One driver, who fancied himself, had the alleged support of Herman, MBSA's technical director, but did himself no favours by adopting what I found to be a quite unpleasant attitude towards my being chosen to run the team. If he couldn't get on with me before we'd even gone racing, it most definitely wouldn't be a relationship made in heaven. I'd earned the right to be in a Honda through my track performances; and also, I feel certain, because of the huge enthusiasm that I had demonstrated for the product in terms of my sales abilities and those of my sales team. It was going to be a tough year, of that I had no doubts, so why should I make it even worse by recruiting some self-opinionated superstar, who was no better than a dozen other drivers I could immediately think of?

Then the solution to the driver choice, presented itself, quite literally. Julian Morris, our best man, who was still living in Johannesburg, invited Liz and I to have supper at his house, just a couple of miles from where we would be staying in Mid Rand. We were shown through to a large snooker room, which had a pub-style bar at one end. Sitting at the bar was none other than Mike O'Sullivan, the Leyland salesman from whom I nearly brought my Triumph TR7 sport car and who was in the next pit garage as driver of the 3.5 litre Rover in the Castrol 9-Hour. Alongside him was his wife, Eileen. I hadn't realised that they were good friends of Julian and his latest wife, Alison (Heather having left the marital home). Looking back, I think that Julian was keen to put Mike in the frame for the vacant seat in the Honda Team. If he had, then it was a smart move, because by the end of the evening, Mike and I had agreed to meet at the new workshops before we flew back to Cape Town.

I made a few phone calls, and it became obvious that Mike would be a good choice for our new team. He now ran a motorsport preparation company, Mosport, with his brother Paddy; and most of the people I spoke to thought that not only would he be a good team mate to have, but that I could do a lot worse than to get him to prepare the two cars.

I knew enough about racing to realise that if I did take Mike on as both driver and technical manager, I was creating a situation that might jeopardise my own racing performance. Would he prepare my car to exactly the same level as his? If he didn't, it wouldn't be the first time that it had happened in the sport. On the other hand, looking at the bigger picture, the primary objective was for Honda to win races, whether it was with my car or my team-mate's. What was important was that the cars were prepared to a high level of performance and reliability. We were now representing Mercedes Benz South Africa, albeit under the guise of Corporate Racing, which was what the new team was now called.

After a great season in the McCarthy Group car, I had a lot of confidence in my own ability. After all, I had ten wins to my name, and the kudos of beating the Toyota works cars in the Killarney endurance race. It was up to me to make sure that I could race at Mike's level.

If I was going to appoint Mike, I would have to disappoint Kevin McBride, with whom I was still talking about the possibility of working for us. I think he was quite glad when it came down to it. He was happy doing what he did, and I don't think he would have enjoyed the pressures that came with working for a motor manufacturer.

Following a couple more meetings with Mike, I came to the conclusion that he would be the ideal person to employ to run the workshop and drive one of the two Honda race cars. He was over the moon and told me that he would put his role at Mosport on ice and employ a replacement, under the watchful eye of his brother, Paddy O'Sullivan. Mike had a wealth of experience in motorsport preparation and, most importantly, knew all the right people for getting the multitude of technical jobs completed, such as installing roll cages into the two Hondas that we would be sent by Mercedes Benz. He also brought with him, a black race mechanic, Willy who would also drive the transporter. I felt as though I was now on top of things and could turn my attention to another, even more important matter, getting married in Cape Town in about 7 weeks' time.

Whilst the biggest worry for couples getting married in Britain is usually the weather, in South Africa, that is rarely the case. On 21 February, it was one of the hottest days of the year. Norman and Penny, who incidentally had been the secretary of the Cliff Richard Fan Club in South Africa, had erected a large marquee in the garden, adjacent to their very tempting swimming pool. With the air temperature being well over 35 degrees centigrade, both the marquee and the pool were essentials, rather than luxuries. Many of our colleagues from Mercedes and McCarthy Group were there on the big day, as of course were our two families.

Unfortunately, a long honeymoon wasn't an option, from a time point of view, as there was so much to be done before the start of the Stannic Group N Championship. We stayed overnight at the beautiful old Cellars Hotel in Constantia and next day flew to Johannesburg, having said goodbye to Nick and Alexandra, Liz's 14 and 11-year-old son and daughter, both of whom would be staying in Cape Town with Liz's former husband during term time and with us during school holidays, which meant them flying up to Johannesburg.

Chapter 21
A Lost Brief-Case, So Near and
Mayhem at Welkom

I'm not sure how we managed to get the two brand new Honda Ballades, that had been delivered to our Wynberg workshops by Mercedes, ready for testing. There was so much to do, from installing the racing seats, safety harnesses to having the cars painted in the Corporate Racing colours of yellow, red, white and blue. Mike proved to be a star and managed the business really well for me; and when it came to all of the technical preparation, his expertise was invaluable.

Then there was the work that had to be done on the transportation vehicle that Mercedes organised for us. If I needed confirmation that I'd chosen the right person to prepare the cars, I only had to see what Mike was able to organise in such a short time. Everything came together, and his level of contacts within the Johannesburg automotive and supplies sector was quite extraordinary.

Eventually, we were ready to start testing. We chose the virtually unused Swartkops Race Circuit, near Pretoria for the initial shakedown and publicity photographs. The cars seemed good, but Mike was keeping a close eye on the opposition, to see what improvements they had made. Driving for Toyota, in their 1.6 litre Twin Cam Conquests, was former F3 driver, Mike White. He was a highly experienced and very fast driver, who had been racing in Europe successfully. He had been the lead driver for Toyota in the Castrol 6-Hours, when we had beaten their works team. We knew that didn't go down well, and we would have to be on our toes, going forward.

One of our serious areas of concern, relating to the increased performance levels that Toyota was seeking, was homologation and the way that Toyota was displaying a high level of flexibility in this respect. In motorsport, homologation is the approval process through which a vehicle, or part, is required to go for certification to be able to race in a specific series. As an example, if a manufacturer wants to run a much wider diameter exhaust system on its race car, it may be necessary to build and sell 50 or more passengers cars with the same modification, maybe calling them GT versions, or similar, to differentiate them from the standard car.

Mercedes were far more reserved and wouldn't just simply change a specification to improve performance and then introduce a different model to meet with the homologation criteria. It gave Toyota a head start. Nevertheless, Mike was doing a great job in preparing the Hondas and was confident that we would still be competitive.

From memory, our first race of the season was at the Aldo Scribante Circuit in Port Elizabeth. Situated right on the Indian Ocean coastline, it was a fairly basic facility, to say the least. Nevertheless, it provided an interesting circuit, and we decided to go down a little earlier than was needed, managing to book a test day at the track. I discovered that one of the major changes required when we travelled from the high altitude of the Highveld to sea level circuits, such as Port Elizabeth and Cape Town, was that the motors had to be reset on the dyno. I was quite staggered to learn that the cars gained about 17% in performance at sea level.

We had booked the team into the Marine Hotel, right on the seafront. On the night that we had arrived, we all went for supper in the hotel's night club. It had been a stressful build-up to this opening race, and we were all quite tired, but it was good to be together over supper. None of us were late turning-in.

It was about three o'clock in the morning when I woke up with a start. Where had I left my briefcase? I'd taken it down to supper with me, because in it was a lot of cash which was usual when we travelled. I remember putting it under my chair at the table. It also contained our racing licenses and a few other documents, without which we wouldn't be allowed to race. I quickly got dressed and ran down to the night club, but, not surprisingly, it was closed. I then ran through to the hotel reception. That was also closed. I eventually found the night manager, and he told me that I would have to wait until morning for him to open up the club. I knew that this meant I wouldn't get any more sleep that night. Not an ideal scenario before our first race.

I asked the manager to look in the reception area to see if anyone had handed in the case. He really didn't want to bother, but I insisted. To my relief, there it was, tucked away under the front desk. What could so easily have been a disastrous start to our new racing season was averted, and I was able to go back to bed and get some meaningful sleep.

Our first race meeting went reasonably well. Nevertheless, it's probably fair to say that if it were a school report, it might have described our performance as promising, but a lot of work still to be done. We were in a pensive mood as we headed off on the long trek back to Johannesburg.

Soon it was time to head to Welkom, a track situated in the Orange Free State. Situated in the middle of some of South Africa's major gold-mines, Welkom was a track unlike anything I'd raced at in the UK. For a start, there was hardly any infrastructure in terms of hotels or even facilities at the track. There was a Holiday Inn, and that was about it.

I'll never forget the greeting that we received on entering the reception area on arrival. It was certainly somewhat different to what we expected, with the uniformed receptionist sitting in a chair, with her feet on the desk in front of her, so that she could more easily continue to cut her toe nails with a big pair of clippers. The clipping process didn't stop as she asked us if we had a booking!

The track itself great, albeit the pit complex was very simplistic and, from a driver's point of view, presented some great challenges. Welkom Circuit boasted a very long back straight, which was approached though a right-left-right chicane, followed by a very fast right-hander.

As we had done at Port Elizabeth, we had opted to do some serious testing the week before the race, booking the track for two-day private usage. On the first day, we notched up some really fast times; and Mike had sorted out the handling on my car, so that it gave me the same feel that I'd benefited from in last season's Honda. Mike ended the day two-tenths of a second quicker than me, but we would have got both front row positions at last year's race. The next day, however, started with somewhat of a disaster!

I had received a phone call from one of the "middle-management" at Mercedes to say that he would be at the track the next morning to monitor our progress. Neither Mike nor I were of the opinion that this was a formal visit, as we realised that this guy was the younger brother of a senior director at the company. He rather fancied himself as a race driver, having done a couple of club races and was very self-opinionated when it came to motorsport. He had been stirring quite a bit about the performance of the cars and of Mike and myself, after the first race meeting. Anyway, he was a Mercedes employee, and he was perfectly entitled to come and watch. What I hadn't expected was that on his arrival, he would ask to try one of the cars. I wasn't happy about this, neither was Mike, but it was a little difficult to refuse when he told us he had been given the OK to do so by his brother. To be sure that it was in order, I made a quick call to MBSA in Pretoria and was told by the person who had been given responsibility for the motorsport programme, that I had the right to refuse the request, but that politically might be advantageous to let him drive the car.

Confident that if anything wrong, I had at least aired my opinions, I set the young lad up in my car and told him to just do two laps before coming back in. I also gave him a rev limit which he should not exceed under any circumstances. Off he went, with Mike and I standing nervously in the pits. At Welkom, there is a double left-hander which precedes a 90 degree right-hander onto the pit straight. As the young guy, who will have to remain nameless, approached the second part of the double left-hander, he realised that he was going too fast and stupidly stood on the brake pedal. We knew exactly what the consequences would be, but there was nothing that we could do, other than let the scenario unfold itself, in what seemed to Mike and I standing there watching, like slow motion.

There was my car, upside down, rolling on to the grass at the edge of the track! We managed to get the door open and let the incredibly red-faced driver clamber out. Nobody said anything for a minute or two whilst we managed to get the car back onto its four wheels. Mike and I didn't know whether to laugh or cry. I think the words "poetic justice" went through both of our minds. Sadly, whatever the rights or wrongs of the situation, it was my car that now looked in somewhat of a sorry state.

I almost felt sorry for the lad, but realising that the forthcoming race meeting was just three days away, that emotion was quickly replaced by another, which was far less forgiving! I can't remember his exact words, but he mumbled something about the car not handling properly and disappeared. Before long, he had climbed into his own car and disappeared. We had work to do, a lot of it, to get my car ready for the race meeting.

Mike, as always, did an amazing job; and when I arrived back at the Welkom circuit for the race weekend, the car looked as good as new. In practice, everything felt fine, and we were both feeling confident that we could put in a good show for the Mercedes visitors who were coming to the race meeting.

In testing, we had worked hard at developing our slip-streaming tactics on the long straight to find that little extra speed. It worked perfectly for us when it came to qualifying. Mike found himself fourth, on the 30 car grid, with me right behind him in sixth, but both less than a half a second off the factory Toyotas, which we knew would be very competitive on the fast Welkom track, as they had a higher top speed than us.

Race day was another scorcher, and Welkom offered little shade for spectators. Despite this, a large crowd had gathered for this highly popular championship. With 30 cars on the grid, it had all the makings of an exciting race. Liz and Eileen sat in the pits, knowing how hard Mike and I had worked to make the Honda's competitive, and how much this race meant to us.

Everything went to plan for the first few laps, and Mike got up into second place, with me in fifth, close on the tail of one of the Toyotas. Then as I turned onto the pit straight, the car suddenly veered to the left, and it quickly became apparent that I had a tyre problem. With 25 cars, all virtually in a long, fast-moving convoy behind me, it wasn't the most convenient place for a puncture, but that's what it turned out to be. A small bolt had done straight into the front left tyre, and my race was over. Standing by the car on the grass verge, I watched the pack come around again, with Mike still in second place. It was as high as he would get. The next time I saw the Honda, it was crawling slowly down the pit lane.

The Honda garage was not a good place to be that afternoon. All the work we'd put in for nothing, but that's motor racing. Mike's problem was apparently caused by the failure of a part in the engine that probably cost about 20p. It was back to the drawing board.

Sadly, that was to the most competitive the Hondas were that season despite all of our efforts to make the cars more competitive. Certain issues with homologation didn't help, including the fact that Toyota introduced a more performance assisting exhaust system, which Mercedes for a variety of reasons wouldn't respond to, but that is not an excuse. The reality was that the Toyota factory team were just better than us that season.

That day, after the two disappointing DNFs, we loaded up the race cars and wandered to one of the corners to watch the remaining couple of races before heading back to the Paddock. What we were about to watch unfold was nothing short of extraordinary.

It was traditional at this Free State Circuit for the track to be opened to the public at the end of each race meeting. The original idea had been to allow spectators to drive their own cars and motor bikes slowly around the track, so that they could get a better feeling of what it was like for the race drivers. That was the idea, but the reality was different, so very different.

It was my first time at a Welkom race meeting. The final race had ended, and we were in the paddock heading for our cars when the relative peace and quiet following the race was suddenly shattered by a bedlam of noise. As we looked across in the direction from which it was coming, we could see that the track was alive with spectators in their road cars and on bikes. We had heard that this always happened after a race meeting, but instead of the steady procession that I was expecting, all hell was let loose. I couldn't believe my eyes as I watched a variety of road cars being chucked around at high speed, obviously racing each other. Then a couple of motor bikes hurtled down the main straight, inches apart from each other. A girl was on the pillion seat of one of them, hanging on to the rider for dear life. The only word that I can think of to describe what was going on that day was "terrifying". I wondered how much alcohol had been consumed under the hot sun all day and what part that was playing in the scenes that we were witnessing. It was nothing less than sheer lunacy.

We got back to the cars and manoeuvred into the traffic jams that were forming at the various exits, onto the public roads. After about 20 minutes or so, we heard sirens and saw three ambulances turning into the circuit. Oh dear, what had happened now. The ambulances raced across the grass where people were walking and tried to get access to the track. In the process, someone was knocked down by one of them.

The ambulances were there, we found out later, because two motorcyclists, one going the reverse way around the race track, collided head-on, resulting in a double fatality. The person hit by the ambulance had been seriously hurt, whilst a motorcyclist had hit a police car outside the circuit and been killed. Probably the worst accident of the day had occurred when a father took his son out onto the track in a Ford Cortina with the sun-roof open. He had tried to emulate the race cars and take the chicane, to which I referred, without lifting, somersaulting the car in the process. I believe that it was the father who died, whilst the son received serious brain damage after being thrown out of the car.

All in all, my first ever race meeting at Welkom, had most definitely been a weekend to forget.

Chapter 22

A Sponsorship Challenge, a Dead Elephant and an Historic Race

As the end of the season approached, I started thinking that it was perhaps time to call a day on my race driving career. Much as I was enjoying racing in these production cars, it was a long way from where I really wanted to be. By now, I was 41 years old. I was also finding the travelling in South Africa rather tedious. The distances to most of the races are vast, and, much as I enjoyed my lifestyle as a professional racer, I wasn't being mentally stimulated.

Whilst these thoughts were in my mind, an opportunity arose that really did stimulate me. Every year, normally in November or December, a motor race was staged at the Kyalami Circuit, which attracted as many people to it as the South African F1 Grand Prix if not more. It comprised an international Group C race. Now one of the most popular categories of historic racing, Group C cars are closed cockpit sports cars, similar to those raced in the top category of the Le Mans 24-Hours. You may have seen Steve McQueen in the 1971 film *Le Mans*, driving a Porsche 917. Although not technically a Group C car, it will give you an idea of the style of car to which I am referring.

Many of these cars were powered by Cosworth V8 F1 engines, others by V12 and V8 Turbos, and it was not unusual for them to be faster than F1 cars in a straight line. One of the most memorable and successful teams to have raced in Group C was sponsored by Rothmans and used Porsche 956s, whilst other manufacturers included Lancia, Jaguar, Nissan, Sauber, Toyota and Mercedes. Amongst the well-known drivers to compete in Group C, you had the likes of Derek Bell, Jacky Ickx, Hans Stuck, Bob Wollek and Manfred Winkelhock.

I'd always wanted to drive one of these extraordinary cars, but like so many young drivers, became brain-washed into wanting to be an F1 driver. When I saw that the race at Kyalami in 1987 would not only be sponsored by Yellow Pages and named the Yellow Pages 500 but would be the last ever international race to be held on the famous Kyalami Grand Prix Circuit before being demolished, demolished, my mind went into overdrive.

News had broken that the owners of Kyalami had sold a lot of the ground on which the track was situated, and it would be used for commercial development. Even in the relatively short period of time that I had known the track, I could see that the outskirts of Johannesburg were spreading rapidly in the direction of Pretoria. New office and factory buildings were appearing more and more along the route of the Ben Schoeman Highway, together with residential housing developments. Kyalami, once known for its beautiful open countryside, was now disappearing amongst architect-designed office blocks and upmarket shopping malls. It didn't come as a big shock when the Kyalami redevelopment programme was announced.

It was normal at that time for a large number of the Group C teams to take part in the end of season event. It didn't count for championship points, but it paid a reasonable entry fee and travel expenses, making it an attractive opportunity for the teams to spend December in the midst of a South African summer. As an extra money-making activity, several of these teams made it known that they would invite South African drivers to share the race-driving with one of their normal professionals, subject of course to them having an appropriate international racing license, a reasonable driving pedigree and a bag of gold! In other words, they would need to bring sponsorship. It was too good an opportunity to miss. I needed to put my business hat on once again.

The Yellow pages 500 event was for a grid of both Group C and Group C2 cars. The latter was a class introduced to offer less expensive racing with cars that were very similar to Group C, but it offered a slightly inferior level of performance. The grid size was expected to be around 30 cars in total. In addition, there would be an extra race the following weekend, but this would be restricted to Group C2 cars only.

My opportunity arrived when I was told that one of the leading C2 teams, PC Automotive, was offering a seat at late notice, due to the driver's father having been taken seriously ill. Patrick Capon, a joint owner of the team, and a highly regarded specialist in old clocks, contacted me from the UK, having heard that I was interested in competing in the Yellow Pages 500. What had motivated him to call, however, wasn't my average race driving skills but rather my above average sponsorship acquisition skills. Patrick told me that there was a drive available in both the Yellow Pages 500 and the following weekend, the Champion Spark Plug Challenge, also at Kyalami but for Group C2 cars alone.

He then told me how much I would have to pay for each event. It was not an insignificant sum of money, to put it mildly, and it had to be paid in Pounds, not SA Rand. If I was going to race in what would be a historic event at Kyalami, I now had less than six weeks to put a deal together to secure enough sponsorship to cover the racing fees and a driving fee for myself.

My task wasn't made any easier by the imminent arrival in South Africa of my aunt and uncle, Don and Joan, both of whom were in their mid-60s and had decided to come and visit my folks, particularly of course my mother, Joan's sister, who was still not at all well. We had agreed that we would collect them at Jan Smuts Airport on their arrival from the UK, and they would stay with us for a week prior to heading up to a private safari camp, not far from the Mozambique border, for a few days. We would then head down to Cape Town to visit my parents. To make life easier for Joan and Don, for these long distance journeys, Liz and I purchased an American, right-hand drive, Chevrolet 5.7 litre Cruiser Van, which was equipped with six aircraft-style seats, air-conditioning and mosquito nets at the windows, absolutely ideal for touring South Africa.

A couple of days prior to their arrival in late September 1987, we received a phone call from Don. He explained that a hurricane level storm had hit England, and that where they lived, Sevenoaks in Kent, was now literally One Oak! He went on to tell me that my aunt had suffered a bad fall, trying to clear up the debris in their garden, resulting in a broken arm. Not what you need before setting off on a 12-hour plane journey.

Concerned as I was for Joan's well-being, I was also worried that trying to initiate, negotiate and close a fairly substantial sponsorship deal wasn't going to be easy in these circumstances. Liz and I were going to be tour-guides for much of the time, and you must also remember that this was in the days before mobile phones, lap tops, e-mails, and all the other digital technology developments that have now made communication so much easier.

I spent two entire days on the phone, trying to secure appointments. Our visitors were arriving in less than ten days' time, and I wanted to identify at least a couple of prospects before heading off to our first destination. Within the next two days, I worked on generating a substantial amount of guaranteed PR and media coverage for a potential sponsor. This is often necessary, to add further value to a proposed sponsorship. I'd been to see the editor of the *Sunday Times*, the primary Sunday newspaper in South Africa. In a similar way to British Sunday papers, it always included a free colour supplement, normally a life-style publication.

My proposal was that with the forthcoming Yellow Pages 500 being a major international sports event within South Africa, the newspapers' readers might find it interesting to hear how a professional race driver, one who is not a famous F1 star, goes about securing the large levels of commercial sponsorship that is needed to secure a drive. The feature wouldn't be about the action on-track, but rather what happens in the in the board-room of potential sponsors. The editor's response was that he didn't have a budget to pay me for this, and secondly, there was no one available to write it at such short notice. I solved both of his problems in one go. I told him that I would write the feature; and that that I didn't need paying. His next question was obvious; then what do you want out of it? My answer was very simple, I wanted a guarantee that the article would be on the centre pages of the magazine, in full colour, and that it would contain a significant-size photograph of the race car adorned in the subsequent sponsor's branding. 'What if you don't get a sponsor?' he asked. I assured him that I would. We agreed to go ahead.

I then went to the offices of a full-colour glossy magazine that was distributed free to up-market households within certain areas of South Africa. The magazine was called *Style*. I did a similar deal, but on the basis of the magazine being keen to cover major social events, such as fashion shows, country fairs, film festivals and similar activities. I pointed out the calibre of many of the international drivers, quite a few with celebrity wives and girlfriends, who would be competing in the Yellow Pages 500 and suggested it would make for an interesting feature with lots of photographic opportunities. After a number of further discussions, it was agreed that they would include a three-page interview with me, including the photos that I insisted upon, but confirmed that they didn't have a budget to pay me. This was fine by me, and it was in-line with my overall strategy.

Finally, I contacted SABC TV, the South African equivalent of the BBC. My meeting was with one of the producers of a prime-time TV chat show called *Graffiti*, presented by Penny Smythe, a very popular TV star. Along similar lines to those I had adopted with the print media, I suggested that an interview with me prior to the race meeting might be of interest to viewers; not because I was in any way famous, but because I was demonstrating that you don't have to be a champion to be a winner.

The week went by too fast, but on Friday, some of my hard work paid off. I was following up my earlier calls and was delighted to find that two of the companies,

I'd contacted, wanted to meet me to discuss the opportunities in more detail, and I was able to book those meetings for the week I returned from my travels.

We duly collected Joan and Don from Jan Smuts Airport and brought them back for a relaxing weekend at our new home, sitting under the palm trees by the pool, sipping South African wine for much of the time. The weather was perfect; and by the time we were ready to leave on the Monday morning, they had lost their ghostly white pallor which made it so easy to recognise them as they pushed their trolleys out of the Arrivals Gate.

Before we knew it, it was time to head north; way beyond the Kruger Park, to a small town called Hoedspruit and from there to an area called Timbavati, known across the world as the home of a famous pride of white lions. The Cruiser Van proved absolutely ideal for the long, hot journey; and despite her arm being in plaster, Joan was able to relax comfortably in the luxurious reclining seats. Don, alert as always, was fascinated as we headed through the most extraordinary scenery in a country that he'd never visited before.

After a long drive, we eventually booked into the Tanda Tula Safari Camp, which was owned by a Greek couple, whom I had met and befriended when I enjoyed a few days there as a guest, the previous year. John and Sally Panos ran a very successful business, Safari-Plan, which comprised three separate camps, each one catering for around 14-24 guests at any one time. Until you have visited the South African "bush", as it's known, it's very difficult to appreciate the vast scale of the region. I mentioned previously that the Kruger Park is about the size of Wales. When you go to Hoedspruit and beyond there is a plethora of wild life camps, but very few of them have fences. What it means is that the wildlife are free to roam, freely and uninterrupted, across swathes of land which stretch for hundreds of miles. Each camp allows herds of elephants, wildebeest, zebra, buffalo, lions, giraffes and a host of other species to follow their natural instincts and cross their land so that their guests can genuinely watch nature in the wild.

The Tanda Tula Camp, where we would spend the week, could host a maximum of 14 guests at any one time. My first visit had been very brief, but despite that, was one that I have never forgotten to this day. My very first glimpse into life in the wild was just so very special. The staff treated everyone as friends; and to go out in the open top jeep, early in the morning, whilst it was still dark, was an awesome experience. So was the smell of a cooked breakfast, wafting through the crisp morning air from a camp that had been set-up for us in a dry riverbed, over ten miles from the camp.

Once we had all unpacked and were sitting in the thatched bar beside the circular swimming pool, Lionel, one of the Rangers, excitedly greeted us with the news that an elephant had died a few miles away. You are so lucky, he explained, adding that this elephant had slipped and fallen sideways into a *donga*, a dry gulley through which water flows during the rainy season. Due to its enormous weight and size, it had been unable to get up from the fall and had suffered a massive heart attack. Lionel also told us that in accordance with the regulations in place because of the increasing poaching activities within the region, they had cut the tusks and feet from the elephant and handed this into the Parks Board, where the ivory could be sold, and the funds used legitimately. As a result, there was this rotting carcass lying in the sun, attracting every predator for miles around.

145

We had a quick breakfast and then jumped in the jeep and headed off to see this unique sight. Sadly, Joan's broken arm was not up to the shaking that the off-road trek would undoubtedly entail, so she opted to spend a relaxed day reading her book beside the pool.

I'm not exaggerating when I say that we could hear the site where the elephant's torso was stretched out in the blazing sun, before we could see it. The hum of millions of flies, big *brommers*, as they call them in South Africa, that were hovering over the carcass, could be heard from about 400 metres away as we headed slowly in the open top jeep towards the clearing where it was all happening. Then the smell hit us! A rotting carcass, suppurating in a temperature up in the high 30s, does have that ability.

Just as we reached the clearing, it started getting dark, despite being about 11 o'clock in the morning. The reason for this was plain to see. The very high trees surrounding the elephant's final resting place were stacked full of vultures, almost blocking out the light. There must have been hundreds sitting in the trees all around, some gorging on bits of the elephant, whilst on the ground a bizarre spectacle was being played out. There must have been about 40 vultures, desperately trying to get off the ground, wings flapping violently, but their stomachs were so full of elephant carcass that they couldn't get off the ground. It had to be seen to be believed.

If you've watched the famous Stewart Grainger and Deborah Kerr movie *King Solomon's Mines*, there is a scene where the key cast members are on safari camping, somewhere in Africa. It's quite comical as they watch what can only be described as a cavalcade of every wild animal you would expect to see, hurtling from right to left in front of their camp site. What we saw that day at Tanda Tula was nothing less than that. Virtually every predator including lions, hyena, jackals, leopards and wild dogs descended on the poor elephant. The lions were amusing to watch, they filled their stomachs with food and laid down in the sun to rest, but should any other animal arrive to get a small bite of the carcass, the growls started and short, quick, threatening runs were made by one or two of the lions on behalf of the others. The piece *de* resistance came when one of the lionesses, who had been feasting on the elephant's rear end, suddenly burst through the bladder and was engulfed in gallons of urine, but without even a flinch, kept on chewing. It had been a very special day, and we'd sat there for the best part of five hours before eventually heading back to camp.

Whilst everyone sat enthralled by the goings on all around us, my mind was also elsewhere for a lot of the time. I mentally went over my search for the sponsorship thousands that I needed to secure the drives with the British Group C racing team and tried to think what else I could do to add value to my sponsorship properties.

We spent a wonderful few days at Tanda Tula, with my aunt and uncle, before heading off through the beautiful scenery of the Eastern Transvaal, heading south, where some 900 miles away, my folks were waiting in Cape Town, looking forward to meeting their overseas guests.

A week later, and we were back in Johannesburg, and the relaxed atmosphere of our home. Whilst Joan and Don recovered from the long journey back, I started preparing for my two meetings. To be honest, it was very difficult to plan, because my first meeting with a company is usually very much exploratory, a balance of outlining the opportunity in very general terms, before then trying to identify some of the issues facing the company which could possibly be helped by an innovative, well-structured sponsorship programme. Until I had gone through that process, anything that I was putting together in my mind would be based on pure assumption. Not the way to go. So I just had to be patient.

Both of the meetings were with CEO of the company. The first was a well-known international computer company, GBS Wang. My second was with a jewellery retailer, Sterns, whose strap-line was "The Nation's Jewellers" and could best be compared to H Samuel in the UK. During the meetings, it became apparent that both companies wanted more coverage on the car than was available to me, but I knew that it was just a matter of negotiation

Seemingly, they were both impressed with the opportunity that I was presenting, particularly liking the guaranteed coverage that I'd put in place. My concerns that it would be very difficult to create a meaningful, measurable business development opportunity, as opposed to simply brand awareness, within such a short space of time, were valid. This meant that my efforts to ensure a way above average level of guaranteed media coverage even more important.

The budgets that I had set for the two weekends varied slightly, due to the varying prestige level of the events, with the Yellow Pages 500 being the jewel in the crown. This helped me arrive at an innovative strategy which I presented to both companies.

The outcome was positive, and I was able to secure the full budget that I needed to cover the team's costs and a personal fee for me. GBS Wang would be the primary sponsor of the team for the Yellow Pages 500; and Sterns the team's primary sponsor in the Champion Spark Plug Group C2 race the following weekend. The various media coverage activities that I had arranged would be further enhanced by showing how we had worked with both sponsors to put together a programme that worked for everyone.

Somehow, despite the various interruptions and difficulties that had to be steered around, the deals had been done, and I could now focus on what I had decided would be my last two races in a driving career that spanned the period between 1974 and 1987. I'd escaped unhurt from a couple of major accidents, and now I just had to enjoy racing the most powerful race car that I had ever sat in. I was relishing the fact that I'd be on the same track as some of the world's leading professional racers. I was also determined that having made the decision to retire, I wouldn't try to be a hero and exceed my limits of capability. That didn't mean that I would give less than 100%, it just meant being a little bit sensible and not wrecking someone else's race.

When race day arrived, Liz and I got to the circuit early to avoid the predictable traffic jams. The weather, as it was more often than not, was perfect. In fact, my only concern was that temperatures of around 35 degrees centigrade were forecast for the start of the race, which in the closed cockpit of the Group C cars would mean it could get up to 50 or 60 degrees. The race would last for around 70 laps, based on speeds achieved in practice. Mike Catlow and I would each be in the car for around 50 minutes. That doesn't sound a long time, but not being physically used to driving a car with some 480 horsepower and handling capabilities to match, I knew that it was going to be a tough session. Of course I had trained as much as I could, but it's time in the car that really counts.

Sitting in the cockpit on the grid, prior to the rolling start, I had to pinch myself to believe that this was really happening to me. I had put in so much effort to secure the sponsorship that I was determined to savour the moment. As was often the case whilst I was racing in South Africa, I got some unpleasant comments from two or three local drivers, who weren't slow to inform me they deserved to be in the car far more than I did, being quicker drivers, in their opinion. It was water off a duck's back, as far as I was concerned; they could also have got off their butts and found some funding, just as I had to.

I'd always thought that the filtering systems on these closed-cockpit sports cars stopped debris, dust and rubber getting into car; but in the long run down to the first corner, by which time the cars around me were reaching approximately 160 miles per hour plus, on that first lap, I found that wasn't the case. As we braked for the third gear Crowthorne Corner, the cockpit was literally invaded by the smell of rubber, burning oil and particles of dust and tyre debris.

My fears that it would be an exhausting race were spot on. Driving this super-quick car was a challenge that I was relishing. Its handling capabilities were sensational, particularly after months of racing a front wheel drive saloon car, as I had been. It was also incredibly hot in the driving seat, and I was glad that I had opted for a full-face balaclava, which absorbed much of the perspiration before it dripped into my eyes.

What was so memorable, however, was being overtaken by the leading C1 cars of Jochen Mass, Bob Wollek and South African Sarel van der Merwe. Their sheer speed and lateness of braking at the end of the straight was something to behold. It was also quite a challenge when racing as quickly as I felt confident, I could see two cars side by side coming up fast behind me into the 90 degree, right-hander Sunset Bend. A couple of times, despite staying off their line, as best I could, I still got lightly sideswiped as they passed me.

With about ten laps to go, my neck muscles gave up the ghost, quite literally. It meant that as I climbed the steep run up to Leeukop corner, which led onto the main straight and braked hard, my head rolled forward; and then as I accelerated through the corner and on to the straight, it jerked back. It was a bizarre sensation that I had never previously experienced. It was also quite worrying as it made it difficult to keep my eyes focussed to where I was heading. My drinks system in the car had also stopped working, which was not ideal.

The last ten laps became increasingly tough; and when I eventually crossed the finish line in 15th place overall out of the 30 starters, I was just about at my limit and only had enough energy to head back to the paddock, where I had two problems to manage. One, my fingers had been gripping the steering wheel so tightly for the last ten laps, that I battled to get them to let go; two, I couldn't find the energy to climb out from the car, I felt so dehydrated. Eventually, my crew came to the rescue; and within a short while, I was feeling good again.

It had been a wonderful experience, one that I wouldn't have swapped for anything. To drive in such prestigious company was in itself something very special and to do so without making any mistakes was a good feeling. I was able to head to the hospitality marquee and meet up with the CEO of GBS Wang and spend the next hour chatting to his guests. The next day, he would be delighted to open the colour supplement of the *Sunday Times* and see a double-page colour photograph of the GBS adorned Royale RP 40, with an accompanying three-page feature article about the sponsorship, how it was put together, and why GBS had decided to enter into it.

Yet again, with two substantial sponsorship deals, Brian competed in the 1987 Yellow Pages 500 Group C International, driving a Royale RP40 for PC Automotive. It was his final event on the famous F1 Grand Prix track, before being partly demolished. It was also Brian's final race before retiring from race-driving, after 14 seasons.

The following Saturday, it was time to race once again. This time the race would be for C2 cars on their own, which meant a smaller grid of 24 cars. My team mate differed in this race. I would be joined by a driver with the unlikely name of Stingbrace. It transpired that he was the manager of a top London hotel, who raced under a pseudonym because he didn't want any publicity that might be associated with the business.

With the experience I'd gained in the Yellow Pages 500, I was more mentally prepared as to what to expect and got a great start, moving up from my starting position on the fourth row of the grid. I felt good in the car and was making up some ground on the two cars ahead, when suddenly there was a misfire which quickly necessitated a visit to the pits. A battery lead had broken and needed a quick change. That was a blow, as I dropped down the field, but I was determined to end on a high note and passed several cars within a few laps.

Liz was the first to see the problem, standing on the pit wall watching as we all headed past her at around 165 mph. She shouted to the crew member standing next to her and pointed to the rear of my car as I flashed by. She could see that the rear wheel on the right hand-side of the car was at an angle to the bodywork. The instant response was that the wheel looked as though it was working itself loose. Without pit to car communication, which we didn't have, there was no way of the guys warning me, other than a Pit Board, which might prove too late. As I braked for Crowthorne Corner, at the end of the straight, the car just hurtled into a spin, which at that speed isn't funny, believe me. The worst part was that there was so much tyre smoke as I spun around that I had no idea where I was heading. I just sat there waiting to hit something solid. I was out of control.

The car came to a stop and I could see that I had spun into the inside grass verge of the wide right-hand bend. How I had avoided either being hit or hitting something else I don't. I'm sure there will be some drivers who read this book who will tell you that they would have taken a different course of action. Good for them, that's all I

149

can say. I obviously didn't have that talent. When I climbed out of the car, I could immediately see that the right rear wheel had collapsed from the suspension. We later discovered that a bolt that secured the rear shock absorber had sheared. Apart from the suspension damage and four ruined tyres, the Group C2 car was undamaged, and I was unhurt. Having subsequently watched the incident on a TV recording, it was obvious that it could all have been so different.

I started the long walk up the hill to the pit lane, reflecting that my racing career was now officially over; nearly 14 years from the day that I first raced my Victoria's Night Club sponsored Formula Ford at Castle Combe.

Chapter 23

An Offer from Mercedes, Instant Dislike and a Cunning Plan

I hadn't set the motor racing world alight. I hadn't followed in the footsteps of my peers, drivers such as Nigel Mansell, Derek Warwick, Geoff Lees or Derek Daly who had gone on to reach the heady heights of a Formula 1 drive, but I honestly believe that I made the most of what was an average talent as a racing driver. By adding that essential ingredient, an ability to secure significant sponsorship, I had probably exceeded my limitations.

My race-driving CV might not have impressed Frank Williams or Ron Denis, but I had won a Championship and a prestigious 6-Hour endurance race. I had also been a Mercedes Benz paid professional driver and had made two competent appearances in a Group C, Cosworth V8 powered race car, in the prestigious Group C international race that marked the end of one of F1's most famous Grand Prix tracks, Kyalami. Importantly, I'd made a lot of friends along the way and was aware that I had also put a few noses out of joint.

Yes, it was definitely the right time to call it a day; after all, I had an unfulfilled ambition to chase. I might not have made it to Formula 1 as a driver, but there might be another way that I could get there. I wasn't going to give up that easily.

Whilst I was in South Africa, I was lucky enough to get involved in some broadcasting. Whilst this included a fair bit of F1 work for SABC TV, I was also introduced to another exciting sport, F1 Powerboat Racing. If you haven't seen it, you really are missing something a bit special. These closed cockpit boats, with long barrow bodies, a huge rear engine producing 400 horsepower and sleek large sponsons on either side, look more like a Formula 1 car than a boat. They are quick, reaching speed of up to 150 mph and accelerate from nought to 62 mph in less than two seconds. The boats race on large lakes and dams, not in the sea.

Liz and I used to travel all over South Africa to commentate on this exhilarating sport. We became great friends with a South African F1 Powerboat Champion, Fred Stynberg and his girlfriend. I recall one particular race that demonstrated how dangerous the sport is. I was down to commentate at a race in Natal, not far from Durban.

Fred was wearing a full-face helmet for the first time in a race. To our dismay, halfway through the race, Fred's boat veered to avoid another, at about a 100 mph. The right-hand side sponson dipped into the water, and the boat cart wheeled before disappearing under the dark, deep waters of the lake. For what seemed like an eternity, all we could see were the ripples on the surface; then a rescue boat arrived, and a diver went over the side into the water. We were told later that Fred had been underwater for nearly 40 seconds. Not that long unless you are under water, upside down, in water so dark that you cannot see where you are and wearing a full-face helmet that is filling up with water. Fred later explained that the first thing you have to do when you go under like that is to let some bubbles out of your mouth, so that you can work out which way is up. Apparently it is all too easy to be totally disorientated due to the somersaulting of the boat and the darkness under water. It makes the hairs stand up on the back of my neck to think of it, even as I'm writing this now.

Another sport on which I regularly commentated in South Africa was speedway. It's a sport I have always loved, but although it has now grown to the level where its major international series is owned by IMG, the American sports marketing company that manages many of the world's top sports stars; in South Africa, at that time it was very basic but fun. Having decided to retire from race driving, I thought seriously about developing my sports broadcasting career and put a few feelers out.

I had been invited to Pretoria to meet Peter Cleary and his team at Mercedes Benz HQ. There was a lot to be discussed, not least of all the future of Corporate Racing, the business that we had set up to run the Honda's in the 1987 Championship. Then there was Mike O'Sullivan. He'd had been a great choice to run the team and the car preparation and had tried relentlessly to get the best out of the cars. That we hadn't hit the levels of success that we had had targeted was due to several factors, most of which were outside his control. I genuinely don't think I let the side down from a driving point of view; I was usually no more than two-tenths of a second behind Mike in qualifying and learned a lot about driving saloon cars from him. The problems lay more with the rigidity of the technical and marketing governance we were experiencing. I'd shown in the previous season what could be achieved with the Honda. The reality was that Toyota hadn't sat on their laurels during the off-season. Neither had Delta, or Opel, as we know it in Europe. Whilst we had been involved in setting up a totally new operation, they had both homologated a few specification changes that made a vital difference from the start of the season.

With the Stannic Group N Championship being so fiercely competitive, the ability to find a quarter of a second a lap was all that it took to make a big difference. Despite all of Mike's efforts, we had always been on the back foot. Mike, I knew, was keen to continue a relationship with Mercedes Benz South Africa, and I tried all I could to make sure that his proposals were met with a positive response.

Once we'd worked out the financial settlements and handover of the company to Mike, my work was done, and I was ready to say my goodbyes to the people within Mercedes who had been very supportive of my efforts to promote Honda over the past couple of years.

I wasn't expecting an invitation from Peter Cleary to have a coffee with him before I left the building. As soon as we had sat down, he got straight to the point of the meeting, asking me what I was planning to do, now that I had called a day on my racing career. When I told him that I seriously didn't have any plans, other than taking a holiday and give the matter some serious thought, he told me about some new plans that Mercedes were about to put into action.

He explained that the Board of Mercedes Benz South Africa was quite concerned that the recent increase in the number of specialist sports car businesses opening up in the major cities was having a detrimental effect on their Official Dealer's sales performance. This didn't come as a huge surprise to me. I had seen the growth of businesses that sold exotic sports cars, usually used cars, such as Bloomsbury Carriage Company, The House of Sports Cars and Ashley's. Many of these cars were taken in on consignment, meaning that a car was left on the showroom floor by the owner, on the basis that if it was sold, the dealership would take a sizeable commission.

Mercedes had been increasingly aware that their dealers were finding it difficult to buy in stock of their own sports cars; and that increasingly, Mercedes sports models were ending up in the hands of these specialist sports car dealers. This was not helping the authorised Mercedes dealerships.

As Peter went on talking about this problem, I was beginning to wonder what it had to do with me. Then he explained, telling me that he had been very impressed with the work that I had carried out for McCarthy Motors as its Honda Sales Manager. He explained that the company was going to open a small number of new Mercedes dealerships in South Africa, which would specialise in the sale and purchase of second-hand exotic sports cars and other specialist high-value models, competing in the market sector currently being dominated by small private companies, such as those I have already mentioned. The new dealerships would operate under the new brand name of Mercedes Silverline, with showrooms in selected prime locations. They would have a different brand identity to the normal Mercedes Dealerships, more fitting to the sale of sports cars such as Ferrari, Aston Martin, Maserati, Porsche and so on.

It was sounding interesting, and I was waiting to hear where I might fit in. I didn't have long to wait.

As ever, Peter came straight to the point, telling me that the first of the Silverline Dealerships within South Africa would be opened in the upmarket Johannesburg northern suburb of Sandton; probably in Sandton City, the enormous shopping mall that dominated the skyline, at that time. The Sandown Motor Group, which operated the existing Mercedes Dealership within the region, would be funding the new concept. Peter then added that he would like me to become Sales Manager of the new business.

The package that I was offered was way above what I would have expected and included the company flying an AMG 300E in from Germany as my company car. In addition to that, Liz, as my wife, would be entitled to a Honda Ballade. Until the new showroom was ready, I would be based at the Sandton branch of Sandown Motors.

There was little doubt in my mind that whilst this wouldn't take me back into motorsport as such, the connection would be there indirectly and I decided that it was too good an offer to turn down. The certainty of our future meant that we could now invest in a house and we moved into an area called Paulshof, still very close to the Kyalami Circuit, but just a few miles from Sandton City.

I had to go and buy a couple of suits and some shirts and ties, which would replace the race team uniform of the past couple of years. I felt quite nervous on my first morning as I sat in the traffic jam heading into work, but I was very much looking forward to what was going to be quite a demanding challenge. Little did I know just how much of a challenge it would turn out to be, but in a different way to what I was expecting.

The first week went OK. I took delivery of my new car, as did Liz hers. Then on the Friday afternoon, I was informed that I was invited to join the management team in the bar at 5:30 p.m. What bar, I remember asking. The Dealer Principal's Bar, was the answer. Apparently this was a regular occurrence on a Friday evening, and as far as I could see from my first attendance, comprised a couple of the management team believing themselves to being very funny, like stand-up comedians, whilst everyone laughed politely. As the drinks flowed, so the laughter got louder. Having avoided alcohol completely whilst I was racing, I wasn't keen to follow the trend and risk picking up a drunk-driving charge on the way back home. I was assured that there were very few roadblocks to this effect and encouraged to follow the herd. It wasn't my style.

Then, on the Monday morning, came the bad news. I was informed that Sandown Motors had taken on a sales director, and I would be reporting to him. OK, I thought, that isn't too much of a problem until I was told who it would be. The person in question was leaving his role at Mercedes Benz South Africa and joining Sandown Motors. I had first met him whilst I was working for McCarthy Motor Group. Whereas I got on really well with most of my contacts within Mercedes Benz, including their management team of Gavin Sharpe and Hans Keisser, based in Cape Town, on the few occasions I had any dealings with this person, I found him pompous and quite rude. He was one of those people who just never listened to what you were saying and talked over you all the time.

The situation wasn't helped when it was announced that most of the Dealership team would be heading off to three-day conference at the Royal Swazi Spa Hotel in Swaziland, me included. I really didn't enjoy the event, particularly the two-faced whinging and moaning that went on behind the scenes. In my opinion, there didn't seem to be room for any innovative thinking and ideas. It seemed to me that the word "change" was not a popular one within the retail motor trade. I recall sitting there, remembering my days with Xerox and the constant input of new ideas and approaches to selling their products. If only some of that company's management team could have been at this conference!

I'd been in the role about five weeks when this new sales director first walked into the showroom. Within two more weeks of dealing with him, I'd had enough. To my dismay, the decisions about the new Silverline branch were being constantly delayed, and I was beginning to wonder if they would ever happen. (I may be wrong in this, but to my knowledge, they never did materialise in the format that I had been assured they would.)

The Friday evening gatherings were now being dominated by one man. I was being treated like a second-hand car salesman by him, and I knew that I had two choices.

Looking back, I think that the situation hadn't been helped by the fact that I'd become used to being my own boss and making my own decisions. However, I still strongly believe had he not been there, I might have been tempted to give it more of a go. It was obvious that he and the Dealer Principal were by now as chummy as you could become; and that, my face, really didn't fit.

I waited for another week to see if things were likely to improve, then one evening drove home from the showroom and told Liz that we would have to take the cars back, because I was going to resign the next day. I wasn't sure what her reaction would be, but I should have done. She told me that she was surprised it had taken this long, adding that I'd been like a bear with a sore tooth for the past few weeks and that she could fully understand why. Her next comment was more down to earth, asking me how we would be able to pay the bond (mortgage) repayments on the house. What I then told her came as a big surprise! When I had finished, she laughed, went into the kitchen and came out with two glasses of wine, suggesting that we should go and sit beside the pool, whilst I told her in detail what my plans involved.

It probably appears that I was a bit headstrong in arriving at my decision to resign after just a couple of months in my new role, and I wouldn't blame anyone for thinking that. However, I had been making plans behind the scenes, once I saw the writing on the wall at the dealership. The more I thought about the situation, the more I knew that I had to get back to working for myself. I certainly didn't consider returning to race-driving, but I did come to my senses and realise that motor racing was my passion, and that I had taken the easy option when offered such a tempting opportunity by Peter Cleary. It had been a mistake; my mistake, and no one else's.

My passion for motorsport was complemented by a genuine interest and enjoyment in training sales people. This had come to the fore in my time with ITT, where I had been the company's UK Sales Training Director. That interest was confirmed when I created the sales training programmes that featured the cast of the BBC TV series *Are You Being Served?* Once I had come to the conclusion that I wasn't enjoying life at Sandown Motors, I racked my brain, trying to find a way that I could combine my passion for racing with the level of satisfaction that training had given me.

The answer came to me, as the best ideas often do, whilst I was lying awake in bed one night, unable to sleep because of the intense heat and the rush of thoughts racing through my mind.

I would start a racing driver school.

To the best of my knowledge, there hadn't ever been one in South Africa. There most definitely wasn't one now. The problem that instantly came to mind was that you needed a race track to be able to run a school, and that the cost of setting up such an operation would be immense. For a start, there were the cars, the equipment to maintain them, and then there was the staff requirement, including instructors. Finally, the cost of advertising and promotion would be considerable.

Wide awake in bed, these initial issues seemed almost insurmountable to me, but in the cold light of day, as I sat in the traffic queuing on the road to the showroom, I realised that the only way forward was to forget looking at such a big overall picture and to break it down into manageable sections. It struck me that the most important factor to be dealt with had to be the use of a racing circuit. This immediately narrowed the scenario down to a manageable level. At that time there, the only race tracks in regular use were in Johannesburg, Port Elizabeth, Cape Town, Lichtenburg, and Welkom. I started looking at the logistics of operation and the potential catchment market, quickly coming to the conclusion that the best place to start such a business would be in the Johannesburg region. Kyalami had been rebuilt into its new modern format, and whilst it offered the best facilities for operating a racing school, it also presented a major problem inasmuch that it would be very demanding as an instructional venue. What I needed initially was a short track, about the size of the Brands Hatch club circuit, one and a quarter miles, where instructing would be much less demanding than on a circuit twice the size. Then I remembered where Mike O'Sullivan and I had carried out the very early testing of the two Honda Group N cars the previous year, the Swartkops circuit, situated midway between Johannesburg and Pretoria. It was a short circuit but ideal for teaching the basic skills. It wasn't being used for racing since having been purchased by a wealthy businessman, David Cohen, who owned and raced a Ford GT 40 in a few historic events. He allowed other historic competitors to use the circuit, albeit that it wasn't licensed with the governing body, the MSA, for actual racing.

Within two days, I had set up a meeting with David and agreed a deal which would allow me to hire the circuit to run a racing school for a certain number of days a month. We agreed on what was effectively a "peppercorn" rental. The track boasted a three-storey control tower from which we could operate and incorporated a room that would make an ideal classroom. On the negative side, it also contained a drive-in cinema, situated in the middle of the circuit, around which the race track ran. It was sited right beside a very fast downhill, then uphill corner, which might prove problematical. The drive-in was no longer in use, but still had the individual car ramps and the audio posts alongside each parking space.

I now had a race track, but no cars. I thought back to my relationship in Cape Town with Anelma, a couple of years ago, and remembered that she had a relative who was the marketing director for Toyota South Africa. I'd met him a couple of times, and he seemed a straight down the line but very approachable person. I called Anelma and checked that she was OK with my approaching him again. I met Francois Laubser the following day and explained what I was planning, adding that I was doing this on a shoestring and wondered if he could help with some race cars. He immediately saw the opportunity that this offered Toyota and promised to give it some thought as to the best way forward.

Within a couple of days, Francois offered me the loan of three of the previous season's fully race-prepared Group N cars that had been so successful in the championship. These were 1600cc Toyota Conquest hatchbacks. They were fitted with all the right equipment, including roll cages, racing seats and full six-point harnesses; and each car was a different colour, important at a school.

Much as I would have liked a number of single-seater Formula Fords, they would have to wait until we were generating revenue. Nevertheless, here I was, within the space of ten days, with a race track and some race cars. I firmly believed that I had put together a solid platform for building an innovative and potentially successful business. What I needed now was some serious sponsorship. I knew that wasn't going to be easy. After all, most South African business personnel probably wouldn't know what a racing driver school was, let alone have any idea as to how that might benefit their companies.

Chapter 24
Back to School, Sponsorship Success, Camel Rookies

Having taken the decision to go back to being an entrepreneur, rather than a corporate employee, I felt as if a great weight had been taken off my shoulders. I was now waking up every morning, really looking forward to the huge challenges that lay ahead, if we were to launch South Africa's first racing driver school. Within a couple of days, I came up with the name for the new business. The Speed International Racing Driver School struck the right chord and I was now in my element putting together innovative plans for securing the funding that I needed. There was no such thing then as Crowd Funding and I didn't want to seek investment as such. Instead, I would adopt the route that I knew best, seeking commercial sponsorship, and set about devising what I felt was an innovative strategy.

Having retired from racing, Brian and his wife, Liz, started South Africa's first racing driver school. Initially operating at the Swartkops Circuit, near Pretoria, the school progressed to the newly rebuilt Kyalami GP Circuit. They are pictured here with one of their very first school race cars, courtesy of Toyota Motorsport

My experience told me that as this was the first school of its kind, few companies in South Africa would fully understand the potential that Speed International offered as a dynamic marketing and business development platform. I came to the conclusion that my first step should be to make contact with the people who had supported my racing programme up to that point. Autoquip was a very successful

157

business, with branches across South Africa. It offered a wide range of high performance motoring and motorsport equipment, including wheels, tyres, exhaust systems, competition seats, safety harnesses, race clothing and helmets. I had developed a good relationship with its CEO, Bruce Coquelle, who was first and foremost a businessman, but he also loved motor racing. He was a totally straight down the line individual and was always seemed keen to help me. I think that from our very first meeting, some years back, he understood that on the occasions that I presented a sponsorship opportunity to his company, it was always based on a potential to sell more products, rather than simply to increase brand awareness, as is usually the case in the majority of motorsport sponsorship proposals, even today.

When I took him out to lunch and outlined my plans for Speed International, he immediately saw the huge business potential and told me that he wanted Autoquip to be involved from the beginning. Right then and there, we agreed a sponsorship deal that, in addition to a fee, would provide Speed International with an on-going supply of items such as open-face helmets, race suits, uniforms for our staff, equipment for the workshops and a lot more. To be successful at my first meeting with a potential sponsor was a great feeling.

Using a similar strategy, I was able to conclude sponsorship deals with Ferodo, for what would be a much-needed supply of competition brake pads, with Sabat for batteries and with Continental for huge cost-saving deal on tyres.

There was one piece of equipment that I needed at Speed International, without which it would be difficult to operate. Due to the sanctions that had been imposed on the country, I was unable to purchase what are best known as tell-tale rev counters. As I knew from my days at the Thruxton and the Jim Russell schools in the UK, it is essential that instructors are able to monitor rev-limits that they have given to novice race-drivers at varying stages of the course. At most racing schools, they were able to achieve this by means of a normal clock-face style rev counter, the sort you see in road cars, which has a second mandatory needle. This needle, normally coloured a bright red, sticks at the maximum revs used and can only be reset by the instructor.

I tried as many sources as I could for a supply of these to fit into our Toyotas but without any luck. Then an idea came into my head. I contacted one of the leading universities in Johannesburg and spoke to the head of their electrical engineering department, explaining my predicament. He immediately showed an interest in trying to help and suggested that he could get a couple of his under-graduates to work on the problem. When it came to discussing costs, he told me that I would need to simply pay for any parts or equipment used. It was a perfect scenario, and I left him to get on with the task.

Now, I was free to concentrate on the marketing of the new school. I had plenty of experience of working with racing driver schools in the UK to understand some of the pitfalls of this type of business. For a start, the very people who would appear to be the prime target, youngsters who wanted to get into race-driving, rarely had the money to pay the not inconsiderable costs of instruction. The real markets at which I decided to aim Speed International were:

- Males and females aged between 25 and 45, who had no intention of become professional race drivers, but had the disposal income to enjoy learning to drive at high speed on a track. Many of these might own a high performance road car.
- Companies that were looking for new activities to use as part of their sales incentive and staff motivation programmes.
- Clubs and associations related to cars and motoring, such as the Ferrari Owners Club and the MG Car Club, that might be keen to book the school exclusively for their members to receive tuition in our cars before using their own expensive vehicles.
- Parents looking for unusual gifts for special occasions for their family members (Red Letter Days didn't exist then!).
- 17–25 year olds who did want to get into motor racing and wanted to test their level of talent before forking our money to buy a race car or kart.

Whilst I was confident in my own ability to generate a great deal of media coverage for the opening of the new business, I realised that it was more important to target this at a wide range of publications and media sources, not just at the obvious motoring and motorsport media. I designed a media strategy that would target as wide a market as possible, not least of all the business, lifestyle, high-worth individuals, automotive and motorsport sectors.

Finally, I needed to focus on a title sponsor for the school. That would be the tough one, as I was sensible enough to realise that whilst Speed International was an innovative new concept and would offer a high level of media coverage, that in itself didn't offer anywhere near enough measurable value to a company in return for the level of fee that I would require. For a start, the track itself was very basic, with little in the way of hospitality facilities; and on top of that, we only had three race cars.

I realised that I would have to be very canny if I was to attract a major brand to become involved with the school and help take it to the next level. It wasn't just simply the fee that was important to me. I knew from experience that by joining forces with a major brand, we would benefit incredibly from the professional level of PR that they would bring as part of the deal. No company would commit to such an involvement as I was seeking and then want it to fail. It was in their interest to put as much resource in as they could, and that was the real value in bringing a title sponsor on-board. We weren't in a position to spend a fortune on advertising, and a major sponsor could do so much to help offset this.

I was also looking for what I usually refer to as "quick win" marketing strategy. In other words, I need to find a way of encouraging someone to sign up for a course straightaway, rather than waiting until they could see how the school was developing. This was particularly true of the youngsters wanting to get into racing, but who, almost by definition, had the lowest level of disposal income.

My mind went into overdrive on this particular issue, as I started putting my plans together and working out a time-schedule as to when we could launch the school.

I haven't mentioned Liz's involvement at this stage, but I must. As I've mentioned before, for someone who had grown up in South Africa, where motor racing isn't at the socially acceptable level that it is in Britain, she took to my four-wheeled world like a duck to water. She thrived on being given a high level of responsibility and took on the task of setting up the administrative systems for the new business, including building a data base of potential customers, both from the business sector and the motor clubs. She also took on the responsibility for fitting out the control tower at the track, which was particularly tough as everything had to be removed at the end of a course, including classroom chairs, white boards and so forth. Then there was the accounting and banking systems to put in place; and finally, the implementation of some of my marketing activities, such as the printing of brochures, badging of instructors' uniforms, caps and so forth. She had also agreed that she would handle all telephone sales enquiries; and finally, but the most important in some ways, the catering at the track. South Africans are renowned for enjoying their food and at a track such as Swartkops, which didn't have a café of any sort, meeting their simple but sizeable culinary requirements was no mean feat.

We had designed an office in the roof area of our new house and came to the conclusion that we should look into the ways in which the purchase of a PC might help our business. Neither of us had any experience whatsoever of these new-fangled pieces of equipment, and we tried to get as much advice as we could. Liz took the lead on this, and I came back from the track one afternoon to find a brand new ARC World computer sitting on the desk in our office. In case you are wondering what was so great about this, I need to remind you that we are talking about the days before anyone had heard of Windows, Google or the Internet. This was pure and simple DOS-operated computing. Believe me, it was not easy! You had to control everything by pushing the F-buttons, even at the end of a line of typing. It was so primitive compared to today's PCs. On the subject of Windows, I have to admit that this new device came very close on more than once occasion on being hurled out of our office window and into the swimming pool. Luckily, Liz had a lot more patience than I did, even if she did occasionally sneak into the first computer game that either of us had experienced, consisting of a game of tennis with the ball bleeping its way from one side of the screen to the other.

Whilst Liz was pressing on with her mountain of responsibilities, I was ready to move forward with my sponsorship acquisition strategy. What I had finally done was to combine the "quick win" requirement that I mentioned, with the approach to a potential title sponsor. I'd also decided upon the company that I felt would be an ideal candidate for my new concept. I'd put together a very simple sponsorship property document, using our new pet computer. I think the process aged me by about ten years!

I achieved my first objective, which was to secure a meeting in Johannesburg with Peter Buckley, Country Manager (South Africa) for R J Reynolds Tobacco Company. You may recall that in 1987, the Lotus Formula 1 Team, for whom Ayrton Senna was driving, ran in the distinctive yellow livery of Camel. The company was also well known for its global Camel Trophy competition, involving Land Rover 4x4 vehicles, all pained in the distinctive Camel livery.

I began our meeting by explaining the Speed International project to Peter, who seemed quite interested in what I was planning. This gave me the confidence to introduce the "quick win" concept on which I had been working. I explained to Peter that my idea was to initiate an annual competition at Speed International, to identify the most promising pupil. However, that same confidence was quickly dispelled when Peter interrupted my flow of ideas and bluntly stated, whilst he could see where this was going, he needed to point out that he had no budget whatsoever for anything of this type. This certainly wasn't the first time that an objection of this type had been put in front of me, and it wouldn't be the last, that was for sure.

I wasn't going to argue with him as I knew that would lead nowhere, so I simply asked if the high-profile Camel Trophy programme was taking up most of his South African budget. He admitted that it was, and I could see from his attitude that it was not only my project that was being rejected. I could fully understand his predicament, as it happens a lot in international operations, where each country is required to contribute its fair share to a high cost multi-country sponsorship programme.

I then asked for his opinion of the project that I had put forward. He quite openly admitted that it was very innovative, and, had he a budget, he might have thought more about a possible involvement of some sort. It was the opening that I had hoped for. I immediately told him I fully appreciated his budget restrictions, but wondered if I might ask a couple of specific questions. He smiled and told me to go ahead. He seemed like an open-minded person, quite rare in some ways. He was actually prepared to listen, which was even rarer.

Here goes, I thought to myself, firing off the first question. I asked him whether or not he would able to supply the school with a large number of Camel-branded T-shirts and baseball-style caps as a promotional activity. He nodded that it might be possible. Then I enquired whether he would be able to find the budget to fly the winner of what I was already referring to as The Camel Rookie of the Year Challenge to the UK and back. He thought for a moment and then again agreed that it might be possible to lose such an item of travel expenditure within his operational budget. I was nearly there!

I took a deep breath and went ahead with my last two questions, the answers to which would determine whether I would be walking out of his office with my tail between my legs or with a smile on my face.

Brian introduced the annual Camel Rookie of the Year Challenge at the new racing school, to identify the top pupil. The winner was flown to the UK for a test in a Camel sponsored Paul Stewart Racing, FF2000 car. Sir Jackie Stewart's son Paul, at the Donington Park Test in 1988, with Brian and Liz.

The first was straightforward. I asked him if he would be able to arrange a test-day in the UK for the winner of the Camel Rookie of the Year Challenge, ideally in the Camel-sponsored Formula Ford 2000, raced in the UK by Paul Stewart, Jackie Stewart's son. I watched his face as he pondered this question. His response was positive, suggesting that R J Reynolds pay them enough as a sponsor to expect them to co-operate with that sort of request. By now Peter was smiling, and I got the impression he was enjoying the journey that I was describing.

It was now time for the big one. I took another deep breath and asked Peter if he would be prepared to allow his external PR agency, which I had researched carefully, to work with us to promote the Camel Rookie of the Year Challenge within South Africa. His answer came quickly, asking me if I had heard what he had said right at the beginning, the fact that he had no budget.

I assured him that I had and asked if I could quickly explain my new proposal.

Half an hour later, I walked out of Peter Buckley's office with a hand-shaken agreement that Camel would be the new sponsors of the Rookie of the Year Challenge for an initial one-year agreement. There would be no sponsorship fee involved, but the school would be supplied with Camel merchandise, as I had proposed. There would be Camel branding on the school cars, a return air ticket to London would be paid for the winner of the Challenge, a test-day with Paul Stewart Racing would be organised at the Donington Park Circuit, near Derby; and finally, it was agreed that Digby Wesson, who ran Camel's external agency in South Africa, would work with me to promote the new competition.

With the exception of a fee, it was everything that I could have possibly hoped for. I knew that on the back of such a prestigious, albeit perceived, sponsorship, I would be able to secure a meaningful fee-paying title sponsor, one that would not conflict in any way with Camel. I had explained the need for such a fee-paying sponsor, and Peter fully understood that, confirming that it would be agreeable to R J Reynolds, subject to my telling him, at a later stage, who it would be.

Wow! This was really happening, and all in the space of less than two months since handing in my resignation at the Mercedes Dealership. I knew right then, even though I hadn't generated a penny in sponsorship fees, that I had made the right decision.

Despite all of my efforts, however, I couldn't put together a strategy that really enthuse me, for securing a title sponsor, so there was no point in just knocking on company doors. I'm the world's worst salesman if I am not totally enthused about what I am offering.

Liz and I talked about the best way forward and came to the conclusion that it would be best to put the sponsorship search on hold until after the launch of Speed International. It turned out to be a good decision.

True to his word, Peter Buckley set up an initial strategy meeting for us both with Digby Wesson, whom I knew from my Kyalami days. Between us, we came up with some great ideas for promoting the launch of the school, effectively on the back of the Camel Rookie of the Year programme. It was amazing, but not surprising, the impact that the Camel name had when talking to media personnel. It was just what I had hoped.

People were now phoning us, having heard rumours about the new school; and Liz once again proved herself to be an accomplished salesperson, convincing the majority of callers to take advantage of the special trial lesson offer that we had thought up. Bearing in mind that this was the first school of its type in South Africa, word got around very quickly.

We took delivery of the cars from Toyota. They looked stunning in their new livery. Then I had to start learning some basic car mechanics, which was far from my comfort zone, but there was no alternative. We just couldn't afford a full-time mechanic to carry out the end of each day's check-over, in respect of possible brake pad changes, tyre changes and other basic maintenance.

Then I had to design the courses and sort out a roster of potential instructors. That wasn't as easy as it might seem. I spent a few hours contacting drivers who I felt had not only the skills, but the communication ability to become good teachers. I was very aware that every person who contacted Speed International was potentially a paying customer. The way in which they were treated, from their first phone enquiry to their initial classroom lesson and subsequent exposure to track driving, was critical to the ultimate success of the business. I often thought back to my early experience at the Brands Hatch "Motor Racing Stables", during which I had been made to feel quite awkward and unwelcome in so many ways. I was determined not to let that happen at Speed International; the slowest, most untalented customer would be treated in the same way as the most promising. I wanted them all to end the day thinking that they had experienced something very special and would go away and tell their contacts.

Amongst the team of instructors whom I eventually gathered together was a South African, Kenny Gray. We had worked together as instructors some ten years before, at the Scorpion Racing Driver School at Thruxton in England and raced against each other in Formula Ford. Prior to an unfortunate track accident, Kenny was one of the quickest Formula Ford drivers I'd come across. With my intention of introducing Formula Fords to the school in due course, he would be a great asset. Other instructors included well known South African racers including Chad Wentzel, Alan Kerwick and Andy Keil, all of whom would prove to be excellent in all aspects of the role.

One of major problems, in those early days, was a logistical one, involving the task of getting three race cars, 24 fold-up chairs, a huge circuit layout whiteboard, catering equipment and supplies, a stack of race helmets and appropriate tools from our house in Paulshof, about 15 miles from Swartkops, to the circuit and then home again each evening. In case you are wondering why we didn't leave much of the stuff there at the track overnight, the answer is very simple. We knew that if we did, it was unlikely to be there the next morning. There were no electric security fences, or armed response patrols or any other form of security, other than an old five-bar gate and wire mesh fencing. I think you can start to see that Liz and I really were taking on a huge challenge in getting this business up and running.

The race cars were street legal but rather noisy. In our very early days, until we got to know our instructors well enough to get one up really early to help with the task, we would have the three cars at my house overnight, where I would work on them. Then in the early morning, to avoid the traffic, Liz and I would drive two of them to the circuit. Once we had unpacked everything else that we managed to get into the cars, we'd drive back home in one car to fetch the third one.

It was exhausting stuff, but we were enjoying ourselves and the interest level in Speed International was increasing dramatically. Our Launch Day, to which we had invited the media to become "guinea-pig" pupils for the day, went incredibly well; and it generated some amazing coverage, including two TV features on the main free-to-air channels, each feature over five minutes in duration.

We knew that we had to pace ourselves and not try to be greedy by running the school every day. We settled on a five-day course, our zero to hero programme, as we called it, once a month, with two individual days of lessons each week. It was still physically tiring. The 24 chairs, all shiny red and embossed with the Speed International logo, had to be hauled up, and then back down, two flights of a quite rickety open staircase on the outside of the Control Tower building. In addition to packing the helmets for the students, Liz had to prepare the catering for the day. One thing was for sure, we were both going to be incredibly fit.

The thing that kept us going through all of this planning and setting up was the fact that not only did we genuinely believe that the school would take off in a big way and soon we would be able to employ staff to take the pressure off us, but most importantly, we were working together, which gave us a lot of pleasure.

Launch Day for Speed International came along very quickly. We had already started to enjoy some enthusiastic media coverage, and the percentage of acceptances from individual media personnel to the opening Media Day was exceptionally high. As Liz and I were asked to line-up with the cars and instructors for the photo sessions, we both felt very proud of our new business.

Despite a request from the instructors that because of the heat, they be allowed to wear branded T-shirts and shorts, instead of the branded, lightweight race suits, I stuck to my guns. I explained to them that customers' perception of the staff was just as important as the level of instruction. When you go to a racing driver school, you expect your instructors to be professionally dressed. Launch photos of instructors in shorts sent out the wrong message.

We received a level of publicity way beyond our expectations; and when SABC TV phone to say that they wanted to come and record a feature for their Graffiti programme, we were over the moon. *CAR* magazine also sent one of their top journalists, Dave Pollock, to do a course at Speed International, resulting in a comprehensive, positive 3-page feature in full colour. The bookings poured in; and whilst Liz was kept busy with managing these, I was kept at full stretch, instructing and then preparing the three race cars.

The deal that I had put together with Camel was one of the best things I could have done. It upped the profile of the school and provided that "quick win" scenario that I had been looking for. To qualify to take part in the Camel Rookie of the Year Challenge, customers had to have completed all three stages into which the course was divided. It was not open to anyone with a full competition license.

The primary concept of the Camel Rookie Challenge was to find the person who was able to drive ten full laps of the Swartkops Circuit at the highest average speed, but with the shortest gap between their fastest lap time and their slowest, within the rev limit that was permitted. This all involved a mathematical calculation, the results of which would then be added to points scored by competitors in an interview with the panel of judges. These interviews would determine a person's motivation and promotability, to go together with their skill levels in the race car.

The completion comprised four qualifying rounds, followed by two semi-finals, with the 24 going through to the final of the Camel Rookie of the Year Challenge.

Chapter 25
Innovation, Judges and Hire Cars

To be able to run the Camel Rookie of the Year Challenge, we needed the tell-tale rev counters that I talked about earlier. I'd given the brief to Wits University to design such a piece of equipment. They came up with something that was not only as good as an imported instrument, from a company such as Stack or VDS, but was actually far better for my purposes.

The finished item was a digital rev-counter in a case about the size of TV remote which fitted under the dashboard on the passenger side of the car. It was linked to the dashboard rev counter. The instructor could set it to zero with a small key, and at the end of a driver's session, could take two readings. One was the maximum revs the driver had used, whilst the other, even more important reading, was the total number of seconds the car had been over the set rev-limit during the session. Why was this so important? Because it prevented a situation in which a driver, who had maybe over-revved on his or her first lap by 500 rev for example, took the view that he or she might as well use that level for the remainder of their session. The ability to detect how many seconds the driver had been over-revving would eradicate that. It was a vital feature, for which I am eternally grateful to Wits University.

I had designed the Camel Rookie of the Year Challenge, based on one simple, but vitally important skill that a racing driver needs, to be able to progress in the sport. I knew that it was quite easy to ask each entrant in the Challenge to set the fastest lap time that they could over a ten lap stint. Then the top few would qualify to the next round and so on until the final. That was far too easy in my opinion. I wanted to add another tough element that would serve them well in any subsequent racing activities. I knew that if a driver had ten laps to set a fast time, there would be at least one or two laps where they almost shut their eyes, took a huge breath and got around a corner at high speed without going off the track. However, ask them to set an identical time again and again and again for ten laps, they would really struggle.

Setting up a race car, to get the best out of it, is a key part of racing. Imagine that a driver asks his race engineer to make a very small change, maybe to an anti-roll bar setting, and then he goes back on the track to try it out. The best way of knowing if it has been a positive change is to check the subsequent lap times. The problem with that, however, is that if a driver has done, shall we say four laps before coming in for the roll bar adjustment and his lap times were:

Lap 1/52.4 secs; Lap 2/53.2 secs; Lap 3/51.8 secs; Lap 4/53.6 secs

Then he goes out again, after the adjustment, for four more laps, achieving times of:

Lap 1/53.2 secs; Lap 2/51.9 secs; Lap 3/54.8 secs; Lap 4/52.4 secs

If the race engineer looks at those times, how can he possibly tell whether his roll bar adjustment has helped or hindered the search for a faster lap time? Imagine the difference if the driver's lap times had looked like this before coming in:

1/52.4 secs; 2/52.6 secs ; 3/52.5 secs ; 4/52.4 secs

Then after the adjustment:

1/52.2 secs; 2/52.3 secs; 3/52.1 secs; 4/52.3 secs

Now, the race engineer can be sure that there is a definite, albeit small improvement.

The ability to turn in lap after lap with a maximum of three-tenths of a second difference between the fastest and the slowest lap is of paramount importance to a race driver. If lap times are all over the place and totally inconsistent, it will always be difficult if not impossible to make adjustments to that race car.

Watch the top F1 drivers in practice and qualifying and see how consistent they are. It's a vital skill, as I think you can see.

With the aid of the new electronic rev-monitors, it enabled me, with the help of a University mathematician, to create a formula that could be applied to every Challenge competitor's performance over ten laps of the Swartkops circuit. It was based on their fastest lap, their slowest lap, the gap between the two and any over revving they had done. In the early heats of the event, it worked better than I had dared hope. It seemed as though our friends at Wits University had done us proud.

The heats and semi-finals went well and we were building up to the Final. I'd decided on our panel of judges, inviting three high-profile members of the South African motorsport and automotive media, Geoff Dalgeish, Dave Trebbett and Mike Winfield all of whom had been incredibly supportive of our Speed International initiative. They were joined by John Kirkpatrick, who had been my instructor, back in 1972, at the world-famous racing Jim Russell Racing Driver School at the Snetterton Circuit in England. John went on to own the school, and we became good friends.

I was able to invite John out to South Africa because of two sponsorships that I had put together on the back of the Camel deal. The first was with Luxavia, a Luxembourg-based airline which operated twice-weekly flights from London to Johannesburg, via Luxembourg. The deal was very simple, inasmuch that it didn't involve any money, but provided Liz and myself with 1st Class travel between London and South Africa for an agreed maximum number of flights per year, which I think was eight. I negotiated that this would also include flying John Kirkpatrick to and from South Africa for the Camel Final.

The second deal that proved very attractive was one that I mentioned earlier with Safari-Plan, the company that ran the Tanda-Tula Safari Camp in the Northern Transvaal, now remained Limpopo Province. The deal was based on my creating awareness of the camp with international motorsport visitors to South Africa. When I mentioned John Kirkpatrick's visit to South Africa to Jon and Sally Panos, the camp's owners, and outlined the proposed media coverage he would be getting, they suggested that Liz and I should bring him up to Tanda Tula for a few days. It made the trip a very attractive one for John, and it clinched the deal. He would come over to RSA as a Camel Final judge, adding huge credibility to our Speed International initiative.

One aspect of the new business for which I hadn't been able to secure sponsorship was the insurance of the three race cars. Nobody wanted to touch it. In the UK, it was now big business, but hadn't been deemed relevant in South Africa. Not being covered was a major concern, and then Liz came up with an idea. She remembered a couple of friend, husband and wife, whom she hadn't seen for quite a while and had a feeling that Gavin was involved in the insurance industry somehow. She made a call; and the next thing I knew, we were having supper with them at our house.

To my amazement, Gavin was really interested in Speed International and asked how he could help us. When we explained our predicament about insurance, he told us that he was sure he could sort something for us. He kept to his word. A phone call early the following week told us that our three cars were now fully insured at what seemed to be a very realistic premium.

We were now very close to day of the Final and making sure that everything was in place. We knew that there would be a lot of media coverage of the event, and that everything had to run like clockwork. The week before the Final, we ran a couple of school days at the track, bearing in mind that we were a business and needed regular revenue.

I was standing in the pit lane, talking to a couple of pupils when I heard a huge screeching of tyres, an engine revving its guts up and then a horrible loud noise like an explosion, followed by the sight of a spiralling dust-cloud. Then total silence!

I jumped in one of the cars and sped around the track to the corner, in front of the drive-in cinema. There it was, one of the school's three race cars, nose down in the grass between the track and the Armco barrier, as if it had dived down from the sky. A figure in white crash helmet was running up the bank, away from me. I couldn't believe my eyes when I saw the state of the car; it looked totalled. Then I decided that I should find out if the driver was OK. He was by now standing in the drive-in cinema area, leaning against of the many speaker posts. His helmet was now off, but his face was just as white as the helmet had been.

From my rather limited conversation with him, it appeared that he had been approaching the left-hand downhill corner too fast. Instead of following the tuition we'd been providing, telling pupils that when that situation arose in a front-wheeled drive car, never to slam the brakes on, he had done exactly the opposite. The car had subsequently hurtled into a 90 degree turn, up the small banking, spun into the air and landed on its nose. What could I say to him, other than to remind him he was very lucky not to have been seriously hurt.

My problems had only just started. The Finals were on the following week, and now we were a car short. Then I remembered the insurance. Liz immediately got on the phone to Gavin. I was glad, because I think I was too much of a coward to explain that just days after insuring the cars, this had happened. To his credit, when Liz had explained what had happened, Gavin's first words were to ask if I was OK. When she assured him that I hadn't been in the car, I'm not sure what his follow-up words might have been!

The car went to the panel-beaters who took one look and told us that it would take about a month to fix, if it wasn't declared a write-off. Now what? We couldn't afford another. I phoned Toyota, but they didn't have any spares car of that specification, race-prepared. There was only one thing to do.

The girl in the car-rental company which I called, and which will remain nameless, seemed quite surprised when I told her that I would like to hire a Toyota Conquest, 16-valve for a week, but that it must be a white one.

To this day, I don't know who was smiling down on us, but it must have been someone quite special. I collected the car from the rental company's office on the Monday morning, took it home, changed all four wheels and tyres to our own stock, changed the pads to Ferodo competition pads and carefully covered the car in sponsor's branding in line with the red and the black cars. Finally, when we got to the track, I took the number plates off. We had had the engine performance checked, and it was on a par with what our engines were putting out. The only problem was that we didn't have a six-point harness fitted.

The first ever Final of the camel Rookie of the Year Challenge went according to plan in just about every way. We managed to sort out the driving schedules so that most of the running was done in the two normal school cars, but the third was essential as a back-up.

The competition was one by a young South African, Gavin Kelsey, who set a searing pace from the start of the day and was a very deserving winner. I think the gap between his fastest and slowest lap was just four-tenths of a second, which for a novice is exceptionally good. The Final went as well as we could have hoped it would and even the hire-car, which I had studiously kept an close eye on all day, stood up to the task. In fact, when I took it back the next day, with all of its original equipment back in place, the assistant who booked it back in, commented on how clean we'd kept it. Then she noticed that the speedometer wasn't working and immediately gave us a small refund! We were very lucky that what could have been a disaster for the school, worked out OK. Three weeks later, the original race car was delivered back to us from the panel beaters, fully restored.

As we left the track that evening, after a long but satisfying day, we met up with one very excited young man, our new Camel Rookie of the Year, Gavin Kelsey. To say that he was excited about his future trip to the UK would be a massive understatement. I wasn't going to tell him, until much later, that it was my intention to offer him a full-time role at Speed International as an instructor.

The next month went quickly, and it was soon time for Liz and me to take our Luxavia flight to the UK. We had decided to go a week ahead of Gavin, as we had a lot to organise over there. The flight presented a welcome opportunity to relax before eventually arriving at Heathrow, where we were met by one of John Kirkpatrick's staff. He'd brought us a Jim Russell Racing School branded Vauxhall Carlton for our personal use during our stay, courtesy of JK himself and Vauxhall, who were the sponsors of his highly successful racing school.

We needed a couple of days off to unwind a little before getting down to work, so we headed up to Ashby De la Zouche, not far from Leicester. It was on our way to Donington Park race circuit where Gavin would be completing a week's course at John's school, as part of his prize.

Ashby is where the famous Battle of Bosworth took place in 1485, right at the end of the Wars of the Roses, in which Henry Tudor defeated and killed Richard the

Third. Wandering around the newly built Battle Centre, Liz and I both commented on how good it was to see history portrayed in such an imaginative manner, with a typical 15th century street scene being recreated, amidst smells of horses and the noise of men in armour, as the troops rode and marched through the local town on their way to battle. We even visited the church where Richard took communion the night before the epic encounter the next day. I enjoyed it, but for Liz, not having seen anything like this before, it was especially fascinating.

At the weekend, Gavin flew into East Midlands Airport from South Africa, where we were all greeted by Tony Jardine, who ran the UK motorsport PR agency that represented R J Reynolds. Tony was there to make arrangements with us for Gavin's test-day with Paul Stewart Racing, another facet of his rookie prize. It was to be held on the Thursday, midway through his week's course at the Jim Russell School and would be filmed for showing back in South Africa, yet another real bonus for Speed International.

Also on Gavin's course that week at Donington Park was Jamie Ireland, whose famous father Innes made his F1 debut with Lotus in 1959. Jamie was a nice kid, and he and Gavin got on well together. Sadly, just four years later, in 1992, Jamie took his own life. I've recently finished reading Damon Hill's excellent autobiography, which gives a rare insight into the difficulties that the child of a highly successful parent can experience. Whilst there are many benefits to balance this with, the mental pressures are not inconsiderable. Innes, Jamie's father had not only been a very talented race driver, but although I never met him, it seems from his peers that he was quite a character, doing things very much in his own way. Sometimes that combination of rare skill and individualism can be a lot to live up to.

Gavin's week at the Jim Russell School ended on the Saturday, with a race day, limited specifically to pupils who had completed a course at the school. It featured the school Formula Ford race cars and proved quite dramatic. Gavin came so close to being crowned the week's champion in the races, by claiming pole position in the Final, only to spin on the first lap. He was gutted at the time, of course, but when he realised just how far he had progressed in the space of a few months, he came to terms with the disappointment.

The test with the Camel-sponsored Formula Ford 2000 had gone well, and once again showed how small the world of motorsport is. The team manager who attended the test that day, along with Paul Stewart himself, was Andy Miller, who went onto became team manager for Stewart F1 in later years. I first met Andy when he was a race engineer for a Formula Ford driver against whom I competed most weekends during my FF1600 career, Rob Coates.

It had been a memorable week for Gavin; and to his delight, when it was over, I offered him the role as a full-time instructor at Speed International. Life couldn't get much better for him at that point in time. Sadly, it wasn't to be too long before it all went wrong for him.

In the space of a year, Liz and I, together with the enthusiastic support of our instructors, had taken an idea that came into my mind as I was driving my Mercedes to another unpleasant day at Sandown Motors and turned it into reality. If this was what we could achieve in our first year, what could we do to better in our next one? If someone had told us what was in store, we would both have been very surprised. For the time being, however, we had to get ourselves back to South Africa, where we had organised the final part of Gavin's prize, a factory drive for Toyota in a

Stannic Group N race. Before we left, however, there was a treat in store for Liz, one which I'm not sure if she saw it in that way. Paul Stewart offered to take us both on a lap of the Donington Park Circuit in his new Ford Cosworth Sierra. Racing drivers rarely do things by halves, and we were treated to two hot laps in Paul's quite rapid car. I'd never driven there before, so it was great experience to sample the infamous Craner Curves. My first thought, as we headed through these downhill sweeps, was that it must be unbelievably scary to tackle this circuit on a racing motorbike, at speed, in the wet. Those guys really earn their money!

A week later, we were back in South Africa, and I was preparing the race cars for yet another course at Swartkops. As I drove into the circuit on our first morning back there, I commented to Liz that although the school was going well and the circuit was ideal for tuition, it wasn't really the ideal venue to attract either a major sponsor who would be able to help us grow the school or new business from the corporate sector.

I think that having been back to Brands Hatch and Donington Park, whilst we were in the UK, it brought home to me how geared up those circuits were commercially. Although we had secured some business from the business world, in the form of sales and staff incentive days, both Liz and I were aware that the catering and facilities were, by necessity, of a basic standard.

We looked at all of the options within South Africa. The Aldo Scribante track in Port Elizabeth was fine as an instructional venue, but in the same way that Swartkops provided very little in terms of customer facilities, Scribante's only real claim to fame was a spectacular view of the Indian Ocean from the track and a truck stop facility through which you had to drive to get to the race circuit. Admittedly this gave spectators and competitors a good view of the hookers marketing their wares quite blatantly as they checked out the truck drivers arriving, but he wasn't really conducive to the image that we wanted to portray to attract business clientele.

Cape Town was better equipped, but didn't offer such a prolific market as Johannesburg, being somewhat seasonal in respect of tourism. Welkom, in the Free State, was a complete no-go from a hospitality point of view, with just one lone hotel close to the track, as we had found out on our recent visit.

There was only one place to consider if we were serious about growing Speed International.

Chapter 26
Kyalami Again, Staff Problems and Trust Broken

The newly refurbished Kyalami Circuit, was now looking quite good, with a series of new hospitality buildings (or *bomas* in Afrikaans), all thatched in African style and offering a relatively high class of interior fittings. Whilst the track, being much longer than Swartkops, would be far more difficult to instruct pupils and would need a new approach to tuition, it offered a professional pit lane and garages, with a facility which would make an excellent technical facility for storing and preparing the race cars. There was one big negative from my point of view. Kyalami was now owned by Motor Racing Enterprises, which I was led to believe boasted Mervyn Key and Laurie McIntosh as two of its directors. I'd had dealings with both of them, back in the early 1980s at Kyalami. They were to hit the South African press headlines in the early 1990s when an OSEA (South African Office of Serious Economic Affairs) team, including its assistant director, as well as lawyers, accountants and police, flew to London to pursue inquiries into Tollgate Holdings, the South African transport group with a London share-listing that collapsed with debts of more than R300 million (pounds 62 million) last year. Mervyn Key was one of those charged with fraud over Tollgate but was subsequently acquitted.

The front man for the Kyalami operation was Dave McGregor, who was a likeable man, with whom I had always got on well. He had been in England on business for a couple of weeks when I was there with our Camel Rookie winner. He joined us at Donington Park for the test-day, and I think, more than most people, recognised how much hard work had gone into establishing Speed International. He was knowledgeable about motorsport and understood sports marketing. My problem was that whilst I had few qualms about dealing with Dave, it was the people to whom he in turn reported that worried me.

We had a couple of exploratory meetings about the growth and potential of Speed International, and he could see that it had all the makings of a very successful business. He was also very aware of my penchant for acquiring sponsorship and fully understood that if we were to operate from the new Kyalami circuit, the chances of my securing a major deal would be greatly enhanced. Eventually we reached the stage of formatting a draft agreement, which would see MRE purchasing Speed International from me, but then retain me as a consultant to run the business. Liz and I mulled it over for a few days and finally agreed that if we wanted to expand the business, it would take a lot of capital, particularly if we were to introduce the single-seater race cars that we felt were necessary to widen our market sector. We both felt reluctant to hand over the reins of a business into which we had put so much effort, but in the world of race driver schools, we knew only too well that the Achilles' Heel is always going to be the race track itself. Without it, you can't operate, but if you only rent it, you are always vulnerable to the whims of the owners. We'd been lucky at Swartkops, but there was no guarantee that the owner might not get a commercial developer wanting to buy the land to build factories or whatever. We couldn't afford to buy the track, so we had to look at the alternatives.

We accepted Dave McGregor's offer and said a very sad goodbye to Swartkops. We had enjoyed some wonderful times there and had such fun with the majority of our customers. Whilst we wouldn't be sorry to forego the task of getting the cars and equipment to the track every time we were operating, or the maintenance at home in the garage every evening, we knew that life was going to change at Kyalami. We hoped it would be for the better.

Once we had made the decision to move, I sat down with Dave McGregor and started planning the future of Speed International in its new surroundings. As I mentioned, Kyalami was looking stunning in its new layout, particularly the paddock area; and one of the first decisions that we made was to utilise the brand new scrutineering facility as our technical workshops and car storage centre. We also took over one of the offices under the new control tower as our administrative base.

I then talked to Dave about expanding the school's fleet of cars, suggesting that we needed a minimum of four Formula Ford race cars, as well as a couple more two-seater instructional cars. I recognised that it would require quite a major capital investment, but I proposed that I should now put together a strategy for acquiring a significant title sponsor for Speed International. Our move to Kyalami offered a totally different set of commercial entitlements to what we were restricted to at Swartkops, and I was confident that I could attract a sizeable fee for such an opportunity.

We had now mastered the complexities of the ARC World PC, but it was good to be able to switch on to a more modern system. The new deal also meant that we no longer had to do the accounting, which was a bonus to both Liz and me. With a full-time staff member, Gavin Kelsey, our Camel Rookie, it meant that he could take some of the work off my plate. The best news of all, by far, was that by employing Mark Durham, to run the technical workshop, I wouldn't have to work on the cars any longer. This had never been my real forte, and I take some pride in the fact that we never had any technical calamities whilst I was carrying out these duties. It didn't mean that I had enjoyed the responsibility!

With these changes in place, I was able to become far more involved in marketing the school, which I was really looking forward to. Just before we had gone over to the UK with Gavin, I had made the decision to invest in a new piece of equipment, which I hoped would help develop increasingly professional sponsorship material. It was a National Panasonic video-mixing and production unit. When we were in England, I had used my JVC camcorder to record a lot of relevant material, including a visit to a race meeting at Brands Hatch, as well as footage of Gavin at the Jim Russell School and his Camel test-day.

The new unit, which required three TV monitors, would allow me to edit all of the material and format it into innovative sales and promotional, adding commentary and sound, as well as captions and titles. It was not the easiest task learning how to use it and being able to produce material to a standard that I felt comfortable with showing to senior management within a potential sponsor.

I had my ups and downs trying to get it right, probably more downs than ups if I'm honest, but the trickiest part came when I tried to add a musical sound track. I couldn't afford any specialised equipment which would enable me to do this, so with invaluable help from Liz, we reached a satisfactory compromise. I had a turntable and amplifier in our lounge at home, situated in an alcove under the open wooden stairs up to what was still my office. By playing a vinyl record on the turntable, I could use a microphone to record it onto a sound cassette, then copy that onto the video sound track. All highly technical, of course! The track that I will always remember as the opening for the video that I was making was Pictures of Matchstick Men by Status Quo. I remember for two reasons, one was a very painful one; I lost track of the number of times I gently lowered the stylus onto the vinyl, then cracked my head on the wooden steps above me as I got up to monitor the recording. Liz eventually came to the rescue and working as a team we finally finished producing a ten minute video presentation that I could easily edit to personalise for showing to specific companies.

Looking back on it all today, it was really Heath Robinson in style, but guess what? It worked and allowed me to secure a high-profile title sponsor for Speed International. The deal over three years was worth SAR7, 50,000 which in 1988 would have converted to approximately £1, 65,000, a level of sponsorship that I think amazed most people at that time. A new imported, full spec 2-litre Honda Prelude would have set you back about SAR22, 500 in 1988.

The company in question was PG Windscreens, one of the country's leading windscreen replacement businesses as well as an OEM supplier. My research had shown that the company was close to a major change to its brand identity and would become PG Autoglass, with a different logo and colour scheme. I was able to demonstrate how Speed International could play a vital role in promoting the new brand identity to the public, the trade and to the media. It would also form a great platform for motivating its sales force.

I couldn't agree the deal on my own, but it was finally approved by the MRE Board. There was one particular provision that had been included, which Dave McGregor had agreed to. It had been previously agreed that Speed International would be given its own building in the paddock, comprising an office, a classroom and a roof viewing area. Within the sponsorship deal, it was stipulated that it would be branded in the title sponsor's livery; and on race days at Kyalami, this could be used by PG Windscreens for customer and staff hospitality.

The contract was signed by both parties and then put away in a drawer for safe-keeping.

The launch of the new PG Windscreens-sponsored Speed International Racing Driver School took place in the largest of the thatched hospitality units, a big double-storey building on the outside of Sunset Corner on the original part of the revamped Grand Prix circuit. It was an exciting occasion, very well-attended; and both Liz and I recognised that the move to Kyalami was indeed the correct decision, even if we did feel that in some ways we had lost our baby.

It was soon time to start preparing for the 1990 Camel Rookie of the Year Challenge, and this year I was able to secure an amazing level of agreed media coverage, including no less than six multi-minute TV features. We used the Camel Rookie programme as the platform on which PG Windscreens would change its identity to PG AutoGlass, in line with the rebranding of its nationwide chain of re-fitment centres.

I haven't yet explained that we now had a different fleet of race cars at the school. We had switched from Toyota to Ford as the preferred vehicle supplier, based on the fact that Toyota didn't have access to single-seater race cars, whereas in Formula Ford, it was an obvious link. We were very grateful to Toyota for having been the OEM that originally had faith in us and supported to support our start-up and first full season. They fully understood our decision, and I think had been pleasantly surprised at the level of publicity Speed International had enjoyed within the motoring media in that first year.

Gavin Kelsey, our Camel Rookie of the Year, was now working at the school as a full-time instructor until he blotted his copybook very badly. I knew that Gavin was keen to race and agreed that he could spend time in between courses, to look for a possible drive or a sponsor. I could understand how much he wanted to build a career on the platform of winning the challenge. One day, he asked me if he could borrow one of the racing school Formula Fords to take part in a race at Swartkops. I had to tell him that he couldn't, as these cars were effectively my business, and we couldn't afford to have one out of action, should he have an incident in the race. He wasn't happy with me, but I stuck to my guns, I had no choice. The business, as I've explained, was now owned by MRE; and when I told Dave McGregor of my decision, he backed me fully.

A month went by, and I received a phone call from the SA Police, in respect of a break-in to one of the school's Ford road cars, a Sierra Estate. I knew nothing about this, and Liz checked out what had happened. It transpired that Gavin had decided to take the Formula Ford, with or without my permission. He solicited the support on my technical manager, then took the race car, on a trailer, towed by the school's Sierra Estate to the Swartkops race meeting. There, he raced the Formula Ford, luckily without incident; but that evening, he left the Sierra outside in the street, and it was broken into. He had managed somehow to keep it all quiet, but didn't realise that all too often these things eventually come to light.

Once I found this out, I had no alternative but to fire him from his job. Both Liz and I felt it was a real kick in the teeth, as we'd done so much for the young guy. It was a very stupid decision on his part.

On the subject of school cars, we made a bold decision in terms of the replacement cars in which instructors could accompany the pupils. We purchased four second-hand Ford Sierra 1600 salon cars; and with the help of Ford and a lot of various suppliers, converted them into modified salon cars, stripping out the interiors and putting in full roll cages, race seats and then adding growling exhaust systems before having them all painted in the new PG Autoglass aquamarine and navy blue livery. They looked and sounded great and achieved the performance target of being quick but manageable to drive. They were within the limits of most average road drivers. That's what you need at a racing school, cars that are suited not just for those customers wanting to learn the skills that might help them into a racing career, but for those who simply want to enjoy a Corporate Day at the track.

In addition to the PG deal, I'd also put together some more sponsorship deals. These included one with Sasol, a former sponsor of the Jordan F1 Team in 1991. The deal comprised them installing a fuel tank in the Paddock at Kyalami and 10,000 litres of fuel a year for the school's use. The only negative from our point of view, was the fact that plans for the exclusive Speed International building had shown no sign of being put in place. This in turn started to become a point of embarrassment in my dealings with Louis Rosseau, Marketing Director of PG Autoglass, and the man who had been so supportive of our efforts to make the sponsorship work for his company.

Eventually it started to become a major issue, and Louis was under pressure from his own board. I tried getting a reaction from the MRE Board, but there seemed to be little interest on their part. I sensed that there was something else going on that was preoccupying their time.

It gradually started to come out that there were some financial irregularities that were under scrutiny, involving a company called Tollgate Holdings, Duros Merchant Bank and some of the Kyalami personnel. What was happening I hadn't a clue, but rumours were flying around, including one that the future of Kyalami as a race circuit was in doubt.

Eventually, Louis asked me to meet him and the CEO of PG Autoglass. He was fully aware that I wasn't now running Speed International, and that Liz and I were both embarrassed at the lack of development of the new building. He told us that sorry as he was, if the MRE board didn't act within a set time, PG Group would pull the plug on the sponsorship. I could totally understand their viewpoint and didn't blame them. It was bad news, however. I had worked hard to secure the deal and knew that if I was running the business, we could have come to a meaningful compromise.

PG Group kept to their word and after the first year, pulled out of the sponsorship deal. It was a devastating blow and what worried me the most was that it would tarnish our reputation when trying to find a replacement sponsor. I was very appreciative when Louis Rosseau, totally unsolicited, sent a letter to me personally, thanking Liz and I for all our efforts to try and ensure that all agreed objectives would be met. He then explained how sorry he was to bring the relationship to an end, through no fault of ours.

Liz and I were both gutted at the way in which this situation had been allowed to develop with MRE. PG Autoglass wasn't some backstreet operation that added nothing to the reputation of the MRE Speed International business, but was one of South Africa's premier companies.

Looking back on this episode, I have sadly become accustomed to seeing significant sponsorships lost because of the short-sighted attitude of people within the sport itself. All too often, the problem lies in the fact that once the deal is struck, complacency takes over; the amount of work that should be undertaken to meet the primary objectives of the sponsor become a hassle, and it starts to go downhill from there. There is an attitude amongst far too many people in sports, all sports, that sponsorship is almost their right. They don't see it as a partnership, despite their protestations, if you dare challenge them.

Had Speed International still been my own business; and I'd such a massive sponsor through my own inadequacies, I would have got straight back out there in the marketplace and tried to find a replacement. My problem, however, was that this was one issue too many with the MRE directors; and quite frankly, I was aware that I had lost confidence in them. They were very bright guys, of that I had no doubts, but could I trust them? I came to the conclusion that I couldn't. This meant that I had two choices: I could stay in place and look for another sponsor, fully aware that the same thing could happen a second time, or I could cut my losses and move on.

It was a bitter pill to swallow, having put in so much hard work to get Speed International to where it was, but I took the decision that unless I could buy the business back from MRE, I didn't want to stay there. Even if I could raise the money, I would still have the same Achilles Heel, the track would be owned by MRE.

Liz and I talked a lot over the next few weeks about this and eventually came to the conclusion that not only would I resign from the company, but that I should continue with my unfulfilled ambition of trying to get to Formula 1; obviously not as a driver, but in a capacity that would allow me to be successful. This would mean leaving South Africa and heading back to Europe. Liz was all for it, as she really looked forward to living in England. The big question that faced me, however, was what to do about my parents.

Chapter 27
Great News, a Criminal Act and Mr Sponsorship

My mother had astonished her surgeon, not only surviving the initial operation to remove a lung but by recovering well and was now nearly two years over his initial three month survival prognosis. They had decided to move back to Johannesburg on the recommendation of Mr Morgan, who felt that the dry Highveld winters would be better for her well-being than in the Cape. They'd moved into a retirement village, and Ken had been offered a job as the resident manager.

Unfortunately, there was a major problem brewing. Whilst they were still living in Cape Town, Ken had been offered a job by a business colleague who had set up his own company, specialising in the installation of lightning conductors on buildings. Ken's role was as sales manager, and he enjoyed the work; but after about a year, it seemed that the business wasn't doing too well. One of the essential employee benefits in South Africa is the contribution towards the spiralling costs of medical insurance. As in the USA, South Africa does not have a national health service; and so for most people, medical insurance is mandatory. For Ken, with the ongoing costs of Eileen's medications increasing quite regularly, medical insurance was a must-have facility.

A letter arrived one morning from the medical insurance company, informing Ken that his medical contributions hadn't been received for some months, and his insurance was now invalid. Ken immediately called me, and we contacted the company, but the bad news only got worse. It seemed that my father wasn't the only member of staff to suffer this problem. It seemed that his supposed business friend had been pocketing the medical insurance contributions of several senior staff. There would be a police investigation, but in the meantime, Ken was no longer covered.

What made it even worse was the fact that because of his age, the company wouldn't insure him in his own right unless it was at a ridiculously high premium. The same went for other companies we approached on his behalf. I'd like to think that this sort of situation couldn't happen in the UK; but at that time in South Africa, it certainly could, and there was no flexibility whatsoever.

We could help financially for a while, but should something major happen, we were in trouble. It made our choice of what to do even more difficult.

Eventually, we all agreed that the answer was for Liz and I to head back to the UK and for Ken and Eileen to follow us, once we were settled and could arrange accommodation for them. Because they had continued paying their UK National Insurance contributions all the time they had been in South Africa, they would have access to the NHS. Nevertheless, it was a worrying time for all of us, and certainly did my mother's health no good at all.

On 31 December 1990, Liz and I flew out of Jan Smuts Airport and headed towards Heathrow, leaving behind us sweltering temperatures of around 35 degrees centigrade. We landed at 6:00 in the morning, having been warned by the pilot that the air temperature at the airport would be a very low minus six degrees. I remember having to scrape the ice off the windscreen of the hire car that we had booked, before setting off to Sevenoaks, where my aunt and uncle, Joan and Don, would repay our South African hospitality by putting us up for our first few weeks.

Liz and I took the opportunity of visiting the Autosport International Show during our first month in the UK. It coincided with the Show taking place at the NEC for the first time and proved invaluable for me in terms of meeting some of my old contacts with the sport. One of these contacts was Mike Blanchet, yet another very talented Formula Ford driver from the mid-1970s era, against whom I'd competed regularly at that time. Mike had by now retired from race driving, which I thought was a great shame, as he could have gone a long way in my opinion. Nevertheless, he was now the managing director of what was then the worlds' largest race car manufacturer, from a revenue perspective. Lola Cars was based in Huntingdon in Cambridgeshire, which was famous for being the constituency of a certain John Major, the British prime minister.

My meeting proved to be very well-timed, and I was invited by Mike to visit him at the Lola Factory to have a chat about some plans afoot within the company. I should point out that when we bumped into each other at the Autosport Show, Mike had immediately referred to me as Mr Sponsorship, so I had a good idea what the purpose of the meeting would probably be. I was right, but in way that I didn't expect.

Chapter 28
Meeting Lola, Lola's Italian Affair and a Great F1 Driver

Before I explain what happened at the subsequent meeting with Mike Blanchet at Lola Cars, it's worth looking at the company itself, to fully understand what it had achieved since its origins back in 1958. The man who started the company was Eric Broadley, who built a sports racing car in his garage in Bromley, owned by the Broadley Family. The car enjoyed a lot of success and eventually led to orders for Eric to build similar cars for paying customers. Eric decided it was a good time to invest his savings into setting up a company, Lola Cars Ltd.

In the 1960s, Lola had built a worldwide reputation for its sports cars, and Eric was contacted by Henry Ford 11 to design Le Mans 24-Hours winning car, which could beat the dominant Ferrari's in this famous race. The subsequent design became known as the Ford GT40.

Suffice to say that it proved to be a clever move, and Lola went on to build iconic cars, such as the Lola T70 sports racing car, examples of which today change hands for seven-figure sums.

Eric's next big venture was into the American single-seater market. Colin Chapman, boss of Lotus, had stunned the Indycar world by winning the world-famous Indy 500 in 1965 with a ground-breaking, rear-engine car driven by Jim Clark. Eric was keen to follow in his footsteps, and succeeded when in 1966, Graham Hill won the prestigious event in a Lola T90.

Having been successful during the 1970s and 1980s in formulae, such as F3000, Formula Ford, and Formula Nippon, Eric took the decision to move further into what he saw as the lucrative American market. He had by then moved his business in the UK to a brand new factory in Huntingdon and took the decision to enter into an agreement with Carl Haas, an American team owner, to set up a Lola agency in the USA. It was to be the start of a long-term, highly successful partnership.

In 1978, Al Unser won the Indy 500, at the wheel of the only Lola in the field. The name Lola was becoming synonymous with racing in the USA, and then in 1990, Lola enjoyed another Indy 500 success, thanks to Dutchman Arie Luyendijk. Lola Cars would go onto dominate the series for the next couple of years, selling up to 35 chassis in a season at its peak.

Mike Blanchet had joined the company as its Sales Manager, doing a great job for Eric Broadley in generating a lot of new business, particularly in Japan. He was eventually appointed as Managing Director of Lola Cars, taking over the duties that I think it's fair to say Eric didn't really enjoy. He was a designer, an engineer primarily; and in the years that I knew Eric, he was never happier than working on technical issues rather than the commercial aspects of the company. It was probably the way in which he differed most from Colin Chapman, who was a very different kettle of fish in that respect.

In 1991, when I had my meeting with Mike, Lola was riding the crest of a wave in America, Europe and Japan, but it seemed that Eric Broadley wanted to get into F1 again. He had enjoyed success back in 1967, when Lola worked with Honda racing to design and build their F1 car. In the hands of John Surtees, the Lola T130 won the 1967 Italian Grand Prix. In 1974, Graham Hill's newly formed F1 team, Embassy Hill, commissioned Lola to build a new car, which evolved into the Hill GH1 in 1975. Sadly, the air crash that killed Graham Hill, Tony Brise and several other team personnel brought the programme to a tragic end.

Lola had another dabble into F1 in 1988 and 1989, when it developed a relationship with the French Larrouse F1 Team, effectively designing and building Lola cars for them, officially entered as Larrousses. In the process, this caused a major wrangle with the FIA, and the team lost all of its Constructor's Championship points. Motors racing can be a very up and down sport, as Eric was finding all too often.

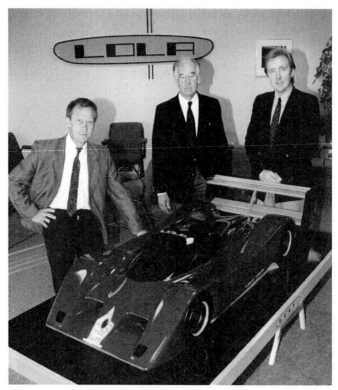

Eric Broadley, Lola Chairman, together with Mike Blanchet, Managing Director, and Brian Sims.

Whilst I was sitting drinking coffee with Mike Blanchet in his office at the new Lola factory in 1991, he explained to me that Eric Broadley now wanted to set up his own factory team and enter the 1993 F1 World Championship as a constructor in

180

its own right. Fate, however, decided that Eric's dream was not going to come to fruition in the way that he had contemplated.

When Mike offered me the role of marketing director for the Lola F1 Team, I had to pinch myself to make sure I wasn't dreaming. Less than six months ago, I'd been running the Speed International Racing Driver School in Johannesburg, organising the 1990 Camel Rookie of the Year Challenge. Now, here I was sitting in Huntingdon, being offered the chance to move into F1 in a dream role, heading up the marketing side of the proposed new team.

Just as things were looking so good, Mike Blanchet was taken seriously ill with a kidney-related issue. For a while, he bravely battled on; although how he managed to fit in his regular dialysis treatment sessions with his travelling schedule in America and Japan, I'll never know. That he was able to, says a lot about the man. Then it all became too much, and he was admitted to hospital, meaning an enforced absence from Lola.

This put a lot of pressure on the F1 programme, much as Mike's management team tried to help, it wasn't easy. The company's business development manager was a really likeable young guy, Nick Langley, who was one of a rare breed inasmuch that he was a qualified engineer, with a talent for sales. His job was to sell race cars, but unlike purchasing a street car, teams didn't just phone and order next years' car. Purchases were based on a number of factors, not least of all, testing sessions at a race track. It was a common sight to see Nick heading off to Heathrow or Stanstead Airport, laden with new development parts for a car that was being tested in France, Italy or even Japan. It was a highly skilled role, requiring both engineering and interpersonal skills, which Nick certainly possessed. Peter Spruce was another member of the team who tried his best to make up for the loss of Mike Blanchet's management skills.

Then out of the blue, Eric took a phone call from Beppe Lucchini, the president of a highly successful Italian steel producer, Lucchini Steel, which was based in Brescia, near Milan. The company was one of the primary steel suppliers to the Italian automotive industry in particular, to Fiat and had been a primary sponsor of the Dallara F1 Team since 1988. Currently the team were running JJ Lehto and Pierluigi Martini as its drivers.

Dallara was a sizeable race car manufacturer itself, based in Parma, Italy, similar in many ways to Lola Cars. It was very much a competitor to Lola Cars and had subsequently entered its own factory team in F1, as Lola was now seeking to do. The company also worked closely with Italian motor manufacturers such as Ferrari, Lancia, Alfa Romeo and Maserati.

For some reason, Beppe Lucchini was keen to switch allegiance to another manufacturer and having heard that Lola was planning to come back into F1 in its own right, thought that it might be worth having an initial discussion about the possibility of a collaborating in some way. The USP that he was offering was an engine supply contract with Ferrari.

Mike, who was now back at work, asked me if I would accompany him to Brescia for the initial meeting with Beppe Lucchini.

Beppe was everything you expected from a wealthy, successful Italian business magnate. His dress sense was immaculate; his office was both spacious and stylish, with photographs on the walls of famous Ferrari F1 drivers and cars. Although we didn't have time to see it, he told us that in the basement of the building he had a collection of Ferraris, including some F1 cars.

The meeting went well for a couple of hours, and then he glanced at his watch. He went on to suggest that although he had planned to take us to his favourite Italian restaurant, as we were getting along so well, would it not be an idea to have a snack lunch in his office whilst we carried on talking. This suited us fine, and when his PA announced that this was ready in the adjacent room, Mike and I walked in, expecting to see some sandwiches and maybe some fruit. That wasn't how Beppe Lucchini did things. Waiting for us was a spread fit for kings, as they say. An amazing selection of breads, cold meats, cheeses, fruit and pastries, together with a range of bottles offering wine, fruit juices and water. The Italians know to do things properly when it comes to food.

We heard from him over lunch, that he could bring two drivers to the team, in addition to the Ferrari engines. His idea was that Lola would design and build the chassis in the UK and that the team would be run out of the existing workshops in Brescia, staffed by the personnel who had been involved, and currently still were working with the Dallara F1 Team.

The drivers that he had lined-up were Michele Alboreto, the former Ferrari F1 Driver who had raced in over 180 Grands Prix by then, with five wins to his name and another Italian, Luca Badoer, the 1992 Formula 3000 Champion. Mike and I had a lot to talk about on the plane home that evening. We could both see the potential benefits of joining forces with Lucchini, particularly in respect of the engine deal that came with it. We weren't sure how Eric Broadley would see it, however, as he had his heart set on his own team. Nevertheless, it was an attractive offer and the benefits of the experience that Lucchini had gained in F1 over the past three years, would be invaluable.

Then Mike's illness hit hard again, and it would be the best part of a year before he was well enough to come back in his full capacity, It was a major blow to the company, but had to be dealt with. The next time I met Beppe Lucchini it was in Eric Broadley's company, again in Brescia. Eric had brought in to the proposed collaboration and was keen to try and wrap up the legal side of things, as well as to get cracking on the design of the new chassis that that would now have to accommodate a Ferrari F1 engine. One of Lola's talented young designers, Mark Williams, was to head up the design programme. It was to be a massive challenge for him, working closely with the Italians, which all of those involved in motorsport, knew wouldn't be as easy as it might appear.

The next meeting that I was involved in took place in Huntingdon, in the Lola Board Room. A group of Italians had flown in for this, partly comprising lawyers who would present the draft joint-venture agreement. In addition, there were several Ferrari-engine personnel to discuss installation requirements with Mark Williams and his team.

I'll never forget the look on the faces of all the Italians when it was announced that lunch would be served in the board room. It comprised a few individual Tesco sandwiches on plates, together with little packs of fruit juice, with plastic straws still taped on the sides. Having been so royally looked after from a catering point of view, in the Beppe's Boardroom in Brescia, I couldn't help but feel somewhat embarrassed.

Despite the best efforts of the Italian lawyers to seemingly drag the legalities out for ever and a day, agreement to the new partnership, between Luchinni and Lola, was eventually reached; and we all toasted the launch of the new Lola BMS Scuderia Italia F1 project, in fruit juice through straws of course!

Whilst the technical team started their work on designing and building the new Lola F1 car in readiness for its 1993 debut season, I was kept busy in another direction. One of the areas in which Mike Blanchet had been very involved was Lola's CART programme in the USA. It was a massive market for the company at that time, worth in excess of £10 million per year. As I explained, Lola had appointed an agent in America, Carl Haas, who was the owner of the championship winning Newman Haas Racing Team that competed in the CART and subsequent Indycar Series from 1983 to 2011. There were two primary reasons for my making several trips to America during 1992. One was to have a Lola presence at some of the key races, so that Lola customer teams didn't feel that there was any lack of interest in their activities. Obviously the company's technical presence was always very much in evidence, but it was also important to meet the team owners and talk about their future plans, gathering any relevant information that would be helpful from a sales point of view.

Chapter 29
A TV Role, a Rock Star and Paul Newman

In the course of my work at Lola in 1982, I received a phone call from Sky Sports in Isleworth, asking whether it was possible for them to come to Huntingdon and shoot a feature on Lola's CART (Championship Auto Racing Teams) involvement in the USA. They explained that they would be broadcasting every CART Round live in the UK, on a Sunday night, throughout the season.

After spending a couple of hours filming at the Lola factory, Diane Keen, the programmes producer asked me if I would like to become the regular *pundit* in the studio for each race, joining Tiff Needell who would be presenting the programme. Tiff was yet another of the Formula Ford drivers whom I knew well from years in that category, so it would be good to work with him.

The way that it worked was that Sky broadcast the live ESPN coverage of each race, mainly on a Sunday evening in the UK, or in the case of the Indy 500, the live ABC Network feed. Tiff and I would be in the Sky studio in Isleworth, next to the Gillette HQ on the Great West Road. We would start the programme from there; and then every time there was a commercial break on ESPN, or a yellow flag incident, we would take over the commentary.

I really took to the new role; and from the comments we got, I think that Tiff and I combined well. I was delighted when I received a call from Simon Reed of Eurosport, after just a few weeks in my new role. He asked me if I would like to become the F1 back-up commentator for F1 races.

Former F1 driver, John Watson, travelled to each race and provided live commentary for them, but often they had quality issues and needed to use their studio feed for a short while. The same applied to coverage of practice and qualifying. With the studio being in Paris, this meant that I was flown on a Friday night from Gatwick to France, put up in a good hotel for two nights and then back to the UK on Sunday evening. Liz was able to join me there on several occasions, and it was a great experience to work with John and Allard Kalfe.

Returning to my TV work for Sky, Diane Keen rang me one day and explained that as Tiff would be competing in the 24 Hours of Le Mans, he would be unable to present the Sunday evening CART Race. She asked me if I felt comfortable about presenting the programme on my own. I didn't hesitate and accepted her offer. I would have Tyler Alexander of McLaren as my guest that week in the studio. However, during the week prior to the broadcast, I received a phone call from an old school friend, asking me if he could possibly come with me on the Sunday evening and watch the programme from within the Sky Sports studio. His name was Ian Gillan; and he was the lead singer for Deep Purple, who of course had a massive hit with Smoke on the Water, incorporating that magical introductory guitar riff.

Ian and I had gone to Hounslow College and were in the same class, and both played for the same football team. We had lost touch when he left to go to Acton Grammar School in 1963, and I left to go to Isleworth Grammar. Our paths crossed in a strange way some 29 years later.

One of Brian's old school friends is Ian Gillan, who went on to become one of the biggest names in rock music, as the lead singer for Deep Purple. Seen here together at the Autosport Show in 1992.

I was working for Lola; and in the course of my sponsorship search, I arranged an appointment to meet the international sales director of Bowring Insurance Group, the UK head office of which was situated across the road from the Tower of London. All I knew was that his name was Chris Godwin. As I walked into his office, we both looked at each other for a second and then broke into a big smile. When I had set up the meeting, it never occurred to me that Chris Godwin might be one of the three Godwin brothers who were at Hounslow College with me back in the 1960s. He recognised the name Brian Sims, but had no idea that I had gone into motorsport as a career and didn't make a connection.

Over lunch, we chatted about our days at school together, and, in the process, Chris made a comment about how well Ian Gillan had done since leaving Hounslow College. I looked blankly at him and asked what Ian had done. It was only when he mentioned Smoke on the Water that the penny droped. I recall Chris commenting that Ian had probably made more money than the rest of the school put together. I asked him if he had a contact number for him, but he didn't. Chris and I have kept in touch since that day, and I have attended many enjoyable school reunions with him.

When I got back to my office at Lola the next day, I called my PA, Penny Banks, into my office and told her that I had an interesting task for her. I explained about Ian Gillan and asked her to find out who his recording company was, and how I could make contact with him. A couple of days later, she told me that she'd made a call to the company, but they wouldn't release any data on Ian, other than to suggest that I send them a fax, which they would forward on to him.

About a month went by, and I was coming to the conclusion that because Ian was now working in such a different strata, the last thing he needed was to re-connect with an old school friend. Then one evening, the phone rang, and it was Ian, apologising for the delay in getting back to me. He was on tour with Deep Purple and currently in Stockholm. He gave me his personal contact details and promised to get in touch when he finished the tour.

True to his word, Liz and I were invited to afternoon tea at his spectacular 16th century Manor House near Leighton Buzzard, where we met his wife Bron and young daughter Grace. What a great guy Ian turned out to be; absolutely no hint of celebrity, at all, just a very happily married family man who loved what he did; music was his passion.

Now he wanted to sit in the Sky Sports studio and watch the motor racing live from America; but when I walked in with him, I got a very odd look from Diane Keen, my producer, who was standing in the studio, talking to some of her team. Ian had taken the opportunity to visit the washroom. Diane then came over to me and asked me if my visitor was, who she thought it was, Ian Gillan of Deep Purple fame? When I confirmed it was and explained why he was there, she told me that she was a huge fan of the group, and there was no way he was going to sit in the studio to watch the programme. I queried why, and she told me that Ian was going be one of my programme guests. As a result, I spent the next three hours sitting with Ian on one side of me, and Tyler Alexander on the other, whilst we chatted about Indycar Racing, interspersed with stories about Ian's colourful life on the road.

Over the years since then, Liz and I have been lucky enough to attend many Deep Purple concerts as guests of Ian and Bron. The last one, at Cape Town's Grand West Casino was particularly memorable with Deep Purple topping the bill that included Uriah Heep and Wishbone Ash. Ian invited us into the dressing room in the interval for drinks and then asked us if we'd like to sit with his wife on the stage for the whole of Deep Purple's second-half performance. We had my stepson Nick and his wife Verné with us. What a fantastic time we had sitting to one side of the stage behind the massive speakers, looking out at the 5000 plus live audience. I quite envied Ian, his life as a rock star. Had the Victims come good, back in 1963, it could have been me! If only that teacher hadn't opened the windows, as I was playing Telstar on the school organ…

Returning to my role in America with Lola, I had another reason for developing a good relationship with Carl Haas. Apart from making sure that in Mike Blanchet's absence, I could stand in for him as best I could, I realised that Carl was incredibly well-connected in respect of the American business sector, and I was hoping that he could introduce me to a few contacts who might see F1 as being a feasible sponsorship option.

Carl was a fascinating character, with a wealth of entertaining anecdotes about motorsport, both in America and beyond. He had joined forces with Paul Newman in 1983, with the legendary Mario Andretti as their driver and a year later won the CART title. In 1989, Mario's son, Michael, joined the team as a driver, partnering his father in a two-car Newman Haas Team. Like father, like son! In 1991, Michael copied his father's achievement and won the CART title for the team.

I recall the first time I met Paul Newman. I'd travelled to the States on behalf of Lola, to watch the CART Race at the Columbus Mid-Ohio Circuit, one of the road tracks, as opposed to the ovals which comprise a fair percentage of the calendar. I parked my hire car and walked over to the Newman-Haas hospitality marquee, aware that the team were busy on track with official practice. Fancying a coffee, I tried without much success, to operate the complex looking piece of equipment on the table in front of me. Suddenly from behind me, a hand shot out and a soft American drawling voice asked me if I needed some help. I turned around, and there was Paul Newman, a smile on his face. He then introduced himself to me, as though I wouldn't know who he was! I knew he wouldn't have a clue about my identity, but I was wrong. He told me that Carl had mentioned that I'd be arriving that day. What a lovely man; totally and utterly without any self-importance or hype, he was just there as a part of the race team; and what really surprised me was that as I got involved with the team over the two days of the race meeting, I saw him walk around the paddock, sometimes through the crowd, and no one pestered him for autographs or photos. The American spectators accepted that at race meetings, he was Paul Newman the team owner and not the star of Butch Cassidy and the Sundance Kid or a hundred other movies.

My next visit to America was to introduce two British businessmen to Carl. They had approached me in the UK to discuss how they could secure a license to produce a video simulation game, featuring the Newman Haas Lola CART Team. One of them was the grandson of the English author Dennis Wheatley, who wrote a high number of occult thrillers, including such titles as *The Devil Rides Out* and *To the Devil a Daughter.*

We landed at O'Hare International in Chicago, where Carl met us in a brand new Mercedes 600 and drove us to the Newman Haas Team workshops in Lincolnshire, Illinois. I never ever saw Carl without a cigar in his mouth. Nothing unusual about that, you may be thinking; a lot of people in those days smoked regularly. They did, but Carl didn't. He simply cut off the end of a new, expensive Havana cigar and stuck it in his mouth, which is where it stayed until he decided it was time to change it for another new one. Carl didn't smoke on doctor's orders.

On one famous occasion, a journalist asked Carl why he didn't cut the expensive Havana cigars in half if he was only going to chew one end before throwing each one away. Carl's reply was very simple and straight to the point, 'Because I don't have to!' was his reply.

On the way from the airport, Carl was very keen to show us his new car. Just as we were getting precariously close to the back of a huge juggernaut, he decided to choose that moment to demonstrate the telephone that was installed, but apparently concealed, in the car. He told us to watch the dashboard, and then he fiddled with something on the steering wheel. I could sense the fear emanating from the two visitors sitting in the back as we got even closer to the truck. Then slowly a phone rose from the dashboard, and Carl lifted the unit from its fitting and dialled his office, telling his PA we were about ten minutes away! We were all delighted when we eventually saw the Newman Haas flag flying from the roof a building and turned into the driveway, before climbing out of the car.

That evening, Carl invited all three of us to his house for supper, together with his wife Bernadette, or Bernie he called her. As you would expect, the house was quite magnificent, built in Lake Forest, Illinois, right on the shoreline of Lake

Michigan. When we arrived, he asked us if we would like a tour of his home. What else could we do but accept, very glad of the opportunity to have a good old nose around!

The first port of call was the garage, where a red Ferrari Berlinetta Boxer sat on a plush carpet. Then it was off to the stunning indoor swimming pool, followed by a somewhat surprising request for us to head upstairs to the bedrooms. The memorable part of this was the sight of the dressing room, with automatic sliding cupboard doors that opened at the touch of a switch, revealing a vast array of men's shoes, all in racks. Then it was on the new shower room, and an unforgettable demonstration of the four separate power jets of water that came from the ceiling, the side walls and then, to everyone's amusement, from the floor.

Bernie didn't join us for supper, probably having experienced enough motor racing conversations to last her a lifetime. Carl told us that he didn't have any children; and I got the impression that for all of his immense wealth and success in the motor racing business, there was a loneliness of sorts within the great man. That evening over a wonderful meal, I feel that I was lucky enough to be given a rare glimpse of the man behind the Carl Haas façade.

Chapter 30

Coffee with a Hollywood Legend, Lola's Bad Year and Dinner with James Hunt

As well as his successes in CART racing, Carl had also ventured into the world of Formula 1. In 1984, he put together a commercial agreement with Beatrice Foods, a US consumer conglomerate, which saw Team Haas (USA) Ltd compete in the 1985 and 1986 F1 World Championship. (In case you are wondering, I should point out at this stage that the Haas F1 Team, which currently competes in the F1 World Championship, has no connection with Carl Haas or his former team in any way.)

The constructor of the new car from Carl's F1 team was officially called Force, but not surprisingly, the cars were entered under the Lola banner, for whom Newman Haas Racing was, of course, its US agent. There was a sad lack of success for the fledgling new team and its drivers Alan Jones (1985) and Patrick Tambay and Eddie Cheever (1986), scoring a total of six world championship points in 20 races over two seasons of racing. Nevertheless, Carl Haas brought a welcome touch of individuality to the pit lane, and I think many people were sorry to witness the lack of success of the programme. It ended in an almost farcical way when the CEO of Beatrice Foods was dismissed, and the board withdrew its funding of the F1 project.

On another visit to America, I was again at Columbus, Mid-Ohio, for a CART race. On this occasion, I was approached in the Paddock by one of the team owners, Rick Galles, who was then running the Mexican driver, Adrian Fernandez, in the CART championship. Rick asked me if I would stop by his motorhome on race-day, as there was someone he wanted me to meet. He added that it was a big-name showbiz celebrity, but he wouldn't tell me who it was. He did, however, explain that he was trying to persuade this person to become a partner in his business, in a similar that Carl Haas had agreed with Paul Newman. The celebrity had asked if he could speak to someone who understood marketing and sponsorship within the sport, and it seemed that my name had appeared on Rick's radar for some reason.

The next morning, I walked across to the Galles Racing motorhome and knocked on the door. Rick pulled it open and beckoned me in. Sitting there on one of the leather couches, wearing a pair of jeans and trainers, with a team baseball cap on his head was none other than Gene Hackman.

For nearly two hours, the three of us sat drinking coffee and talking about the way in which sponsorship in motor racing worked, the funding levels required and costs of running a team in the CART Championship. As I'd found with Paul Newman, Gene was such a laid-back individual, and it was an absolute pleasure to meet and talk with him. It felt quite surreal sitting there talking about racing as opposed to his film career in Hollywood. Hopefully I hadn't put him off the world of racing in some way, but for whatever reason, Rick Galles and Gene Hackman never did put a deal together!

My next task was back in Europe, where Eric Broadley and I attended the Hungarian F1 Grand Prix for the sole purpose of announcing the new F1 partnership between Lola and BMS. This presented the first demonstration of Beppe Lucchini's powerful links with Ferrari, as we were invited to hold the media launch in the prestigious Ferrari F1 Team's hospitality area. It was quite a moment to enjoy, and I could feel the pride flowing from the famous man himself, as his dream had come true, albeit in a slightly different format to what he had originally expected, a full-blown Lola F1 Team. Nevertheless, it was a day for the memory banks, and it really brought it home to me that I was now in F1, in my own right; thanks to Eric and Mike Blanchet, who gave me the chance that I'd been looking for.

Sadly, the performance of the new car when it took to the track for the first time, at the beginning of the 1993 campaign, failed to live up to expectations despite the benefit of being powered by Ferrari V12 engines direct from the factory. It was to be a cruel learning curve for Lola.

On a more positive note, it introduced me to one of the most special people with whom I have had the pleasure of working, Michele Alboreto. He had been contracted by Beppe Lucchini, to bring his wealth of experience to the fledgling team. Despite never winning the world championship, Michele, who was now 37 years of age, was runner-up in 1985 to Alain Prost and had won five F1 Grand Prix. He had also secured victory in the prestigious Sebring 12-Hours, been a member of Lancia's World Championship sports car team for several years, securing numerous victories and was now back in F1 with Lola. With a brand new Lola F1 chassis to sort out, it was agreed by both Beppe and Eric that his vast experience would be vital to the success of the project.

I got to know Michele well during the 1993 season, and it was heart-breaking to see such a talented driver struggling to come to terms with what was inherently flawed race car. I recall that the very first time he saw the new car assembled at the inaugural test day, his reaction was that it looked far too big and clumsy. The test did little to change his tune and when Luca Badoer, a highly rated young Italian driver who had won the 1992 Formula 3000 Championship, no mean feat, also agreed with Alboreto's comments, we got the feeling that we were in for an interesting season.

Ironically for me, the first Grand Prix of the new season was the South African race at Kyalami. It was home from home in a way for me, and I was looking forward to going back there in my new capacity as the marketing director of an F1 Team. I remember being asked to organise cars in Johannesburg for Michele and Luca. I contacted one of my mates who was running an Alfa Romeo dealership and lined up a couple of top of the range vehicles for our two drivers.

The race wasn't encouraging for the team, with Michele qualifying in a lowly 25th position on the grid, whilst Luca sat alongside him in 26th place, hardly setting the world alight. Neither car would finish the race, with Luca suffering gearbox problems after just 20 laps, and Michele retiring on lap 55 with engine issues.

Michele had asked me if I would drive him back to the hotel later that afternoon, and it was fascinating for me to listen to his opinions and suggestions about the car's performance. He had strong views as to the primary cause of the problem. He told me that it was a total lack of aerodynamic down force. He also thought the car too cumbersome. There was going to be a lot of head scratching back at the team's two bases, Huntingdon and Brescia.

I'm not going to explain what happened in each Grand Prix that season, suffice to say that things didn't improve. What I witnessed that year was an increasing stressful situation in which the Italian team manager, race engineers and both drivers were convinced that the primary problem was a lack of down force, endorsed by their data statistics from the previous seasons, which was related to the Dallara chassis. On the other side of the fence, as it were, was Eric Broadley and his team, who were convinced that the problem was one of mechanical grip or rather a lack of mechanical grip. For me, a non-technical person, I could only look on in despair as the ante was upped. The further into the season we got, the worse the atmosphere between the two camps became.

In that era of F1, we had an innovation called pre-qualifying. In other words, difficult as it might be to believe today, there were more teams and cars in F1 than the maximum number allowed on individual race tracks. Qualifying was not like today, with Q1, Q2 and Q3 to determine the grid, but rather a straight shoot-out between every single car to fill the maximum number of grid places permitted. This meant that quite often up to ten cars might fail to qualify, and that was their weekend over.

During that awful season, 1993, between them the two Lola's failed to qualify no less than seven times and retired because of technical issues a further 11 times. I remember one of the darkest moments being at the British Grand Prix which was held at the Donnington Park Circuit that year. The race became famous for the amazing performance in very wet conditions, of Ayrton Senna in his McLaren, but for Michele, despite actually running to the end of the Grand Prix; it had been a nightmare. In his own words, he told me that he was suffering such bad understeer, or pushing as it's known in America, that he wanted to retire the car on the third lap, but found it impossible to negotiate the hairpin that preceded the entry to the pit lane, so bad was the understeer, so he had to just keep going. He ended up in 11th place, the last finisher, some six laps down from Senna, the race winner. He went on to ask the question why nobody at Lola seemed to take any notice of his views on what was wrong with the car.

In a sad way, I think everyone was glad to reach the end of the season. There were no winners in the battle between the Italian side of the team and the UK, just losers. I felt desperately sorry for Eric Broadley, who so wanted to see his beloved Lola brand make its mark in the modern era of F1. When the season was over, we were sitting in his office chatting one afternoon, he told me that if he could sell Lola tomorrow, he would then head off to Lymington in Hampshire, where his yacht was moored and spend his time enjoying his other passion, sailing. I could see that he had enough of F1.

Year 1993 was a memorable for me in many ways, not least of all because it was the last time I met James Hunt. You may recall that back in 1981, I'd organised a Deutz-sponsored tractor race at Kyalami, on the morning of what should have been the 1981 South African F1 G1 Grand Prix. Due to political wrangles involving Bernie Ecclestone of FOCA and Jean Marie Balestre of FISA, the race was downgraded at the last moment and didn't count for world championship points. James had agreed to drive one of the 24 tractors, he but hadn't appeared on the race morning. He had most definitely appeared at the party I held at my house opposite the race track, and what a great pleasure it had been to meet one of F1's greatest characters. I hadn't seen him again since then, so when Tony Jardine invited me to join him and James for dinner the night before the 1993 South African Grand Prix. I was delighted to accept.

With Max Mosley's help, Brian became Manager of the Kyalami F1 Circuit. In 1981, Brian secured sponsorship with German tractor manufacturer Deutz, enabling South African female racer, Desire Wilson, to drive for Ken Tyrrell, in the SA Grand Prix. Sadly, the race didn't count for Championship points, due to a bitter row between FISA and FOCA.

During the evening I spent with James and Tony, it became very apparent that this was a different James Hunt to the one whom I'd met at my party. It came out in conversation that he was finding life tough financially, as you can read in the excellent book on James Hunt by Maurice Hamilton. Whilst some people might find the story depressing in some ways, I took a positive view after meeting him that evening. What I feel I experienced that evening was the real James Hunt, not trying to impress anyone, happy to talk about the ways in which his life had changed and how many of his supposed friends had deserted him when the money ran out. I thought back to the letter that he'd personally sent me after failing to turn up at the Charity tractor race all those years before. I knew then, that under the rather feral playboy image, there was someone rather special. He didn't have to write that letter to me. A number of so called F1 celebrities wouldn't have bothered because I couldn't be of any use to them. I feel so privileged that I spent that very special evening with James and Tony Jardine.

On 15 June 1993, three months later, James passed away, leaving a void in the sport that has never really been filled. He would have been so proud of his son Freddie, who is now enjoying increasing success in sports cars, often run by Brookspeed, the team owned by a friend of mine, Martin Braybrook. He often tells me how incredibly similar Freddie is to his famous father and what a good driver he is. Many years later, in 2016, I was asked to contribute my comments about James

Hunt on one of a series of paintings by Mark Dickens, based on every F1 World Champion. The entire collection was ultimately purchased by Sebastian Vettel.

In 2016, Mark Dickens, the British painter, was commissioned to create a set of paintings of every F1 World Champion. Brian was proud to be invited to add some words about James Hunt on the British World Champion's portrait, as well as on Jody Scheckter's.

That season, 1993, I spent a lot of time involved with Lola's F1 efforts, from which it was sadly impossible to derive much pleasure. However, what I did enjoy a lot were the few occasions when I was able to attend some of the CART Rounds in America. Having won the 1992 World F1 Championship for Williams, Nigel Mansell had stunned the motor racing world by announcing that he had concluded a deal with Carl Haas to drive for Newman Haas Racing in the CART Championship the very next year.

In my opinion, Nigel Mansell is one of the most under-rated Grand Prix drivers of all time. I might upset a few people by saying this, but if he had been Brazilian or Italian, he would have been lauded far more than he was as a Brummie, with his distinctive accent. As I was to discover, F1 has a very high level of snobbery within certain sectors of the sport, including the British media. Nigel wore his heart on his sleeve; and if you're a Brit, that doesn't go down too well.

One or two of his F1 team mates were also more adapt than he was in playing mind games. I recall the incredible animosity between Nigel and Nelson Piquet when they were at Williams together. For a driver to start slagging off his team mate's wife, as Piquet did quite blatantly about Roseanne Mansell, was totally unacceptable in my book. I'd known Roseanne and Nigel since 1974; and besides being a lovely person in her own right, without the incredible level of support that she provided for Nigel, he would never have reached the levels of the sport that he did. At the time, quite a few people in F1 thought Piquet's comments were rather amusing, but that only goes to endorse my views. It also highlighted a major difference that I was to discover between F1 racing and racing in CART. In America, drivers' wives, girlfriends and children were made far more welcome by the teams and the media, whereas in F1, I always felt that they were tolerated, at best, and cold-shouldered in many cases.

Having seen for myself how different the scene was in America, I personally hoped that Nigel might fit into CART and enjoy himself better than he had perhaps in F1. That he could deliver on the ovals, as well as the street and road tracks, was never in doubt in my mind.

Confident as I was that Nigel would show fans of CART racing, as well as the hyper critical F1 community, just how good a driver he was, I don't think I was alone in being overwhelmed at the level of his talent, bravery and dedication in his first ever season in America. What was so amazing was that in his first season, contrary to what most people expected, it wasn't the traditional road circuits where he excelled. Instead, it was the tough, demanding and unforgiving oval tracks, such as Phoenix, where a huge accident in practice nearly put paid to the rest of his season, or Milwaukee, which hosts the famous Milwaukee 200.

I had the pleasure to be at Milwaukee in late May when Nigel blitzed a grid that included two other F1 world champions, Mario Andretti and Emerson Fittipaldi, to win this famous race. Having been to quite a few oval races in America, I found them fascinating. The common complaint when you speak to European motorsport fans is that oval track racing is boring. Yes, of course it can be, any form of racing can be; and, my goodness, hasn't Formula 1 been going through a long spell of some very boring racing during the past few seasons?

Liz, my wife, is a great yardstick when it comes to putting across a balanced view of watching motorsport. She has certainly done a fair bit of it in our 33 years together. From circuits like Welkom, in the Orange Free State in South Africa when I raced for Mercedes Benz, to Kyalami at the South African Grand Prix, as well as many other F1 events during my years with Benetton F1 and Lola F1, Liz has seen it all. She would be the first to tell you that she has been least impressed of all with F1, which she found very pretentious and unfriendly.

In 1999, she was given the opportunity to check out the difference between F1 and CART, when we were invited by Derek Walker, boss of the CART team, Walker Racing, to a weekend at the Nazareth Speedway in Nazareth, Pennsylvania. I was in the latter stages of negotiating a representation deal with Derek, at the time.

Having stopped in Bethlehem for breakfast on our way through to the circuit, an experience in itself, we arrived mid-morning on the Friday's practice session. As we headed into the centre field to meet Derek and his race driver, Gil de Ferran, we were greeted by the most ear-piercing screech of metal on concrete as Al Unser Junior lost control of his Penske and scraped the wall for about 250 yards before coming to rest, fortunately unhurt, in the middle of the track. It immediately brought home the speeds these cars were reaching on this one-mile oval.

On race day, Derek suggested that we'd be better going up into the "bleaches" to watch and see all the action. What immediately fascinated Liz was the consumption within the packed stands, of huge hot dogs, oozing yellow mustard and blood like ketchup, much of which was being transferred with gay abandon onto a variety of brightly coloured shirts.

The racing itself was something to behold, with Helio Castro Neves and eventual winner, Juan Pablo Montoya, continually wheel-banging as they vied for the lead, lap after lap. The central tower displayed the race positions, keeping everyone totally up to speed as to how the race was unfolding. I worried that Liz would soon tire of the action, but the longer the race went on, the more excited she became. After the race, we headed back to our hotel, and she told me that was one of the most exciting race-meetings she'd ever been to. For a start, she explained she was able to see the whole race unfolding, unlike F1, where you see the cars hurtle past every one minutes 30 seconds or so. At most Grand Prix, she added, you spend more time watching the action on the big screens than you do on the race track in front of you. She found that with oval track racing you got to watch the whole race unfolding, whilst the PA commentary, combined with the clearly visible control tower information meant that you could monitor everything that was happening on track.

During one of my visits to America, I sat having a coffee with Mario Andretti, and we talked about the differences between the two forms of racing, CART and F1. He, of course, has been hugely successful in both. What he told me was very simple. In America, he said, we race for the fans; in Europe, you race for the media. It was an interesting viewpoint, and I think he summed it up very well.

Eventually, 1993 came to an end. It had been a formative year for me, and I still continue to look back at that era and count myself very lucky that I was able to not only gain so much valuable experience of motorsport on a truly international scale, but that I had met so many incredible people within the sport. The sport, to me, has always been about the people in it rather than the technology that today is dominating so much of it. Maybe that's why I think that so many of F1s current issues would be far more easily resolved by marketing experts than leaving it in the hands of technologists.

Chapter 31
A Tragic Loss, Max and Bernie's Shock Plan and a Bold New Venture

As we moved into 1994, everyone at Lola Race Cars was delighted to hear that its Managing Director Mike Blanchet would soon be back on the scene on a regular basis. His business acumen had been greatly missed during his relatively long absence; and whilst everyone had chipped in as best they could, it had a bearing on some of the problems now facing the company. It has to be said though that the mood amongst the 140 or so staff was rather despondent after the disastrous F1 season that the company had endured. It goes without saying that both parties, Lola and BMS Scuderia Italia, decided to bring their relationship to an end.

No one was more disappointed than Michele Alboreto. I had invited him to be my guest at the Autosport Show dinner in January, courtesy of Selenia Oils, a company that I had approached for sponsorship. They had arranged for the Maserati sports car that Michele had raced in the World Endurance Championship to be on their stand at the show. Everyone at our table found Michele to be the most enjoyable of guest, and he kept us all entertained with wonderful stories of his time as an F1 driver at Ferrari. One in particular has always stayed in my mind. Just after he and his wife Nadia had their first child, Naomi, apparently Enzo Ferrari invited them to supper in his private apartment. Michele explained that it was rather like being summoned by the headmaster at school to his study, such was the awe in which the drivers held the great man. Enzo had told Nadia how he looked upon his drivers very much like his own sons, and how incredibly proud he was of Michelle and his new baby daughter. He then handed Nadia a small packet which, she discovered, contained the keys to a brand new Ferrari road car. A token, Enzo Ferrari stated, of his love for Michele, Nadia and the new arrival.

The next time that I met Michele was at Silverstone in 2000. I was walking along the front of all the transporters parked outside the garages in the paddock. It was a round of the World Sportscar Championship, and Michele was driving for Audi. Suddenly, I heard my name being called. I looked around, and there he was, wearing a long, warm-looking overcoat, running towards me from the paddock entrance. He greeted me like an old friend, which surprised me as I was just one of hundreds of people with whom he had worked over the years. He asked me if I had enjoyed working with Benetton F1, and what I thought of Flavio Briatore. He went on to tell me his personal thoughts about the man. They weren't favourable, to say the least.

In 2001, Michele lost his life in a crash whilst testing an Audi R8 race car at the Lausitzring in Germany, following a tyre blow-out. Knowing, from the short time I spent with him, how important his family was to him, I can't begin to imagine how badly the tragedy must have affected his wife and two daughters. Motor racing is an incredible sport, with some extraordinary highs and lows. Michele was one of the most likeable individuals I have had the pleasure of knowing in my motorsport career.

Back at Lola Cars in Huntingdon, we saw less and less of Eric Broadley. He indulged himself in his passion for sailing and who could blame him. The whole F1 fiasco had left a bitter taste in his mouth and for someone so passionate about his business and his workforce, 1993 had hit him hard.

In addition to everything I've talked about with F1, there was a problem on the horizon in the USA, with Lola's primary competitor in Europe, Reynard Motorsport, based at Bicester, now making in-roads into Lola's lucrative American market by designing and producing highly competitive race cars for the CART Championship. This included eventually persuading Lola's leading Indycar designer, Bruce Ashmore, to set up and run a North American operation for them, based in Indianapolis.

Then came another potential body blow for Lola and Eric. It started one morning, when his secretary Jane brought us both a coffee, as we sat talking in his office about a few relevant issues. She put the latest copy of *Autosport* on his desk and suggested that we looked at the page she'd folded over. Eric read the headline at the top of the page and then passed it to me, with an expression on his face that said this was all we needed right now. I knew it was something serious.

There it was, I can still picture it in my mind, the headline that no one at Lola wanted to see: *Max and Bernie to Make F3000 a Control Formula*. The implications of this single statement were alarming, which was what Eric was referring to. Formula 3000 had been introduced by the FIA in 1985 to be the category just one step below Formula 1. The cars looked very much like F1 cars, but weren't quite as quick. The F3000 specifications allowed and encouraged a choice of chassis, engine, transmission, brakes and many other parts. This meant that there was a healthy competition between many different companies. In addition, the way that teams ran F3000 was to amortise the cars over two seasons. In other words, teams would buy a new car every second year, a major cost reduction policy.

F3000 quickly became the category that attracted young designers and engineers, where they could cut their teeth before hopefully moving up into the full-scale battle-field that was Formula 1.

As one of the leading F3000 constructors, it could have a serious and detrimental effect on Lola's current orders and future business. This wouldn't affect only us, but all businesses involved in the Formula. I found it incredible that such a statement could be issued by the sport's governing body, without any prior discussion with the companies heavily involved. These included Reynard, Ralt, Cosworth, Zytek and many others. The reality facing everyone if Max and Bernie got their way was that those existing suppliers who failed to secure exclusive supply contracts would undoubtedly be forced to lay-off many highly skilled workers.

Another worry was that by adopting a control formula policy which, through a tender process, would identify one specific chassis supplier, one brake supplier and so on, would mean that the competition aspect would disappear, and young designers would lose a great opportunity to prove their worth to potential F1 employers. Yet another "control formula" would do nothing to help them, and there were already too many such categories.

Another negative factor of the Ecclestone, Mosley statement was that teams were already phoning and asking us put their orders for new cars on hold. It was understandable, as they didn't want to buy a car which they would normally expect to amortise over two years, to become obsolete at the end of just one season, if the new "control formula" was brought in. All in all, it was a very worrying problem. With Lola CEO, Mike Blanchet still not fit enough to return right then, I proposed to Eric that I should call Adrian Reynard and suggest that he and I set up a meeting with FIA President Max Mosley, to outline our concerns. Although we were competitors in the F3000 market, this threatened move would have serious implications for both of our companies.

In his Kensington office, Max listened intently to what Adrian and I had to say and then explained that he was worried about F3000 budgets having increased dramatically. He felt that drastic action was needed; hence, the new regulations. After taking on-board our point that prior consultation should have been entered into, Max advised us to arrange a meeting, involving all companies working in F3000 and to endeavour to agree a series of major cost-cutting measures which he would seriously consider. It seemed sensible, but then I didn't know how difficult it would be to make this happen.

Trying to persuade everyone involved in F3000 to sit around a table, to forget their day-to-day rivalries and to look at the bigger picture was a nightmare!

In the process of trying to put this forum together, it made me realise that the British motorsport sector was supposedly a world-leading industry, and yet it had no forum for such discussion. Furthermore, there was no mechanism in place for motorsport industry leaders to discuss rule and regulation changes with the sport's governing body. The industry had no representative body to protect and promote the interests of its thousands of businesses of all sizes. There was a total lack of any industry data or statistics about the size of the industry or the number of people employed. It was done by thumb-sucking. Even more to the point came the realisation that there was actually no such thing as the British motorsport industry in its own right, formally recognised by the government. Companies working in motorsport were seen to be add-ons to the automotive industry. The more I delved into this situation, the more I realised that although everyone casually referred to the UK being the world leader in terms of the motorsport industry, the reality was that there were no industry statistics in respect of turnover, exports percentages or even the number of employees. Perhaps even more worrying was the absence of a clearly laid out industry career path for youngsters wanting to become high-performance engineers or technicians within motorsport.

The reality was that our industry was successful without really knowing why. So how best these concerns could be addressed? It didn't need rocket science to work out that the British motorsport industry needed government recognition as an industry in its own right, separate from the automotive industry. To achieve this I believed that what was needed was the formation of its own representative trade body. Looking back at that time, I'm really not sure what made me take on the task of trying to achieve just that, but that's exactly what I decided to do.

Chapter 32

Tea at the House of Lords, a New Industry and a Lancaster House Invitation

I knew from my experience and success in sponsorship acquisition that one of the most daunting problems I would face was not just generating enough funding to set up such a new organisation but convincing people of the need for such an initiative. Even more difficult would be the task of convincing people that this was about the business of motorsport and not another of the schemes that keep appearing to find the next British F1 Champion. It wouldn't be easy, and I needed help. I turned to the business world, thinking that there would be more understanding there about my objectives in terms of securing business partners capable of helping me set up and launch such an organisation. The first company I approached was Andersen Consulting, now known as Accenture.

I had previously approached Andersen Consulting in the UK to become a potential Lola F1 sponsor. They were sponsors of Newman Haas Racing in America, and Carl Haas, during one of my visits to Chicago, agreed to introduce me to a senior level person within their London office. He did just that, and I arranged a meeting with Rob Baldock, who was a partner in the organisation. Unfortunately, we hadn't been able to agree a deal, but it was more to do with timing than anything else.

When I called Rob again, this time briefly outlining my ideas for setting up a motorsport industry representative organisation, he was immediately very interested. We then met to discuss the concept in more detail. When he heard that I had already gathered support from some individual individuals within the industry, he suggested that we should invite them to a presentation at Andersen's head office in London, with a view to agreeing how we might move forward with my concept.

The subsequent meeting went extremely well, and it wasn't long before we had Andersen's agreement to support the organisation that I had named The Motorsport Industry Association, MIA for short.

In that meeting, we all agreed that the first step would be to form a steering committee of influential motorsport industry contacts. Rob then volunteered to serve on a steering committee if I could pull one together. This was a huge positive step forward, as I knew that unless we could firmly position the proposed organisation as being about business, not about racing drivers, it would flounder and die. Having Andersen Consulting as the primary sponsor would ensure that high level of business credibility.

The Steering Committee that we set up comprised:
- Rob Baldock partner at Andersen Consulting
- Richard Scammell MBE CEO of Cosworth Racing
- Ralph Firman CEO of Van Diemen International
- Tony Schulp publishing director of Haymarket/Autosport Group
- John Kirkpatrick CEO of Jim Russell Racing Driver School
- Tony Panaro CEO of Euro Northern Travel/Motorsport Tours
- Brian Sims (chairman) marketing & PR director of Lola F1

Every one of these influential figures agreed that there was a very real need within the motorsport industry for an organisation of the kind I had proposed. The Motorsport Industry Association was about to take shape. It was a very special feeling to know that such an experienced group of industry leaders had bought into my vision.

To have such an experienced steering committee took a lot of the weight off my shoulders, as I knew that my own level of business acumen was nowhere near at a level that would be needed as we moved the organisation forward to meet the many needs of the industry. I was a professional salesman, and of that I was very proud, with a huge level of enthusiasm and ideas for the growth of the new organisation, but I had never had a formal business education; so to have Rob Baldock, from outside of our industry, but with vast experience in business management, growth and development was a huge bonus.

The first thing that Rob did for us was to introduce the committee to two business colleagues whom he felt might be persuaded to help the MIA. Thanks to this introduction, we were able to enter into favourable partnership agreements with global law firm Norton Rose agreeing to manage the incorporation of the MIA; and Rawlinson Hunter, international financial and tax experts, agreeing to carry out our financial audits.

I was also able to secure an affiliation agreement with Society of Motor Manufacturers and Traders, feeling it would further enhance our credibility. Many of their members companies, such as Cosworth and Ford, were heavily involved in motorsport and agreed that it would be in their interest to also become members of a representative body such as the MIA, to promote and protect their interests in the coming years.

Within six months of my first meeting with Rob Baldock, the MIA was launched at Andersen Consulting's prestigious European HQ in Arundel Street, London. Hosted by well-known Brands Hatch motorsport commentator and a good friend of mine, Brian Jones, and attended by about 60 people, including many media personnel. I was able to outline the primary objectives of this new organisation, which included:

- Gaining formal recognition of motorsport as an industry in its own right.
- Providing a forum for businesses operating within the industry.
- Providing industry statistics.
- Promoting and protecting the interests of businesses operating within the industry.
- Providing educational career paths and qualifications within the industry.

The resulting positive media coverage was really encouraging, but I should have realised that it would have a downside. We started receiving negative feedback from a few industry people who clearly had no intention of seeing the bigger picture. One in particular was Tony Fletcher, the CEO of Premier Fuel Systems. He also chaired AMRA, an organisation that was basically set up to manage the distribution of trade passes at motorsport events. I met with him and suggested that he might like to serve on the MIA Committee, representing AMRA, which he agreed to. What I hadn't bargained on was that he and a couple of other AMRA members would use their best efforts to undermine what the MIA was trying to achieve. This came to a head during an MIA Committee meeting in the SMMT's London HQ, at which the late Ernie Thompson, SMMT CEO, was voicing his support of our aims and objectives. Following a pro-AMRA, anti-MIA intervention, Fletcher was immediately asked to resign from the Committee. I personally found this incident so sad and pointless. He didn't seem able to accept the fact that the MIA had been created as an "umbrella" organisation for the motorsport industry, and that it wasn't competing in any way shape or form with AMRA.

Within a month of the MIA launching, we had over 20 member companies on-board, including totally unsolicited membership applications from Alan Gow's TOCA organisation and from the Benetton F1 Team. Ford and Cosworth had also joined, as had Van Diemen International, at that time, the world's largest volume manufacturer of race cars. We always knew that growing the membership would be a tough job, as with most new organisations. The attitude of many people, which I could understand, was that they would wait to see who else joined, before making the decision to do so themselves.

Having been appointed as the CEO of the MIA, registered as a non-profit making organisation, I needed to spend all my time helping to achieve the objectives that we had set ourselves. I took the decision to resign from Lola and focus on the MIA. Funds were obviously very low in those early days despite amazing generosity from Andersen, Cosworth, Ford, Gordon Bruce and Van Diemen. To her credit, Liz agreed to go back to work so that I could afford to focus on MIA matters entirely.

At our first full Committee Meeting, which I recall was at the Dorchester Hotel, I raised the topic of looking for a "quick-win" membership benefit that we would help answer the question that so often was put forward, "What's in it for me?" We were all finding that too many companies were sitting on the fence, waiting until we had some 40 or 50 members in place, before they would sign up. This included Ron Dennis at McLaren.

I had arranged an appointment to meet Ron at his Woking office. When I arrived, the first thing he said to me was that he only had a few minutes, as Alain Prost was waiting to see him. Having briefly explained why we had set up the MIA, I told Ron that I was fully aware that the MIA needed McLaren far more than McLaren needed the MIA, at this stage of its existence, but that unless the likes of McLaren supported the launch of such an organisation, it would be tough to get other smaller companies to join. Sadly, it was water off a duck's back to the boss of McLaren, and I never heard from him after our meeting. He didn't have the courtesy to let me know if McLaren was in or not. I should have realised that he was far too important to waste time with this fledgling organisation as it was then. However, as you will hear in due course, it didn't stop McLaren taking advantage of the MIA to promote their own interests, still without joining the organisation, which really didn't impress me!

As a Committee, we were still looking for that magical "quick win" element to make membership more attractive. I had more time to think about this than the rest of the Committee, who had their own businesses to run; and I eventually put a proposal to them, suggesting that we should launch an annual MIA Business Achievement Awards programme. Awards would be presented at a reception for which MIA members could buy tickets at a preferential rate. With a range of Award categories, including Small Business of the Year, Export Achievement of the Year and Technical Achievement the Year, we hoped that it might attract companies that are keen to achieve some form of recognition. When Rob Baldock, by then MIA chairman, persuaded Andersen Consulting to sponsor the top award, we knew that we were onto a winner.

The inaugural MIA Business Awards were held at the Rothley Court Hotel in Leicestershire, for which Liz and I managed to sell 100 tickets at £40 each, meaning that we would break even, at worst. The Anderson Consulting Award that evening went to Prodrive and was accepted by its chairman, David Richards. With several senior Andersen Consulting partners and guests attending the event, I hoped that he would be positive about the MIA in his acceptance speech.

In 1994, Brian established the Motorsport Industry Association, with sponsorship from Andersen Consulting, now known as Accenture. Prodrive's CEO, David Richards (left), was presented with the primary Award at the inaugural MIA Business Achievement Awards. A year later, the event was held at the House of Lords, thanks to the help of Lord Astor of Hever, whom Brian had invited to become the MIA's Honorary President.

He was positive, but didn't leave it at that. Upon receiving the Award, David Richards made the comment that, delighted as he was to receive the MIA/Andersen Consulting Award, which included an element of consultancy services, he felt that Prodrive could probably teach Andersen more than Andersen could teach Prodrive. Which wasn't exactly what the Andersen Consulting directors had expected to hear.

As a Committee, another issue that we recognised was the need for a high-profile honorary MIA President, who could open doors into government and industry. A solution presented itself when I was invited by Cosworth to be the guest speaker at a conference held at Silverstone, to which a group of all-party peers and lords were present. Having talked about the organisation that I'd set up and the reasons for its existence, I was able to meet some of the guests. One in particular expressed great interest at the launch of the MIA, Lord Astor of Hever. Having chatted for some time about the aims and objectives of the organisation, he asked if there was anything that he could do to help us achieve these.

When I reported back to my committee, we all agreed that there was a role which could well provide Lord Astor with an opportunity to help the MIA. It was our belief that he would make a great honorary president, and I agreed to get back in touch with him to propose this.

After leaving a message for him with his PA, Tracy, I was stuck in a jam on the M25 when he called back. I explained that we had come up with a proposal and would like to meet with him. He suggested that we met up for tea the following week at the house. When I asked him where he lived, there was a no reply for a moment; then he responded with the comment that he meant the House of Lords, not his private house!

The following week, I joined him in the House of Lords private restaurant, where we discussed my proposal about becoming our honorary president. He agreed to think about this and then offered to take me on a tour of the House of Lords, which, as you can imagine, proved a fascinating experience. A few days later, Lord Astor called me again and, to my delight, agreed that he would be pleased to accept our invitation to become Honorary President of the MIA. Then he added that it was conditional upon him being able to help in a practical way, as opposed to simply becoming a figurehead. He waited for my response.

Brian, in the Jordan F1 car, with Lord Astor of Hever (MIA Honorary President) seated on the car. In 2019, the MIA celebrates its 25th anniversary and still hosts its annual Awards Reception at this prestigious location.

I don't know where the thought came from, I hadn't pre-planned it, but I found myself suggesting that there was a way in which he could immediately help us in a practical way. I told him about the success of our inaugural MIA Business Achievement Awards evening at the Rothley Court Hotel and suggested that if he could arrange for our next awards reception to be hosted at the House of Lords, it would be a huge step forward for our organisation. I held my breath!

His response was that he very much doubted that a commercial event could be held at the House of Lords. I wasn't surprised, to be honest, but thought it worthwhile persevering and asked if he could try. To his credit, Lord Astor said that he would ask Black Rod, the official responsible for such matters.

Two days later, I heard from Lord Astor, and he relayed some great news to me. Yes, Black Rod had agreed that we could host the MIA Reception at the House of Lords, on the Monday evening in July, following the British F1 Grand Prix weekend at Silverstone. The venue would be the Cholmondeley Room, with a private terrace overlooking the Thames. He went to explain that we could have two race cars on display in the courtyard, but there must be no tobacco advertising on them, and there must be no commercial promotion of the event. All in all, it really was a dream come true, and I was so grateful to Lord Astor for his efforts to secure this extraordinary booking for the MIA.

I think I can speak for all the members of the Steering Committee in saying that when we eventually arrived at the House of Lords on that very special day in July, there was a great feeling of pride in what we had achieved. Not only had we started such a worthwhile and much-needed organisation, but we had managed to secure one of the most prestigious and iconic venues that one could imagine for hosting the MIA Business Achievement Awards Reception. Little did we know then, that the event would continue to be held there on an annual basis for the next 24 years and hopefully for many more to come.

Then, just over a year later, in 1995, totally out of the blue, I received a phone call from the President of the Board of Trade, Ian Lang. He explained that the following year, 1996, had been designated the official centenary of the automobile in the UK; and that in his official capacity, he would be speaking at several major events being staged to celebrate the achievement of the motor industry in that 100 years. He was battling, he told me, to find stories of the current success of the motor industry, which in the mid-1990s, was not at its peak, to put it mildly. He went on to say that he had, on the other hand, come across many stories about the success of the British motorsport sector, before eventually hearing about the formation of the MIA. He then put a proposal to me, asking if I would like to attend a dinner at Lancaster House, next door to Buckingham Palace, with the theme "What can the world-leading British motorsport industry do to help other British industry sectors?" He added that I should put together a guest list of 11 other representatives from my industry, including Formula 1.

Amongst those I invited was McLaren's CEO, Martin Whitmarsh, even though I was tempted to omit McLaren, as they still hadn't joined the MIA, but I preferred to look at the bigger picture. Other people whom I invited included Patrick Head from Williams F1, David Richards from Prodrive, as well as Committee members Dick Scammell MBE, Ralph Firman and John Kirkpatrick. At this fascinating meeting, we came to the conclusion that the best way in which the motorsport industry could help other industry sectors, would be to use young people's proven passion and excitement for motorsport to encourage them into much-needed engineering and technical skills training.

I must relate the way in which the meeting started. Before getting down to the nitty-gritty, Tim Eggar, the minister of mineral affairs, who stood in for Ian Laing at the last minute, suggested that before asking for our thoughts on the main topic, which was to look at ways in which we could help other industry sectors, he would like to ask each one of us what the government could do to help our companies, specifically. The answers were all interesting, mainly linked to cutting unnecessary red tape, helping with R&D tax exemptions and similar assistance. However, when the question was put to Martin Whitmarsh of McLaren, the answer came out as bold as brass. He told the minister that the best way it could help McLaren would be to help overturn the Green Belt veto on the plans for building McLaren's new headquarters at a site in Woking. In the circumstances, as they weren't even members of the MIA, I thought it was out of order, but when it comes to thick skins, F1 takes some beating. I'm not sure if McLaren ever joined the MIA.

When it came to Patrick Head, Williams F1 technical director, he told the minister that the best way they could help Williams was to keep their nose out of it. Williams didn't need financial help, he confirmed, explained that the only way that the government might be able to help would be to cut some of the red tape that affected so much of their activities.

The way in which we eventually proposed that we could best help other industry sectors was to use the proven attraction of motorsport to young people, to encourage them into engineering and technical skills training. Education and training was one of the original objectives of the MIA, announced in my speech at the official launch in 1994.

Just two years after this meeting at Lancaster House, the world's first dedicated motorsport engineering degree course was launched in the UK, at the Swansea Institute, by Roger Dowden and his engineering team. Things move quickly within the motorsport industry. Today, some 17 UK universities now offer motorsport engineering degrees. Of these, Oxford Brookes University is one of the leading suppliers of graduates to Grand Prix teams, including Ferrari F1. In fact, in 2018, Oxford Brookes could boast that it had graduates currently in every F1 Team. Some achievement!

By the end of 1996, the MIA was becoming very high-profile. The problem was that it still wasn't generating enough income to support a full-time administrative office. My efforts to secure funding from UKTI were well received, but such matters take time, and we needed to make a plan urgently!

We felt that we couldn't keep increasing membership subscriptions, as there were so many small businesses within our industry that just wouldn't be able to afford them. I started talking to the department of trade and industry about potential grants. In fairness, everyone I met was very positive about the MIA, but that's about as far as it went.

Everyone on the Steering Committee worked hard to find ways of raising the necessary finance that would help us set up an administrative office, but I think the problem was that none of us had any prior experience of running a non-profit organisation of this kind.

Some of the Steering Committee members helped financially, in particular, Dick Scammel of Cosworth and Ralph Firman of Van Diemen, both of whom were also very helpful to Liz and myself. Liz kept working to allow me to continue my full-time efforts on behalf of the MIA, but it couldn't go on forever like this. After discussing matters with my committee, I reluctantly took the decision to stand down as CEO and suggested that we find a replacement, someone in a position to initially take on the role without pay but with the expertise to put a funding programme in place.

It was Ralph Firman who put a name forward as a potential candidate. He had met Chris Aylett, who had been running the Sports and Allied Industries Trade Association successfully for some years previously. It made sense to bring someone in with such a relevant level of experience, and it was agreed that I should meet Chris for an initial chat at his home in Warwick.

I liked what I heard from him, and after a meeting with the committee, it was agreed that a proposal would be put to him to take on the role of CEO of the MIA. It was good choice in many ways, and Chris went about the task with a high level of enthusiasm and, most importantly, knowledge and experience of how to develop a business strategy that would enable growth and development through sound financial planning.

The MIA has now reached its 25th anniversary, and it has gone from to strength under Chris Aylett's relentless efforts to grow the motorsport industry. After a few years of excellent service in his role as the Honorary President, Lord Astor stood down, due to his political activities taking up an increasing amount of his time, but I am delighted to say that he eventually returned to the MIA in the same role a few years later.

Chapter 33
A Surprising Lunch Invitation, Back to F1 and a Close Shave

From a personal viewpoint, I was at a loss as to what to do next. The MIA had been my life for nearly four years, and now I was no longer involved in the role. Then, as often happens, I took a call, out of the blue, from someone I had met through my involvement with Lola F1. His name was Tony Webb, and he was a director of API, a sports marketing agency that I had engaged in my role with the F1 Team, to help us generate international sponsorship. API was owned by the Olympic silver medallist, Alan Pascoe, who had been the captain of the British Team in the 1970s. Alan's competed in both the 110 m and 400 m hurdles, as well as the men's 4 x 400 m relay.

Tony asked me what I was doing and was surprised when I told him about resigning from the MIA. He told me that he wanted my help with a certain matter and asked if I would join him for lunch the following week in Guildford. He added that he would be accompanied by someone else whom I knew, but hadn't met for many years. He wouldn't tell me who it was. It sounded intriguing.

I arrived at the restaurant and was delighted to see that my host was already there. Sitting next to Tony Webb was Matthew Argenti, another of the band of Formula Ford 1600 drivers who competed in the highly popular category back in the mid-1970s. Although I had met Matthew on occasions, we didn't really know each other that well. I knew that he had been a very quick driver and runner-up in a championship that was won by a certain Mr Mansell. I also knew that he had been good at securing sponsorship, which was something we had in common; and that after he retired from driving, he had joined IMG, the global sports marketing corporation that was owned by Mark McCormack. IMG represented, and still does, many of the world's top sports stars and sports properties.

It was great to meet up again with Matthew, as it was with Tony Webb, who also worked in the field of sports sponsorship, albeit in track and field rather than motorsport. In fact, Tony, in his role with API, was one of the most successful sports marketing personnel within European and British athletics. However, when Tony explained the purpose of the meeting, it was not what I was expecting. He told me, in confidence, that API had been approached by the Benetton F1 Team to discuss the possibility of becoming the team's exclusive sponsorship acquisition agency. It was a big step into the unknown for API, with athletics being its primary area of operation, which was not surprising, given Alan Pascoe's background. However, driven very much by Matthew, with his motorsport and IMG background, a deal had been struck. It meant that with immediate effect, August 1996, API would help the

F1 World Championship winning team secure sponsorship, on the basis of a healthy commission on all deals secured.

Then Matthew took over the conversation and told me that to be successful in acquiring the Benetton F1 account, API had been required to put down a half million pound guarantee. What this meant is that if in the first year, API did not deliver a sponsorship worth more than half a million pounds, it would forfeit the guarantee. A sobering thought.

Having outlined this scenario, Tony explained that the reason they wanted to meet me was to ask if I could recommend anyone who might be interested in joining API to go out and secure sponsorship, lots of it, for the Benetton Team.

The timing couldn't have been better! I felt it was a role which was made for me and immediately pointed this out to Matthew and Tony, asking them if I fitted their brief for the new position. We left the restaurant in Guildford together and said our goodbyes, but not before they told me that they would be in touch very soon.

I must admit that although I was delighted to join API in June of that year, I was very aware that I was taking on a huge task. I kept my nerves to a minimum by telling myself that there was no reason why I should fail; after all, F1 offered a lot more commercial opportunities than say Formula 3, British Touring Cars or the World Endurance Championship. Then I remembered the £500,000 guarantee that API had put down. No pressures, then, in my new capacity as head of motorsport for API!

Liz and I were living in Southampton at that time, which necessitated a daily commute to London for me, a 140 mile round trip, via the M3, to Drury Lane and the API Head Office. The big difference then, as opposed to today, is that I could leave home at six o'clock each morning, before the traffic really started; and on arrival, park in an NCP in Drury Lane, where I would put the seat right back and have a 30-minute kip before walking along the road to a delightful café where I would enjoy a light breakfast before heading into the office at around a 8:45. Can you imagine doing that today with the traffic levels we live with?

I remember my first morning at API and a meeting with Alan Pascoe himself. He confirmed that my priority was to try and secure a sponsorship deal to clear that half a million pound guarantee. There was no ambiguity!

It so happened that during the first week in my new role, I received a call from Benetton F1, inviting me to sit in a sponsorship presentation that the marketing team would be making to Gillette the following week. It would be really helpful to see for myself how an F1 team manage this critical presentation, and I had no hesitation in accepting their offer.

In my mind, I had always imagined what it would be like to watch the marketing department of a top F1 Team in full stride, delivering a stunning sponsorship presentation. I was about to find out. We were scheduled to meet Risto Myler, Gillette's European Marketing Director, at the Gillette Building, on the Great West Road in Isleworth, the one with the tall brick tower. You can't miss it if you're heading in or out of London from Heathrow Airport, avoiding the M4.

I wasn't introduced to Risto, but sat at the back of the room whilst Benetton's official supplier manager ran through the presentation. I found it totally underwhelming. He delivered the slides in a professional manner, but what surprised me was the lack of depth and innovative thinking in the overall strategy, or should I say lack of a strategy. It was simply a collection of slides outlining what F1 is, how many people watch it on TV, where the races are held and pictures of the Benetton race car, painted in Gillette's colour scheme, with GILLETTE in white, down the side of the car.

On several occasions, I watched Risto checking his watch and more than once stifle a yawn. The presentation was centred on the usual three benefits of a sponsorship, namely brand awareness, hospitality and PR. I was quite shocked at what I saw. It wasn't what I had expected at this level of the sport. As the meeting came to an end, with Risto thanking Jonathan Bancroft and promising to "think it over", I would have put a large bet on the outcome being a polite "No thank you". In fact, I did take a gamble, making an excuse to stay behind whilst the Benetton personnel went down to reception. I quickly introduced myself to Risto, explaining my agency role, and asked a direct question as to whether he had been bored by the presentation. He smiled and asked me if it showed. Yes, I told him, adding that he wasn't the only one as I too had found it totally underwhelming. He then explained that every year, nearly all of the F1 Teams approach Gillette for sponsorship. Every year, he continued, they leave empty-handed. His next comment was a real eye-opener for me. He went on to tell me he knew that Gillette should probably be in F1, in some guise or other, but had so far been unable to come up with viable reason to be involved, one that would help them sell more products. The teams all present wonderful images to us, he continued, showing their cars and personnel emblazoned with Gillette livery, as if we don't know what F1 can offer. They don't seem to grasp that we have all the brand awareness we want and should that change, there are far more economical ways of generating brand awareness than through motor racing.

I then asked Risto if I could meet with him the following week, to listen to his views on some of the future issues facing Gillette in terms of marketing and business development. He looked doubtful, but when I promised it would take no more than an hour, he eventually agreed.

I was nervous when the day of the meeting arrived. A potential deal with one of the most high-profile global brands was both exciting and a little scary. I found Risto to be a friendly, relaxed individual and very frank in replying to my questions. I conducted our meeting in a similar way to that which I had adopted, right at the beginning of my motorsport career. I asked quite a few pertinent questions about Gillette, and the issues facing the company in the years to come, listening carefully to Risto's replies. As I was absorbing all of this information, I was also filtering and matching it with some of the capabilities that sponsorship could potentially offer.

After a fair number of questions, to which he gave me some useful background information, Risto touched on a topic that really grabbed my attention, telling me that one of Gillette's biggest concerns was the increasingly high costs of producing TV product commercials, followed by the equally high cost of placing them on TV channels at prime time. This was just the sort of information I'd been looking for. I had identified a major issue. Now all I had to do was to find a way of using F1 as an innovative platform for providing a solution to the problem.

On the way back to my office, sitting in the tube, I found myself thinking back to my first ever sponsorship deal, the one with Victoria's night club. That had been a case of identifying a need, membership subscription sales and finding a potential way of fulfilling that need. The only difference would be the value of the deal!

Before leaving Gillette, I arranged a second meeting with Risto; this time, the focus would be on presenting a tailored, costed proposal, based on those points that he agreed were important to him. All I had to do before that meeting was to come up with a possible solution.

I'd now been working for Alan Pascoe' agency for about six weeks and been learning a lot about putting together effective PowerPoint presentations, under the careful guidance of the two people who had recruited me, that day in the Guildford restaurant.

We put our heads together on the Gillette opportunity and came up with an idea that might provide a way of meeting Gillette's needs. We set up a meeting with John Postlethwaite, Benetton's Marketing Director at that time, and put the concept to him. It went down well, and he gave us the OK to start preparing a presentation based on the ideas that we had put to him.

Our idea was very simple, but then I suppose that many good ideas in business are just that. From my in-depth conversation with Risto Myler, I had gained confirmation from him that race-car branding held no interest, so there was no point in giving them any. Instead, in return for a sponsorship fee, we opted to provide Gillette with the commercial rights which would allow them to produce a TV lifestyle documentary series, featuring behind-the-scenes look at a world championship-winning F1 team.

We initially suggested that it probably constituted 6 x 30 minute episodes. We contacted Sunset and Vine, the international TV production company, and got a quotation for the filming and production of such a series. This would be centred on the Benetton F1 Team, allowing Sunset and Vine to film and interview personnel, including the team's race drivers, in the factory, in the paddock and the pits, but not, under any circumstances, on the track. The reason for this is that within F1, all TV coverage was then owned by FOM; in other words, under Bernie's control. The cost of a license to film on track would have been prohibitive.

What we then proposed, with the help of some experienced TV producers introduced by John Postlethwaite, was that Gillette should market the proposed new documentary series at Sportel, the TV conference in Monaco. We knew that in around 129 countries, F1 races are shown, either live, deferred or in highlights format. Putting it simply, Gillette could offer every host-broadcaster the rights to show *A Year in the Fast Lane,* as we had proposed the series should be called, on their channels for free. There were some important conditions to this.

Firstly, the series had to be shown mid-week at prime-time, targeting the demographics that Gillette had specified. Secondly, and most importantly, they had to agree that in return for being given the six episodes, they would show Gillette TV commercials at the top, middle and tail of the 30 minute documentary at either free or very reduced rates.

Two weeks after my last meeting with Risto, I went back to the Gillette UK headquarters to present our proposals in full, feeling quietly confident that there would be a favourable response. Little did I expect Alan Boath, the UK president of Gillette, to be sitting in the meeting room, alongside Risto Myler. Having introduced himself, he proceeded to issue a stern warning. He explained that he was a huge fan of F1, but for that very reason, he would be the most difficult person to persuade that Gillette should be involved in F1. He was adamant that nobody in Gillette would point a finger at him and accuse him of making decisions based on his own enthusiasm for the sport.

210

I have to admit that my earlier confidence rather diminished at Alan's surprise intervention, but I had no alternative other than to move on to the proposals that we had put together. During our presentation, Alan sat quietly with an expression that would have been perfect in a Poker game, giving nothing away. Eventually, after running through the key points of the presentation, I suggested that it would be interesting to look at a "what-if" scenario. I suggested that we should look at the figures based on just 25 % of the 129 broadcasters taking up Gillette's offer. Alan took out his pocket calculator and spent a minute or two keying in figures before holding the calculator up to allow Risto to read it. The Finnish Marketing Director raised his eyebrows at Alan, who in turn, came up with a line that I will never forget. 'It's a no-brainer isn't it? Let's do it!'

Subject to contract, I had successfully acquired my first ever F1 sponsorship deal, a multi-million pound agreement. What made it so special for me was the fact that every F1 team had been trying to get Gillette on board, according to Risto Myler and Alan Boath. Interestingly, in the UK, ITV took up Gillette's offer and subsequently broadcast the entire documentary series over 6 weeks, mid-week at prime time, with the agreed amount of advertising.

After this exciting meeting came the hardest part of all, dealing with Gillette's American lawyers to put the contract together. We had some difficult moments, right up to the last minute and even on Christmas Eve, were still battling a few points by phone. Nevertheless, the deal was signed off. Gillette agreed that we would put a small amount of branding on the rear wing endplates, purely for association purposes, and to fit in with an in-store consumer competition that they were launching, based on the TV documentary.

Long after the deal had been done, I kept in touch with Alan Boath, and we enjoyed some enjoyable lunches together. On one such occasion, he told me that I was the only sales person who had walked into the office of the president of the shaving division of Gillette with a beard, sold the company a deal costing a few million pounds and then walked away, still with a beard!

API's Alan Pascoe was now a very happy man. In one deal, just four months after joining the company, I had negated the need for API to pay the half-million pound guarantee to Benetton's Flavio Briatore and earned the company a good chunk of commission.

Chapter 34

A Hanging Offence, a Cold Call to Memphis and a New Sponsor in F1

Within a few weeks, the goodwill that I had built up with Benetton F1 by securing the Gillette deal quickly disappeared. Such is the way of F1, as I'll explain.

I'd been so excited when the opportunity to represent an F1 team came to fruition. For a start, it offered me the chance to prove to myself that my sponsorship-acquisition skills, honed in my own racing career both in the UK and South Africa would bring success in the fiercely competitive world of Grand Prix racing. I was also looking forward to working within an F1 team environment, albeit as the employee of a sports marketing agency. It was not the pleasurable experience that I had expected.

Many years before I joined API, I had the pleasure of attending a prestigious sponsorship conference in Johannesburg. It had been organised by a South African company, owned by golfer Gary Player's son. The VIP guest at the event was none other than Mark McCormack, the founder of IMG, one of the world's most successful sports marketing companies. I'd read McCormack's excellent book many times. It was called *What They Don't Teach You at Havard Business School*, and I don't mind admitting that the man became my role model as I developed my own career in sports marketing.

To my huge disappointment, however, the conference had turned into a rather embarrassing disaster. The audience comprised many leading figures from within the South African business and sports sectors, all of whom had paid a fairly hefty fee to be present. By lunchtime, many were asking for a refund, so upset were they with the way the conference was going. One speaker in particular was targeted, leading to someone within the audience standing up and telling him that along with many others present, he took great exception to South African business leaders being treated as though they were "country cousins". Eventually, one of the event organisers took to the stage to issue an abject apology.

This wasn't what I had expected when I had purchased tickets for myself and my guest, the Marketing Director of Total Oil RSA, one of my racing sponsors. He wasn't impressed, and like most people there, thought it was a very disappointing conference. I had been so looking forward to learning from McCormack, someone whom I saw as the leader in his field. I suppose the only lesson that I learned was that even the very best in the business can get it wrong if they take their eye off the ball.

Now I was in the world of F1, and I genuinely believed that I could learn so much from watching the professionals at work. I'd read the excellent sponsorship book written by Guy Edwards, but apart from that, there was a sad lack of material that would help me develop my own acquisition skills. I was really hungry for knowledge.

I have always been a great believer that enthusiasm is an essential part of being in selling. If you aren't genuinely enthusiastic about the product or service that you are selling, why bother? Rather go and find something that does enthuse you. Unfortunately, the reality was that my first experience of working within a F1 Team was not what I had expected. In fact, I'll go so far as saying that it was downright unpleasant. One incident in particular will always remain in my memory.

API's Matthew Argenti and Tony Webb introduced me to one of their contacts from the world of athletics. Roger Rinke was the representative of a leading German sports marketing agency with whom they did a lot of work. One of the agency's clients was Krombacher Beer, and I was keen to talk to the company about Benetton F1. Following some initial phone discussions with Roger Rinke, I was able to secure a meeting with Krombacher's marketing director, two of his colleagues and Roger himself. We agreed to meet for breakfast at the Dorint Hotel, on the Friday morning of the forthcoming German F1 Grand Prix at the Nurburgring, before heading into the Benetton motorhome area to watch Official Practice. The hotel sits virtually at the side of the starting grid at the famous race track.

It was common practice for the F1 teams to leave paddock passes for their guests with the concierge of the hotel for collection. I was duly handed an envelope with my name on the front. On the front, alongside my name, was the handwritten note "6 x Paddock Passes". Strange, I'd only asked for five, but I would have to sort this out later. I went back through to the restaurant where my guests were sitting and handed out the passes to each one of them and kept a pass for myself. There were definitely only five passes, not 6. I should point out at this stage that Team Paddock Passes are like gold dust within F1. Anyway, we finished breakfast and made our way into the paddock, via the security gates, where the passes had to be swiped. Apparently, the info on each pass could be monitored in the FOM offices.

Having secured ground-breaking, multi-million pound sponsorships for the Benetton F1 team with FedEx and Gillette, Brian was on hand to watch their driver, Jean Alesi, launch the FedEX deal at the British Grand Prix at Silverstone in 1997.

213

The meeting with the Krombacher management team went reasonably well. After watching Gerhard Berger and Jean Alesi put the two Benetton B197s through their paces, we walked back together to the car park, where I collected the four passes from Roger and the three Krombacher guests before waving them goodbye and heading back into the circuit and the Benetton motor home.

I eventually found the girl who worked within Benetton F1's marketing department and had responsibility at a race weekend for handing out the relevant paddock passes. I told her that although the envelope she had left for me showed six passes, there in fact only five. I handed back four of these, retaining mine. Her reaction quite shocked me. I was told in a very forceful way that there were definitely six passes in the envelope when she handed it to the hotel concierge, adding that if I had lost one, I would be in big trouble with the team and with Bernie, as these passes were so important within the overall scheme of things valuable. I resented being spoken to like a naughty schoolboy, assuring the young lady that I hadn't lost the pass. I might as well have saved my breath. In her eyes I was guilty, and there was no appeal. For the next couple of weeks, on the occasions that I visited the marketing department office at the Benetton facility at Enstone, I was given the silent treatment by her and a couple of other members of the marketing personnel. I really didn't appreciate it.

The strained atmosphere continued for about four weeks, then one day the team's Marketing Director, David Warren, informed me that the mystery of the lost pass had been resolved. It seemed that one of the staff members, who had been working in the concierge department of the Dorint Hotel on the race weekend, was steaming open many of the envelopes that had been left by the team, before removing a pass from each one. These were then being sold on to his contacts who were prepared to pay to gain access to the paddock. You have to be very clever to beat the F1 security system. This person obviously wasn't, as he was caught in the process. His name, unfortunately, was Schumacher!

I had expected that once this information had been distributed, I would be due an apology from a couple of people, one lady in particular but that was expecting far too much. Nothing more was ever said about the incident, and there wasn't even a hint of an apology.

I admit to never enjoying my subsequent visits to the Benetton marketing department. I didn't hide the fact that I was passionate about F1, and that didn't seem to go down well with some of the personnel, who rather looked down their nose at me. In case you are thinking that I was being far too sensitive, you'll see later that my opinion was echoed by the marketing director of a new sponsor that I brought to the team, a major global brand, who took great exception to being called a "bloody petrol-head" by one young lady at Benetton, eventually taking the sponsorship deal to another team.

On a positive note, I was making interesting progress in my efforts to acquire another major sponsor for the F1 team. In line with a sales strategy that I had used before, I was targeting one specific industry sector. My research indicated that the freight/parcel delivery sector offered great potential, and this meant companies such as DHL, UPS, FedEx and ParcelForce Worldwide. In 1996, none of these companies were involved in F1 as official sponsors despite many teams knocking on their door each year, trying to tempt them into the sport.

My approach involved trying to arrange meetings at the British head office of each of the leading six companies, including those listed above. To my frustration, it didn't get me anywhere. I came to the conclusion that I must have been doing something wrong. A few days of reflection made me realise that I was thinking too small. Thinking about it, F1 offered a global platform to the right company. There I was, trying to excite the British marketing personnel of these global giants when I should have been taking the bigger picture into account. It was time to go back to the drawing board.

Within a week or so, I was on the case again, but this time researching the global HQ's of the companies that I had targeted. UPS proved to be the most difficult to contact, and when I did eventually speak to someone at a senior level, they were adamant that there was no interest whatsoever in F1. I took a different approach to DHL, using a third-party contact, an American named Barry Chappel, to introduce me to the CEO of their Middle East operation. It was a smart move and before long we had arranged a meeting at the Hilton in Park Lane, where he was due to stay for a week on business. I outlined my reasons for wanting to approach DHL on a global basis and showed him some of the research that I had carried out on the size of the business-to-business opportunity that I could deliver. He agreed to move the opportunity upwards within the company and get back to me with a further meeting.

I must tell you about an incident that took place at the Hilton Hotel in Park Lane, as I arrived for the meeting. I should explain that Barry Chappel, who had brokered the meeting, is very American, drives a Rolls Royce Corniche, as does his wife, and he lives in Westport, Connecticut. On several occasions, he picked me up at JFK in the Roller when I flew in from the UK. As an aside, he was a good buddy of Carl Haas. On this particular occasion, Barry arrived just after me, which meant that we were about ten minutes early for the meeting with the DHL contact. He strode across to where I was standing and I saw that he was wearing an overcoat and a leather cowboy-style Stetson.

On seeing me, he took his hat off, stuck it on my head and explained that he had told Ari, whom he had only met once before, that he would recognise Barry by his Cowboy hat. Barry, it seemed, wanted to head quickly around the corner to do some shopping at Trumpers, the famous Royal barber shop in Curzon Street. If Ari arrives early, shouted Barry, heading out of the hotel, he'll spot the hat and introduce himself. That was that. I took the wretched hat off, put it prominently on the coffee table in front of me and waited. Ari did eventually spot it, and we then hada serious meeting.

With the DHL approach now past first base, it was time to focus on a couple of other companies. The first was FedEx. I researched a lot of relevant information, including all of their existing sponsorship activities and tried, without any joy, to get through by phone to their Head of Sponsorship, a lady by the name of Nancy Altenburg. I knew that they sponsored the Orange Bowl, but no motorsport at that time.

I then changed direction and eventually managed to speak to one of the guys in the marketing department, at the company's Memphis head office. He was the first person out of the many to whom I spoke, who knew anything about Formula 1. For the next few weeks, I continued talking to him about the way in which FedEx operated, including how the decision-making process worked geographically and who determined it. I also got a lot of feedback of their plans to enter into a motorsport partnership in the US, which involved a transportation agreement, meaning that FedEx would be appointed by CART as its Official Transportation Partner, moving race cars to a range of destinations across the United States and Canada.

Having got as much information as I could from my contact in America, it was time to carry out some more research; this time into the amount of freight and courier business that the existing 42 Benetton F1 team partners and official suppliers generated in their own right. That might not sound too taxing, but you have to remember that in 1996, Google was still a couple of years away. Much of my research over many years was done in the reference section of my local library.

Having eventually gathered together most of the information I needed from the Benetton Group and its F1 Team partners, I started work on designing a sales strategy that would bring one of most high-profile and successful global corporations into F1 as a business partner to the Benetton F1 Team.

The tough bit was about to begin. I felt that I had gathered together all of the information that I needed to put together a compelling case for FedEx to become a major business partner. The question now was how to get a meeting at a very senior level with FedEx.

I got back to my contact at FedEx in Memphis and asked for some more guidance. I needed to know who he felt was the person to effectively "champion" any potential deal between Benetton F1 and FedEx, in respect of what would be considered by the American company to be a global sports sponsorship opportunity. His advice was that the geographic region most likely to benefit from an F1 deal would be Europe, Middle East and Africa. He added that the regional office was in Brussels and gave me the contact details of the marketing and the sales directors. I hadn't quite finished; I needed to get the contact details of their respective personal assistants, which he quickly looked up for me. I thanked him profusely for all of his help and asked him if we could return the favour in any way. He said that he would like to work in Britain at some stage, to further his own sports marketing career ambitions and would be really grateful for any introductions. He mentioned that he hoped to be in the UK within a few months on a holiday. I promised that if he provided me with dates of travel, I would organise a meeting with our chairman, Alan Pascoe. I also told him that if we did the FedEx deal that I was working on, we would arrange for him to go to a Grand Prix as a VIP guest.

I really felt as though I was on the case now. I had assimilated all the background information that I needed, and it just remained to get that all important meeting. Over the years that I had been acquiring sponsorship, I had developed my own way of doing this, one which has worked for me on many occasions.

I have explained the method to many people on the training courses that I've delivered on sponsorship acquisition, as well as to several business people within my extensive contact network. I'm sure that quite a few of these people don't believe that I go about it this way and that some consider it a tacky approach to a company. Well, I can assure everyone that I am being totally truthful and that I can't help it if some people find it tacky. It isn't, believe me. What it's all about is treating people with the respect that they deserve. How can that be tacky?

The way that I have got many key meetings in a company is actually very simple and straightforward. In my opinion, it is the most obvious way to open a communication channel with a company and far from being tacky, it is highly professional and highly respectful of a person within a business, whether male or female, who in most cases has their finger on the pulse of what goes on in that company.

Think of it this way. If you phone to speak to the marketing director, the chances are that you will be put through to his PA. You then ask for a meeting with her boss. She will no doubt tell you to either put the reason why you wish to meet him, in an e-mail or in the post. This is what happened to me in my early career, and I found that the chances of going any further are quite slim, mainly because until you have had a meeting with the person, you'll only be able to send a generic outline of the sponsorship opportunity, in which you are effectively assuming what the company might get out of the sponsorship. That, to me, is the wrong way to go about things.

My way works very simply. Instead of asking the PA to put me through to her boss, I ask her if I could either set up a meeting with her or a phone conversation with her, on the basis that I would like to seek her opinion as to how best to present my business-development opportunity to the marketing director. Is that tacky? I don't think so. I'm not trying to chat her up; I'm respecting her level of ability to eventually be able to guide me in the right direction within the company or alternatively by telling me that the opportunity fails to address the current needs of the company.

With this in mind, I began by phoning Diane Castille, who was the PA to Paul Evans, Marketing Director of FedEx EMEA. When I asked her if we could talk, her reaction was one of surprise, which is what I usually find. She was more than happy to arrange a time later in the day for a conversation.

We had a 20 minute discussion later on, during which I briefly outlined the potential business development opportunity that I had created. I asked her if she thought that it was both relevant and feasible to present this to her boss. She immediately saw the potential and suggested that if I should confirm our conversation in an e-mail, listing in bullet points the strategy that I had outlined to her. She promised that she would take it in personally to Paul, mentioning our discussion, and do her very best to get me a meeting with him as soon as possible. My e-mail started with the words, 'Last year, the Benetton Group of companies spent $(X) millions on courier and freight business, whilst the other 42 business partners (sponsors and official suppliers) in the Benetton F1 Team spent an estimated $(Y) millions. I would like to meet you to discuss ways in which we can help FedEx secure an increased share of that business…"

The following day, Diane called me with some potential dates for a meeting with Paul and also Bob Elliott, who was then Sales Director for FedEx EMEA, eventually to be appointed its president.

The meeting was scheduled for 2:30 p.m. at the FedEx European HQ, situated on the outskirts of Brussels Airport. It was a foul day weather-wise, but I arrived in plenty of time for the meeting. Diane herself came down to reception to greet me, which gave me another chance of thanking her for being so helpful. Then she told me that she had some bad news. She looked highly embarrassed as she explained that Paul and Bob had been summoned to an urgent client meeting. They sent their apologies and asked if I could arrange another time to meet them.

I was far from happy, as you can imagine, but it wasn't the messenger's fault; I told her not to worry and let's look at a diary. It was at that moment that the time I had spent initially talking to her really paid dividends. Out of the blue, she suggested that there might be another way forward and asked me if was prepared to wait until

5:30 p.m., which was apparently the time Paula and Bob expected to get back from the client meeting. She assured me that she would get me at least half an hour with them, at that time. She also offered to get me on a much later flight home. I thanked her yet again and accepted the offer.

It proved to be a long afternoon, with the rain driving against the glass doors of the reception area. Diane kept me filled up with coffee, but I couldn't find any more interesting magazines to read than a six month out-of-date issue of *Golf Weekly.*

Eventually, the clock ticked around to show 5:30. Diane came downstairs with a smile on her face, telling me that Paul and Bob had arrived back and would send for me in about five minutes. Once again, my faith in PAs had been proved correct. Treat them with the respect they merit and not as obstacles; you'll be surprised at just how powerful many of them turn out to be.

Another example of this came about when I approached Colgate-Palmolive to discuss F1 sponsorship. I followed my normal way of working and got through to the PA to the CEO in their UK headquarters. She was extremely helpful, and after a long phone conversation, arranged an introduction to the appropriate person at a senior level. Unfortunately, for a number of reasons, we weren't able to put a deal together at that time. However, a couple of weeks later, to my surprise, I received a phone call from that same PA.

She told me that she had just heard that my proposals had been declined, but wanted to thank me personally for the way I had involved her from the start and for treating her like an intelligent human being in an important role within Colgate-Palmolive. She went on to say that most sales people treated her as though she was an obstacle in the route to a meeting with the CEO. She finished the call by saying that she was sorry that a deal couldn't be done, but if ever I wanted to approach the company with another opportunity, to call her, and she would try to help. That call meant a lot to me and endorsed my views about getting people on your side.

Thanks to Diane Castille's efforts, I eventually met with FedEx's Paul Evans and Bob Elliott in Brussels at about 5:45 that evening and had been told by Diane that it would only be for 30 minutes. I had prepared a PowerPoint presentation to show them , but after a couple of minutes of running through the early slides, I could see they weren't focussing in the way I had hoped, so I closed the lid of my lap and started a conversation about the company. You could say that the floodgates opened. They told me that they get so many F1 proposals that probably know more about F1 than Bernie Ecclestone does. We started talking about FedEx, and they started opening up about some of the major issues, sales wise. They also wanted to talk about my e-mail, via Diane, that had got me the meeting. Yes, they said, your opening line grabbed us both. We do want to know how we can increase our sales as you mentioned. One and a half hours later, the meeting came to an end, with agreement from both of the FedEx guys that I had presented a fascinating business-development opportunity, and that they definitely wanted to continue our discussions. I proposed that the next step should be a visit to the Benetton F1 Headquarters in Enstone to meet Flavio Briatore and John Postlethwaite.

It had been a long day, but a rewarding one, and I was really looking forward to meeting Paul and Bob in a couple of weeks' time.

Interestingly, whilst these discussions were going on with Benetton, I was also talking to DHL. You may recall that I had targeted several companies in this industry sector when I set out my sales strategy. My contact within DHL in the Middle East,

Sarraf had been very helpful and introduced me in turn to the marketing director EMEA, who was based in the UK. I should point out at this stage that during my meeting with FedEx in Brussels, I had made it very clear that I was talking to several other companies within their industry sector.

One of the many advantages I had found with targeting a specific industry sector is that very often, what works for one company also works well for another. If you think about it, that's not really surprising.

The DHL discussions progressed well, and within a couple of months, I was beginning to think that there was a very real chance that we would end up with a substantial sponsorship agreement for Benetton. Which one it would be was still not clear. I had a couple more positive meetings in Brussels with Paul Evans, then Matthew Argenti, my CEO at API; and I met with John Postlethwaite, Benetton's F1 marketing director, to discuss what else we could to ensure that we signed up one of these global corporations. As I mentioned earlier, at that time, none of the companies we had targeted had been involved in F1, so it would be real coup to put a deal together with one of them.

My first cold-call to Fedex in Memphis had been made during the third week of January 1997. By late March, discussions with both FedEx and DHL were going well. Then Paul Evans called and invited me to lunch in Brussels. He told me that he was finding some opposition to the proposed Benetton deal from their American board. Their argument was that they had now agreed an official transportation partnership with the CART Championship (Indycars), and that the other FedEx regions could use that as their business-development platform.

Paul explained to me that if we were going to get the green light for the proposed Benetton F1 sponsorship, I would have to help him produce an internal document to be shown to the FedEx board members, supporting EMEA's case for going ahead. It wouldn't be easy, he assured me. Nevertheless, I spent the best part of a week putting the document together to Paul's satisfaction. Our argument was based on the fact that whilst FedEx was a high-profile brand in America, it still hadn't made the same impact in EMEA countries. Whilst CART racing was shown on main American TV channels, it wasn't popular within the UK.

It was agreed at API that I should go with Paul to present the document in Memphis. I would be accompanied by Matthew Wheeler, an API board director, on the basis that he would add further credibility to our cause.

The FedEx HQ in Memphis is impressive, as is FedEx airport, which boasts a fleet of FedEx branded planes, totalling more than that of British Airways. Together with Paul Evans, who had flown in from Brussels, we met David Schoenfeldt, a senior board member based in Memphis, and Nancy Altenburg, FedEx's sponsorship manager.

The meeting went well, but we would have to wait for a final decision. Paul Evans and Bob Elliott had done a good job in generating support for the other global regions on-board, and it was now a case of waiting for the USA feedback.

Prior to heading back to London, Matthew Wheeler and I took some time to visit Gracelands in Memphis, which was well worth the effort. What an extraordinary man Elvis was. The number of people that day who were queuing to get in was staggering. The very next day, I received a phone call from David King, DHL's Business Development Director and the man with whom I was now dealing, telling me that they had put our sponsorship proposal to the board the previous day; and to everyone's delight, it had been agreed. This now meant that DHL could go ahead with final negotiations with Benetton F1. I couldn't believe what I was hearing; two potential sponsorship deals on the table, but only room for one of them, as a primary condition of both would be that they would be granted category exclusivity. In other words, no other freight/ courier or logistics company could enter into an agreement with the team.

Talking this over with Mathew Wheeler, we agreed that I would get back to both FedEx and DHL, explaining what had happened. As I had kept both parties informed at all times, there should be no big surprise at this outcome from either company.

It was now early April. I called Paul at FedEx and explained the situation, then David King at DHL. Neither sounded surprised at developments and told me that they would get back to me, as a matter of urgency. They both kept to their word. Paul made contact first and made a suggestion that would hopefully break the deadlock. He proposed that instead of waiting for the start of the 1998 F1 season, FedEx would like to announce their sponsorship at The British Grand Prix at Silverstone and to compete in that event and the remaining Grand Prix races on the 1997 calendar.

When I spoke to Chris King at DHL, he agreed to get back to me to see if they could match this. It didn't take long for him to call me to explain that regrettably DHL would not approve the deal now, in 1997, as it was planned for activation in 1998.

So, there it was, I had put together my biggest ever sponsorship deal, being worth £15 million. It was the first in F1 with any of the global parcels companies and was my second multi-million pound sponsorship deal for Benetton F1, on behalf of Alan Pascoe's agency. This had all happened within a period of ten months.

When Jean Alesi climbed into the Benetton car, now resplendent in its new FedEx and Gillette branding, and drove from inside the pit garage, through a stack of large FedEx brown boxes into the Pit Lane to formally announce the new sponsorship, it all seemed surreal to me. A couple of months later, Gerhard Berger drove the car to an unexpected victory in the German F1 Grand Prix at the Hockenheim Circuit, and I was there to witness the scenes of delight amongst the FedEx and Gillette personnel who had come to add their support to the Benetton F1 team.

I was particularly pleased for Paul Evans and Bob Elliott, who had both taken on the responsibility of bringing this giant corporation into F1 for the first time. They had put their necks on the block, and to see the grins on their faces as Berger crossed the line was worth all of the hard work that had gone into bringing the FedEx deal to a successful conclusion.

I would like to say that the team went from strength to strength after that initial victory in Germany, but unfortunately, it was the other way round. To watch the team struggle was not good, and changes were needed. The first to go was Flavio Briatore, the Team Principal. He had enjoyed massive success with Michael Schumacher at the wheel, winning the Constructors' World Championship and the Drivers' Championship, but with Michael's departure, things started to go downhill. I found Briatore a strange man to deal with, seemingly never happy unless his face was in every photograph or TV picture. Even when I had delivered the FedEx and Gillette sponsorship deals to Benetton, I never got a word of appreciation from him.

More importantly, both Paul Evans and Bob Elliott commented to me how often he had just totally ignored them in the Pit Lane.

This all fitted in with the unfriendly atmosphere I found at Benetton F1 whenever I visited the Enstone Technical Centre or had meetings with potential sponsors at races. If the team had been doing well, I could have put up with it, but to me, it seemed that the decline in the team's performance level wasn't helped by the unfriendly attitude that permeated the team.

Briatore's successor was David Richards, of Prodrive fame. The first thing that he did upon his arrival was to build a new office suite for himself, rather than to take over Briatore's former office. I first met David Richards when I presented him with the MIA Outstanding Achievement Award, back in 1994.

The next time we spoke was in his new role as CEO of Benetton F1. I was still with the API Agency and met with Paul Evans on a regular basis, usually in Brussels. I found it a good way of monitoring FedEx's view of how the sponsorship was going. It was becoming obvious to me that there were certain aspects of the agreement that weren't being dealt with by the team to Paul's satisfaction. One in particular, related to the various meetings with key Benetton Group personnel that had been promised by Briatore, as a way of increasing their market share of freight and courier business. This had been an important part of the deal that I had negotiated with them. There was never a guarantee of business, but there was a guarantee of meetings with key decision-making Benetton managers, with responsibility for freight and courier engagement. Paul was complaining to me that few of these had been delivered. I was in a tricky situation because I didn't work for Benetton and had no say in what they did or didn't deliver within the agreement. The best that I could do was to bring the concerns to Benetton's attention.

Paul was also unhappy with the way in which some of the young girls within the marketing department had treated a few of FedEx's guests at race meetings. One was overheard calling Paul a "bloody petrol head", because he was interested in the technical issues that were plaguing the team. I knew just what Paul was unhappy about.

At one of the Grand Prix, I think it was Hockenheim, I spoke to David Richards about a few of the concerns that Paul had relayed to me. Richard's immediate response was to tell me that FedEx were becoming too fussy for their own good and were a pain in the butt. I found this comment quite extraordinary and voiced my opinion. I asked him if he realised that with tobacco on its way out of the sport, F1 would need to start attracting companies such as FedEx, which had the potential financially to take over the role of title sponsorship of the teams. Yes, they would be more demanding than the tobacco sponsors, wanting measurable and sustainable business-development opportunities. F1 Teams had it easy up to then, now they would have to work a lot harder if they were going to attract the FedEx's of this world. We failed to agree on this point.

Interestingly, during one of my visits to FedEx in Memphis, I was sitting in a meeting room with a couple of their directors and a man, whom I didn't recognise, walked in. It turned out to be Fred Smith, the man who started Federal Express and still personally owned 9% of the shares. I was briefly introduced and that was that. However, David Scheonfeldt turned to me and explained that when he had mentioned the fact that FedEx was going to sponsor the Benetton Team, Fred Smith's first comment was to ask how much it would cost to buy the team! As I stood listening to David Richard's words complaining about FedEx being too high-maintenance, Fred Smith's words came back to me.

Chapter 35
An IndyCar Deal, a New Owner and
a Year in Hell

I have spent a lot of time training senior executives within other sports associations in the skills of sponsorship acquisition, in my capacity as a Visiting Fellow for the World Academy of Sport. These include the International Cricket Council, the International Paralympic Committee and World Rugby. In many cases, I have found them to be way ahead of motorsport in understanding what the corporate world demands from sponsorship in today's changing world. In my opinion, from a marketing perspective, motorsport is still living in the dark ages.

My fears were not without foundation and FedEx eventually pulled the plug on their sponsorship agreement with Benetton F1 after just two seasons. They moved on to a sponsorship deal with the Ferrari F1 Team, nearly doubling their spend, in the process. This gave me no pleasure at all, having worked so hard to bring this amazing company into F1 for the first time. Whilst I was pleased to see FedEx stay in the sport for many years, heading to McLaren after Ferrari, which is where they stayed until pulling out of F1 altogether, I was totally unimpressed at the way they were treated at Benetton F1. As it turned out, David Richards was soon replaced by Benetton F1 and Rocco Benetton became its new Chief Executive. The team that had been world champions just a few years before were now sadly sliding down the grid. I found it very sad to watch, having been so enthusiastic about the potential.

Whilst this was going on in F1, back at the Drury Lane offices of API, the financial success of the two motorsport deals that I had initiated had been noted. API had earned a high level of commission on both the Gillette and FedEx deals. Subsequently, I was invited to a meeting with Matthew Argenti and Matthew Wheeler. They asked me what I thought the chances were of securing a similar representation deal with a leading team in CART racing in the United States of America. I should point out that they had an office in New York and were quite heavily involved in the rapid spread of soccer across the country. I told them that I was confident of being able to gain such an agreement, provided that they, in turn, could show the team in question that that they were capable of bringing in the deals, as I had on behalf of Benetton F1.

No sooner had we agreed the way in which this could work, that I was on a plane to New York, where I would meet Gary Hopkins, CEO of API in the US. Because of the time that I had spent in America with Lola Race Cars, I knew a lot of people there in the sport. Within a couple of months, I had put together a worldwide representation agreement with Walker Racing, one of the leading Indycar teams (The series was actually called Championship Auto Racing Teams, shortened to CART, but that can become confusing. There was a split which saw CART take on Indycar, and that nearly led to the demise of both series).

I had met Derek Walker, Team Principal, in my earlier visits to America. His driver was also someone I knew well from his time in the UK, Brazilian Gil de Ferran, who, incidentally, has just joined McLaren F1 as its Sporting Director, to try to get the famous marquee out of the mire it seems to be in at present. We got along well together, and I felt that it should be possible to generate a serious level of sponsorship to replace the current Valvoline deal, which was coming to an end.

After discussing the situation with Gary Hopkins and also the guys back in the UK, we decided to move forward and thrashed out a great deal with Derek Walker. API (USA) then employed a salesperson to work exclusively on the Walker Racing account, with help from me when required. A young American guy was selected by Gary Hopkins, and although he hadn't worked in a senior sponsorship acquisition role before, he came across as being very professional. It was understood that I would try to oversee the relationship with Derek, but remain based in the UK. Unfortunately, the young rookie turned out to be a salesman who preferred researching potential sponsors rather than trying to arrange meetings with them. I've met quite a few of these over the years.

However, that rather paled into insignificance when Alan Pascoe announced that he had sold his company, API. I was in London when the news broke. Alan called all the staff into a meeting room at API's London head office, where he told us that he had sold the company to an American advertising group, called InterPublic. He explained that the group comprised a number of leading agencies, including McCann Erikson and the Lowe Group, and had now decided to establish its own international sports marketing company, to take on the likes of IMG.

There was a shocked silence around the room, as Alan continued. The fact was that API had been a good company to work for and to suddenly hear that we might now all be working for a large American conglomerate would take a while to sink in. As I sat on the train that evening, heading home, I wondered what the future would hold for me in the light of the dramatic announcement.

In the weeks following Alan Pascoe's surprising announcement, I learned more about the future plans of the new company, which we had been informed would be called Octagon. As you can imagine, I was particularly concerned about the existing motorsport accounts, Benetton F1 and the recently negotiated representation deal with Walker Racing in America.

The first inkling of what would be happening came when we learned that there would be a separate division of Octagon set up to manage its motorsport activities. It would be called Octagon Motorsport and would be run by the Flammini brothers, Mauricio and Paolo. They were the commercial rights holders of the World Superbike Championship and operated from their offices in central Rome. Mauricio had a motorsport background, having raced in F2 quite successfully, whilst his younger brother came from the banking world, in some capacity.

The first time I met them was at the new offices they had taken on in London, in Upper Brooke Street, just off Park Lane. There, Mathew Argenti and I were introduced to Paolo Flammini and told what our future roles would be if we stayed on in the new company.

Matthew would become European Motorsport Director, based in London, whilst I was offered the role of USA Motorsport Director, based in Stamford, Connecticut.

The next step was a meeting with Mauricio Flammini in London; then a couple of weeks later, Matthew and I flew into Rome, to be greeted by Paolo in his new Mercedes Coupe. We were taken out to lunch at a superb seafood restaurant right on the coast and joined again by Mauricio. So far, everything was looking quite exciting, and we went along with it all. Our remuneration packages were presented to us, and from my point of view, were very acceptable. Obviously, in my case, it included an international relocation element.

Realising that there was the often tricky matter of USA visa applications to be organised, I was under rather more pressure than Matthew. Liz and I had talked a lot about the potential overseas opportunity and came to the conclusion that it would be a good career move and also an exciting option for us both on a personal basis. I formally agreed the terms and conditions that were involved and started the practical process of getting the immigration paperwork sorted. There was also the matter of our house in Southampton to be sold or let.

In the meantime, I was spending quite a lot of time on trips to and from America, trying to sort out housing, offices and also my business strategy. Liz accompanied me on a couple of these trips and helped me start looking for a suitable property to rent. In between trips to America, I was based at the Upper Brooke Street offices in London, with Matthew Argenti. It was during this time that the alarm bells started ringing for us both. Paolo Flammini spent quite a lot of time in the London office, and it didn't take him long to really start irritating us, with what we both felt was a petty attitude.

Between us, Mathew and I had about 50 years of experience in the motorsport marketing sector, in senior roles, but Paolo started treating us as if we were young rookies. He would behave more like a school-teacher than a company director and seemed totally unaware that the way he ran his business in Italy wasn't working in the UK. I could see that he was continually winding Matthew Argenti up by regularly tapping his finger on his desk and asking him how many phone calls he had made that day. He seemed to forget that Matthew had been the managing director of the API sales division and had brought in a lot of major sponsors for the company.

Eventually, our USA visas arrived, and Liz and I were able to move to America. We found a suitable place to live on the outskirts of Stamford and were looking forward to beginning this new phase of our life together. My new office was in a small block adjacent to the head office of the World Wrestling Association and on the opposite side of the street to another sports marketing group, Advantage, which had also been purchased by Octagon.

When I headed to work on my first morning, I had some immediate concerns to deal with, relating to the Benetton F1 Team and also to Walker Racing. Despite many attempts to get Paolo Flammini to discuss what was happening to those accounts, I was still none the wiser. I had been instructed not to talk to either client until certain details of Octagon Motorsport had been made public. It wasn't the way I liked to do business; in my opinion, a lack of communication is all too often the root of major issues within companies.

Eventually, I had a phone conversation with Paolo and asked him what exactly he was expecting of me in this new role, as there had been very little communication in terms of strategy. To my astonishment, his reply was very simple. He told me that I was there to secure sponsors for the World Superbike Championship and that was it. It was not my job to worry what was happening to Benetton F1 and Walker

Racing. Again, I felt that he was treating me like a trainee salesman, just as he had with Matthew Argenti.

I spent a couple of days thinking this through before sending him a communication expressing my concerns at the way the goalposts had been moved since we discussed my role when we were in London. There was no way that I would have moved to America to be a sales person seeking sponsorship for motorbike racing. I couldn't see the logic in paying me a high salary and then tasking me to sell a property that I knew little about and had never sold before. What I had been led to believe was very different when I agreed to the American move.

The reply came back from Mauricio this time and was quite vitriolic, suggesting that I shouldn't call myself a salesman as I was obviously scared of getting out into the business world. He added that I would do exactly what Paolo, his brother, told me to do or else he'd find someone who could.

I called Matthew in London and outlined what had happened. He was as shocked as I was. Then he explained that he was also having major problems, albeit in a different way, with the Flamminis. He suggested that I should call Matthew Wheeler, also in London. You may recall that he was the API director who accompanied me to FedEx in Memphis. He had been very heavily involved in the sale of API to the InterPublic Group and was also the person who had asked me to try and secure a representation deal with a leading Indycar team.

I called Matthew Wheeler and sent him copies of the communications that I had received from the Flamminis. He didn't seem surprised, which seemed a bit odd. He asked me to bear with him whilst he looked into the matter. In the meantime, he suggested, I should get to know the senior management team at Octagon's USA head office, which was situated on one of the top floors in the Grace Building in the Avenue of the Americas.

I took his advice and headed to New York, where I met several key figures within the Interpublic group. These included Les Delano, who had officially retired; but because of his motorsport background and close relationship to Frank Lowe, who had sold the Lowe Group to Interpublic in 1990, was still playing a role in developing the global strategy for Octagon Motorsport. Les had been racing Porsche's for many years and was a good friend of former F1 Grand Prix driver, Skip Barber. Skip had by now retired from racing but was the owner of a highly successful racing driver school, so we had a lot in common. I was initially introduced to Skip by Les Delano, and he invited Liz and me to travel up to New England to visit his school. I was highly impressed at what I saw, and Skip and I found that we had a lot in common, including some serious concerns about the way in which Octagon Motorsport was heading. He told me about the plans for Octagon Motorsport to set up a new professional sports car championship in America and explained that he had been asked to consult on the project. He asked for my opinion of the proposed series. I had to admit that I was dubious, as sports car racing at that time really wasn't capturing the public's imagination.

During our stay, Skip admitted that he thought that we were heading in the wrong direction. When I mentioned my worries about Benetton and Walker Racing, he sympathised with me and couldn't understand why two such potentially lucrative properties seemed so unimportant to the Flamminis.

When we got back to Stamford after a fascinating couple of days with Skip Barber, I received a message to call Matthew Wheeler. What he told me wasn't what

I wanted to hear. Apparently I wasn't the only former API employee to be very unhappy with the way things were going. He had spoken to Matthew Argenti and a couple of other people and got a similar story. He admitted to there being a problem. His suggestion took me by surprise. He asked me if I would fly to London at the weekend, so that we could have a meaningful discussion. He also suggested that I should bring Liz with me.

I very much appreciated Wheeler's honesty when we met up at his London office that weekend. He didn't try to pretend that there wasn't a problem, but took the stance that there was little chance of the Flammini's being moved on at this early stage in the company's growth; so in reality, I had two choices. The first was to go with the flow and hope that things might get better, or I could cut my losses, take a very generous pay-out and come back to the UK to find a new job. He added that with my track record, that shouldn't be too difficult.

I chose the latter path of action, which within a few days proved to be the correct decision. I made a few calls and learned that David Warren, who was the current Marketing Director at Benetton F1, had announced his resignation to take up a new role with AllSport Management, based in Geneva. AllSport was the company appointed by Bernie Ecclestone to manage F1 hospitality and track advertising. It was headed up by Paddy McNally, whom I knew from my Kyalami days. Paddy then worked for Phillip Morris International, owners of the Marlboro cigarette brand. It was Paddy who came down to South Africa to agree all of the Marlboro track advertising and promotional activities, prior to the South African Grand Prix.

I called David and asked if Rocco Benetton, now the CEO of the Benetton F1 team, had appointed David's successor. When he told me that they were still looking, I put my name forward. A few days later, I received a phone call from Rocco in which we discussed my suitability for the role. To my delight, he was happy to take David Warren's recommendation that I could do the job, and we agreed a package there and then. It was decided that my title would be Commercial Director, so as not to be confused with team's Marketing Services Director.

It was strange feeling to be back at Benetton, not as an agent this time but actually empowered to take decisions and put my ideas into practice. If there was a negative, it was that the team were still not performing well on the track. Jean Alesi and Gerhard Berger had been replaced as drivers by Giancarlo Fisichella and Alex Wurz. They weren't the problem, but the car seemingly was. Pat Symonds was still the team's Technical Director, so what was going wrong was not clear.

One of the young managers who would be working for me within the marketing department had introduced a lead on a possible sponsorship agreement before I started. I saw it as a priority to try to convert this lead into a deal. The company in question was Marconi. Unfortunately, Benetton's on-track performances were not exactly helping me in this mission. It took a lot of work to put the deal to bed. In my experience, until a sponsorship is signed, sealed and the first instalment received, it's not a deal.

Eventually after about six weeks, I was delighted to hear from Mike Abbott of Marconi that the board had endorsed a significant multi-million pound three-year sponsorship deal over a three year period. I hoped it might be the fillip that the team needed to kick start the season, but it seemed that little was going to improve matters in that respect.

Delighted as I was to be in my new role with the Benetton F1 team, as opposed to simply being an agent on their behalf, I once again felt that there was something intrinsically wrong with the atmosphere at Enstone, the team's impressive technical centre. It was difficult to put a finger on exactly what it was, but I had felt it when I first visited the centre in my API days, and nothing had changed. Maybe it was the clinical coldness of the design of the facility, but I don't think so. I think it was something in the attitude of the personnel. It may have been the performance of the team that was causing it, who knows, but something wasn't right.

I remember talking about it with Matthew Argenti on a couple of occasions, and he agreed with me, having been there on several occasions. Another person to comment on it had been Paul Evans from FedEx, which is one of the reasons he had moved the sponsorship away to Ferrari F1. I tend to be quite sensitive in picking up on a negative atmosphere within a room of people, and I certainly detected negative vibes in that building amongst many of the personnel. Whether it emanated from the very top, I don't know; all I can say is that it wasn't a very pleasant atmosphere to work in. For a start, if you expressed a passion for motorsport, many of the marketing team that I inherited looked down their noses at you. They also made it clear on many occasion that they just saw their role simply as a job. The heritage of the sports meant nothing to them.

Not that it really mattered too much, because one afternoon, Pat Symonds summoned everyone to the downstairs staff restaurant and informed us that Benetton F1 had been sold, lock stock and barrel to Renault. If that wasn't bad enough, the next announcement caused a distinct groan. It was stated that a new CEO had been appointed and would be taking over the company with effect from the following Monday. The new CEO would be none other than Flavio Briatore, the man who had been replaced by Benetton a couple of years previously.

Everyone within the marketing and marketing services department was very concerned. In the relatively short time that he was there, Rocco Benetton had made some worthwhile changes in the way that sponsors' needs were looked after. One change was to set up a marketing services team, the role of which was to manage all of the various needs of existing sponsors. Kate Linnell had joined in the capacity of Marketing Services Director, whilst I was now employed as Commercial Director to run the sponsorship acquisition team. With three major sponsors being brought on board within the space of two years, albeit two were acquired during my API time, we were certainly pulling our weight.

In my opinion, the problems at Benetton F1 were not marketing related. Considering how poorly the team had been running on the track, I think that the marketing department, across all of its activities, were doing an excellent job. It didn't take rocket science to realise that the root of the problems affecting the team's performance lay elsewhere.

Life is very often unfair, and this proved to be the case at Benetton. The first steps that Flavio took, when arrived as CEO, were mainly directed at the marketing department, the sector of the company that really didn't need major changes. It was plain to see that Flavio, having been replaced at the instigation of Benetton, would most likely want to change anything Rocco had put together. As it turned out, that is exactly what happened, with the highly effective marketing and marketing services department being dismantled within a month of his arrival.

I recall being summoned to a meeting with Flavio, at which he bluntly informed me that he wanted younger people involved in the marketing department. I queried this with him, referring to my track record in doing deals for the team. I might as well have been talking to a brick wall. There was little else that I could do, but make sure I secured a good severance package and the commission that I was entitled to being paid to me. I know why Flavio didn't want someone there who could initiate and close these multi-million pound deals; it was because he preferred to do them himself. I could never understand how the boss of one F1 team could be allowed to have management contracts with drivers in other F1 teams. Imagine in football, a manager also being a player-agent, representing the interests of players in competitive teams. That's F1 for you.

I heard that the next person to go was Kate Linnell, the Marketing Services Director. Yet again, there seemed neither rhyme nor reason as to why she should be fired, as she was doing a good job. Kate moved on to become marketing director at Aston Villa FC, and I had lunch with her at Villa Park a few months into the job. She seemed to be enjoying the role, but still felt bitter about the way that Flavio had behaved in terminating her employment at Benetton F1. Tragically, that was the last time that I saw Kate. She died a couple of years later, tragically young and having only fairly recently married one of the Benetton F1 technical team.

Whatever the reasons, I was now out of a job. My first thought was to contact the other F1 teams, but I decided against that on the basis that I had been 100% Benetton for nearly five years, and to conjure up the same level of enthusiasm for another team would be difficult. I needed a break.

Out of the blue, an opportunity arose which would give me the break from motorsport that I was seeking, but at the same time, offered an exciting challenge. It came about one weekend when Liz and I went to stay with some friends, David and Jan Clayton, who then lived in a small village called Draycott in the Clay. I first met David when he was the PR manager of Goodyear Tyre Company, based in Wolverhampton.

I'd been a trainee manager for Goodyear Tyre Company in the 1970s and was delighted when I heard that the board had announced a major sponsorship of my football club, Wolverhampton Wanderers Football Club, better known as Wolves, who I'd supported since 1957. The other exciting news at the time was that David had subsequently left the employ of Goodyear to become the new Commercial Director of Wolverhampton Wanderers.

During the years that David was at Molineux, home of Wolves FC, Liz and I enjoyed a lot of excellent hospitality at matches, but all good things come to an end; and he eventually left the famous club to take on a similar role at Nottingham Forest. His next and final move was into a different sport, rugby union, where he became the CEO of Leicester Tigers RFC. David was to spend 12 years in that role before eventually retiring.

He and his wife, Jan, have developed a great friendship with us over the years; and when he learned about my departure from Benetton F1, he invited us both to spend a weekend with them. Little did I know what was to come out of our time spent together.

Chapter 36
Goodbye F1, the Deals Keep Coming and Is It 2002 or 1802?

David and I were sitting outside on a warm summer evening, talking about the scenario at Benetton, when he asked me what I was going to do next. I outlined my reasons for wanting a short break from Formula 1, adding that I was looking for a new challenge. We chatted about different options within motorsport for a while, including my possibly setting up a driver management company. It was something that had been in my mind for a while, but I wasn't sure that it was really my cup of tea. I didn't think I would have the patience to deal with some of the precocious brats for a start, but worse still, would be dealing with the fathers!

We spent a few more minutes talking over a glass wine, before David came out with an interesting question, asking me whether I had considered taking my sponsorship acquisition skills into another sport. I had to admit that I hadn't, believing that motorsport was where I had a track record and that is where I should stay. He went on to explain to me that rugby union was going through some challenging times, since turning professional in the late 1990s. Now that clubs had to pay salaries to their players, there was a drastic need for them to become far more commercially astute in the skills of generating revenue. I interrupted, telling him that I knew nothing about rugby union, other than what I had seen from watching a few England games on TV.

David responded by telling me that my lack of knowledge would actually be an advantage, as I wouldn't be bogged down by all of the traditions and baggage of the amateur game. He believed that my background in F1, which was widely regarded as one of the most commercially astute sports, would stand me in good stead within rugby.

I have to admit that I didn't exactly jump up and down with excitement; but when David asked me if I would like him to put out a few feelers, I agreed to seriously consider any options that might arise.

It didn't take long for him to get back to me, explaining that he had spoken to Andrew Brownsword, the new owner of Bath Rugby. Andrew was keen to meet me, and we set up an appointment for the following week. Bath was definitely one of the stalwarts of the amateur game, but had serious concerns about moving into the professional era. During the lead-up to the meeting, I gave the Bath Rugby situation a lot of thought and found myself warming to it. It would be an interesting challenge to see if could put together sponsorship deals in a totally different environment. After talking it over with Liz, we both agreed that a break from motorsport, in which I'd then been involved for well over 30 years, might be a good thing.

I met Andrew and Ed Goodall, his financial director, and they told me of their great plans for taking Bath Rugby into the new professional game, and how the financial side of the game was now so critical to success on the pitch. It was an interesting meeting, particularly when Ed Goodall told me that he was still doing the accounts by hand. IT hadn't really made its presence felt at Bath Rugby at that time. Online ticketing was conspicuous by its absence. It didn't take long to realise that this was indeed going to be a major challenge.

I had been informed that within the laws of rugby union, certainly at that time, only three sponsors' logos or branding were allowed on the players team shirts. The major sponsor of Bath Rugby was Blackthorn Cider, whose head office was nearby in Trowbridge. Its Managing Director was Rob McNevin, who was a really likeable person, and we found that we had a lot in common. He had an interesting background, having previously been employed by Guinness (Diageo Group) to look after its Kaliber non-alcoholic beer sponsorship of Andy Rouse's BTCC Ford Sierra Team in the late '80s. This gave us a great platform on which to build a good working relationship.

My first home match at Bath Rugby was one that will forever remain etched in my mind. Blackthorn, Bath's title sponsor, had decided to use this particular game to entertain staff, guests and guest. There were 175 in total, occupying the clubs largest hospitality facility at the REC, Bath's famous stadium which is situated alongside the River Avon, which runs through the beautiful city.

As the players ran out onto the pitch for the start of the game, I noticed two things. Firstly, they were in their away shirts of gold and black, instead of their blue and white home kit. Secondly, and more importantly, there was no Blackthorn branding on the front of the player's shirts. I immediately rang the kit-man at the club and explained what had happened. To my astonishment, he was completely laid back and relaxed about everything, telling me that they had been playing in France, where alcohol advertising is banned and that the other shirts hadn't come back from the laundry, or some similar excuse, so they were using what they had available. That was that!

I suggested that it might be very wise to ensure that they had the right kit available for halftime, unless the club wanted a breach of contract lawsuit to be thrown at them by Blackthorn. I couldn't believe the explosion of words that followed. I was told to take my F****** F1 ways and go away, or words to that effect.

Halftime came and went, but the shirts hadn't been changed! I managed to get Rob McNevin on his mobile phone, later that evening, and asked him if we could meet on Monday morning at his office. Unfortunately, he had been forced to attend an important meeting over the weekend of the match and had missed the hospitality event at the rugby. I wasn't sure whether that was a good or bad thing.

Rob and I met on the Monday morning at his Bristol office. He had by now received an account of the events the day before.

Fortunately, between us, we sorted out the matter in an amicable way. This meant giving him a few extra entitlements, such as player appearance days, which avoided the likelihood of breach of contract litigation. It was an extraordinary start to my role at Bath Rugby and should have given me a warning as what to expect. I'd left the world of Formula 1 and was now taking my first steps into the very new world of professional rugby union. It was to be quite an adventure.

My office was in the main admin building of Bath Rugby, in Argyle Street, which incorporates the famous shop-lined bridge over the River Avon. Despite being rather dilapidated, the building was of the typical Bath style and just across the road from the official Bath Rugby retail shop. The REC, the actual ground where home matches were played, could hardly be called a stadium in the true sense. Literally on the banks of the Avon, it comprised two permanent stands, one which incorporated 26 hospitality boxes and a large individual suite. The other stand which was 90 degrees adjacent to that was quite old, but offered some welcome shelter from the inclement conditions that often prevailed. The remaining two stands that completed the four sides of the pitch were temporary stands, as I was to find out one day at the end of the season, when I looked out of the window from our office building; and to my amazement, I saw that they had disappeared. I was informed that the REC becomes part of the Bath Festival cricket ground pitch during the summer months. The total seating capacity at the REC during the rugby season was 8,200.

I have to admit that I found the game of rugby to be very different to that of football; not just in the blatantly obvious ways in respect of the shape of the ball and the fact that handling works in one game and not the other, but in the type of people it attracts. I have always been a football man, from the very first match that my granddad took me to back in 1955, which was at Griffin Park to watch the home side, Brentford. We watched the game in style, seated in the Directors' Box, with his chum Harry Davies, then the Chairman of Brentford FC. During my teens, I went to nearly every home game at Griffin Park, where the maximum attendance was around 11,800. No luxury of the Directors' Box in those days. Together with Keith Adcock, a good mate of mine from school, I would head off to the ground on the moped that my folks had bought me; and we'd watch the gallant efforts of the Bees, as they were known, to gain promotion from the Fourth Division. Today, a top ten Championship team, Brentford, are close to moving to a brand new 20,000 seater stadium, being built a mile or so away from their famous Griffin Park home.

On the subject of football, despite my links with Brentford FC, I have been a Wolverhampton Wanderers supporter since I was about 11. It probably seems a strange choice for someone who was born and lived close to Chiswick, in West London. The reason is fairly straightforward. For some reason, as a youngster, my football idol was Billy Wright, then Captain of England and of Wolverhampton Wanderers. Wolves were one of the top teams in England at that time, winning the League twice and the FA Cup in a spell of heady success. It was as simple as that. As I am writing this book, my beloved Wolves have just won the Championship, been promoted to the Premier League and are through to the semi-finals of the FA Cup. Over the years, I have followed Wolves through thick and thin, from the depths of virtually going out of existence in the 1980s to watching them win the Sherpa Van Trophy at Wembley. There was none of the fashionable support that exists today, with people only supporting a side when it's winning. With Wolves, there have been more downs than ups, but that's why sensible parents tell their children to be careful who they choose to support, because it will have to last a lifetime.

Returning to my Bath Rugby experiences, it didn't take long to work out that Rugby Union supporters tend to be far less boisterous than their football counterparts. They definitely tend to be less partisan, and keep a more level head on their shoulders. They are also far more likely to congratulate the opposition if they play some good rugby. They don't castigate referees, as we football fans most decidedly do. They still get very emotional about their team, but I think I can safely say that they show more balance in that respect.

Bath Rugby had been one of the leading rugby union clubs in the amateur days and produced many famous internationals, including Jeremy Guscott, Ben Clark, Mike Catt and Mike Tindall, a player who not only played for England, but he has also married into the Royal Family. Hard as I tried, the one aspect of the game that I really battled with whilst watching the Bath team play their league games, was the rules of Rugby Union, or, as I was told in no uncertain terms by Bath's accounts manager, the "laws" of the game. Nevertheless, I tried to attend as many games as I could. What made matters worse was that I seemed to get a different answer from whoever I asked about almost any refereeing decision. I eventually gave up trying to understand some of the finer details of the game and just worried about the score.

More importantly, away from the pitch, I was rapidly coming to the conclusion that in commercial terms, Bath Rugby was operating in the dark ages. My first realisation of this came when I met Ed Goodall, the financial director, and he confirmed my earlier assumption that he did all of the books by hand. It wasn't that Ed was doing a bad job; it was just a shock to the system not to see more than a couple of very old looking PCs in the main offices. I asked about online ticketing and got blank looks, as I did with contact databases, sales figures and so on.

There was a Bath Rugby website, but not of a standard that I would have expected. I then asked what the club did to attract young supporters. The answer was effectively to send out a type-written newsletter once a month, which must have had the youngsters sitting with bated breath waiting for the document to drop through their letter box.

All in all, it seemed that there was a great opportunity at Bath Rugby to make a difference. However, I quickly came to the conclusion that the priority was to bring on two major sponsors, in addition to the existing Blackthorn relationship. Within the new commercial regulations set by Premier Rugby, only three sponsors were allowed on team shirts. This meant that at Bath, with Blackthorn already on-board, we could only have two more. It didn't need rocket science to work out the first category that I should target. With no IT infrastructure, the club was extremely limited in what it could achieve commercially. This would require a high level of expenditure if the club was to invest in an IT system. That wasn't the only consideration, however. It seemed sensible to seek an IT sponsor who would not only provide funding for the equipment required, either in kind or financially, but would provide the high level of expertise in setting up the systems that a modern-day sports club, like Bath Rugby, would need to operate commercially.

Rugby Union might seem strange to me, but acquiring sponsorship wasn't and I was able to put a significant deal together with Northgate Information Systems, formerly McDonnell Douglas Information Systems. What I believed was the most important factor was that Northgate had agreed to conduct a complete IT audit at the club, something that was desperately needed. Once this had been done, they were able to evaluate the true financial value of the agreement. With a little bit of compromise, we were able to arrive at deal that would last three years and see the club put on to a sound footing for the growth and development that it expected in the new professional era.

The next sponsorship that I put in place, running alongside Northgate, was for a mobile phone network to be put in place. Mobile phones weren't in use in any organised way at Bath Rugby, despite a request by the head coach, Jon Callard, who wanted to use mobiles as the strategic platform for communicating with his players in terms of notifying training schedules, fitness checks, diet updates and other similar matters.

Jon had a good contact at Orange, but I felt this would be missing a great opportunity to achieve another objective in my commercial strategy. I had discovered that the average age of Bath Rugby supporters was around 47. That seemed very high, and with no real focus on trying to attract junior supporters, I felt that a serious risk factor existed. It had been stated by the directors that as the costs of running a top flight professional rugby club escalated, there would be a need to grow the spectator attendance at league and cup matches. Although this would be difficult because of council restrictions at the REC, it had to be faced. It struck me that when targeting new sponsors, there should be a focus on companies that would enhance the attraction of Bath Rugby to young people. With this in mind, I suggested that if we could secure a sponsorship deal with Virgin Mobile, whose head office was in nearby Trowbridge, I was confident that their PR support of the partnership would undoubtedly be of a young, trendy nature. It was just what we needed and reminded me of the ways in which Camel had helped us build our racing school in South Africa, by providing the services of their PR agency. It was just what we needed.

That's exactly what happened. With the help of my young salesman, Rob Bennett, we were able to put a major sponsorship deal together with Virgin Mobile. Not only would it deliver the network that was required by Jon Callard, but the launch would be a high-profile affair. It was held at the REC and involved a number of promotional girls, huge inflatable mobile phones and a lot of media coverage.

The players loved the event, and it was designed to appeal to a younger audience. The only problem was that it had upset a couple of the trustees, who had been in place for many years until the recent switch to Bath Rugby becoming a professional club. They still owned around 25% of the new organisation. As I recall, two separate issues sparked off the problem.

First of all, the trustees were rather unhappy with Virgin Mobile's full-page advertisement in the match-day programme. It comprised a sketch of a rather sexy young lady, with her tongue licking her lips in a suggestive way. The caption read: 'Virgin Mobile … Sponsors of Bath Rugby … Lick 'em Boys!'

Whilst most people thought it humorous, some of the trustees didn't.

Then there was another issue. I had come up with a way of generating income from the Player Awards event, an annual event during which the traditional awards were presented to players, voted for by supporters. Every rugby club probably had such an event. Now that Bath Rugby was a professional club and needed to generate revenue to meet players' salaries and all the other costs that would be involved, I felt that such an event offered a great revenue-generating opportunity.

Having spoken to Tom Walkinshaw, owner of Gloucester Rugby and Malcolm Pearce, owner of Bristol Shoguns, I suggested that it might be a good idea to host a combined event at which the player awards would be presented. I proposed it should be held at the Marriott Hotel in Bristol and be called: A Gala Evening to Celebrate Rugby in the West of England. I'd been in touch with the Bristol-based TV channel, HTV, and they had agreed in principle to cover the event. I would secure a major sponsor for the event, which would ensure that there would be a significant financial reward for all three of the West of England clubs. It seemed everyone was happy. All, that is, except the Bath Rugby trustees.

A couple of weeks went by, and then I received a phone call from the president and vice president of the trustees, asking for a meeting with me. 'Not a problem,' I responded.

After a few mumbles about the Virgin Mobile advertisement that had appeared in the programme, the topic moved on to the new gala event that I was planning. To my surprise, although we were sitting informally in my office, with coffee and biscuits on a tray on my desk, the two trustees wanted to formalise the meeting by addressing all conversation through the president. It wasn't an ideal scenario.

After I had explained that it was my job to bring in commercial revenue with which to take Bath into the new professional era, it was made very clear that the trustees weren't happy about the awards gala. I stood my ground, but was then asked a question along the lines of my thoughts about making this "wretched" gala evening an all-male event. I kept a serious face and tried to explain that it would not be possible, based on three factors. One, it was the year 2000, not 1900. Two, that the players would not thank me for banning their wives and girlfriends from the event. Three, I was not prepared to tell the female brand manager of the company who had agreed to sponsor the gala evening, that she couldn't attend the event herself.

Then I heard what can only be described as a classic reaction. It was put to me that as an experienced marketing person, I should be able to come up with some wording on the tickets for the gala that indicated that women would be accepted but would not be welcome!

My first reaction was that the comments were a joke. They weren't, as I could see from their faces.

It wasn't too long before I was the villain of the peace once again. This time, it was with the managing director, Bob Calleja. I was having lunch with him one day, in the small restaurant opposite the offices where we worked. I casually mentioned that as we now had two major sponsors on-board, it might be an idea to spend a little bit of money in sprucing the offices up a little, in particular the reception where visitors often came in. His response was that I should know better than to let our sponsors think that we have some money, by decorating the offices. It would give then the wrong idea about the club. We had to look as though we needed more help financially.

I couldn't believe what I was hearing and tried to explain that companies of the stature of Virgin Media and Northgate didn't think that way. I wasn't suggesting we went totally over the top, but they wanted to be associated with success, not failure, and our reception looked run down and grubby, which it did. He stormed out of the restaurant and didn't speak to me for the rest of the day.

The next day, I completed my final sponsorship deal for Bath Rugby. In an attempt to spice up the Junior Supporters Club and make it far exciting and meaningful, I secured an innovative sponsorship deal with the Walt Disney Store Group. This allowed us to create a Junior Supporters web site with competitions and events, many of them organised at the Walt Disney Store in Bath.

Sadly, that too was criticised, I was told by the MD that not all youngsters had access to the internet and that I was creating elitism at Bath Rugby. It seemed that whatever I tried to do was wrong.

By now, I had just about had enough and made the decision to leave Bath Rugby to those who knew more about rugby than I obviously did. It had been a challenge, and one that I felt I had risen to. I'm sure that as I left the offices for the last time, there were a few smiles around the place. At least the club was now online, and the mobile phone era had arrived in Argyle Street.

I'd enjoyed some of my time at Bath Rugby, but the level of frustration caused by an attitude that was based on finding it easier to say NO than YES. It really got me down. Had it encouraged me to head back to motorsport once more? I guess it had.

Chapter 37

Going Green, the New Scientist
and a Gangster Proposition

After some consultancy work for a couple of junior teams, I was seriously thinking about heading back to Formula 1. I can't say that I was jumping up and down with excitement at the thought, although I'd really enjoyed the time I spent working with Rocco Benetton. I also knew that I could definitely put the big deals together at the very top echelon of the sport, that wasn't the issue. It was just that I had found too many of the people working in F1, so far up their own backsides, that I couldn't really warm to the reality of working with them again.

Don't get me wrong, I'd met some fantastic people in Grand Prix racing over the years, many of the drivers for a start. A little later in the book, I'll talk about some of them, but it was the marketing side of the sport that bugged me most. Too many people there though that by putting on an F1 Team shirt, they were stepping on to a pedestal. They seemed to forget that, however, money-driven F1 might have become, it was basically no different to the Formula Ford racing I'd so enjoyed a few years back. It was motor racing, for God's sake, with bigger and faster cars. That's why so many of us had done the hard work to get into the business that was our passion. That's why David Kennedy and Derek Daly went to Australia and worked in the diamond mines during the winter months to earn enough money to be on the grid the following season, and why Nigel and Roseanne Mansell sold their property to fund a last-gasp season of F3 to get into the top flight of racing. Too many of the marketing and stereotypical PR youngsters I came across, thought it was all about looking good and being seen amongst some celebrities. Wrong! Hopefully, we'll never forget that even at the very top level, motor racing should be about what happens on the track. All the glamour and razzmatazz in the world can't change that.

There was one category of motor racing in which I'd never been involved and that was one of the most famous races of all, the 24 Hours of Le Mans. This was not through any lack of interest, but very simply because the opportunity had never arisen. In 2003, a phone call from a PR consultant, Janice Minton, would bring about such an opportunity. She told me that she had a client who was trying to secure an entry at Le Mans in 2004. I knew that was a tough job in itself. The AOC, the organisation running the event, are very strict as to who can and who can't race in the 24 Hours. She went on to tell me that John was planning to enter a car in the LMP1 category, but with a special dispensation to allow him to run the car on bio-ethanol, produced from sugar-beet and potatoes. In the absence of a category for environmentally friendly race cars, John was hoping they would allow his entry. She then invited me to a meeting with John and her to discuss ways in which I might be able to help add commercial expertise to the programme.

I asked Janice if this was the John McNeil who had brought a Group C car to South Africa on a couple of occasions, to run in the annual Group C international at Kyalami. When she confirmed that it was, I told her that I'd be delighted to accept the invitation.

We met at his laboratory in Kent. By profession, John was a scientist, specialising in renewable fuels technology. He provided a lot more details of his intention to run a Reynard LMP1 sports car in 2004, fitted with a Judd V-10 F1 engine, which in itself sounded quite exciting, but when he talked about the use of renewable fuel, I could straightaway see the commercial potential.

John himself was, and still is, a scientist first and foremost, but in his search for ways of promoting the capabilities and validity of renewable fuels, John decided to combine his scientific work, with his long-time passion for motor racing. In particular, he enjoyed sports car endurance racing, which is how I came to originally meet him when he ran a team in the Group C event at Kyalami in 1987, a race in which I was competing.

John wanted to use the Le Mans race to deliver a message that "green" fuel does not have to mean slow speeds and potential unreliability. In other words, by running one of the fastest sports cars in the world, in the world's most famous, toughest endurance race, it would demonstrate that "green" could be fast, exciting and reliable. He had created Team Nasamax as a platform for setting up the race programme.

I listened to John's incredible high level of enthusiasm for the project and promised him that I would think over his invitation to become involved. The more I thought about the potential for John's Le Mans entry, the more excited I became, and I eventually rang him to agree a deal.

The race team workshops were located close to his scientific research laboratories in Sittingbourne, Kent and; it became quite a common occurrence to see TV or film crews arriving to shoot documentaries about the bio-ethanol-powered race car. In particular, education programmes for school children seemed to be very popular in this respect.

John and I worked on a strategy as to how we could attract sponsorship. I was confident that at a time when there was so much media discussion and coverage of the green-fuel debate in evidence, a highly innovative project of this type would provide an excellent "corporate social responsibility"-based sponsorship platform for the right company. I proposed that, as a first step, we should we create some serious credibility for the Team Nasamax programme by generating extensive, guaranteed media coverage in specific business, scientific and educational categories. The strategy of generating a high level of guaranteed media coverage has been successful for me on so many occasions, as a vital step in acquiring meaningful levels of sponsorship. You have to be very careful with this, however, because by involving one media source, you might put off half a dozen others who feel snubbed. However, handled sensitively, it can work very well.

One particular media source that I targeted would be a very tough one to crack. The most popular scientific publication at that time was *The New Scientist* magazine, which had very successfully found a way of building its appeal to a wide cross-section of readers, instead of what so easily could be a very small, niche sector. This had been done by popularising its scientific content, without it becoming demeaning in any way.

My first contact with the editorial staff resulted in a definite lack of interest. To them, a feature on anything related to motorsport was as attractive as a feature of beef farming would be to a Vegan publication. Nevertheless, when I managed to explain more about the Nasamax project, to their credit, the powers that be decided that they would allow me the chance to personally meet them, to try and convince them as to why it might not be as stupid an idea, as it might first appear.

Not only did they agree after our meeting that it might just be an innovative, alternative take on a subject that they normally veto, but agreed that it warranted sending a senior reporter to the race in France to write a four-page feature on the first bio-ethanol car to race in one of the world's most famous races. The first part of the strategy was in place.

A meeting with the *Daily Telegraph* science editor was the next target. The meeting also generated a high level of interest and resulted not only in agreement that there would be a meaningful feature within the non-sports pages of a national daily, but also an innovative reader-competition based on the feature and offering a weekend at the Le mans 24-Hours as the guests of *The Daily Telegraph* and Team Nasamax.

There was one more call to make before I felt confident that I had a good platform on which to launch the sales strategy; that was to the London HQ of the Climate Group. I'd come across this organisation in my research and felt that a contact at a senior level might well be helpful in identifying companies with a specific interest in promoting their environmental credentials. Its primary objective was to act as a catalyst to take innovation and solutions to scale, by bringing together powerful networks of businesses and governments that shift global markets and policies.

My meeting was with Steve Howard, the CEO at that time, and I was delighted to find him genuinely interested in the Nasamax project, once I had outlined its full scope. It was helpful being able to explain to him that *The New Scientist* was already on-board with Nasamax, as was the *Daily Telegraph*. I suggested to Steve that the Climate Group could also benefit from entering into a relationship with us. It was satisfying to know that once again, the strategy I'd set out of developing high level credibility before plunging in to a sales campaign was paying dividends.

You should remember that this was all happening about 15 years ago, in 2003/4. The huge acceleration in interest in environmental matters that we have subsequently witnessed was really only just beginning to gather momentum at that time. Electric cars were mostly still in their prototype stages, and the thought of a global Grand Prix series for electric F1-style cars was a long way off.

What John McNeil was trying to do at Le Mans with Team Nasamax, in 2004, was ground-breaking; and I don't think he ever got the credit that his perseverance and vision merited. Yes, there was a diesel car also in the mix at Le Mans, but bio-ethanol, that really was going to a totally new level. My gut feeling was that companies would fall over themselves to be involved in such a newsworthy programme.

To my great disappointment, as well as John McNeil's, we quickly found that back in 2004, we were ahead of our time. I was able to meet a lot of major companies, and I can honestly say that the majority of them told us that they found the Nasamax opportunity both highly innovative and extremely worthwhile. However, when it came to talking about the ways in which they could become commercial partners, there was always a major budget issue. At that time, although many people will probably argue with me on this, the majority of companies in the UK were only on the verge of realising the importance of the word "perception" when it came to structuring their marketing policies. By this, I mean that compared to today, there was nowhere near the same level of importance placed on the views of their shareholders, staff, customers and the media in respect of social and environmental issues. Corporate Social Responsibility was nowhere near as important then as it is today.

John McNeil and I were repeatedly being told by marketing directors, that much as they felt the Nasamax programme was something that they would like to be involved in, it didn't fit in to their current marketing strategies, which of course meant that they didn't have an appropriate budget. When we asked which department within the company would be more likely to have a budget for what we now call CSR matters, the answer was invariably that if one existed, it was far too small to look at a project of the scope of Nasamax.

Despite the high level of TV coverage of the ground breaking technology, the support of the Climate Group, which to our delight included the use of their distinctive branding on the race car, the involvement with *The New Scientist* and with the *Daily Telegraph*, we failed to find anyone with the long-term vision to become involved with us. I know that this probably sounds like an excuse for poor selling, and I am not for one minute suggesting that if I could do it all over again, I might have taken a different route, as we all know, hindsight is a valuable tool. I still feel that I let John down in respect of not finding that major sponsor that the programme needed, but very much appreciate the fact that John knew how hard I had tried and told me that he fully understood what I was coming up against in my approaches to companies at that time.

The great news is that as a team, against all the odds, we gained an official entry which would allow us to race in the 24-Hours of Le Man. In the process, the Nasamax car became the first ever, powered by a renewable fuel, to complete the full 24-Hours of Le Mans. In the process, it also set the highest top speed in the race, of nearly 350 kph. In this way, John McNeil demonstrated to the world that green power doesn't mean slow or unreliable. He was very brave to take on this huge challenge and deserved the extremely positive media coverage that ensued, particularly within the internationally popular *New Scientist* magazine, which ran an extensive, very complimentary feature on the ground-breaking Nasamax project. It was, apparently, the first time the magazine had ever covered motorsport in any way.

I very much enjoyed working with John McNeil; and despite some of the frustrations we encountered, we also had some fun along the way. A couple of memories in particular come to mind. The first one being a request from the primary school in Arnage, which is a small town in France, situated close to the Le Mans Circuit. Arnage Corner is one of the main features of the race track, and in a letter to the team, one of the school's teachers explained that her pupils wanted to set up an educational project, linked to the famous race that they witnessed each year, visually and most definitely, audibly! They had chosen the Nasamax Team as being of specific interest because of the unique environmental aspect of the programme. As part of the proposed involvement, the school wanted to "sponsor" the car and in return, had arranged that on one of the days leading up to the race, the car would be on display in the town square, and the team would officially be welcomed by the

Mayor of Arnage. This was yet another of the many innovative PR opportunities that abounded around Team Nasamax. It was a "no-brainer", and John McNeil happily agreed to the school's request.

The car was duly put on display; and, in a memorable ceremony, the mayor of Arnage wished the team every success in the forthcoming race and thanked them for their much appreciated support of the school. To John's obvious delight, he was then presented with a tapestry that the children had designed. It featured the distinctive green and black Nasamax Reynard sports car, below which were the words:

Thank You Team Nasamax for Helping to Save Our Planet
The Fastest Potatoes in the World!

This was in recognition of the bio-ethanol's production from sugar-beet and potatoes. The tapestry was proudly hung on the garage wall for the duration of the 2004 race and attracted an amazing level of interest in the process.

Mind you, there was a time leading up to the 24-Hours when John and I wondered if either of us would actually be alive for the 2004 Le Mans. I'm not joking! I think we both started to wonder what we'd let ourselves in for when we accepted an invitation to attend a meeting in Milan.

It all started one morning when John called me to say that he had received a rather strange e-mail that he was going to forward to me for my comments. When it came through, I immediately noticed that it had been sent by someone whose English wasn't too good. It showed the sender as being an Italian sounding name, which I have to admit to forgetting, but it mentioned that he was the assistant to Mr Lev Levenson, who was a high-profile dealer in diamonds, based in Israel. He went on to explain that every year, Mr Levenson, for tax purposes, liked to allocate large sums of money to projects that specifically interested him. In the past, it seemed that this had included buying art treasures, properties and charities. This year he wanted to look at sponsorship in motor racing, having read of the Nasamax bio-ethanol project and found it interesting.

The e-mail then went on to say that Mr Levenson would be attending a private clinic in Milan for some medical treatment. He wondered if it would be possible for us to meet him whilst he was there.

I called John back. We had both came to the conclusion that this all sounded a bit odd, to put it mildly. In our considerable experience within motorsport, it was quite unusual for a company to make contact with a team in this way and ask them to come and talk about sponsorship. Having said that, we both agreed that we should try to find out a bit more about Lev Levenson, before declining the meeting.

We both carried out what could be called "due diligence" and realised that not only did he exist, but that he was a high-profile diamond dealer. I suggested that I should try to get the assistant, who had sent the e-mail, to call me so that I could ask some questions.

I did express the opinion to John that much as I thought this was probably a hoax, I didn't want to turn the chance down and then read in the paper, one day, that some racing team had just announced a major sponsorship with a company specialising in diamonds. Red face or what? If there is one thing I have learned in my 45-year career in motorsport, it's not to make assumptions about who is, or isn't, a potential sponsor until you have checked it out properly.

I eventually managed to speak to someone who informed me that they were Mr Levenson's personal assistant, and after a lot of pre-amble, managed to determine the level of monetary investment that we might be looking at. It seemed that a figure of around $5 million would be a possibility for the first season. It wasn't an amount to be sneezed at, both John and I agreed. With recognition that it might be a complete waste of time, John suggested that for the cost of a couple of tickets to Milan and hotel bookings, it would be worth taking a chance. As he explained, it will give us a chance to have a good chat about the programme to date and a nice Italian meal. So, off to Milan we flew.

We had been told to call the "assistant" when we arrived at our hotel, and he would then explain where the meeting would take place. A bit strange, we thought, but he told us that he still needed to book somewhere. I was beginning to get an odd feeling that this wasn't going to a straightforward meeting, and was quite glad to have John with me, there in Milan. I normally attend sponsorship meetings on my own, but we were realising that this was not going to be a normal sponsorship meeting.

By breakfast next morning, we still hadn't heard a word and were both thinking that our suspicion of a hoax was probably correct. Then a call came through for me from the assistant. It made us even more suspicious. It seemed that Mr Levenson wouldn't now be able to meet us, due to a change in his medical treatment scheduling, but he had asked two of his colleagues to engage with us. We were then asked to go to a restaurant, just a few hundred metres walk from the hotel where we were staying, and they would meet us there.

John and I looked each other and just laughed at the situation. It really did look as though our expectations were almost certainly right. It was a hoax. The problem now was that we still had quite a while before our return flight, and neither of us fancied sitting at the airport for the afternoon, so we agreed that we had nothing to lose by heading to the restaurant indicated as the meeting place. If the Levenson "team" didn't show, we could still enjoy some good pasta.

As we had both learned, from watching too many TV dramas, we opted to sit in a coffee shop across the road from the designated restaurant, checking out the scene, as they say. We waited and waited and then about 15 minutes after the appointed time, just as we were about to cross the road and enter the restaurant, we spotted three young dudes walking towards us, all dressed in what looked like Armani shiny suits, white shirts and colourful ties. The oldest of the three looked about 22; the youngest about 19. They walked over and introduced themselves, then nodded to the restaurant door where someone resembling a manager had now appeared and held open the doors for us. We followed our hosts through the main restaurant into a small alcove at the back where a table had been laid. Coffees arrived, but there was no mention of any food being available.

Where was this going, we were asking ourselves?

It was obvious that it wasn't going to be a long meeting, when the oldest guy indicated that he would get straight to the point and outline the opportunity that existed for us. We weren't even offered a coffee. What he proposed was that "they" would sponsor the Nasamax Team, initially for one year, but if it worked well, it could be an on-going arrangement. They would pay us $5 million. They didn't require branding of any sort on the car. We could spend the 5 million in any way that we wanted, but by the end of the season, we would reimburse them $2 million but in the equivalent exchange into Euros. In other words, we would have 12 months use of $5 million, but needed to return $2 million, in cash, in Euros. John and I looked at one another, and it was obvious we both fully understood what was being proposed to us.

As if we needed further proof, the youngest-looking member of the trio leant across the table, put his hand into his inside jacket pocket. 'I will show you that we are serious,' he whispered to us. At this stage, I think both John and I fully expected a gun to appear. It didn't, but what was in his hand when it slowly re-appeared was a great fat wad of what looked like brand new bank notes, I think it was in €50 denominations. There are plenty more of those available, he told us.

What followed was a very determined effort on their part to make sure that we wouldn't leave the restaurant until we had agreed to their proposal. It wasn't up to me to make decisions at this stage of the situation. It was totally in John's hands, and he did his best to stall any decision-making on the basis that he would have to go back to his business partners and put the opportunity to them. That didn't satisfy them, and the bombardment began. The word "persistence" would be one way of describing the level of verbal persuasion that John; and I were subjected to, for what was probably about half an hour. Then as quickly as the meeting had started, it was all over, with a final confirmation that if we weren't happy about this being a "kosher" deal, it could be arranged that a senior bank official in Milan would countersign our agreement.

When John and I eventually got out of the restaurant, I think that we both felt a little drained. It had certainly been an interesting trip to Italy, one that we would both remember for quite a while.

It didn't stop there, however. For the next two weeks or so, my phone didn't stop ringing. I took the first few calls and explained to the assistant that we wouldn't be moving ahead with the proposed arrangement. That didn't seem acceptable to him, but eventually, after a quite a while, I think he got the message loud and clear.

Strangely enough, a couple of years later, I heard a story that someone from a fairly high-profile race team had been shot whilst trying to run from a bank in Milan. I never heard anything more about that; but after our episode in Milan, nothing would surprise me.

Chapter 38
A1 Grand Prix, a South African Involvement and working with John Surtees

Whilst I was thinking about the best way to get back into F1, I received a phone call from John Surtees CBE, the only man to win the world championship on two and four wheels. John was then in his early 70s and still running his business from an office in Edenbridge, Kent, which is where he had run his own F1 team in the 1970s. He sounded very excited about a new motor racing series that was being launched and wanted to know when I could meet with him to talk about it. He mentioned that Paul O'Brien was working with him in his Edenbridge office, and it was Paul who had suggested making contact with me. I knew both Paul and his brother Mike, who were well-known, popular individuals within the motor-racing fraternity.

I was keen to hear more about the new series that john had mentioned. Over a coffee, John told me all about the new A1 Grand Prix series, which was being launched by none other than Sheikh Maktoum Hasher Maktoum Al Maktoum of Dubai. He explained that the teams within the series would be competing for the World Cup of Motorsport, and the primary difference to any other motorsport series in existence would be that each team would represent an individual nation. He was obviously enthralled with the new concept and went into great detail about the way in which it would work. He told me that A1GP would be a one-make, single-seater series, comprising 12 rounds over an eight month period, starting in September and finishing in April. Venues included the UK, South Africa, Dubai, Mexico and Brazil. As John delightfully put it, A1GP would be chasing the sun!

Another big difference to most other racing series was that in A1GP, each individual team would be available as a franchise, meaning that investors would be sought to buy individual teams. In the case of the GBR team, John told me, a hedge-fund expert from the city, Tony Clements, had been one of the first to put down such a fee. He went to explain that Tony's daughter, Katie, would be involved in the marketing aspects of the team; and another young girl, Victoria Henley, would be handling the PR. John still hadn't told me exactly what his involvement with A1GP would be, but I didn't have to wait much longer. It transpired that each team would have a team principal, ideally a motorsport personality, whose role would be similar to manage all aspects relating to the actual racing side of the operation. John told me that he been asked by Tony Clements to become the Team Principal of A1 Grand Prix Team GBR.

John was to be in good company, with many other illustrious names having been recruited as Principals, including former F1 drivers, such as Alan Jones (A1 Australia), Emerson Fittipaldi (A1 Brazil) and Jan Lammers (A1 Netherlands). He hadn't finished with the surprises, however.

He outlined the way in which all of the teams' cars would be stored centrally, in a huge, new purpose-built factory at Silverstone Circuit, where the technical teams would be allowed to work on the cars during the off-season. Then, once the season had started, using specially designed, constructed and branded freight-storage containers, the race cars and equipment would be flown in an A1GP charted airliner to each international circuit. It was going to be very much a global circus, touring the world and delivering race meetings wherever it stopped.

By this stage, I wanted to know more about the man behind A1GP and where the money came from. Call me a sceptic, but I had by then been around motorsport long enough to know that fairy godmothers in motorsport, are all too often followed by the bailiffs, at best, and the police at worst. John Surtees took a similar viewpoint, it seemed. He still had his own concerns, but did his best to outline to me the way that it all worked.

My ears pricked up when I suddenly heard the two words, South Africa, coming into the conversation with some regularity. Two individuals in particular seemed to be very involved from that country, Tony Teixeira and Brian Menell. I knew that Brian Menell was part of the Menell family, which founded one of South Africa's most successful mining and industrial conglomerates, AngloVaal. That seemed solid enough, but who was Teixeira? I would have to do some digging on that front.

Nevertheless, when John said that he would like to recommend to the A1 Team owner, Tony Clements, that I should become marketing director of the team, I was happy in principle to go along with it. A week went by and then I was invited to a meeting at the team's new offices in London. Nothing on the cheap with A1GP it seemed, as I stood outside the Sloane Street office block, which I discovered housed not only the British team, but was also the HQ of the A1 Group. I later learned that the close proximity of the offices to the Intercontinental Hotel, owned by the Maktoum family and where Hasher Maktoum stayed when in London, might have something to do with the choice. Then again, Harrods was just across the road, like having our own convenience store!

I must have said all the right things at the meeting with John, Tony Clements and his daughter, together with another person, who was introduced as Wade Cherwayko, the franchise owner of A1 Team Canada. The gas and oil industries were given to me as his business interests. This was all getting very interesting, I recall thinking. They confirmed my appointment as marketing director, and we were on our way. John walked downstairs with me as I left to catch my train, that famous wry smile spread across his face as he put his hand on my shoulder and told me that this would either be a very exciting adventure or another motor-racing fairy tale. I knew exactly what he meant.

The opening race of the A1GP season was to be staged on the 25th September 2005, at Brands Hatch's famous Grand Prix circuit. Before that, however, I was invited to a big conference at which we would be given a marketing presentation by two more South Africans, Stephen Watson and Simon Robinson. The RSA link was beginning to look more than just a coincidence. It turned out that Simon was the head of sponsorship or something similar and Stephen the global general manager. I was by now intrigued.

The presentation was indeed an eye-opener, as John and I agreed afterwards. With the exceptional quality of the all the promotional material that was being dished out, I was expecting something very special when it came to the subject of sponsorship. The franchise owners had all invested heavily, to the tune of several million dollars, I was told. Sponsorship would be the way that they would get their money back, the assembled audience was told. Then came my first big surprise, as we were told about the A1 GP sponsorship acquisition strategy, supported by the most expensive sales material, which would bring in millions of dollars. The strategy involved a sales tool, one which I have to admit I have never used in my career. It effectively comprised a rate card, pure and simple. In case the words "rate-card" sound more appropriate to an advertising salesman, you would be dead right; and that's what it was, a very expensively designed and produced rate card, showing all the spaces on the car and allowing these spaces to be sold in normal advertising fashion. In other words, all of these investors who had come to learn how to get their return on this particular investment, most of whom had never been involved in sports marketing, were being shown how sponsorship was sold in the days of tobacco, when brand awareness, hospitality and PR were the only demands of the sponsor.

To say that I was shocked wouldn't begin to explain how I felt. Then, as if it couldn't get any worse, figures of two to three million dollars were being mentioned when questions about the level of sponsorship expectation in year one were being asked by investors. It was at that precise moment I realised that we had a major problem ahead. One of the most common areas of dispute in sponsorship agreements comes from a difference in the levels of expectation between the commercial rights holder and the sponsor. One of the classic examples of this came back in 1997, when Lola Race Cars dipped their toes back into F1 again, just four years after the disastrous joint-venture with BMS Scuderia Italia. An innovative sponsorship deal between Lola and MasterCard lasted just one race into the season, with "financial and technical" issues being cited as the reason for Lola withdrawing from the world championship. To start with, the car failed to qualify for the Grand Prix by a huge margin, followed by a deal-breaking misunderstanding of the financial terms within the terms of the multi-million pound MasterCard sponsorship.

Such was the embarrassment caused to the sponsor in the process, that MasterCard's USA-based head of sponsorship invited several of the leading F1 teams to the Portman Hotel in London to present to her their options as to the best way forward for MasterCard in terms of damage limitation. At the time I was working at Benetton, on behalf of the API Agency, and, together with John Postlethwaite of Benetton F1, we put forward our proposal. This was based on MasterCard simply spending the balance of the season with us at Benetton F1, without any fee being involved, purely as a way of allowing its marketing personnel the unique opportunity to observe F1 from the inside. They could then eventually make a decision, based on that knowledge, as to the potential ways forward. It wasn't to be, however, and MasterCard chose to see out the 1997 season with Eddie Jordan's team. I can't recall them being involved as major sponsors in F1 again, but I may be wrong.

In a similar way, I feared that the levels of financial expectation being put out by A1's sponsorship experts, coupled with what I believed to be a highly ineffective way of approaching its acquisition, would most likely end in tears. For a start, no one knew what the TV viewing stats would be for this totally new series. Despite this, the sponsorship experts were, in my professional opinion, basing far too much of their advice to A1 franchise holders, on TV-generated brand awareness being the main reason why sponsors would invest in the teams.

I could see huge potential for sponsorship, but not in Year One, and certainly not based on brand awareness. To me, the real potential lay in teams working closely with their individual government trade departments to build dynamic, innovative and sustainable global business-development platforms for companies. But when I put these views forward in a positive way, I was outnumbered. People were being fooled by the enormous amounts of money being spent on so many aspects of A1GP, including the Brand Guidelines, Sponsorship Guidelines and so much other promotional material. Exciting and dramatic-looking race cars abounded, all decked out in their national colours. Big name sports and political figures were brought into add to the spectacle. I can't blame people for not wanting to be brought down to reality; after all, most of the people putting in the money were totally new to this wonderful, colourful sport of ours. They didn't want anyone spoiling the party, that was for sure.

In the case of A1 Team GBR, it was no different. When John and I sat down to talk about the realities of sponsorship acquisition during the first season, we applied our knowledge and experience. As an example, we looked at other existing race series, such as GP2, then the stepping-stone support race at many of the F1 Grand Prix. One of our drivers at Benetton F1, Giancarlo Fisichella, had just launched his own team in GP2. The fee being asked to become the team's title sponsor was considerably less than that being forecast by A1GP gurus as being feasible for lesser sponsorship options within A1. Bear in mind that GP2 was by then a well-established series, competing at many of the F1 Grand Prix events throughout the season and having a proven pedigree, whereas everything about A1GP was unknown. It made no sense at all.

I could see that if I tried to explain the reality of the situation, I would be told that I was being negative. Far from being negative, however, I was very excited about the potential future of this brand new concept of racing. The sponsorship potential was very real, but it would take time; and it would take education of both the corporate sector and the teams themselves to design and implement sponsorship strategies that were based on reality, and the vision of a new business development platform. Sadly, no one wanted to hear that.

Any doubts that A1GP would struggle were dispelled at the opening race of the inaugural season, held at Brands Hatch. It was a stunning event, assisted by beautiful weather. An estimated crowd of over 65,000 spectators turned up to watch the teams from the UK, Portugal, Brazil, Australia, Pakistan, Mexico, and a hosts of other nations take their first step in what would be an eight-month long battle to win the coveted World Cup of Motorsport. The racing at Brands Hatch was exciting, and when the son of a famous former F1 World Champion, Nelson Piquet Junior, proudly waved the Brazilian flag to be announced A1's first-ever race winner, it was a popular victory. The celebrations in the Pangea at Brands Hatch continued well into the night.

What's the Pangea, you might wonder?

Well, F1 has the Paddock Club, which is where the serious hospitality at Grand Prix is conducted at a price in excess of $3,500 per head for a three-day pass. It's where the big sponsors go to entertain their guests, as well as the many celebrities invited by the F1 teams to generate even more publicity than their competitors.

The A1GP had the Pangea, cleverly named after the hypothetical supercontinent that included all current land masses believed to have been in existence before the continents broke apart during the Triassic and Jurassic Periods. As a World Cup of Motorsport, you can see why A1GP used the word Pangea to describe the one place at a race meeting where all the nations (or teams) came together to socialise and meet up. They certainly got that right. What the cost of setting up the quality of hospitality that was available I have no idea, but if the intention was to make the Paddock Club look ordinary, I suppose you could say that they got it right, certainly at the first few events of that debut season in 2005–2006. It was entertaining of the very highest standard.

The problem with the Pangea was that it made a rod for the organisers own back inasmuch that whilst at Brands Hatch it was chock-a-block full, the contrast was extraordinary when it came to the third round of the championship, held at the former F1 Grand prix Circuit of Estorial in Portugal. Although a highly rated venue in terms of being so close to the coast, when race day arrived, you could almost count the number of paying guests on one hand. The Pangea was as stunning as it had been at Brands, except that the number of guests was a mere faction. I dread to think of the food wastage that day.

I'd been under a lot of pressure to bring in some big sponsors. It came from the top, with Tony Clements having heard from the A1 sponsorship exponents how relatively easy it would be to bring on board the major corporates. You can't blame him. He'd done nothing but write out cheques so far in his new A1 existence, and when A1 Team Malaysia announced that Proton would be the primary sponsor of the team, it must have seemed to the A1 franchise holders that this was going to be better than winning the lottery. Indeed, for many countries in which their level of sports participation was very limited, such as Malaysia, A1GP offered a unique sponsorship opportunity to attract its major businesses. It was a lot less expensive than F1, for example. However, in the UK and those other countries, which boasted a proliferation of sports sponsorship across a wide range of top flight sports, the reality was that A1GP was way down the list in terms of value and proven effectiveness. To Ireland, for example, A1 offered a rare commercial sports opportunity, whilst to Germany, it wasn't. Suddenly, the longer-term sponsorship strategies that I had outlined as being the way to go, and which had activated wisely nodding heads of appreciation, were no longer the name of the game as it became obvious from the viewing and attendance figures that A1 wasn't quite the instant success that had been predicted. I was now being asked where the deals were for A1GP. It seemed that all and sundry were now sports marketing experts and couldn't understand why I wasn't bring in deals by the bucket load.

What I had predicted was now coming to fruition. I was told that my efforts to involve UKT&I were too long-term. This was a great shame, because I was generating serious interest and knew that together, we could potentially create a dynamic platform for us to talk to British businesses, proposing a global strategy of business-development opportunities, using A1 Team GBR as the catalyst. In an effort to help, I brought in a company called AC Lighting, a company that supplied exterior lighting effects to the BT Tower in London, as well as to the Natural History Museum and even the Rolling Stones Tours. It wasn't a huge deal, but then it wasn't a huge series, at that stage. The main thing was that in addition to an annual fee, AC Lighting would buy hospitality at many of the races, through the team's coffers.

True to their word, AC Lighting came to many races with a high number of guests and staff, until I received a serious complaint from within A1 Team GBR relating to the fact that some of AC's guests were displaying tattoos whilst in the Pangea, and this was not acceptable! The fact that in one fair swoop, that probably ruled out 65% of the people in the United Kingdom, seemed totally unimportant within the exciting new world of A1 Team GBR.

In an attempt to accelerate revenue income, I arranged a meeting with Peter Dare, the head of SkySport's sponsorship team. With this digital giant being the host broadcaster of A1 within the UK, it was in their interest to generate as much broadcast sponsorship as possible. My suggestion to Peter was that we should identify a few companies that we considered potential targets for a joint approach, offering an innovative package incorporating the GBR team and Sky Sports. He really liked the idea, and we put a shortlist together.

We were well into the season now. I'd been down to Durban where the A1 Grand Prix comprised a street race along the Indian Ocean beach front. It had to be one of the most scenic race tracks in the world, with the individual team's hospitality facilities backing onto the ocean. Through my contacts at UKT&I in South Africa, we organised a reception for the British Team in association with the deputy mayor of Durban, Logie Naidoo, the man responsible for staging this innovative race. It was a test run to see if the concept worked. If it did, then this would be on offer to potential A1 Team GBR sponsors at other races, as part of their sponsorship packages. I hoped that the powers-that-be would be able to see where I was coming from with my strategy. I hoped in vain!

A quick word about the South African Team. The franchise holder was a highly successful black businessman, Tokyo Sexwale, one of the close associates of Nelson Mandela throughout their period of imprisonment on Robben Island. He went on to become the premier of Gauteng Province, before entering the commercial sector in a number of various roles, all of which combined to make him a very wealthy and influential man.

In his A1GP Team RSA role, he was assisted by Dana Cooper who became the team's CEO. For the inaugural 2006-2007 season, Sexwale entered into an agreement with the high-profile French team, DAMS to prepare their car. DAMS, run by Jean Paul Driot, was one of Europe's most successful single-seater teams at that time. Despite enlisting a number of highly-acclaimed drivers over the season, including Tomas Scheckter (Jody's son), Stephen Simpson, Adrian Zaugg and British F3 Champion, Alan van der Merwe, the South African team never really lived up to its full potential.

It did, however, attract a number of major sponsors, mainly due to Sexwale's extraordinary connections with the rapidly changing South African business sector. These included the banking giant, ABSA.

I personally got on well with Tokyo and Dana. Once they had heard that my wife was South African, whenever we meet up at the track Tokyo would put his arm around me and jokingly tell me that I should be changing hats and leaving the British A1 Team. There were many times during the course of that unbelievable first A1GP season when I felt like doing just that!

As many people who have worked closely with John Surtees will tell you, although he was one of the greats of motorsport, on both two and four wheels, he certainly wasn't always the easiest person to work with. I could see that as the season wore on, he was coming under increasing pressure from the franchise holder to deliver, both in terms of dollars and track performance. Everyone was now under pressure to deliver, not just commercially.

It had all started so well for A1 Team GBR in the opening round at Brands Hatch, with Robbie Kerr leading from Nelson Piquet Junior, but a failed battery destroyed his chances of victory. In Dubai, he was leading until being passed by the French team's car of Nicolas Lapierre. Then, in the first of the two races on the streets of Durban, Kerr secured his first win, but in the second and main race, technical gremlins led to his retirement.

The pressure that Surtees was under was then directed in my direction. As is so often the case in motorsport, the buck stops with the sponsorship acquisition person. It's easy to blame him or her, on the basis that if only there was more money coming in, all the other problems and issues that were contributing to the team's performance could be solved. Having been in the business some 30 years or so by then, I had a broad back when it came to this sort of pressure. It was part of the game. In fairness, I had a track record which I think most people in the know would have agreed was a bit special, but you can't guarantee success every time.

What really made me angry was that the criticism within A1 Team GBR started coming from people within the team who had absolutely no knowledge or understanding of motorsport marketing. As part of my role, I was trying to also help such people understand how sponsorship worked, and that it wasn't simply based on brand awareness, hospitality and PR but rather on creating measurable and sustainable business-development opportunities, as I had in so many of my deals, including FedEx, SodaStream and Gillette. The problem that I encountered, however, was that the A1GP sponsorship gurus were telling everyone a different story, supported by the rate card sponsorship material that was being bandied about left right and centre.

On the other hand, the feedback that I was now getting from Peter Dare and the Sky Sports sponsorship tea, who were out there trying to generate interest in the marketplace, confirmed what I had been worried about. The TV-viewing figures, apart from that opening round at Brands Hatch, were nothing short of disastrous. Whether this was due to the broadcast times of the races, many of which were in the Southern Hemisphere and shown late at night in the UK or simply a lack of interest in A1GP, it was difficult to tell. What it meant, however, was that if a team had based a sponsorship strategy on brand awareness alone, as was being recommended, the figures just didn't stand up to close scrutiny.

As a result, we had a bizarre situation in which the A1GP Franchise Holders, who had to rely on what they were being told by A1GP personnel, because many of them had no sports marketing experience, were putting on more and more pressure. They didn't want to hear what was being told to them by experienced sponsorship acquisition personnel, such as Mark Gallagher, principal of A1 GP Team Ireland, or me. When I had been doing deals for Benetton, Mark had been doing the same for Eddie Jordan and knew what he was talking about. On more than one occasion, Mark and I sat sharing our concerns over a coffee in the paddock. The underlying issue was that people didn't want to hear what we were telling them, it didn't fit in with their expectations or hopes.

It got to the stage where I really wasn't getting any enjoyment out of my role at A1 Team GBR. I know that John Surtees was feeling the same in many because he told me. He was in a difficult position inasmuch that he had to get the money out of the franchise holder to be able to pay the team preparing the car. This meant Arden in the first season, before John set up an in-house team in year two. In addition to paying the technical team, all of the other costs had to be covered, including travel, hospitality and salaries. As a result, John was between a rock and a hard place. On the one hand, he knew the reality of the situation and having run his own F1 team for many years, John understood the real world of commercial sponsorship, accepting that what I was saying wasn't bullshit. On the other, he had to appease those holding the purse strings. I didn't envy him his role. I must admit.

When my contract came to end in 2006, I had no desire to sign up for more of the same. When I told John, he told me that he fully understood where I was coming from and thanked me for the efforts that he knew only too well I had put in. The bottom line, as he explained, was that there were people involved who knew it all; and no matter how much experience was involved, you weren't going to change their mind.

As we all know, A1GP didn't last very long. In September 2006, Sheikh Maktoum Hasher Maktoum Al Maktoum of Dubai sold his shares in A1GP to a company called RAB Capital. A South African, Tony Teixeira, took control of the series. With Teixeira at the helm, the series gradually progressed into an untimely liquidation in 2009. In the process, the decision had been made to introduce a new race car which would be powered by a Ferrari engine. Despite a number of experienced motorsport industry personnel advising against this move at such an early stage in the growth of the series, the changeover went ahead.

The opening round of the 2009-2010 A1GP season was scheduled for Queensland, Australia and had been underwritten by the Queensland State Government. Due to major issues with the transportation of the cars and with other matters, the Australian organisers announced its cancellation, just five days before the scheduled opening day of the race meeting. This was deemed necessary in the absence of any communication from A1 in the UK.

Then it was announced that the races in China and Malaysia would be cancelled. Finally, cancellation of the final round in Holland put the entire future of the series into doubt.

What followed was a long string of legal claims and counter claims, as well as a couple of attempts to revive the ailing series, but all to no avail. A1GP is now yet another sad saga that in the history of our wonderful sport.

From a purely personal point of view, I was very disappointed that what had the potential to be a fantastic, innovative and unique championship ended its days in such a farcical manner. I know that a lot of people lost a lot of money. Many of them I know well, and there remains amongst them a feeling of bitterness in the way that money was wasted within A1GP by people who wouldn't listen to those who genuinely wanted the concept to work.

I, for one, really wanted it to work and genuinely tried my best to help the investors grasp an understanding of what was going wrong, but I felt personally abused by some of the attitudes that resulted from people realising that they stood to lose a lot of money.

Interestingly, some years after the demise of A1 GP, I was walking through the Paddock at Silverstone at a round of the Word Endurance Championship, when I bumped in Katie Clements, working then, as I believe she still does, for Julian Jacobi's GP Sports Management. She seemed pleased to see me and asked how I was. When I told her that I'd just returned from four years in South Africa, and that things were going well, she told me that she was genuinely glad, adding that she wanted to apologise to me on behalf of Tony, her father and others involved in running Team A1 GBR for the way that I had been treated during those opening couple of years. She went on to say that they should have listened to me about my concerns and recommendations. Apparently both Katie and her father had lost a serious amount of money as a result of their investment in A1.

I told Katie that I very much appreciated and accepted her apologies. It wasn't something that she had to do, and I didn't prompt her to do so. I saw it as an indication of a person with a sense of decency, and I know that she will do well under the tutorage of Julian Jacobi. I would like to think and hope that I was able to help her, in some small way, to generate an interest in the commercial side of motorsport and, in particular, successful sponsorship acquisition.

Before moving on from A1GP, I must mention John's son, Henry. I met him on several occasions during that first year of A1GP, when he accompanied the British team to several of the races. In particular, I recall sitting in the team's hospitality building in the Paddock at the Estoril Circuit in Portugal, chatting to Henry and Jane, John's lovely wife. I was very impressed that, unlike some of the precocious brats that grace motorsport paddocks today, Henry was a laid-back, almost old-fashioned type of a lad, who was never happier than when he had a book in his hand. He loved reading, and that was so good to see. He wasn't pushy or egotistical, just a normal boy with whom you could have a pleasant conversation about a wide range of topics. What John and Jane must have gone through after that fateful day at Brands Hatch when young Henry lost his life in someone else's accident in an F2 race, I can't even begin to imagine. I will always remember those conversations with Henry very fondly.

I met up again with John in 2016, when he called me to say that he had bought the Buckmore Park Karting Circuit in Kent and invited me to the official launch. Over a coffee, we chatted about those extraordinary A1GP days. We then moved on to more pressing matters, and he asked me if I would consider running a training course on the Practice Day of the first major national race day that season. The topic would be sponsorship acquisition! It was great to know that despite the trials and tribulations of A1GP, John knew that my experience and expertise in acquiring sponsorship hadn't been diminished in any way. I went ahead and ran the course for him. It was to be the last time that I saw him.

In 2006, Brian became Marketing Director of the British A1 Grand Prix team, working with the late John Surtees CBE. Whilst with the team at the Estoril Circuit in Portugal, he met up with Keke Rosberg, some 22 years after working with him in South Africa.

John Surtees passed away in 2017. He was always his own man and achieved in his lifetime what most people only dream of. Yes, we had our disagreements, and he could be very abrasive, but he knew his business inside out and had a wonderful sense of humour. I feel privileged to have worked alongside him, and I must add to that his long serving PA, Sharron, who had the patience of a saint!

Chapter 39
A Call for Help, a Feasibility Study and a Return to South Africa

After my stint in A1, I didn't have to wait long for my next challenge to come along. It came in the form of a phone call from a South African, Nico Vermeulen. He introduced himself as being the CEO of an organisation called NAAMSA. I knew of it from my time in that country and realised that it stood for The National Association of Automobile Manufacturers of South Africa. As its web site still explains, NAAMSA represents the collective, non-competitive interests of the new motor vehicle industry in South Africa. It comprises 22 companies involved in the production of cars and commercial vehicles, collectively employing about 30,000 people.

He explained that that he knew of me, from my days at McCarthy Motors, the Mercedes and Honda dealership group, as well as from my motor racing activities in South Africa, including my very successful school, Speed International at Kyalami. He went on to tell me that many of his member companies were involved one way or another in motorsport activities, as a way of promoting their primary business activities. From what he was telling me, it seemed that there was a general sense of dissatisfaction at the way that motorsport in South Africa was being run, and that it was on the decline.

What he told me didn't come as much of a surprise, I have to admit. I had kept in touch with many of my contacts within the sport in South Africa and had heard similar views from them. Nico then asked me if I was likely to be coming to South Africa in the near future. He knew that Liz and I had family there. When I responded by telling him that we were actually planning a trip within the next two months, he asked if we could possibly meet up and discuss matters.

Liz and I duly stopped off in Johannesburg on our way to Cape Town, and I had lunch with Nico. His reaction to my initial thought process was very positive. I had explained that from my ten years in RSA, nearly all of which were tied up with motor racing, it had become blindingly obvious that motorsport was now perceived by a large number of South Africans, both black and white, to be the plaything of a minority of white males, most of whom who could afford to participate in the various categories of the sport. I also added that it was generally considered fairly down-market, from a social point of view.

He smiled at my comments, but asked me to carry on. I then got onto the subject of the governing body of motorsport within South Africa, the MSA, or Motorsport South Africa to give it its full name. I commented on the fact that I had tried on many occasions to enter into dialogue with the directors of the MSA about ways of taking the sport forward, but had always met a brick wall.

Nico thanked me for my honest and forthright opinions, before bluntly asking me what I felt would be the way to bring about change. I spent about half an hour outlining what I believed to be the best way of moving motorsport forward within South Africa, after which he assured me that he would report back to his Board on our meeting and would be back in touch whilst I was still there.

My advice had been very simple. I told him that in my personal opinion, motor racing would never be taken seriously in the rapidly changing South Africa until was structured and run as an industry sector in its own right. You may have heard those words somewhere before! As I detailed in an earlier chapter, back in 1994, I had launched the Motorsport Industry Association, at the London UK head office of Accenture (or Andersen Consulting as it was then known). I had explained that within the UK, motorsport at that time was not a formally recognised industry sector in its own right, and many people believed that until it was, it would battle to generate the levels of investment it needed to keep its perceived position as a world leader. The MIA is now 24 years old and has played critical role in the outstanding growth and development of the British and also, international, motorsport industry.

When I spelt out my ideas to Nico, they were based on the experiences that I gained some from starting the MIA in Britain, back in 1994, rather just a collection of vague ideas as to what might improve South African motorsport.

Before leaving South Africa to return home, I spoke again to Nico, and he asked me how I would go about bringing about similar changes within motorsport in RSA. He sounded somewhat surprised when I told him that during my stay, I'd had an initial phone discussion with Wayne Furphy, CEO of Accenture in South Africa, during which I outlined my background in the UK; and my involvement in the formation of the MIA, with Accenture's backing.

I had followed this up with a face-to-face meeting with him, in which he explained how he was keen for Accenture to get much closer to the South African automotive industry and asked if there was any way that we might be able to work together in some way. It was an opening that I had seized upon. Wayne and I were then able to put together an agreement which would see Accenture sponsoring a feasibility study in respect of my creating an organisation similar in many ways to the MIA, aimed at formalising a South African motorsport industry. The deal we reached included four 2-week visits to South Africa for Liz and me, including our flights and accommodation. We would be based at Accenture's Woodmead HQ in Johannesburg, be provided with a hire car, an office and secretarial back-up.

When I had finished outlining this to Nico, in our phone conversation, there was silence at the other end of the phone. Then Nico responded. I think he used one word … Wow!

I hadn't finished, however. I then explained to him that I had managed to set up an important meeting the very next day in Johannesburg that would hopefully add a high level of credibility and support to the feasibility study that I was going to undertake. He asked who the meeting was with.

It's with the Chairman of MCI, Mr Cyril Ramaphosa, I replied. Little did I realise that the man with whom I had arranged a meeting, would go on to become the President of South Africa in 2018, replacing Jacob Zuma.

I had first met Cyril Ramapahosa when I was introduced to him at the 1993 South African F1 Grand Prix, in my capacity of Marketing Director of the Lola BMS Scuderia Italia Team. However, at the time I arranged to meet him, he was also in-charge of South Africa's Black Empowerment programme (BEE). I realised that his opinion of my plan to formalise a South African motorsport industry would be very important to the feasibility study that I was about to embark upon.

I had initially made contact with his PA and explained that I was in South Africa for another couple of days and would like to arrange a meeting with Mr Ramaphosa. She initially laughed and said that his diary was booked solid for two months ahead. She then asked me what the meeting would be about. I told her that I had the pleasure of meeting Cyril during the 1993 F1 Grand Prix at Kyalami, and that he told me he liked motorsport. I explained that the meeting was about setting up a programme in South Africa to encourage black youngsters into engineering and technical skills training, through motorsport. She told me that she would personally tell her boss that I had phoned, but added that I shouldn't expect too much. An hour later, she called me back and said that she didn't know what it was about motor racing, but whatever it was, it worked! If I could be at Mr Ramaphosa's Sandton office at 10:00 the next morning, he would see me for half an hour.

I was there on time, and we started talking about my plans. He surprised me by telling me that he had checked out my background and was fully aware of the MIA, and what it had achieved. In particular, he was interested in the educational side of its activities. We spent some time talking about the potential for young blacks to set up small businesses allied to the motorsport industry, such as building race car trailers, engine tuning, tyre fitting and many other commercial activities. As we shook hands at the end of the meeting, which had exceeded the proposed 30 minutes by over an hour, he told me that he would send me a letter confirming his support of my ideas. I had got off to a flying start, way beyond my expectations.

When I got back to the UK, I waited for the letter to arrive; but after a week or so, and it hadn't turned up, I called his PA, and she apologised for not having sent it through. It arrived the following week. What he told me in the letter was that he saw the formation of a South African motorsport industry would, in his opinion, provide innovative and dynamic opportunities not only to learn some engineering and technical skills training, but also to subsequently set up small businesses, providing support services in a range of different motorsport activities.

I couldn't believe what had happened in such a short space of time, but it was now time for Liz and I to fly back to the UK, take stock and make our plans for implementing the feasibility study.

We had been really chuffed at what we had found on our latest visit to South Africa. There had been enormous change in the country, not simply from the obvious political changes, but even more importantly in the attitude of the people, of all South Africans, of all racial types. You could actually feel the positive swell of support for the changes that Nelson Mandela had brought about. Wherever you went, whether to a shopping mall, a restaurant, a coffee shop or just queuing in the bank, there was a different feeling about the place. People were smiling. It probably sounds very naïve, but it wasn't just me; it was a tangible emotive swell of people's belief that Mandela had achieved the impossible and through his leadership would bring about bloodless change within South Africa.

Liz was born in South Africa, she'd gone to school there, she'd grown up there, and now she was seeing amazing changes taking hold of the country. She was delighted to be getting involved in a programme that in its own small way might start to create real opportunities for young black youngsters to embark on a career that would offer them exciting employment opportunities. Yes, she told me, let's go back and try to make a difference!

Nico had told me that motorsport was on the wane in South Africa, which was sad to hear. It had always been a very well-supported sport, but it seemed that times were changing. Through motorsport, I'd been lucky enough to enjoy some great times in South Africa. Now I was being presented with a unique opportunity to use the experience that I'd gained in my early MIA days, to develop training and education programmes for previously disadvantaged youngsters, using motorsport as the attraction.

One of my first steps on starting my feasibility study was to introduce myself to the UKT&I personnel in South Africa. I'd developed a good relationship with the organisation over many years in the UK, and I knew that if I explained what I was now trying to achieve in South Africa, they might well be able to support my initiative. There was indeed a high level of interest, and I knew that I could rely on their help as things developed.

With their introduction, I was able to meet some key figures in the RSA government. However, I wasn't expecting a rather embarrassing situation that developed in that respect. One of the senior figures in the South African Dept of Trade and Industry (DTI), with whom I was discussing my plans for setting up a South African motorsport industry sector, commented that despite my telling him that I had started the MIA in the UK, they could find no trace of me on the MIA web site. Puzzled, I looked for myself and sure enough there was absolutely no mention of my role whatsoever in the history of the MIA. This caused me considerable embarrassment, as you can probably imagine. To sort this out, I had to contact and gain the support of my original committee members. Even then, it took quite a while for this to be rectified.

Chapter 40

Vested Interests, a Lack of Respect and Important Industry Support

I've already described how and why I set up the Motorsport industry Association in 1994, but it came as a big surprise to me that day in South Africa, when I saw that I had been written out of the organisation's history. It was to be another 5 years before a possible reason for this became apparent. In October 2013, I was back in the UK. One morning, I received a communication from the MIA office.

I'm not sure why I was sent this communication, but as it was addressed to me, I opened it. Its purpose was to solicit support for Chris Aylett to be formally recognised with an honour for his work in building up the MIA to the powerful and successful organisation that it is today. The letter would be sent to the relevant Cabinet Office, with several letters of support. I was asked if I would support the application.

I want to get one thing clear, straight away, I have absolutely no problem in principle with Chris Aylett being awarded the MBE or whatever is deemed appropriate to recognise his achievements in building up the motorsport industry to where it is now, through his work with the Motorsport Industry Association. I have never done anything but confirm that, in my opinion, Chris has done a good job, one that I could never have done.

Looking back, however, I was the person who came up with the concept of the MIA, did the hard slog with my Steering Committee, brought Accenture on board with Rob Baldock's help, created the MIA awards programme and through my contact, Lord Astor of Hever, secured the House of Lords as the venue. I also introduced Lord Astor as the MIA Honorary President, and through Ian Laing, I invited the guests to the Lancaster House event that resulted in a focus on academic qualifications within our industry. That is as far as I went ... I could never have taken the MIA from that point, to where it is today. So I take my hat off to Chris for that.

So why was I, together with my Steering Committee members, written out of the MIA's history?

When I initially opened the letter requesting support, I looked through the two letters that accompanied this request. Both were from former Chairmen of the MIA. The first letter was based on the writer's involvement with the MIA, which started when his company became a member in 1998, four years after I founded the association, and at the same time that Chris Aylett took over my role as CEO, after I stood down. Aylett had been recommended as a possible replacement by a valued member of my original steering committee, Ralph Firman, CEO of Van Diemen International. I personally interviewed Chris and considered that he would be an ideal candidate, having previous experience of running a trade association. It provided a fair description of the work that Chris had put in to build the MIA to its current level.

The second letter was the one that really disappointed and hurt me.

I had first met the writer when he was the sales manager of the company in question in 1994 when I visited the company at the invitation of its owner, who had wanted to hear more about the Motorsport Industry Association and was very happy to join, fully supporting the objectives that my steering committee had outlined.

Later that year, the inaugural MIA Business Achievement Awards Reception was held at the Rothley Court Hotel, near Leicester. We sold all the tickets for the event, meaning that over a hundred people attended. The major award, the MIA Outstanding Achievement Award, was sponsored by Andersen Consulting and presented to David Richards, CEO of Prodrive. Interestingly, the MIA Export Achievement Award was won by the company to which I have just referred. A delighted Sales Manager came up to accept the unique trophy from me. Having been at the event all evening, he couldn't but help recognise some of the most influential figures from our industry who had braved some foul weather to support the first MIA Awards event.

Within the first year of its existence, we had well over 30 impressive members including Cosworth, Ford Motor Company and Benetton F1 and TOCA.

So when this individual, in his October 2013 letter of support for Chris Aylett's honour, describes the early years of the MIA in the following way, you can imagine the feelings of my steering committee members, as well as my own, when it got into our hands.

"Our company first joined the MIA in 1994, when our company had 95 employees and a turnover of just £12 million. At the time, the MIA had less than a dozen members and was really struggling to attract new companies and to grow, despite the ever increasing importance of the sector to the UK economy.

However, since Chris became the CEO of the MIA in 1998, he managed to put together the diverse interests of our industry and has without a doubt made a substantial and sustained contribution to the UK economy and balance of payments.

It came as a kick in the face for nearly four years of hard work that my original steering committee put in to create something that had never even been thought of, let alone tried. He seems to forget that prior to 1994, the motorsport industry was not even officially recognised as a sector in its own right. It was simply considered a part of the motor industry. In fact, he seems to have very short, or maybe selective, memory. I was the person who left my position as marketing director of Lola Cars F1 Team to start the MIA, having recognised the urgent need for such an initiative, following what was seen as a major threat to the motorsport industry by the sport's governing body. Liz went out to work, so that I could afford to give up my Lola job and work full-time on building the MIA.

At the formal launch of the MIA at the Arundel Street head office of Andersen Consulting in 1994, I clearly laid out the objectives and purpose of the new organisation. I have it all on video record.

It was tough getting out there into companies and persuading of the need for such an organisation, but between us, we achieved a huge amount in those first three years; and yes, we were proud of what we had achieved by the time Chris Aylett came on board. Being brutally honest, a lot of the really hard work had already done by then.

It would have taken nothing away from Chris Aylett's subsequent successes for this person to have refrained from his negative comments. For a fellow professional in the motorsport industry to treat his peers in this way was both uncalled for and in poor taste.

It was my decision to stand down after three years at the helm of the MIA. The organisation wasn't yet in a position financially to employ a full-time CEO. In addition, I recognised that I didn't have the skillset to run a trade association despite having had the vision to start it. Ways of generating income from government and similar sources were beyond my level of experience.

It was me who interviewed Chris Aylett and recommended him as being suitable. He then came on board and took the MIA from the level at which it was operating in 1998, to where it is today. He has done a great job, of that I have no doubt. Whether he deserves an honour is not for me to say. What I will say, however, is that I take great exception to the attempts that were made to delete from history my involvement in the MIA's formation and formative years, as well as that of Richard Scammel, Ralph Firman, Tony Schulp, John Kirkpatrick, Rob Baldock and Gordon Bruce in their capacity on the Steering Committee.

Eventually, after this saga, I was appointed an Honorary Life Member of the MIA, one of three with Lord Astor and Rob Baldock. Sadly, recognition that has to be given begrudgingly, doesn't have the same impact as that given with goodwill.

Maybe I am totally wrong for thinking that there might be a connection between the application for an Honour, which I have described and my being written out of the MIA's history. If I am, I apologise.

Despite the issue that I have just described, I was eventually able to convince the South African government officials of my legitimate involvement in the formation of the Motorsport Industry Association in the UK. Bear in mind that at this stage, I was carrying out a feasibility study in respect of setting up in South Africa a similar organisation to the MIA. I was only too aware that its objectives would need to be very different from those that I had outlined in the UK. For a start, although there hadn't been a formalised motorsport industry sector in its own right in the UK at that time, there was a recognised motorsport sector, albeit formally operating within the overall motor industry.

In South Africa, on the other hand, motorsport had been on the decline for some time, in terms of the number of people watching it, media coverage and even participation. It's strange when you think that back in the 1960s and very early 1970s, South Africa had its own thriving domestic F1 championship, with drivers such as Dave Charlton, Guy Tumner, Roy Klomfass, Eddie Keizan, Ian Scheckter and Basil van Rooyen. Many of these would also make appearances in the F1 World Championship. Its decline was down to a combination of factors, including political pressures and a rapidly decreasing value of the Rand, coupled with the increasing cost of buying and running F1 cars, as well as the loss of tobacco sponsorship.

I was of the opinion that my priority in South Africa was not so much the formalisation of the industry itself but rather looking at the introduction of educational initiatives. I knew that if companies were asked to invest in education, particularly related to much-needed engineering and technical skills training, it would be preferable to investing in motorsport, as such. The key, in my opinion, was to use motorsport as a way of encouraging young people into engineering.

However, I also remembered Nico Vermeulen's comments about the motor manufacturers being disappointed with the way motorsport was being run in the country. Maybe there was an opportunity to look at a different starting point, one involving the manufacturers. However, I was convinced that the most feasible starting point would be to start with education.

As was the case in Britain, there was a huge shortage of youngsters choosing that career path in South Africa, both male and female. I discovered that the most effective qualification for thousands of black youngsters in technical colleges was that of being a car mechanic, and that was about it. I recalled my conversation with Cyril Ramaphosa and his excitement when I talked about the potential that motorsport engineering offered for those studying to be a car mechanic. It would provide the inspiration that they needed to carry on studying, he agreed. The problem was that with so many youngsters in South Africa giving up maths at the age of 12, there was a lot of preliminary work to be done.

It was time to gain reaction to my proposals, relating to a formalised motorsport industry, from companies that operated within motorsport already. Luckily, I knew many of the owners and directors of businesses that fitted that category. I visited about three dozen in total across the country, the majority in Johannesburg. I was very surprised at the positive response I got from so many of them to my ideas about forming a South African motorsport industry with its own educational programmes. Amongst them were three very good friends, all of whom had supported my racing school initiative from the very beginning, as well as my own racing activities before that. Bruce Coquelle was the chairman of Autoquip, one of South Africa's leading tyre and wheel suppliers, as well as the stockist of a lot of racing equipment, much of it imported. Brian Smith was the CEO of the Western Province Motor Club, which managed the extremely popular Killarney Circuit in Cape Town. Then there was Owen Ashley, who was also based in Cape Town and had been Toyota's Motorsport Manager earlier in his career. He was widely regarded as South Africa's leading motorsport engineer and designer, with his own company based at Killarney. All three agreed with my objectives and offered to serve on a steering committee if I decided to move to South Africa and set up a South African equivalent of the MIA. Other leading individuals in various sectors whom I spent time with included Iqbal Sharma, Head of the Department of Trade and Industry in Pretoria, Mansoor Mohammed, Business Development Director at the City of Cape Town, and many leading figures from the academic and educational sector.

My four trips, within Accenture's agreed sponsorship, soon came to an end, and it was time for us both to head back home to England and make sense of it all. Liz had managed all of the meeting notes and other administrative work involved in the feasibility study, and between us, we had a lot of work to do.

Chapter 41
A Big Decision, Two Major Sponsorships and a Genuine Need for Change

It took us about a month to make up our minds about the opportunity in South Africa. It's true to say that we had some very mixed feelings about going back. On one hand, it was Liz's home country. Her son Nick, my stepson, was now involved in the family business in Cape Town, which was run by his father; so for her, the attraction of spending time with Nick, his wife Verné and their daughter Lexi was very strong. On the other hand, it would be a major upheaval for us both. We knew all about moving country, having not only moved back to the UK from South Africa, but then moving to Connecticut, USA, with Octagon Motorsports before returning to the UK, just under a year later. It's not easy, that's for sure.

Of course, it wasn't just about our personal feelings in respect of relocating to South Africa. We had to be very sure that we could achieve our primary aim of establishing a motor sport industry there. I think we were both concerned as to how much practical support we'd get from the government. My feasibility study had included several meetings with key government individuals, but I've learned the hard way that talk is cheap, particularly in South Africa. Would the outpouring of positive words that we had both heard, be converted into the high level of assistance that we would need?

Eventually, we came to a joint decision, which was based on a change of heart as to where the new organisation should be located. I'd assumed that the obvious place would be in the northern suburbs of Johannesburg, close to the Kyalami race track. As I thought about it in more detail, a major doubt crept into my mind. Kyalami might always have been considered the heart of motorsport in South Africa, but the more I looked at its recent history, the more I realised that it came with a lot of baggage. Where a lot of money is involved, there will always be people who will use whatever means they can to get more than their fair share. The more I delved into some of the dubious goings-on that had surrounded motorsport in Gauteng Province over the years, around which there had been a high level of media coverage, the more I started questioning if it was the ideal place to launch a new initiative which I was adamant would be 100% above board.

I called quite a few people whom I knew in South Africa, to get their reaction to my thought process. I have to say that I was quite surprised when the majority of them agreed with my views. They felt as I did, that it might be a good thing to find a new base for my initiative, to avoid it immediately being tarred with the same brush as some other motorsport-related initiatives.

So what were the options? In my opinion there was only one, when it really came down to it. The Western Province Motor Club had always done a very good job of staging motor racing at the Killarney Circuit in Cape Town. Killarney has the status of being the second oldest racing circuit in South Africa. Only the East London Grand Prix Circuit predates it. Try as I might, I couldn't find any evidence of there being any significant baggage associated with motorsport in the Western Cape. In fact, I found just the opposite. The chairman of the WPMC was Denis Joubert, a former racer and a professional architect. I knew Denis quite well, and we seemed to get on very well. I trusted him, and I trusted his views on the sport in South Africa. Interestingly, his son Deon was a successful professional racing driver and had been my co-driver in the Honda when we won our class in the Castrol 6-Hour Endurance Race at Killarney, back in 1985.

I spoke to several more influential people within the motorsport sector, before finally coming down on favour of the Western Cape as being the most suitable location in which to base the launch of the new motorsport industry initiative. In the end, it was really a no-brainer, because I simply couldn't afford the risk of what I was planning being tainted by the unfortunate antics of a few individuals in the recent history of the sport in Gauteng.

Once I was sure about the proposed location, it made it much easier for Liz and me to make the big decision. I think we both felt happier about heading to the Western Cape and being close to our family in the process. Once we made the decision, the pressure was off, and we realised that it was time to open a good bottle of South African wine and toast our new future.

It was a strange feeling returning to live in a country that we had left 17 year earlier, but within a few weeks, it seemed as if we hadn't been away. It was good to meet up with a lot of the drivers I knew from the days when I had been racing with them. What did surprise me was how many of them were still actively involved in driving. Quite a few were by now in their late 50s, early 60s. Willie Hepburn was even older.

I opted to go to the first race meeting that I was able to at the Killarney Circuit. It was like entering a time warp, with everything still looking very much the same as I remembered from the days when I must have taken in over a hundred races at the delightful track. It gave me a chance to meet Brian Smith, who had taken over from Denis Joubert as CEO of the Western Province Motor Club. Brian's background was interesting, having previously been the CEO of GUD Filters, a company based at the huge Atlantic complex on the Atlantic coastline of the Western Cape. We had spoken on the phone during the feasibility study, but I had never met him before. Brian was a huge motorsport enthusiast and raced an Alfa Romeo, but he was primarily a businessman; and when I spoke to him about my plans, he expressed a high level of interest and promised his support.

The same day, I met Owen Ashley, who ran his own race car engineering business in premises within the Killarney Circuit. I'd spent some time with him during one of my recent visits to South Africa, whilst carrying out my feasibility study. Like Brian, he could immediately see what I was trying to achieve and had also promised his support. They were both delighted that I had chosen the Western Cape as being the catalyst from which I would launch my strategy. They both felt that, for too long, Killarney had sucked the hind tit when it came to government support for motorsport within South Africa.

Much as I enjoyed my day at Killarney, time was of the essence. I knew that unless I could secure some serious financial support, all of my plans would come to nothing. The next step would be to meet with some of the influential figures within the business world.

As I was busy planning my target list of business contacts, I received an interesting invitation. The business school of Cape Town University asked me if I would be the guest speaker at a regular monthly business lunch that they hosted. They specifically wanted me to talk about my plans that had brought me to South Africa. It was perfect timing and would give me the potential opportunity to make some new contacts.

On the day of the event, Liz was asked if she would hand out some brochures that I'd put together. In the process, one of the guests told her that he unfortunately wouldn't be able to attend the talk, as he had an urgent meeting to attend. He added that he was keen to hear what I had to say and gave Liz his business card, suggesting that I should phone him. His name was Gareth Shaw, and he was a senior manager at Petro SA. I have to admit that I wasn't sure what Petro SA was all about, at that time.

When I got home, I did some research on Petro SA, and what I found out came as a big surprise to me. The Petroleum Oil and Gas Corporation of South Africa, to give it its full name, the National Oil Company of South Africa and a subsidiary of the Central Energy Fund, was wholly owned by the State. Its listed core business activities included the production of synthetic fuels from offshore gas at one of the world's largest gas-to-liquid refineries, situated in Mossel Bay, on the Indian Ocean coast.

It didn't take me long to secure a meeting with Gareth at Petro SA's head office in Parow, a suburb of Cape Town. He turned to be a really interesting guy, and we had a great chat about his role at PetroSA, and what I was doing in South Africa. He quickly grasped the importance of what I wanted to achieve and suggested that it might be worth my while talking to Petro SA about potential commercial opportunities. It was too good an opportunity to waste, and I immediately asked him if he could set up such a meeting.

A week or so went by, and then Gareth called me, asking if I would be able to have a breakfast meeting with him at the Radisson Hotel in Cape Town the following week. When I accepted his invitation, he told me that he would be bringing Dr Nompumelelo Siswana with him. He explained that in her role as Vice-President of Petro SA, she would be the best possible person to present my ideas to.

I had a lot of work to do, before the meeting, in putting together a document that outlined my objectives. Not that I minded, this was an amazing opportunity to speak to someone at such a high level in a business that could well prove extremely relevant. Thank you, Gareth Shaw!

Dr Siswana proved to be a fascinating lady, who told me that she had been forced to leave South Africa back in the apartheid era to study chemical engineering in Australia. She had eventually returned, highly qualified, to join Petro SA. What immediately became obvious at our first meeting was that she had a great sense of humour, and the three of us were soon talking as though we'd known each other for ages.

I listened carefully as she told me of some of the aims and objectives of PetroSA, and why she believed that there could be some potential benefits for the company in the motorsport industry project that I was in South Africa to launch. Under any other circumstances, I would have suggested that I should go away and develop a personalised proposal for her as to how this might work, but this meeting was developing at a much faster rate than I had expected. The meeting came to an end after about two hours, with a basic agreement that Petro SA would be on board with the organisation that I would be setting up. It was a stunning morning's work, and I thanked Gareth profusely for having set it up for me.

The most important aspect of the proposed relationship was not the money that it brought with it, but rather the extremely high level of credibility that would result from having this high-profile government backing. In addition, as I always try to explain to people, you cannot put too high a value on the PR support that invariably is put in place by the sponsor.

I knew that I now had a superb platform on which to acquire other commercial partners. I also recognised that my decision to locate to Cape Town was being vindicated, with the head office of Petro SA being right there.

A week or two later, I heard from another company that I had approached during one of my visits in 2006 to Johannesburg. I had been to the South African head office of Dell, the IT giant, and met their Sales Director, Rob Nunn. What was very much an exploratory meeting had been set up for me by the managing director of Accenture, Wayne Furphy. Once again, my relationship over the years with Accenture was paying dividends.

Rob told me that in principal, Dell would be very keen to work with me in helping achieve my objectives in South Africa. He explained that with there being a very high level of CSR in my strategy, with engineering and technical skills training for young black student being at the heart of it, he felt that the Dell Foundation would be the most appropriate partner and would arrange a meeting for me with Delano de Witt, head of the Dell Foundation.

Rob was true to his word, and I met Delano when he was in Cape Town. We were able to agree a deal that worked well for both parties, and I realised that we were making surprisingly good progress, within a very short space of time.

Yet another advantage of working closely with two international organisations of the calibre of Petro SA and the Dell Foundation, was the fact that I could seek advice at a very high level. Both Dr Siswana of Petro SA and Rob Nunn of Dell were very good in this respect. Both were also both very well connected; and if I needed to make contact with somebody at a company, there was a good chance that they might know them, or know someone who did.

It was now time to start talking at government level, and I managed to secure a meeting with Iqbal Sharma, who was the Head of the Department of Trade and Industry. I found him to be extremely supportive of my plans to create a South African motorsport industry, and when I proposed that he might like to play a role in the official launch event, which I was already giving thought to, he told me that there was a good possibility.

We were now ready to form an appropriate legal entity that would allow us to operate. With much appreciated advice from Petro SA's legal department, we structured the South African Motorsport Industry Association as a Section 21 company, meaning it was a not-for-profit company that cannot distribute shares or pay dividends to members.

You may think that I was being over sensitive, but having witnessed some very creative accounting within the motorsport sector whilst in South Africa previously, I was determined that everything we did with SAMIA, the name we had given to the new company, would be totally and utterly above board. I was delighted when Dr Siswana accepted my invitation to join the board of SAMIA. We then appointed highly respected Afrikaans auditors, De Villiers Broodrk, which would add even more credibility

Another director, whom I appointed to the board of SAMIA in my capacity as CEO, was Bez Sangari. Bez was the CEO of Sangari Education SA, a very successful business supplying engineering tuition equipment to schools, colleges and universities. He was also the South African franchise holder of Formula 1 in schools. I had spent quite a lot of time with Bez, outlining my plans and objectives for the development of a South African motorsport industry as the platform for developing engineering and technical skills training. He was extremely supportive and proposed that it might be appropriate for me to become a director of his F1 in Schools organisation. As I personally knew Andrew Denford, the man who had come up with the "F1 in Schools" concept in the UK, I was pleased to accept Bez's invitation.

F1 in Schools is a really innovative educational programme that Andrew, himself a qualified mechanical engineer, had put together. It has been running since 1999 and now operates in 40 countries around the world. Its primary objective has always been to use the attraction of motor racing to encourage young schoolchildren between the ages of 10 and 16 to become excited about engineering and to seriously consider a career in that sphere. It's well-worth taking a look on Google and finding out more about it.

I knew that the College of Cape Town, one of the city's leading further education and training facilities, ran the F1 in Schools programme very successfully. What I didn't know was that I was about to be invited by Jannie Isaacs, Principal of the college, to be the guest speaker at its annual graduation ceremony. It was all happening, and much of it was down to word getting around about my plans for the future of a motorsport industry in South Africa.

The College offered a number of courses across a range of subjects, but one of the most popular was for youngsters wanting to embark on a career as a motor mechanic, the majority of whom were black or brown. The qualification that they could gain on their course would help them secure much needed employment. I was asked by Jannie to attend their specific graduation and deliver a 30 minute talk, which he described as needing to be *inspirational*. No pressure there, then!

On the day of the graduation, there were about 450 people in the main auditorium, and I was seated on the stage, alongside the Principal and the Dean of the college. As I sat down, dressed in the blue academic robes that Jannie had insisted upon, he leant across to me and, with a big smile on his face, informed me that if I looked around the hall, I would see that mine was the only white face there. He went on to tell me that in the case of, virtually, every graduate receiving their diploma that morning, their qualification would be the first ever achieved in their families. It was very moving to hear that, and I responded to Jannie by telling him that the very people whom I was meant to be inspiring were, in reality, inspiring me!

Chapter 42
Illegal Street Racing, Ferrari Star Flies in and National Newspaper Signs-Up

The day at the College of Cape Town really opened my eyes and made me even more determined than ever to get the motorsport industry project off the ground. I knew that it could make a huge difference, not only in terms of education and career development, but also in helping to reduce another major problem within the city, street racing. This was claiming the lives of far too many youngsters, mainly from the Cape Malay community.

A love of cars is not unusual amongst teenagers, but you only had to drive around Cape Town to see the root of the problem. There were hundreds of older cars that had been re-built, with a range of performance enhancing accessories and engine-tuning kits. Many, which had been lowered, had enormous rear wings attached, massively wide and noisy exhaust systems fitted as well as new alloy wheels with low profile tyres. In most cases, the cars had been enhanced by a colourful, garish paint job. Some of these cars were already high-performance models, but with all of the extra tuning, they were now lethal, in the wrong hands.

The racing was, of course, illegal, but it was held on some of the city's main roads very late at night, into the early hours of the morning. Locals were telling me that it was almost a weekly occurrence to read in the newspapers that there had been a serious crash involving some of the street-racers. These incidents were often fatal, sometimes with totally innocent people getting caught up in them.

Many people put it down to boredom, others to drugs and gang-related issues.

It was my belief that with a little imagination and support, we could use the obvious attraction of high-performance driving and engine-tuning to encourage many of these young people into skills training, through the introduction of motorsport and high-performance engineering skills training programmes. If we added to that, an opportunity to run technical centres, open in the evenings, where they could learn about motorsport simulation and e-gaming, with the chance to also build and then drive, high-tech simulators, we might be able to encourage them off the streets. At the same, there was a good chance that they would learn the skills would help them secure meaningful employment. It was worth a try; that was for sure.

In the meantime, there was the small task of launching the new South African Motorsport Industry Association (SAMIA). With Petro SA's help, we were able to secure a prestigious conference venue in the Cape Town Waterfront area, guaranteed to attract a high number of media personnel. It took me back 13 years, to the launch of the MIA at the head office of Accenture in London. I don't suppose that there have been many people who have had the pleasure of a launching two motorsport industry associations in their lifetime!

I invited the British Trade Commissioner for South Africa, Brian Gallagher, and his deputy, Debbie Dixon. I had learned the value of working closely with UK Trade and Investment from my MIA days, but I wasn't sure whether it would work quite the same overseas. To my delight, Brian and Debbie, both accepted their invitation to attend the launch, as did their local manager, Sandra Warne. I think the fact that I'd invited Iqbal Sharma from the South African DTI may have helped build credibility for the event. I was really appreciative of all their support for this new initiative.

The launch went off without a hitch, and we got some extensive media coverage, not only in the motorsport and automotive media, which we probably expected, but in the business media as well. Dr Nompumelelo Siswana from Petro SA was superb and just so incredibly enthusiastic about the objectives of our new organisation. Delano de Witt and his daughter Petra De Witt, who both ran the Dell Foundation, made the journey to Cape Town from Pretoria, which was an added bonus.

There was also a very good turn-out at the launch from many influential figures from within the motorsport sector, although I was very disappointed that no one from Motorsport South Africa, the sport's governing body, took the trouble to attend. I think it may possibly have been because I had taken the important decision of establishing the offices of SAMIA in the Western Cape, as opposed to Gauteng Province. Nevertheless, it was another signal to me that I'd made the right decision. If you recall, it was a meeting with Nico Vermeuelen, the CEO of NAAMSA that had prompted me to come back to South Africa. He had told me how concerned the auto-manufacturers were with the way that motorsport was being run in South Africa. I really did believe that if this new organisation was going to succeed, it had to be seen to be making a totally fresh start, away from the same old names and faces who had been involved in some of the less successful projects within the sport.

The launch opened up a new network of worthwhile contacts for me, and I was so grateful for the tremendous support I received from many of the people whom I had known for years, most of whom came down to the Cape for the event.

Now it was time to start the really hard work. Our membership was already looking impressive, but it was important that SAMIA delivered some of its promises fairly quickly. With this in mind, I realised that not only would I have to make a special effort to ensure that the Johannesburg motorsport fraternity felt included and involved, but that our members could quickly see the benefits of their subscriptions. In other words, we needed to introduce a "quick win".

This is where my experience, gained in starting the MIA, came into play. Why not introduce a similar concept to the MIA Business Achievement Awards? This had proved a highly successful initiative when we launched it in our first year and is still as popular as ever, some 24 years later. Of course, it would be difficult to find a venue with the same historic prestige as the House of Lords, but in principle, it seemed a good idea. I spoke to Pumi, which is how Dr Nompumelelo Siswana liked to be called, about the idea, as well as Delano de Witt. They both agreed that it made a lot of sense.

I put some thought into targeting another sponsor, one that wouldn't conflict in any way with Petro SA and Dell, but would help us generate a high-profile for the proposed awards programme. It didn't take me long to arrive at an ideal candidate, and I set about arranging a meeting with Mark Smyth, the motor industry editor for South Africa's primary business newspaper, *Business Day.*

As I thought might well be the case, there was little interest when I first started my explanation about SAMIA. As Mark pointed out, motorsport in South Africa was in decline and of little interest to the black community. However, he perked up considerably when I showed him the letter that Cyril Ramaphosa had sent to me. By the time I had explained about my meeting with Nico Vermeulen of NAAMSA, he was listening intently. He found the fact that I had successfully set up the MIA in Britain as being highly significant. Mark and I had a fairly long and interesting meeting, after which he agreed to present my proposals to the board.

These were centred on the opportunity for *Business Day* to become SAMIA's media partner, presenting it with the exclusive opportunity to be involved from the very start in the formalisation of a new industry sector within South Africa. In addition, *Business Day* would be involved in the launch of the SAMIA Business Achievement Awards.

Mark told me that the one question that would be asked by the Board Members concerned the cost of becoming our media partner. He doubted that there would be a budget available, as sponsorship was not part of the paper's marketing strategy. I had fully expected this, from the research that I had done. I was ready with a response and proposed that in the first year of the agreement, *Business Day* should provide SAMIA with an agreed level of advertising within the paper throughout the year.

This would allow us to promote the new SAMIA Business Achievement Awards in a way that our small budget wouldn't allow. With *Business Day* being the major business publication in South Africa, this represented a high value for us. I knew that we would get a significant level of editorial content, in addition, as the story of SAMIA unfolded. It really was a win-win scenario, and I hoped their board members, who were considering my proposals, thought the same.

Mark called me within the week and told me that we needed to meet, as he had some good news to deliver. It transpired that the board had agreed to everything that we had proposed. I knew at that stage that we were on the right course with SAMIA. To get South Africa's leading business newspaper to become our media partner was a massive step forward.

Since our launch in Cape Town, I'd been aware that we needed to host a major event in Johannesburg to balance our involvement with the motorsport sector in South Africa. I also had to recognise that Gauteng Province was the main business location in the country. To stage the inaugural SAMIA Business Achievement Awards reception, in Johannesburg, seemed to make a lot of sense.

South Africans were used to travelling between the two cities. By air, it took about two hours, whereas by car, it was a journey of about 1350 kilometres. For many years, I used to thoroughly enjoy the drive and on many occasions drove straight through from Jo'burg to Cape Town or vice versa, with just a couple of convenience breaks. However, as I grew older, an overnight stop had to be built in. I think the quickest time in which I completed the journey was around 11.5 hours, sticking to speed limits.

The venue that we selected for the awards reception was the Centurion Hotel, situated very close to the Centurion cricket stadium, almost mid-way between Johannesburg and Pretoria. It would be convenient for people to travel from either city, with a distance of approximately 35 miles between the two. The government personnel, whom we invited, were mainly based in Pretoria; and as we were very keen for them to attend, Centurion was an ideal choice.

There was one more person who I wanted to invite to the awards reception. However, to get them there, I would need to ask Pumi for some financial help.

When I was racing Formula Fords in the UK, back in the 1970s, South African Rory Byrne had just joined Royale, one of the leading Formula Ford constructors. The company had been bought in 1973 by Alan Cornock, who would eventually become a good friend of mine and worked on my steering committee in the formative days of the Motorsport Industry Association. Together with his wife, Sheila, Alan was determined to make a success of his new company, previously owned by Bob King. He was aware that he needed an innovative engineer, as King had been filling that role himself. Rory Byrne was the man in whom Alan put his faith. He was to stay with Royal for four years, but his obvious talent would lead to him heading upwards to a higher category of racing. When the Toleman Group approached Rory, they convinced him of their ambitious plans, and he joined them to work on their F2 programme. It was a good move, and Toleman subsequently finished 1st and 2nd in the 1980 European F2 championship, in the hands of Brian Henton and a young Derek Warwick. Alex Hawkridge, chairman of the Toleman Group, took what was a brave decision to head to F1, with Henton and Warwick staying on as drivers. The Rory Byrne designed TG181 appeared in 1981, but it wasn't until 1983 that the team won its first world championship points, ten in total, in the hands of Derek Warwick. It was enough to attract the services in 1984 of a young driver from Brazil, Ayrton Senna.

In 1985, the Toleman team received a major sponsorship from the Benetton Group. It was to be a significant step forward, because a short time later, the Italian clothing giant decided to enter F1 in its own right. It made an offer for the Toleman F1 team, which was accepted by Alex Hawkridge and the team become Benetton F1. Rory Byrne continued as chief designer. At the Mexican Grand Prix in 1986, Gerhard Berger took his, the Benetton Team's and Rory Byrne's first victory in F1.

The rest, as they say is history. Rory, working with Flavio Briatore at Benetton F1, when the team won the 1995 F1 Constructors World Championship, in the hands of Michael Schumacher, who took the drivers' title.

Rory left Benetton at the end of that incredible season and eventually re-joined Michael Schumacher at Ferrari. In 1999, a Byrne-designed Ferrari won the F1 Constructors' World Championship. It was the famous Italian manufacturer's first such title in 17 years. By the end of 2004, Byrne had achieved an incredible level of success at Ferrari, designing the cars that Michael drove to 71 victories, six consecutive constructors' titles and five consecutive drivers' titles.

I had been lucky enough to know Rory when I was racing Formula Fords in the UK, and he was designing Formula Fords for Royale. At the time, he was also helping a young South African Formula Ford driver, Roy Klomfass, with whom I spent quite a lot of time when I eventually moved back to South Africa.

I explained all of this to Pumi and asked her whether it would be possible for Petro SA to pay for Rory's airfare and hotel accommodation if I could persuade him to be our special guest at the inaugural SAMIA awards reception. She came back to me very quickly and told me to go ahead.

That was probably the easy part of my strategy. Now I had to believe that Ferrari F1's chief designer would firstly even remember me, as it had been a long, long time since we last met. Then I had to persuade him to fly from Maranello in Italy to Johannesburg to attend an event held by a new organisation that he would never have heard of. It shouldn't be too difficult!

If there was one skill that I possessed, it was something I initially learned at school and then honed over the years through necessity; the ability to compose persuasive text, whether an e-mail, a letter or any other type of document. I knew that this one would have to be one of the best that I'd ever written. As I usually do, I decided on a combination of initial phone call followed by an e-mail.

I also knew that I needed a bit of luck!

The combination seemed to work and I eventually had a very positive phone conversation with Ferrari F1's chief designer. He seemed genuinely interested in what we had created with SAMIA, particularly after I told him how I had started the Motorsport Industry Association back in 1994. He knew about the MIA, and this obviously added to the credibility of the South African initiative. Once I mentioned the letter of support from Cyril Ramaphosa, Rory told me he'd be very happy to attend.

It says a lot about the man that he was prepared to find time in what was obviously a hectic F1 schedule to fly to South Africa and support an initiative that was geared to helping young South Africans to build careers in engineering and technical skills training.

I only wish that some of the other influential figures, whom I would come across in my efforts to gain support for the programme, had showed a similar attitude to Rory Byrne's. Sadly, too many people only wanted to know what was in it for them.

Chapter 43
A Lot of Talk, Shenanigans at a University and Still No Action

Rory Byrne arrived at the hotel where the SAMIA Awards Reception was being held, in quite a bad way, following a long flight from Italy, and we could see straightaway that he was suffering from a nasty bout of flu. Had he gone straight to his room and slept for a couple of hours, I would have understood, but he was a real trooper. Not only did he spend time with me discussing how our interview would go and agreeing what he could and what he couldn't talk about, but he also gave two quite long interviews for the TV channels that were covering the event. He then found the energy from somewhere to talk to many of the guests who had arrived early and who were busting a gut to just say hello to such an iconic South African.

With support from Cyril Ramaphosa, now the RSA President, and with sponsorship from Accenture, Brian and Liz returned to South Africa in 2007, to set up the SA Motorsport Industry Association (SAMIA). It primary objective was to encourage young black students into engineering and technical skills training. He invited Ferrari's F1's Chief Designer, South African Rory Byrne, to the inaugural SAMIA Awards Reception in Johannesburg

The inaugural SAMIA Awards Reception was a huge success, of that there was no doubt. The Rory Byrne interview worked really well, and the large audience were enthralled to hear first-hand what it was like to work with Michael Schumacher, as Rory had done so successfully over so many Grand Prix. I remember feeling at one stage that the interview was becoming a little too technical for what was a very diverse audience, and so I asked Rory what he thought defined Michael Schumacher as being better than any other driver with whom he had worked. His answer was very straightforward. He told me that it was Michael's incredible ability to multi-task that set him apart from other drivers. He expanded on this by relating some of the in-car conversations between Michael and Ross Brawn, often to change strategy in the middle of a race. As an example, Ross would tell Michael that they were switching from a two to a three-stop strategy and asked Michael to find a second lap for three laps before pitting to come back out in the right position. Michael would now be on qualifying pace to do this, but he could still make changes on the car as he was driving on the limit, whilst at the same time asking Ross about other driver's strategies, lap times and other relevant information.

Rory then added another comment about Michael; a short, sharp comment that Michael worked at his job harder than any other driver he knew.

Another key area of interest to Rory was our plan to use the proven attraction of motorsport to encourage kids into engineering and technical skills training, as well as giving up the street-racing activities that were claiming so many young lives. His message to young black South African was very clear and echoed the sentiments that I had been continually presenting. He told the audience and media personnel present that he had never seen a job advertisement for racing drivers, but there were hundreds of job opportunities advertised for race engineers, technicians, aerodynamicists, telemetry specialists and a host of other technical positions, for those with the right qualifications. He emphasised that there was absolutely no reason why any young black student at any of the technical colleges couldn't one day work in F1, providing they worked hard and were determined to succeed. He then added that they must also work hard at maths, and not do what so many youngsters were doing by giving maths up at the age of 12. He finished by adding his support for SAMIA, and what it was trying to achieve within South Africa.

Rory then stayed on to present every single SAMIA Business Achievement Award winner with their trophies, posed for photographs, signed autographs until eventually, he just had to turn in. I cannot give him enough credit for what he had done to help us stage our first awards reception. Everyone who had met him felt the same, particularly Dr Nompumelelo Siswana of Petro SA, who had made the trip from Italy possible by authorising the necessary funding.

I mentioned that Rory had presented the award winners with their trophies. There was one young man in the audience who was feeling rather nervous about the fact that Ferrari F1's Chief Designer was taking more than a token glance at the trophies before presenting them. His name was Bryn Saunders; and at the time, he was an intern at Advanced Composites, a company in the Western Cape that specialised in composite materials manufacturing. The company was a SAMIA member, and I asked them if they would like to design and build a highly innovative trophy for us to present to each award winner.

The MD decided it would be a great experience for Bryn to take responsibility for this. The young lad called me a month or so later and asked me to look at what he had come up with. I was really impressed with what he designed and the quality of the prototype that he showed me. It was made totally of black carbon fibre with a dark grey weave running through it. Its design comprised a cube base, about three inches in height and four in width, with a curled flag effect emanating from it, about ten inches in height. The recipient's name was engraved on a matt silver plate on the front of the cube. I could balance it on my little finger; it was so light in weight. It was not only a wonderful representation of our industry but, as far as trophies go, unique.

I invited Bryn Saunders to the awards reception. I watched his face when Rory Byrne asked me where the trophies had been made, as he was handed the first one to present to a winner. It was a picture! I could see that he didn't know whether the Ferrari designer was going to criticise the design or the production, or whether he was actually going to praise it.

Rory was fascinated by the quality of the trophy and asked Bryn and his colleagues from Advanced Composites how the flag furls had been created without any evidence of what he called "bubbling". He then added that Ferrari had been finding problem in doing something similar! To say that Bryn was chuffed would be a huge understatement. Not surprisingly, Bryn has subsequently built a very good career for himself but not in motor racing.

The media coverage that our inaugural awards received was way more than we could have expected. It included two TV interviews on SABC TV News, as well as a host of articles in the motoring and motorsport publication. *Business Day's* coverage was superb, and I knew that it was a newspaper that would have landed on the desk of thousands of influential South African businessmen and women. It was also well-read in government circles.

Brian was successful in acquiring a substantial, long term sponsorship for his Speed International Racing School, with PG Windscreen Group. The Launch was shown on the SABC TV News, and no less than seven TV features about the school were shown during its first twelve months of operation.

Liz and I were feeling pretty exhausted by the end of the event, but that was one of the great things about being able to work together, as we had for many years. Working as a team suited us both. In the same way that we had built the racing school, Speed International, we were now working on a totally different type of project, but one that was giving us a great deal of personal satisfaction that we were heading in the right direction. Of course, there was a long way still to go; and the next step was to meet the Premier of the Western Cape, Alan Winde, as well as Mansoor Mohammed, the Business Development Director for the City of Cape Town. It was now time for all of the early interest in SAMIA to be turned into practical support. There was no way that the annual subscriptions from our members, even with the Petro SA sponsorship, could fund what we wanted to achieve.

The city and the province were both making excited noises about the fact that this new industry sector was being based in the Western Cape and not, as was usually the case, in Gauteng Province. That was all well and good, but I made it very clear that unless they came to the party in some way, I had made the wrong decision. What I was proposing was that, between us, we identified some government-owned land which could be used to build a motorsport industry engineering technical centre, comprising a technical college, a motorsport simulator centre and an environmental motorsport unit. If we could be given the land, I knew that I could find the investment to build the facilities, which would be run by one of the existing technical colleges, ideally the College of Cape Town; but the key factor was giving it a motorsport identity of its own, to make it attractive to youngsters, rather than just being perceived as another education facility.

It also had to be capable of exciting the kids who were out street racing and encouraging them to want to come and learn about motorsport engineering. We had to get the message across that there was a very real chance of eventually working in the South African motorsport industry, as Cyril Ramaphosa had predicted. It was, of course, conditional upon our ability to generate government recognition of this sector in its own right. I was very confident that with the help of NAAMSA, we could achieve this. It was land that we needed, and there seemed plenty of that from our initial research. The big question was whether we could overcome the vast amount of red tape for which government departments are famous. I would have to get on to Iqbal Sharma in Pretoria and solicit the help of his department of trade and industry. After all, he had waxed lyrical about SAMIA as the keynote speaker at its launch, just a few months previously. I was disappointed that there had been no follow up from him or his associates despite promising at the launch that he was very much on our side and would do what he could to help drive things forward.

I spent quite a lot of time talking to people within the academic community as to how we could gain their buy-in to the proposals that we were making to government. Whilst we were getting a lot of support and practical help from the Jannie Isaacs at the College of Cape Town, I also needed to look at the potential for university level involvement. The obvious place to start was the Cape Peninsular University of Technology, based in Bellville, a district of Cape Town. CPUT, as it was called, perhaps rather unfortunately, was a very impressive facility, with over 30,000 students. It had been formed by merging the Cape Technikon and various independent colleges. It boasted five separate campuses.

I met with its head of engineering and asked him whether there was an interest in the possibility of introducing motorsport engineering degrees at CPUT. If so, how could we go about it? I knew that it would invariably be a long process, but I needed to know if it was feasible. It was no good getting the technical colleges excited in motorsport engineering if there was no chance that students could progress to degree level. His response was very positive, and I came away from our first meeting quite enthused.

On the way back in the car, a thought came into my head which I felt could well speed up the process that had been explained to me. I knew that one of the leading universities in Britain that offered motorsport engineering was Oxford Brookes, and, I recall reading that it was embarking on the construction of a new £10 million engineering centre, in which motorsport engineering would play a key role. What if I could persuade Brookes to work with me in some way to help CPUT introduce motorsport engineering? I realised that I was getting into what was virgin territory for me, and I knew very little about the workings of the academic world, but so what? I knew that it was education that could help solve some of the issues I was facing in South Africa. Surely, there were people who would see what I was trying to achieve and be able to point me in the right direction, even if I was treading on a few toes in the process.

The next day I called Oxford Brookes University and to my delight, spoke to someone who sounded quite interested in my story. Mike Meechan. He told me that he would talk to the university's head of mechanical engineering about my South African involvement and get back to me. It transpired that the head he referred to was Geoff Goddard, formerly of Cosworth F1, member of the Motorsport Industry Association.

Following several more phone calls, there was agreement that Oxford Brookes would most definitely be interested in looking at ways in which they could help CPUT if there was a desire on their part to look at the feasibility of introducing motorsport engineering. It was encouraging news. I was due to return to the UK for other reasons and fitted in a meeting at Oxford Brookes with Geoff Goddard, Mike Meechan and a couple of his colleagues. It resulted in further confirmation that Brookes would be very keen to work with a South African University to help them set up a motorsport engineering programme.

When I got back to South Africa, I decided to call Debbie Dixon of UKT&I whom I'd met at the SAMIA Launch in Cape Town, together with her boss, Brian Gallagher, the British Trade Commissioner. I updated Debbie on the various meetings and discussions that had been taking place and asked if there was any way that I could get a grant of some kind to take the CPUT head of mechanical engineering to visit Oxford Brookes and meet Geoff Goddard and his colleagues with a view to developing a potential relationship. She promised to discuss the matter with Brian Gallagher and find out if there was anything they could suggest. I knew that she would do her best; she is such an enthusiastic person.

My confidence in Debbie wasn't misplaced. She came back to me, having spoken to Brian Gallagher, with some good news. UKT&I would cover the travel and accommodation costs of two representatives of the Cape Peninsular University of Technology visiting Oxford Brookes for a meeting with some key individuals, including Geoff Goddard.

When I made contact with CPUT again, I was given some surprising news. The head of engineering, with whom I'd been dealing, had left the university and taken up the role of Director of the Engineering Council of South Africa. It was a blow, because we had got on well together, and he was very supportive of the SAMIA initiative.

He wasn't replaced immediately, but one of the lecturers was appointed to the role on a temporary basis. I quickly made an appointment to see him as I wanted to strike whilst the iron was hot.

I have to say that my first impression of the stand-in wasn't too favourable. It seemed to me that he was more intent on showing me how important he was in the overall scheme of things, than wanting to discuss what I had arranged with UKT&I. I put it down to insecurity. Whereas his predecessor spoke to me enthusiastically about the way forward, the new man simply threw up a list of negatives in respect of the potential relationship with SAMIA. I hadn't yet told him of the offer from the UK about visiting Oxford Brookes. Before I was able to do so, he ended our meeting, but not before taking about five minutes to tell me how busy he was. To me, that is like a red rag to a bull! Far too many people hide behind that comment of being SO busy and then explaining why to the point where you can't help thinking that if they spent less time telling you how busy they were, they'd have the time to talk to you briefly.

A week or so later, I was able to arrange another meeting with him, this time joined by another lecturer from the engineering department. I found him a bit more positive than his colleague had been previously. When I outlined the possibility of arranging a meeting at Brookes, there was little interest, however. They explained that there was a lack of available budget. It seemed an appropriate time to mention the potential offer from UKT&I, in respect of paying travel costs. Suddenly the entire mood of the meeting changed and in a total turnabout, a level of enthusiasm for my proposals could be detected. The meeting ended with agreement that we would meet again, once this had been discussed internally.

I didn't have to wait long. A couple of days after that meeting, I received a call from the temporary head of engineering, inviting Liz and me to attend the university's forthcoming graduation ceremony. How quickly things can change, I thought.

It was an impressive graduation event, the second I'd been invited to during my first year back in South Africa and was followed by a buffet lunch, during which we were introduced to some other key figures at the university. It was obvious from our discussions over lunch that there was a high degree of excitement about the chance for the two lecturers to visit Oxford Brookes.

I didn't hear anything more about the proposed UK trip for a week or so, but when I did, it unexpectedly came from Sandra Warne, the manager of the British Trade Consulate office in Cape Town. It seemed that two people from CPUT, whose names she gave me, had been to her office wanting to contact Brian Gallagher and Debbie Dixon. They explained that they were going to visit Oxford Brookes University in the UK, paid for by UKT&I. They then suggested that instead of this being administered through SAMIA, UKT&I should cut SAMIA and myself completely out of the arrangements for the visit and deal directly with them, in terms of the travel and accommodation expenses.

As you can imagine, I wasn't too impressed. Unfortunately for them, when this information was fed back to Brian Gallagher, he immediately phoned me, told me what was being suggested and confirmed that the two individuals had been sent packing in no uncertain terms.

277

Liz was able to provide a possible explanation. She told me that whilst we had been having our buffet lunch after the graduation ceremony, she had been chatting to the wife of one of the two lecturers in question. During the conversation, it became clear that her husband was very keen to get a job in Britain, and she mentioned that he was excited about the opportunity to visit a British university!

There was another reason. I had explained from the very start of my discussions with the head of engineering that if we were to help CPUT establish a motorsport engineering degree programme, there would need to be a consultancy fee paid to SAMIA. This was made totally clear, and no one could say that they weren't aware of this. By cutting out SAMIA, they obviously thought that they could do a deal direct with Oxford Brookes and UKT&I.

This wasn't how I did business, and when I told Dr Nompumelelo Siswana, and other members of our board, they felt exactly the same. There were other universities in Cape Town, and we took the decision to look elsewhere. Sadly, the damage had been done, and it killed any chance of a relationship, without causing a lot of drama by going over the heads of those involved.

On a positive note, our membership was increasing, and we were busy planning the second SAMIA Business Achievement Awards reception. This one, we decided, would be held in the Western Cape, and we finalised a favourable deal to host it at the business school faculty of Stellenbosch University.

In the meantime, we were still busy with our efforts to find a suitable site for building the proposed motorsport technology centre, as well as securing government recognition of motorsport as an industry sector in its own right. We had some very influential SAMIA members involved in this second quest, but it seemed that Iqbal Sharma at the DTI had lost interest in trying to help us. Pumi, in her role as vice president of the state-owned PetroSA, did her best to pull whatever strings she could. Her feedback was that whilst there was a lot of support for what we were trying to achieve, nobody in government wanted to put their head above the parapet.

We realised that one of our biggest problems was the task of convincing people that we were talking about the business of motorsport, as opposed to the sport itself. As I've previously mentioned, the sport was perceived as being very much for whites, not blacks. The message that we were trying to get across was that SAMIA's primary objectives was to introduce engineering and technical skills training, specifically for black youngsters, which could lead to employment within the motorsport and high-performance engineering. In other words, it was about perception.

In terms of the land search, we were very much in the hands of two people, Mansoor Mohammed, at the City of Cape Town and Alan Winde, at the provincial government of the Western Cape. Both were in very senior roles, and both kept telling me how much they were trying to help find a location that would be practical for what we wanted. One proposed venue was an unused Ministry of Defence area of land in Goodwood, on the outskirts of Cape Town. It would have been ideal location in my opinion, inasmuch that it was right in the heart of the street racing community and would have been an ideal area from which to recruit students. I spoke to Jannie Isaacs at the College of Cape Town about it, and he also felt it would be a good choice. Unfortunately, that's as far as the Goodwood proposal went. I may be wrong, but I was starting to get the feeling that there were a lot of hidden agendas in place with the provincial government, most of them politically motivated.

Whilst SAMIA was getting a lot of good media coverage and great support from most of its members, I was becoming impatient with the lack of progress from the DTI and also in respect of the land issue. I wanted SAMIA to bring about an initiative that really would help black youngsters. I knew from my experience as a director of F1 in Schools, that a fascination with motorsport amongst school kids transcended racial groups. Many of the F1 in Schools teams were from township schools, very often helped by teams from some of the top schools in the country, which in itself was great to see. I was amazed by how many of them knew about F1, even though they had little chance to watch in on TV.

You may be thinking that I was being over optimistic in my belief in the power of motorsport to excite these particular youngsters, who were coming from a previously disadvantaged background. I had no doubts in my mind that I would be proved right. I also knew that it was worth trying, because it was blatantly clear that the existing way of doing things wasn't working.

I soon started thinking that I should look outside the Western Cape, becoming very frustrated at the lack of progress that I was experiencing. In the Free State, the province that had Bloemfontein as its principal city, there had been a race track close to a small town called Welkom. I had raced there on many occasions. It was situated in the heart of the gold mining area in South Africa and had very few, if any, restrictions in terms of noise or usage. Then, in a move that I am sure the Free State government regretted for a long time, they were persuaded to invest a huge sum of money in building a new motor racing circuit at the venue, both a huge Indy car style oval track which replicated the track at Las Vegas in the USA, as well as a new road circuit. A lot of money was spent in building this to internationally acceptable standards, including superb TV control facilities and a massive pit complex, which many Grand Prix circuits would have been proud of.

The person who had persuaded the provincial government to build this excellent motorsport venue was none other than Bobby Hartslief, the South African who had headed up the consortium that bought the Kyalami Grand Prix Circuit at Kyalami back in 1980, employing me as its manager. Once the new circuit at Welkom was ready, in 1999, and changed its name to Phakisa Raceway, Bobby, who had returned to South Africa after a spell overseas, convinced the owners (the Free State government) to host a South African Round of the World MotoGP Championship for motorcycles. Once the contract with Dorna, the Right Holders to MotoGP, had supposedly expired in 2004, the government found that it wasn't as easy to extract itself from the contract, as they had expected.

In 2009, I made contact with the Free State government and arranged two meetings; one was with the manager of the track, who had been appointed by the Free State government; the other was with one of the government ministers, who will have to remain nameless.

My proposal, which had secured the meetings, was that with the venue losing money, as I had been assured it was, it might make sense to look at locating the SAMIA Technology Centre at Phakisa and working together to generate motorsport industry-related usage.

I was taken on a tour of the Phakisa facility and was both impressed at the layout and buildings despite the fact that it had an overall appearance of neglect. The track worried me a lot more, with evidence of major problems in the near future. However,

I wasn't looking at running a commercial motor racing track, so that wasn't in itself a serious concern.

I had seen enough to recognise that if we could find a way of developing a joint project between SAMIA and the Free State government, it could prove to be the break-through that I had been pursuing. The Western Cape government and the City of Cape Town would only have themselves to blame if we were able to find what we wanted elsewhere. OK, a venue in the middle of the Free State would not have been my first choice, but if it meant getting the programme up and running, then so be it.

Chapter 44
Meeting a Minister, Tacking Potholes and Getting Nowhere Fast

Liz accompanied me on the nine hour drive to Phakisa, and after touring the race track, we stayed overnight in a Bloemfontein hotel, to be ready for my 7:45 meeting the next morning, with the minister, at his office in the city.

I arrived at his office five minutes early and was shown into the reception area. An hour later, I was still there; and when I asked his PA what time he was likely to arrive, I simply got a shrug of her shoulders. Another hour went by, and eventually he arrived. There was no apology of any sort, just an indication that I should go into his office.

The first 30 minutes or so were taken up by him, showing me his new mobile phone, laptop and, from the window, his new car. The opportunity to get down to a serious discussion eventually arrived, and I was able to outline my thoughts about establishing the SAMIA Technology Centre at Phakisa. He listened patiently and then asked me a question.

'Why are you doing this SAMIA thing?'

I explained my reasons and added that my experience in establishing the MIA in Britain had led me to believe that my experience in developing engineering and technical skills training for young people, through the use of motorsport, would work well in South Africa.

'What's in it for you?' was his next question.

I showed him the paperwork that confirmed SAMIA as a Section 21 company, together with its Board members, including Dr Siswana of PetroSA and Delano de Witt from the Dell Foundation and, finally, my salary as CEO. He looked at it carefully and commented that he didn't think it was much of a salary. Then he fired his next question at me, asking me to tell him what was in it for him if he agreed to my proposals.

I obviously misunderstood what he was asking me. I replied that hopefully it would be the same level of satisfaction that I would also get from helping young blacks into technical skills training and, eventually, jobs through the attraction of motorsport. In addition, I added, it could help get them off the streets at night.

He looked at me and told me that is not what he meant and repeated his question. 'What's in it for me?'

I repeated my answer, adding that it would also help offset the costs of running the circuit, which was apparently losing money, hand over fist. What else could I say? At that point, he stood up and made it clear that the meeting was over and left the room. I never heard from him again, and he never returned my calls. It would seem that I hadn't come up with the answer that he was looking for.

The journey home was a long one; not just because the meeting hadn't ended in the way that I had hoped, but because the much of the road between Kroonstad and Kimberley was in such a bad state that we could only average about 25 mph. We had to traverse potholes the size of which I have never seen before. The sun went down in the Free State much earlier than further south in the Western Cape. I dreaded getting a puncture and having to fix it in the dark, but eventually, we arrived at our hotel nearly an hour and a half later than scheduled, but relieved to have made it safely.

As Liz and I sat down to enjoy a glass of excellent South African Merlot, we both knew that we had a lot of thinking to do about where we went from here, in terms of SAMIA. When we made the decision in 2006 to return to South Africa to set up SAMIA, we asked my father, Ken, if he would like to come with us. He was by then 83. My mother, Eileen, had died earlier that year, so Ken was staying with us in Hampshire. It took him at least three seconds to accept our invitation. We had arrived in South Africa on 8 January 2007.

Now, nearly four years after I had agreed the feasibility study with Accenture, we sat in the hotel after our disappointing meeting in Bloemfontein and looked back at what we had achieved, and what still needed to be done.

We had launched SAMIA and secured three major partners in PetroSA, the Dell Foundation and *Business Day*. We had created the SAMIA Business Achievement Awards and held our first event. We had been successful in bringing Rory Byrne from Ferrari F1 into South Africa as our special guest. We had ensured that the South African motorsport industry now had a voice and a doorway into the government in Pretoria as well as the Provincial Government of the Western Cape and the City of Cape Town. We had a good number of SAMIA members, representing a reasonable percentage of the industry. We had a strong board made up of influential industry personnel. We had created a high level of media coverage, especially through our partnership with *Business Day.*

All of this had been achieved with only one full-time person on board. I'd had a great deal of help from many other people, including Liz, who was as enthusiastic about achieving our original aims and objectives as I was. Owen Ashley, Bruce Coquelle, Brian Smith, Bez Sangari, Delano de Wit, Rob Nunn and, of course, Dr Siswana , all played a vital role in getting us to where we were.

I was very frustrated that although I was constantly being told that we had achieved a great deal in the time we had been there, I felt that we should be further along the route to our key objective of gaining formal government recognition for our industry.

Bez Sangari, one of our directors, had lived in South Africa for many years and built a substantial business in the education sector. He had been very supportive throughout the four feasibility study visits that I'd made in 2006 and continued to do so once SAMIA had been launched, in his capacity as a director. We talked a great deal about the ways in which we could speed up our progress. I also talked at length to Pumi. They were both of the opinion that it was quite normal in South Africa for any dealings with the government to take a long time. They added that it was even more difficult for me, as I was only had Permanent Resident status as opposed to South African citizenship. I also didn't really understand the internal politics that played such a major part of getting any support from government. I was very helpful to have such stalwarts to rely on, and I accepted that I just had to continue to knock down some of the doors that I was finding so difficult to open.

I kept on with that task and, as I had been doing for some time, attended many meetings with people, such as Felicity Purchase and Mansoor Mohammed , at the City of Cape Town, and Alan Winde at the provincial government. I think that they were all sincere in supporting my SAMIA initiative, but were either unwilling to take on the mantle of securing meaningful, practical help, or else had no real idea of which box this fitted into.

Then, before I knew it, it was time for our second SAMIA Business Achievement Awards reception, at the Stellenbosch Business School. Having managed to tempt Rory Byrne, Ferrari F1's Chief Designer to be our special guest at the inaugural reception in 2009, I had set the bar very high in terms of matching that for 2010.

Bearing in mind that SAMIA was all about the business side of motorsport, it was important that our guest should clearly reflect that. There was one name that kept going through my head as being an ideal candidate; Brian Gallagher, the British trade commissioner. He was a very warm and outward going person who was fully aware of how I had set up the Motorsport Industry Association (MIA) in the UK, some 16 years previously. He understood what had been achieved in that time, in respect of developing the industry sector into world-leading status, worth over £9 billion.

My committee liked the idea, and when I subsequently invited him as our guest speaker, Brian was delighted to accept. We agreed that the format I'd used with Rory Byrne, an on-stage interview as opposed to a conventional talk, would be more interesting and would mean that he had less preparation to do. As he was shortly due to end his four-year stint in South Africa, prior to moving to a similar role in Beijing, it was an important consideration for him, adding that that he and his wife were spending a lot of time trying to learn Mandarin.

We were looking forward to the event, and, despite it being in the middle of the South African winter, we were blessed with good weather. We had a very high level of acceptance to our invitations, and it was great to see so many people arriving. In particular, it was encouraging to see that the Minister of Education in the Western Cape government, Donald Grant, was in attendance, as was the CEO of Petro SA, Mr Sipho Mkhize. Sadly, Iqbal Sharma, DTI director, didn't make the trip from Pretoria. Another very special guest was my father, who amazingly had recovered from a very serious illness and was determined, at the age of 87, to be there to support Liz and me.

The interview with Brian Gallagher proved to be a winner. Some high-profile people might have had a fascinating career, but are unable to simply stand and talk about their achievements, their life and their views and opinions. Brian was a very good speaker, but, as often happens with an on-stage interview format, the audience gets to know so much more about the person. This was very much the case with Brian Gallagher, as we talked about his former career as a professional football referee, and his various travels around the world. It transpired that Brian once showed Alex Ferguson a red card in a match that he was refereeing! He was tremendously supportive of what we were trying to achieve with SAMIA and kept referring to what I had done in the UK, in founding the MIA.

Once again, Dr Nompumelelo Siswana was a real star and did a lot of lobbying on our behalf throughout the evening. All in all, it was a great evening, turned into a very special one when Petro SA CEO, Sipho Mkhize, stood up to address the audience. He referred specifically to the government and City of Cape Town attendees, telling them that Petro SA had supported SAMIA, a dynamic organisation as he referred to it, two years, but that it now needed other people to step up to the challenge and provide the financial and political support that was needed to take us to the next level.

Just a few weeks after the SAMIA Awards reception, I was shocked to learn that Sipho Mkhize's employment as CEO of PetroSA had been terminated with immediate effect. I immediately rang Pumi, but she knew no more about it than anyone else, other than the fact that Mikhize had apparently notified Petro SA of his intention to challenge his dismissal.

I have to admit that this news, coming as it did on top of the experience that I had in Bloemfontein and some of the shenanigans I had witnessed in my dealings with CPUT, was beginning to wear me down. What really made me angry was that whilst all of the talk, more talk and even yet more talk was going on, kids were still being killed through street racing in the Western Cape, and youngsters were missing out on the chance to set themselves higher levels of inspiration than simply being a basic car mechanic.

Then some more shocking news arrived. Owen Ashley, one of the most supportive of my board members was diagnosed with terminal cancer. Owen was not only a very talented race car designer, but also a great supporter of young drivers. He had gone to school in Cape Town with one of Liz's three brothers and had lived just across the road in Rondebosch. Owen attended our next board meeting, but he sadly passed away a few weeks later at the young age of 63. I will never forget the tremendous level of support that he gave to me, personally, when I sometimes felt that I was getting nowhere with my efforts to bring about change within the motorsport industry in South Africa. Most importantly, he was brutally honest and didn't always tell me what I wanted to hear. He would often sit and have a quick chat with me over a coffee, in his Killarney workshop, telling me that there were too many people in the motorsport industry in South Africa who didn't want to see change.

In another conversation, he also told me that one of the problems I was facing was that I was English and had been very successful in building a racing career in South Africa, country based on my ability to secure serious levels of sponsorship, rather than on my driving talent or technical abilities. He added that there were a lot of people in motorsport in South Africa who resented the fact that I had started South Africa's first ever professional racing school (at Kyalami) and made it such a success. They seriously believed that there were better race drivers than me out there, and it should have been one of them that started such a school, not me.

I can't say that I was surprised at what Owen told me, I knew that a lot of people didn't like the level of publicity I was able to secure for my sponsorship deals. Neither did they like it when I was able to win races, as I did in my years with Honda. There was a sense of resentment.

Owen had been a good friend to me and to Liz. He was as straight as they come and wouldn't pussy foot around. He had his opinions and wasn't afraid to voice them.

I feel privileged to have had him on the board of SAMIA and as a friend. South African motorsport lost a very special man when he died.

In the weeks that followed the SAMIA Awards event, Liz and I spent a lot of time discussing the way forward. In particular, I talked to Bez Sangari a great deal about the situation, asking him to give me his honest opinion as to how we could get more practical support from government. Eventually, I put a question to him that had been brewing in my mind for a while. I asked him if he thought that SAMIA could move on quicker and get more support if a black person was at the helm.

He thought about it carefully before giving me his answer. 'Yes,' he told me, 'I think you may be right.' He told me that he knew of a young black businessman whom he thought might possibly fit the bill, asking me if I would like him to approach him.

I suggested that we should think carefully about it for a couple more weeks, whilst I sounded out some other opinions.

The first person I spoke to after Bez was Dr Siswana. She told me that in her opinion, it might possibly make a difference if we could find a black person to run SAMIA, but added that no one would have the level of experience that I had. On the other hand, she agreed that she was very frustrated with the attitude of government, especially at the provincial level. Sadly, now that Sipho Mkhize had been sacked, one of our biggest supporters had gone, and she didn't know what was going to happen within Petro SA.

Then we had a break-in at our house one night. It was quite an unpleasant experience, as were sleeping, until Liz woke, having heard a noise. She got up and saw the guy hiding in the garden, our window having been forced open. He was within a couple of metres of where she was standing. She immediately rang the alarm bell on our security system, and within a few seconds, an armed response guard arrived and gave chase, but the guy had climbed the fence and gone. It shook Lizzie up very badly, as so many house break-ins in South Africa tend to end in violence, assault or rape.

The next day we set about arranging something that we had both agreed we would never do. We had electrified wire security fitted around the entire property. Before leaving the UK, we had both said that we didn't want to live in a place more akin to Fort Knox than a private residence. We'd been told we were being over sensitive, but that had been our choice. Now we knew that it had to be done.

A couple of weeks later, we were due to spend a week in England. One of the places that we were going to was Oxford Brookes, to try and look at other ways of working with a South African partner university after our issues with CPUT. We stayed in a small hotel about a mile from the city centre. It was a very mild evening in July, and we walked into Oxford, had a wonderful meal before walking around the city, and later, catching a bus back to our hotel. We sat in our room and relaxed with a glass of wine, commenting on how nice it had been to be able to walk out at night, as we had done without worrying all the time that you might be mugged.

Liz summed it up very concisely. 'It might be my country,' she said, 'but I seriously don't want to go back to living behind burglar bars and electric fencing, with armed patrols driving back and forth outside our house. It scares me! Yes, I know that England has its crime problems, but we're not living in constant fear, only going out if you can take the car and even then, worrying about car hi-jacking.'

It didn't help that Nick and Verne, Liz's son and daughter in-law, suffered a worrying break-in, not long after ours. This time, four intruders actually got into the house in Pinelands, a suburb of Cape Town, whilst Nick and Verne and their two youngsters, aged three and seven, were sleeping. Fortunately, the intruders were disturbed and got out without being able to resort to violence.

I had to agree with Liz; being back in England put the high level of security that everyone has to endure in South Africa into perspective. You live with it on a daily basis and get used to it. It's only when you experience a different way of living, that you realise how much it actually affects you.

We also had the responsibility of looking after my dad. After his illness, despite being amazingly self-reliant, we knew that we couldn't be there 24 hours a day for him. We did quite a lot of travelling within the country, and I wasn't keen about him being in the house on his own. Fortunately, we'd managed to find a really special retirement village, very close to us. He had his own small one-storey house, access to the swimming pool and gardens. Most importantly, there was a medical centre, which meant immediate attention if Ken used his panic button.

Another major factor was very high security, as it was a walled and gated village, but with spectacular views across the valley to the mountains of Franschoek and Stellenbosch. He was very happy there, making some good friends with whom he enjoyed regular evenings at the bar. We often joined him there, and it was good to see that his illness hadn't affected his love of South African wine.

Liz loves England and gets very annoyed when people here continually whinge and moan about so many aspects of British life. Her view is that people don't realise how lucky they are to live in a country which has the National Health Service, and effectively a safety net if things go drastically wrong. In South Africa, that most definitely isn't the case. There is no safety net. As she also says, you can walk the streets here in the UK with the knowledge that you will be safe, unless you are very unlucky. Until such basic rights are no longer there, you don't really appreciate them.

We talked that evening for a long time and agreed that despite our personal feelings about heading back to, we couldn't just walk away from South Africa whilst we had a job to do. A week later, we flew back in Cape Town, where I spent the first week calling all of the contacts that I had made in the provincial government, the DTI and the City of Cape Town. I wanted to know if there had been any further progress in their attempts to move closer to the objectives that we had agreed upon as being important. I was disappointed to learn that nothing had moved forward at all.

I then called Bez Sangari, in Johannesburg, and we had a further discussion about his search for a potential black CEO to take over my role. Although very busy with his own business, he had put out some feelers and told me that he still had someone in mind. His views on this being the best way forward hadn't changed.

We had another issue to deal with in respect of PetroSA. Dr Siswana rang me to talk about the renewal of our initial two year agreement, in the light of the CEO's recent dismissal. She said that it was unlikely it would now be dealt with as a matter of urgency, which in South Africa meant that we could be waiting another year before a decision was made.

I talked to my committee and told them of Bez's views about securing a new CEO. I added that I had come to the opinion that I was banging my head against the proverbial brick wall in trying to progress SAMIA's objectives at the levels I had reached. I had tried to get Cyril Ramaphosa to follow up our very positive meeting and subsequent letter, by putting me in front of some government officials who had the power to make things happen, but it seemed that whilst he was still in agreement with what I was trying to do, his business activities had to take priority.

I made my recommendation to the Board of SAMIA that I should announce my resignation to the membership and hand over the reins to Dr Siswana and Bez Sangari until a suitable replacement was found. I also explained that the goings on at Petro SA meant that we would have to cut our costs, as their sponsorship was unlikely to be renewed. This was another reason why I couldn't continue, as SAMIA wouldn't be able to meet my salary, as modest as it was.

It was a tough decision to make, but it had always been our understanding that I would stand down eventually to allow a South African to run the association. It just meant that we were a year short of our original timeline in that respect. The accounts of the Section 21 Company were brought right up to date, and I took all of the relevant files and paperwork to Bez in Johannesburg.

I had a lot of confidence in my board members, particularly Bruce Coquelle and Brian Smith, to act in the interests of SAMIA and its members, as well as Dr Siswana and Bez on a practical basis. They were all successful and experienced business people, who shared my vision for the growth and development of a South African motorsport industry. They had told me, in no uncertain terms, that Liz and I should be proud of what we had achieved in both identifying the need for such an initiative and then bringing it to fruition in such a high profile way. They thought it disappointing that there was such a lack of vision amongst so many of the people who could have ensured that we achieved our objectives in respect of our much needed educational and social objectives, as well as economic.

Now that I knew that SAMIA was in good hands, it was time for Liz and me to plan our future. Liz was torn between two options. Most of her family, including her brothers Graham and John were in South Africa, as was her twin, Peter; whereas her daughter, Alexandra, and her British husband Paul, were now living in Auckland. From a personal point of view, Liz was happiest in the UK.

As for my views, I had always loved living in South Africa. However, I realised that unless I made a lot of money very quickly, the thought of retiring out there really wasn't attractive. As I explained, there is no safety net and older people are very numerable, in more ways than one. Very good friends of ours, Jon and Sally Panos, who owned the game camps that we had visited on a regular basis in the north of South Africa, were driven out of the country by three vicious attacks on Jon in their house in a Johannesburg suburb. They moved to Galway Bay in Ireland, where they now live in total safety.

We spoke to my dad, but although he was very happy in his retirement village, he made it clear that he didn't want to stay in South Africa if we left. We eventually reached the decision that we would sell the house we had bought in Cape Town and return to the UK. It wasn't an easy decision, and I think we both felt that had we been ten years younger, we would probably have stayed. I was by then 64 years of age, which in South Africa creates yet another barrier to the likes of private medical insurance and health care. I also recognised that although my UK pension could be paid into South Africa, it would never increase.

Do we regret going back there in 2006? The answer is no. We were able to spend nearly four years with Liz's family, which wouldn't have happened had we not moved back. Ken received some excellent medical care that undoubtedly saved his life, but it was at a very high cost, financially. Liz and I were able to share some quality time with him in wonderful weather, enjoying some stunning scenery; and he got to meet the two grandchildren, which really delighted him.

OK, so you could argue that we had failed to achieve what we had hoped for, but we laid the foundations for someone with better qualifications to build SAMIA onwards and upwards. In many ways, it was very similar to what had happened with the MIA in Britain. I had the vision and determination to create the Motorsport Industry Association; and in three years, built a solid platform on which to grow it before recognising that it needed a different set of skills to build it further from there. It's frustrating in some ways, but that's me. I suppose I like being a pioneer. That reminds me of a comment I once heard. You can tell a pioneer by the arrows in his back!

Chapter 45
Sad News from South Africa, Facing Reality and Handing Over the Reins

We had only been back in England for about three months when the shocking news came through from South Africa that Bruce Coquelle, a close friend, SAMIA board member and Chairman of the Autoquip Group had died. I knew that he had been ill, but had no idea that his illness was terminal. It hit me very hard when I heard, particularly coming so close to the passing of Owen Ashley.

The bad news didn't end there. I needed to speak to Brian Smith about a couple of SAMIA matters. As I've mentioned, he was the CEO of the Western Province Motor Club, the organisation that ran motorsport at the Killarney Circuit in Cape Town. The receptionist answered my call, and I asked or Brian. 'He's not here' was her blunt reply, to which I responded by asking if he would be in later in the day. 'No' came the answer, 'He's dead!' Those were the exact words!

I'm rarely at a loss for words, but on that occasion, I was totally unsure what to say. I got very little information from the person who had answered my call, so I rang another friend, who worked closely with Brian, and he confirmed that Brian had indeed passed away. He had also been in his early 60s.

In the space of a few months, three board members of SAMIA had died, all of a similar age. It wouldn't only be SAMIA, however, that would feel their loss greatly, but South African motorsport in general; such was their level of involvement. To say that it completely knocked the wind out my sails would be an understatement.

I called Pumi Siswana, and she was as upset about the news as I was. She had met all three men through her work with SAMIA and had found them to be both charming and knowledgeable. I wondered what would now happen with SAMIA, as did Pumi. Neither of us felt like pursuing matters right then, we needed a to a take stock for a short while.

The more I thought about the consequences of losing three stalwarts of the board, the more concerned I became. I was no longer involved in a director capacity, but I feared that without the driving force that Brian, Owen and Bruce brought to the SAMIA board, it was probably asking too much of Bez Sangari to pull it back together.

On the other hand, I realised that no one is indispensable. If Bez could recruit the new CEO, there were plenty of talented, senior and influential figures within the South African motorsport sector who could take over on the board and continue the work that we had started. I had made my choice, and it wasn't fair to now go back and interfere with the future of the association.

I'd like to say that as the months went by, I received news that the new SAMIA CEO had been appointed; and that after the shock of losing three Board members, suitable replacements had been appointed. I would like to say that, but I can't. It just didn't happen. It would appear that the enthusiasm for pursuing the aims and objectives of this unique, ground-breaking organisation wasn't sustainable without its key personnel. Sadly, eight years on from my departure, SAMIA is just a memory.

I still feel guilty in some ways. Maybe I shouldn't have stood down when I did, but when I made my decision, I did so because I genuinely believed that with a black South African at the helm, SAMIA would become more acceptable to many of the people who stood in the way of our progress.

Those people to whom I am referring know who they are; I hope that they feel proud of their lack of decisive action. By now, if they had pulled their finger out, we could be seeing a meaningful number of black youngsters building careers in an exciting new industry sector. They should also reflect on the number of lives that might have been saved in illegal street racing accidents, had we been able to develop the race car simulation centre that was a part of the overall strategy.

Both Liz and I feel sad that South Africa is obviously in a bad way, with increasing violence, failing utilities and an increase in the numbers of people leaving. It makes me very sad, but also extremely angry. Apartheid might have been removed from the statute books, but it has been replaced by another major issue; the huge gap between the rich and the poor. This time it's nothing to do with black and white. It's about those who are making fortunes, and those who have been left way behind.

Having witnessed the self-serving attitudes of many of the people who could have helped us make a significant difference to the lives of many black youngsters, I fear for the future of a country that has so much to offer. When I compare the optimism that was shared by millions of people when Nelson Mandella set out his vision for a fair society, back in those early days of his presidency, to the anger, frustration and bitterness now being experienced, it is not a good feeling.

Chapter 46

Another Sponsorship, the AMR-One failure and Lunch with a Dame

I spent the first year back from South Africa working with a motor racing team, based near Royal Tunbridge Wells. Jota Motorsport was run by a very talented young guy, Sam Hignett, who had spent time as a race driver in sports car events before realising that his real skill was in running a motor-racing team and building a successful business in the process.

Jota, at that time was an official Aston Partner Team, running, and winning, with an Aston Martin GT4 in races, such as the Spa 24-Hours and the Britcar Silverstone 24-Hours. In addition, it was developing a great relationship with Mazda, creating a GT4 racing version of the highly successful road sport car, the MX-5.

Within a few months, I had put together a significant sponsorship deal for the Aston Martin programme, with Hiscox, the international insurance group. However, my major target was to help Jota secure the high level of sponsorship required to compete in the Le Mans 24-Hours, with the AMR-One, an Aston Martin race car, of which only six would be built. The car would compete in the highly competitive LMP1 category of the race. Built totally by David Richard's Prodrive, the AMR-One would be using a bespoke 2.0 litre turbocharged engine.

At a cost of several million pounds, the car wasn't cheap, that was for sure, which is why major sponsorship was needed.

I saw this as a very attainable challenge, but as I had done successfully on many previous occasions, I came to the conclusion that it would require an innovative sales strategy. We would need a large budget, and a conventional sponsorship deal would be difficult.

The strategy that I eventually came up with was based on a concept I had used in South Africa to acquire a sizeable sponsorship for the new racing school that I was opening at Kyalami. You could call it a "loss-leader" concept, meaning that to secure two other major sponsors, you sometimes have to bring in a key company or organisation which provides a very attractive catalyst to the other two, albeit that you may have sacrifice a normal fee in the process. This was the case with Camel, when I opened my racing school in South Africa. The relatively small deal that I secured with RJ Reynolds Tobacco was pivotal in securing a very large deal with PG Windscreen Group.

I got in touch with one of my extensive network of contacts, Lord Digby Jones of Birmingham, whom I'd met at the World Cup breakfast in Cape Town in 2010. He, in turn, invited me to a function at the O2 in London, together with another guest, Christopher Rodrigues CBE, Chairman of the British Tourist Board, whom I had told Lord Digby that I wanted to meet.

I was able to set up a subsequent meeting with Christopher and outlined my strategy to him. He liked my ideas and agreed in principal, subject to the other partners coming on board. My next port of call was a meeting with the CEO of Harrods, Michael Ward. My contact within Harrods secured this for me, and I knew that Michael was a car enthusiast and, at that time, a Porsche driver.

I just needed one more "partner". I arranged a meeting with a person with UKT&I whom I'd met when he was working for them in South Africa. He was now based in their Victoria Street offices and liked the ideas that I outlined, as had the others. Now I was ready to develop a full-blown proposal on how I saw a joint involvement with the Aston Martin AMR-One debut at Le Mans in 2012, being mutually beneficial to all four prospective partners. It was geared to bringing in the full amount of budget required. I'm not going to explain how the deal works, that information stays in my head and has to be paid for but suffice to say it had worked for me in a similar way before, on several occasions.

In the same way that engine builders don't give away all the details of how they build a very quick unit for a team, I like to keep some of my more innovative sponsorship strategies in my head.

It was still a year away, but in 2011, the AMR-One would make its first Le Mans appearance in 2011 during the Le Mans Test Day. It proved much slower than the other LMP1 category cars. Both cars, however, were sent to Spa to continue testing for Le Mans. Then came the big test; the 2011 Le Mans 24-Hours. What took place in the French classic was most definitely not what we needed in terms of impressing our potential 2012 partners. One AMR-One car retired after just two laps, the other after four.

Not surprisingly, amongst the partners that I had brought together, there was a reluctance to continue the programme that I had so successfully pitched to everyone. One of the keys to the entire strategy was that the AMR-One was the first ever LMP1 car totally built by Aston Martin. Only six units would be built, and two of those would appear in Harrods before and after the world-famous Le Mans 24-Hours in 2012.

It was now obvious that the AMR-one programme would not continue, certainly not until a lot of work had been done. It would be almost impossible to simply transfer my sponsorship strategy to another motor racing programme. What I had devised fitted the AMR-One project perfectly and was tailor made for it. Reluctantly, I had to accept that through no fault of mine, I had lost the opportunity to earn a lot of commission. There was no reason for me to stay on at Jota Sport.

Before I finally took the decision to leave, however, I was contacted by Lorraine Ellison MBE, who worked closely with Lord Digby Jones of Birmingham. I have worked with Lorraine on several occasions, one of which was in Sao Paolo. In the early days of the MIA, I was invited to be a guest speaker at a British Ambassadorial conference in Brazil. I was going to be in that country with the Benetton F1 Team, and so I was able to accept. The theme of the conference was British engineering excellence, and it had a strong motorsport industry influence, coinciding with the Brazilian Grand Prix.

After the conference, which had been attended by Lorraine, in her role as a consultant to UKT&I, she explained to me that she would be bringing a reciprocal Brazilian trade mission to the UK, later in the year, and wondered if they could visit the Benetton F1 team. I had agreed to this, and it turned out to be a very successful and worthwhile visit.

As I've mentioned, I had met Lord Digby on several occasions, one of which was at a UKT&I Breakfast, in Cape Town, on the morning of England's 2010 World Cup game in the City. He was joined by Boris Johnson, which made for an interesting pairing. Lord Digby is an avid Aston Villa fan and also on the board of Leicester Tigers Rugby Club, where my great friend, David Clayton, was the CEO for 12 years, until recently retiring.

The reason for Lorraine contacting me in 2011 was quite surprising. Apparently, Lord Digby and Lorraine were acting as business advisers to Dame Kelly Holmes. She had expressed an ambition to take up motor racing, as from 2012, having been successful in a Channel 4 reality style TV programme, called *Famous and Fearless*, in which she did extremely well. This had involved an element of stunt driving, including a car flip. Lorraine asked me if I could help put something together for Kelly, as both she and Lord Digby trusted my experience and understanding of the motorsport world. They didn't want her exploited or put at risk in any way.

I met Dame Kelly on several occasions and found her a friendly and likeable person, but without doubt, she also had a tough streak, as one would expect of a double-gold Olympic champion. With the help of Mazda, we were able to offer her a season's racing in the Mazda 5 Series, which would have been a great way to learn the ropes of motorsport. However, when she realised the amount of time that she would have to commit if she wanted to be successful, and of course she did, it was obvious to her that there would be a major clash with her intensive and various commitments linked to the London 2012 Olympics. She had little choice but to decline Mazda's generous offer.

It was shame, as I think she would have done very well, but in the circumstances, she was right to focus on other things.

Chapter 47
An Academic Invitation, Porsche, Dallara and Cruise Ships

Another opportunity quickly presented itself to me, once I had decided to leave Jota, one that was to take me into a totally new and untried area of activity. A phone call from a Professor Alan Hutchinson at Oxford Brookes University offered me an unusual opportunity. He invited me to become a member of the Industrial Advisory Board that had been set up by the School of Mechanical Engineering. My reaction when he called me, was to immediately suggest that he had got hold of the wrong person, as I had very little technical understanding of motorsport. He assured me that he hadn't and went on to say that the advisory board comprised a high number of very bright, technical people, but lacked the commercial nous that was needed to present balanced judgements on issues.

I was flattered and soon attended my first board meeting. To my great surprise, I was able to contribute far more than I had expected and found it a fascinating experience to meet a range of such highly intelligent individuals from a range of business backgrounds. Within a couple of months, I was asked by one of the university personnel on the board, David Hartley, if I would be interested in acting as a consultant to the mechanical engineering department, in respect of its motorsport industry activities.

He arranged for me to meet Dr Gareth Neighbour, the head of department, who told me about the increasing reputation that the department was gaining for producing excellent motorsport engineering graduates, including those at MSc level. He went on to tell me that Oxford Brookes now had graduates in the majority of the F1 teams.

The building in which the department was housed had been designed and built specifically for it, some five years earlier, and boasted four-engine dyno rooms, as well as its own four-post rig, for advanced chassis and suspension development work. I had visited Brookes just after it was opened, during one of my trips from South Africa, and it was good to hear how successful it was becoming on an international scale. I heard from Gareth that its real strength was the hands-on style tuition, working on many of the race cars that adorned the workshops. These included F1, CART and F3 cars.

The objective was to ensure that when students left to head into the motorsport industry, in whatever capacity that might be, not only were they technically adept but also had an in-depth understanding and acceptance of the motorsport industry ethos. As Bernie Ecclestone has always said, it's no good delivering a vital component of the race car thirty seconds after the race has started. Delivery on time is a key factor in the success of the UK motorsport industry.

I asked Gareth why he had suggested that I should come on board as a consultant. It seemed that the primary reason was to benefit from my wide ranging understanding of the motorsport industry and my extensive contact network. He was hoping that I would be able to develop strong relationships with leading companies within the motorsport industry and F1, to help increase the credibility of Oxford Brookes globally. In the process, he believed, it would make it easier to attract new students each year, as well as increasing their subsequent recruitment into the motorsport industry. It sounded an exciting challenge, and it wasn't long before I had my first success.

I've mentioned Nick Langley before. You may recall that he and I worked together at Lola Cars in Huntingdon. Nick eventually left Lola and spent 12 years working for a company that took over Lola's mantle as the world's largest race car manufacturer (revenue-wise). Dallara is an Italian company, based in Parma, but now with a recently opened USA operation in Indiana, which is involved in building race cars for a range of international series. Many of these are one-make series. I've listed a few of the categories, to give you an idea of how successful Dallara has become.

- Indycar
- Indy Lights
- World Series 3.5
- Formula 2
- Formula 3
- Sports Cars

Dallara not only operates within the confines of motor racing but also does a lot of consultancy work within the automotive sector, having its own wind tunnel with clients that include Ferrari, Maserati and Fiat.

Nick kindly introduced me to Andrea Toso, the head of R&D and also Country Manager for the USA. I was subsequently invited to their factory, in Parma, to meet him. It was fascinating to go on a tour of the facility with Andrea, who has been in motorsport most of his career. I was able to see the new race car simulator that had been designed with the help of Ferrari F1, which is designed to provide engineering solutions, just as much as for the more conventional race-driver training. I understand that Pirelli use it for a lot of tyre simulation work in F1.

Andrea and I had a very worthwhile meeting, and he expressed serious interest in my proposal that we should look at developing a working relationship between his company and Oxford Brookes. We agreed that he would visit our facility at Wheatley Campus just outside Oxford, as soon as possible.

A month later, on a beautiful summer's evening, Andrea was sitting with Gareth and me, enjoying a long conversation over a beer or two at a country pub, just down the road from the university. It was the start of a long relationship between Dallara and Oxford Brookes that would be based on an innovative electric race car project for our graduates and also resulted in Andrea Toso becoming a member of our Industrial Advisory Board.

Another of the many successful partnerships that I was able to bring together for Oxford Brookes was with Porsche GB, in respect of its Porsche Carrera Cup GB programme. To have an exact replica of the Porsche LMP1 car that won Le Mans in 2017 on display at the University Open day was a real bonus for the department of mechanical engineering. The Porsche relationship was yet another milestone on the way to Oxford Brookes being perceived as the world's leading motorsport engineering university.

The university marked its 150th anniversary a couple of years ago, and one of the events that were staged as part of the official celebrations was a Motorsport Industry Forum. It was held in the magnificent new John Brookes building, at the Headington Campus, in the heart of Oxford. I was asked to chair the panel of VIPs that we had assembled for the evening. It comprised: John Surtees CBE; Andrea Toso of Dallara; Mark Williams, former Head of F1 Engineering at McLaren; Gavin Ward, Red Bull F1 aerodynamicist; Mark Preston, team principal Cheetah Formula-E Team and Frank Bachmann, CEO of BMW Mini UK. We had a specially invited audience of around 250 guests, and it proved to be a fascinating event during which we covered a lot of topics.

If anyone had told me that I would one day be giving three half-day lectures each year to a 110 MSc in motorsport engineering students, from all over the world, most of who will be employed in F1, I would have run a mile. I am not a technical person by any stretch of the imagination, but that's what I have now done for the last four years.

It came about one day when I was talking to Gareth Neighbour. I told him that in my opinion, in motor racing, an understanding of how to secure funding through sponsorship is a big plus, whether you are a marketing person, an engineer, a head of department, a racing driver, an event organiser or whatever. He asked why it was important for an engineer. I explained that there were several reasons. As an example, I suggested that as an engineer, you might well run one day your own racing or rallying team and need to understand how to fund it. You don't necessarily need to be able to go out and find the money yourself, but if you understand how it is done, you can interact better with the person whose responsibility it is.

Then there is the relationship with sponsors. Very often, senior company figures within a potential sponsor are invited to tour the F1 team where you are working as a design engineer. If they stop and talk to you, as can often happen, knowledge of how sponsorship works may help you guide the conversation in a positive way. I know that, because I've witnessed it happening.

You may be the head of a technical department within an F1 Team. As the season passes the half-way point, you find that you have no budget left for some new software that you feel is vitally important. You talk to the CEO, who tells you that if you want it, it will have to be sponsored in some way. Knowledge of the potential benefits that you can offer a potential sponsor can often prove a great help in talking to the marketing department, whose help you are going to need.

Another reason why it can help is that the existing and potential sponsors may well have an entitlement within their contract that allows them to bring their staff, or clients, for a factory tour on a certain number of days per year. It's normal for the visitors to stop and talk to staff during the tour. Your knowledge of the sponsorship process can prove very helpful to the team. For example, if you can hold a meaningful conversation with a potential sponsor's managing director about ways in which they might benefit from sponsorship in respect of a technical perspective. The more confident you are, the better it will be.

Gareth went away after our conversation, and a few days later, he asked me if I would be able to put a module together on "sponsorship acquisition for engineers" to include in their syllabus. It was a challenge that excited me. Later that year, I ran the first of the three half-day sessions. I was surprisingly nervous beforehand, worrying what sort of reception I would get as a marketing person, lecturing MSc engineers on sponsorship acquisition. In their world, there is a right answer and an incorrect answer to the majority of situations, whereas in marketing, it's a grey world, with no definite rights or wrongs, only opinions. I always say that if I found that by wearing a tartan kilt and playing the bagpipes, I could get more interest in meetings with prospective sponsors, then that would be the right way for me to do it. It's all about adopting the approach that works best for you. No right way and no wrong way!

I needn't have worried; the course went down extremely well, and I have now run it for the past four years. Many of the students talk to me afterwards and tell me how interesting and helpful they have found it. In particular, quite a few of them are now looking at the role of sales engineers in the motorsport industry as a career option. Most of them weren't aware that such a role existed in motorsport. I always tell them about Nick Langley, who is one of the best sales engineers in our industry.

Dr Gareth Neighbour went on to become Professor Gareth Neighbour; and a while later, he left Oxford Brookes University. He then took on the role of Head of Engineering and Build at Birmingham City University. Our paths crossed again very recently, as you'll discover in the last chapter of the book. I think that it was a considerable loss to Oxford Brookes when he left. He was a person who could make things happen, and he would always fight his corner, for the good of the department. You need someone like that. I was sorry to see him go. We have, however, kept in contact and become good friends.

I must mention one other person, whom I have worked with for some three years at Oxford Brookes, Gordana Collier, Programme Lead for the MSc Motorsport Engineering course. Working in the field of academia has had its moments, I must admit; for example, that I find the level of communication quite unacceptable on many occasions. People go on leave or perhaps a day off and never leave a message on their voice mails. As a result, you can phone for three days on the trot and get no reply, only to find that the person to whom you need to speak is in Iceland for a week's conference.

What I like about Gordana and some of her work colleagues is the high level of enthusiasm that they maintain, particularly in respect of the students. As I always say, the only thing more contagious than enthusiasm is a lack of it. The project which has really improved at Oxford Brookes since Gordana came on board is Formula Student, a programme that involves students designing and building a race car from scratch in the course of one year. They compete in a series of technical tests and practical completion at Silverstone annually. Formula Student is owned in the UK by the Institute of Mechanical Engineers and is highly regarded by the top motor racing teams when it comes to engineering recruitment.

I have taken the decision to end my consultancy agreement with Oxford Brookes after five very-enjoyable and stimulating years. There are a lot of changes in the pipe line, and I have been disappointed to find that the focus on motorsport engineering is, in my opinion, no longer at the level I feel is necessary to maintain its world-leading status. A lot of people have worked very hard to build the reputation that

Oxford Brookes now enjoys within the motorsport industry worldwide. Unless that level of motivation is continued, a reputation can very easily slip. I sincerely hope that that doesn't happen. Oxford Brookes has been a very special place to work, and I have learned so much from the amazing students with whom I have had the pleasure of working over the five years.

It seems, however, that my academic career isn't over. I will be taking on a new challenge very soon with a university that has very quickly established itself as a leading player in the field of motorsport engineering. As an added bonus, the university is in the same city as my favourite football team, which has just achieved Premier League status. The city of Wolverhampton is definitely on the up!

I must thank Gordana for introducing me to a chance to add a new skill to my portfolio. She mentioned one day, over a coffee, that a colleague of hers had become a guest speaker on cruise ships, and she asked if I had ever thought of doing this. I hadn't, but once I started researching the way forward, I came into contact with one of the agencies who offer to represent potential speakers. I made contact, outlining my career background and the topic that I felt would be entertaining, as well as interesting, to a very mixed audience on a cruise ship.

Brian has recently become a popular celebrity speaker on cruise liners, talking about his career in business and sport.

To my astonishment, within a week, I had my first booking. I was invited to join a ship that was on a world-cruise and asked to deliver six different 45-minute presentations during its last two weeks. It meant flying to Hurghada in Egypt, to pick up the ship, which would proceed through the Suez Canal, to Crete, Malta, Malaga and Lisbon before berthing in Southampton, just a 30 minute drive from where I live.

It was an experience that I won't forget in a hurry. I am the first to admit that neither Liz nor I have ever yearned to go on a cruise. I don't know why, it just hasn't appealed, preferring to do our own thing when we travel. The big difference, however, was that this one didn't cost us anything other than our bar bill, at staff prices. The flights to Egypt there were included. Mind you, I had to put a powerful and entertaining visual presentation together, which took me a long, long time to design and create.

I have two overwhelming memories of that first cruise. One was the people who had spent four months on the ship, eating and lazing in the sun, talking at the restaurant tables about nothing other than food and when the next opportunity to eat was scheduled. The even more vivid memory was of a 12 hour Force 10 storm in the Bay of Biscay on the way home. I was so ill that Liz eventually had to send for the doctor, who gave me an injection to try to relieve my sufferings. In the process, one particular strong wave caused the ship to lurch so badly that as I was laying on my bed in our suite, I saw Liz lifted from her feet and thrown against the wall, cracking her head badly before landing very painfully on her coccyx. She had managed to avoid the sea-sickness, but ended up with a sore head and back. The next morning, we met the captain, who confirmed that it had been a very bad storm, with a lot of the crew becoming very ill, always a sign of just how rough it was.

Back home, I spoke to my doctor, who suggested that for my next trip, I should try using a patch. I didn't know such things existed for sea-sickness, but I was happy to try anything to avoid a repeat of my maiden voyage problems. We have done two more cruises in the past few months, and I can thoroughly recommend the patches. They certainly worked for me. Come to think of it, maybe the pharmaceutical company involved might be interested in sponsorship!

I've now completed three speaking engagements on cruise ships, in the past year. Our last cruise included a visit to the Historic F1 Grand Prix at Monaco, which was, without doubt, one of the most enjoyable race meetings that I have ever attended.

I can fully understand why so many people love cruising, but I can't say that it has really changed our minds. Liz and I much prefer a self-catering cottage in the South West of France, where we can relax and travel as the mood takes us.

Chapter 48
Special Drivers, Being Positive and Looking Back

Having been lucky enough to work in motorsport for over 40 years, I've witnessed a huge amount of change; not just in the racing itself, but in the way that it is presented, both live and by the media. I've met many of the people running different categories of the sport, as well as a high number of competitors. Then there is the rapidly increasing level of change that is currently being brought about by environmental pressures.

I love change, let me make that clear. I only have to look back at my year spent with Bath Rugby to see the negative impact that stubborn resistance to change can bring about. However, that doesn't mean that because something is new, it must automatically be better than that which it replaces. Music is a great example of what I am saying. Some of the greatest music ever heard was composed in the 18th and 19th centuries. Is the music in our current charts better than that of the Beatles, Roy Orbison, Elvis Presley and Dusty Springfield and Queen? There is a tendency amongst young people to believe that it is, just because it's new.

Take Formula 1, for example. Has there been a golden age of F1, or are we currently in one? Personally, I don't think we are, but that's only my personal opinion. However, in the process of my career, I've had the pleasure of watching and often working with many of the real characters who have made our sport so great over the decades. I'm not just talking about F1 but across motorsport in general over the years. These are some of the people who have made an impression on me over the years, each with a very short reason as to why.

Jim Clark:

One of the very first F1 drivers I ever watched race on TV and one of the best ever. I cried when he was killed.

Graham Hill:

The best entertainer in F1; his TV interviews on BBC TV with Jackie Stewart were hilarious. Probably not a natural racer like Clark, but what determination.

Jochen Rindt:

He was my idol for several years. I can still recall my shock when I saw the newspaper headline about his Monza accident whilst I was on holiday in Spain. In F2 and then F1, he gave everything in a race car. He and his beautiful wife, Nina, typified that era of F1.

James Hunt:

My memories of partying with him at my house in South Africa in 1981, and then dining with him three months before he passed away in 1993, will always be very special. *RUSH*, the movie, says it all. A character in every way.

Manfred Winkelhock:

A regular at the South African F1 Grand Prix, who was not only a fast driver but another wonderful character, who would talk to anyone about his love of the sport. He was always surrounded by Lufthansa crew at the Kyalami Ranch Hotel around Grand Prix time!

Jochen Mass:

Once my neighbour in Cape Town, he just so obviously loves driving race cars, whether modern or historic. He was, and still is, a superb sports car driver, whom I had the pleasure, and privilege, of being overtaken by on the track. Never too busy to talk to you, another gentleman of the track.

Geoff Lees:

One of the most talented Formula Ford drivers I had the pleasure to meet and race against, but also a sad reminder that without money, talent is not always a guarantee of success in our increasingly elitist sport. Made good in Japan, but should have been in F1.

Derek Daly:

I think the word "character" might have been invented for Derek. We worked together at the Thruxton Racing School in 1977, and I raced against him in Formula Ford. He was always entertaining on the track, not that I saw much of him. He was too quick!

Stirling Moss:

I remember watching him race, on a black and white TV in the 1960s, with commentary from Raymond Baxter and John Bolster. He truly is a wonderful person and a real gentleman. Meeting him on many occasions has been a great pleasure, with so many amazing anecdotes to hear.

Roy Klomfass:

We met racing in Formula Ford on many occasions, when he was in the same team as Rupert Keegan, then became friends in South Africa, his home country. He was a great friend of Rory Byrne, who helped him in his early days. I was very sad when I heard of his tragic death. A fun guy who never quite fulfilled his potential.

Gil de Ferran:

Another driver to find success in America, following a European grounding. Gil won the CART Championship for Derek Walker. Having been a passenger in a road car, driven by Gil around the Homestead Oval in Florida, I can see why! Gil is now the Sporting Director at McLaren F1.

Brian spent a considerable amount of time in America on behalf of Lola. Here he is seen with CART Champion, Gil de Ferran at the Homestead Oval in Florida, having just been taken for a lap of the track.

Rupert Keegan:

He was one of the most colourful of all Formula Ford drivers. He would be sideways for much of the time but still very quick. We never knew what was coming next from Rupert. Controversial Durex and *Penthouse Magazine* sponsorships in F1 fitted his personality well.

Mario Andretti:

I had the pleasure of watching him race in CART (Indycar) on many occasions, including at his own Nazareth Circuit, as well as meeting him through my work in the US for Lola. My laps alongside him in an Audi TT around Brands Hatch were unforgettable.

Felippe Massa:

A talented Grand Prix driver, who, throughout his F1 career, always remained very approachable and normal. Success never went to his head. He was so much better than he is sometimes given credit for and was never afraid to include and involve his family in his career. I sincerely hope he enjoys Formula E now. He deserves it.

Michael Schumacher:

What can I say that hasn't been said? He has been just so special, in so many ways. Tragic.

Keke Rosberg:

I had the pleasure to work with Keke in South Africa in early 1980s, another driver who can truly be described as a character. Blindingly fast in cars that were so different to today's F1 machinery. Brave and a chain-smoker then! A character at a time when F1 was great fun but very dangerous.

Jacques Laffitte:

I spent a week at Monza, interviewing Jacques for a South African magazine. An under-rated driver, who was the opposite in a race car to what he was out of it. A relaxed, laid-back character, whose first thought on his arrival off the plane was always to find his golf clubs.

Derek Warwick:

What a Formula Ford driver this guy was before taking the same talent into F2, F1 and then as the World Sports Car Champion. I even bought a road car from his Southampton dealership, so trustworthy too! A real gentleman.

Tom Pryce:

I had the pleasure of watching him throw his Shadow, spectacularly, through Clubhouse Corner, lap after lap, at Kyalami, in the 1975 South African Grand Prix. I wish he hadn't been at that same circuit in 1977. Tragic.

Mike Wilds:

When I was racing in Formula Ford, as a novice, I remember watching Mike's distinctive Dempster-sponsored F3 car on the same programme. Have known him for a long time, they don't come any better than Mike.

Ian Scheckter:

I got to know Ian well during my years spent racing in South Africa. Not only a huge talent but a great character who always put on a spectacular show for the crowd. In my opinion, he could and should have been an F1 champion, like his brother.

Sarel van der Merwe:

He is almost certainly the greatest all-round motorsport driver I've known. Multi-time South African champion in rallying, saloon cars and winner of the Dayton 24-Hours in a Group C-style sports car. Sarel is a brilliant driver and a fun guy away from the track.

Peter Gethin:

I interviewed Peter at Kyalami when he was the team manager for Toleman F1 in 1984, managing his young Brazilian driver, Ayrton Senna. I loved watching Peter race in F5000, which took a lot of bravery and a special talent, before going on to F1, where he won the closest ever finish at Monza.

Alex Zinardi:

I met Alex at Donington for the first time when he was racing sports cars. A great guy, who went on to show the world just how brave and determined he was, following his terrible Indycar accident in Germany. He is a lot more than just a superb former racer, being also a double-gold para-olympian. A genuine Boys' Own character.

David Purley:

Another Boys' Own type of character. I witnessed his terrible Silverstone accident, as well as his bravery in trying to rescue Roger Williamson from his burning race car. A short but colourful life.

Geoff Smailes:

A South African Formula Ford driver, who plied his trade in England. I raced against him a lot and was never sure whether he was just faster than me or a lot braver. Geoff was a wild character to watch on the track, and a good friend off it.

Nigel Mansell:

Having raced against Nigel for a whole season in Formula Ford, I have nothing but admiration for this guy and his wife, Roseanne. Like Liz and myself, a real team! Nigel was fast, brave and thoughtful. I also spent a lot of time with him when he competed in a Lola in Indycar. I still don't think he gets the full credit he deserves.

Emerson Fittipaldi:

I followed his career from those early days in Formula Ford when he first arrived in the UK from Brazil, then in F3 and upwards. I got to know him whilst we worked together in A1GP. A lovely man.

John Surtees:

I've said it all in the book, John was someone very special. He was certainly a character, in every sense of the word.

Matthew Argenti:

One of my best mates. Yet another product of the mid 1970's Formula Ford talent production line, a very quick racing driver who should have gone further. We both eventually went in the same sports marketing direction and found ourselves working together many years later. I think he retired from driving too early.

Mike Blanchet:

Yet another superb Formula Ford driver. Mike was a very talented racing driver, who I believe would have gone much further up the ladder with a good sponsorship manager behind him. A wonderful person, who gave me my first chance to work for a Formula 1 team when he was CEO of Lola Race Cars. Mike is a very popular character within the motorsport industry.

***

There aren't many advantages of growing old, but one is being able to look back over a long career. I started my story, sitting on my bike outside the gates of the Southampton branch of Greenham Tool Company, on a bitterly cold morning in January 1964. A lot has happened since that day.

Had a fortune-teller told me then that I would race cars for a living, eventually reaching the heady heights of Formula 1, not as a driver but as the marketing director of a world championship-winning Grand Prix Team, I would have told them not to give up the day job!

As I explained, throughout my childhood, I knew that I would one day become a pilot in the Royal Air Force. It came as a huge shock when I couldn't deliver that scenario. I wonder now whether the gods may have been looking down on me that morning in Southampton and taken pity on me, aware of my disappointment, by instilling in me a fascination with motor racing. If they did, what a shame they didn't give me the talent of Jim Clark, Michael Schumacher or Jackie Stewart. That was cruel.

But maybe they did help. Not by favouring me with amazing race driving skills, but by helping Lotus F1 boss, Colin Chapman, acquire the Gold Leaf Team Lotus sponsorship deal in 1968, a deal that changed the face of motorsport forever. Maybe the gods, in their wisdom, set me on a career path which would enable me to learn those same skills that Chapman had. My years at Greenhams, Goodyear, Mary Quant, Xerox and ITT were all part of the plan.

Our lives are forged very much by our school teachers, parents, families, people we work with, husbands or wives and our friends. At an early age, I knew that life was for living. Regrettably, money was rarely my goal. I just knew that I didn't want to get to retirement age, and wish I'd done more with my life.

Maybe my feeling this way was the result of a family tragedy when I was just a 12-year-old. One morning, as I was getting ready for school, the phone rang in our house in Isleworth. I can clearly recall my mother answering it, then calling my dad to the phone. It was obvious something was wrong. He put the phone down, kissed my mother and then grabbed his car keys and ran out to the garage. My mother took me into the lounge, telling me that my grandfather, Ken's dad, had been taken ill and was in hospital. It was the morning of his retirement from Kodak, where he had worked for much of his life as a machine operator. The work he was doing had been considered important to the war effort, and he had stayed there throughout the Second World War. Now he was 65, about to retire that day and looking forward so much to moving into the new bungalow in Pevensey Bay, that he and my gran, Ruth, had scrimped and saved for.

Sadly, it wasn't to be. That afternoon, I was collected from school by my other gran and told the news that Frederick had passed away, having suffered a heart attack, even before Ken had arrived at the hospital. He would never see the completed bungalow that he had spent his hard life working for.

Maybe that affected my outlook on life, I can't say, or maybe there is some Romani blood in the family, who knows? Both Liz and I like change, that's who we are. As long as that change is something we can share, we're happy.

I've been incredibly fortunate inasmuch that Liz and I have shared so many wonderful adventures together during our 33 years and continue to do so. I love the fact that Liz choose to travel with me on many of my business trips, usually heading off into the local town to enjoy some sightseeing and maybe do some shopping. It makes my life so much more enjoyable; and having worked with me in much of my motorsport career, she knows most of my business friends and contacts.

When I secured my first-ever sponsorship, with Victoria's Night Club, I must admit that I had no idea where it would take me. Only mid-way through my second season, as I got some good results with my new car, did I think about a possible professional career. Formula 1, even!

The reality, of course, was that I didn't have the level of racing skills required. However, it didn't stop me from wanting to get to Formula 1. Once I accepted that I wasn't good enough as a driver to get there, I became even more determined that I would achieve my ambition, whatever it took.

I came to an important conclusion, deciding that I would do my very best to get as far in motor racing, as my limited driving talent would allow. It wouldn't be Formula 1, but that no longer mattered. I somehow knew that I would get there, and be successful, but not as a driver.

Looking back, it had dawned on me that the more positive I became about the direction in which I was heading, the more the opportunities kept presenting themselves. Maybe it was just a case of my recognising the opportunities that were already there. All I know is that having decided to continue race driving, at least for the foreseeable future, the more I would require increasing amounts of sponsorship. In turn, the more successful I was at acquiring that sponsorship, the more my reputation for doing so increased.

I've explained how my racing career developed from that point in time, and how I eventually reached the heady heights of racing in international Group C events before retiring and starting my own racing driver school.

Finally, the opportunity to move into F1 presented itself, as I knew it would, and I was confident that I could be successful. It wasn't in the glamorous role of a racing driver, as I had once expected, but in a business suit, sitting in the boardrooms of companies across the world persuading to part with millions of dollars. What really mattered was that I was successful at what I was doing.

I had developed my one real skill and made it work for me in so many ways. Always a professional salesman, I've travelled a long way from sharing a room in digs, all those years ago back in Southampton. I hope that by example, I've shown a lot of people that you don't have to be a champion to be a winner.

Chapter 49
Recognition

Having often referred to opportunities presenting themselves, I was completely taken aback at the beginning of 2018, when an e-mail arrived from a totally unexpected source. It was from Birmingham City University and read as follows:

I am delighted to write to you on behalf of Birmingham City University to invite you to receive the honorary award of Doctor of the University (D. Univ) ... in recognition of your outstanding achievements within the motorsport industry.

I took a few days to sink in, not least of all because I never went to University. Although I was a consultant to Oxford Brookes University for the past five years, I had always thought that honorary doctorates were something other people received. For me, this was something very special, and I learnt that Professor Gareth Neighbour, now Head of School for Engineering and the Built Environment at BCU, was partly responsible for bringing this about.

As I have explained, he played a vital role in developing Oxford Brookes into one the world's leading motorsport engineering universities, and, in my opinion, it was a case of Birmingham City University's gain and Oxford Brookes loss.

Although I have attended a couple of university graduation ceremonies, purely as a guest on both occasions, I really didn't know what to expect on the day that I would receive my award.

I found out that Birmingham City University currently has around 24,000 students taught across four facilities, including 2,500 overseas students. The graduation ceremony, which is held twice a year, takes place in the city's Symphony Hall. It was Bruce Welch, of the Shadows, who recently told me that he had played there on several occasions; and that, it was, without doubt, one of Europe's finest concert halls because of its outstanding acoustics.

Nearly six months after receiving that official invitation, I headed up to Birmingham for the big day. Once there, I was taken for a quick run through of the procedures, and I was able to see for myself the amazing size and majesty of the Symphony Hall, 2262 seats in total. I don't know how many were there for the graduation, but with 650 students receiving awards, it must have been close to capacity, with all of the family members.

The chancellor of the university is Sir Lenny Henry, and what a great character, with a huge talent for enthusing the students. As I sat on the stage throughout the presentations to all 650 students, I could see how he put each one at ease and made them feel so special. It was a joy to watch.

After I had received my honorary doctorate, I was invited to give a short address to the audience. Using motorsport as the theme, I stressed the importance of realising that talent alone rarely guarantees success; but that if you add determination to that talent, it can become an unstoppable force.

To have received such unexpected recognition, at this stage of my career, is something very special to me. I take the view that it's not just for me, but also for Liz, who has been involved in so many of my motorsport-related adventures. Without Liz's help, enthusiasm, confidence and encouragement, I couldn't have launched the MIA or established South Africa's first racing-driver school or launched the South African version of the MIA or written this and previous books.

We have always operated as a team; we're determined to continue in that way for as long as we can.

END